Critical Essays on
LAURENCE STERNE

CRITICAL ESSAYS
ON
BRITISH LITERATURE

Zack Bowen, General Editor
University of Miami

Critical Essays on

LAURENCE STERNE

edited by

MELVYN NEW

G. K. Hall & Co.

New York

G. K. Hall & Co.

1633 Broadway
New York, NY 10019

Library of Congress Cataloging-in-Publication Data

Critical essays on Laurence Sterne / edited by Melvyn New.
    p. cm.—(Critical essays on British literature)
    Includes bibliographical references (p.   ) and index.
    ISBN 0-7838-0040-1 (alk. paper)
    1. Sterne, Laurence, 1713–1768—Criticism and interpretation.
  I. New, Melvyn.   II. Series
  PR3716.C68   1998
  823'.6—dc21   97-34645
                                                          CIP

This paper meets the requirements of ANSI/NISO Z3948–1992
Permanence of Paper.
10 9 8 7 6 5 4 3 2

Printed in the United States of America

For the New generation of readers, the grandchildren,
Emily, Felicia, Michael, Hannah, and Kohei

Contents

General Editor's Note

♦

The Critical Essays on British Literature series provides a variety of approaches to both classical and contemporary writers of Britain and Ireland. The formats of the volumes in the series vary with the thematic designs of individual editors and with the amount and nature of existing reviews and criticism, augmented where appropriate by original essays by recognized authorities. It is hoped that each volume will develop a new and unique overall perspective on its particular subject.

Melvyn New's collection consists of the most important Sterne criticism to appear in essay form during the last 15 years as well as four new essays and an essay translated especially for this volume. New's delightful introduction to the subject is simultaneously an expression of his views on Sterne, on the interpretation of Sterne, and on literary criticism in general. New's scholarship is interwoven with an explanation of his thematic organization of the collected essays in four categories of investigation: the intertextual, skeptical, erotical, and ethical Sterne.

ZACK BOWEN
University of Miami

Publisher's Note

◆

Producing a volume that contains both newly commissioned and reprinted material presents the publisher with the challenge of balancing the desire to achieve stylistic consistency with the need to preserve the integrity of works first published elsewhere. In the Critical Essays series, essays commissioned especially for a particular volume are edited to be consistent with G. K. Hall's house style; reprinted essays appear in the style in which they were first published, with only typographical errors corrected. Consequently, shifts in style from one essay to another are the result of our efforts to be faithful to each text as it was originally published.

Notes on the References

For the sake of uniformity, all citations of *Tristram Shandy* are to the *Florida Edition: Tristram Shandy: The Text*, vols. I and II, ed. Melvyn New and Joan New (Gainesville, Fla.: University Press of Florida, 1978), and to *The Notes* (1984), vol. III, ed. Melvyn New with Richard A. Davies and W. G. Day, cited throughout the volume as *TS*.

All references to *A Sentimental Journey* are to the edition by Gardner D. Stout (Berkeley: University of California Press, 1967), cited throughout the volume as *ASJ*.

All references to Sterne's sermons are to the *Florida Edition: The Sermons*, vols. IV and V, ed. Melvyn New (Gainesville, Fla.: University Press of Florida, 1996), cited throughout the volume as *Sermons*.

Introduction:
Four Faces of Laurence Sterne

MELVYN NEW

Laurence Sterne's dismissal of criticism, artistic or literary, is well known: "Grant me patience, just heaven!——Of all the cants which are canted in this canting world,——though the cant of hypocrites may be the worst,—— the cant of criticism is the most tormenting" (*TS,* III.xii.214). Toward compilers of criticism—or of any other body of knowledge—he is equally unkind:

> thus my fellow labourers and associates in this great harvest of our learning, now ripening before our eyes; thus it is, by slow steps of casual increase, that our knowledge, physical, metaphysical, physiological, polemical, nautical, mathematical, ænigmatical, technical, biographical, romantical, chemical, and obstetrical, with fifty other branches of it, (most of 'em ending, as these do, in *ical*) have, for these two last centuries and more, gradually been creeping upwards towards that Ακμη of their perfections, from which, if we may form a conjecture from the advances of these last seven years, we cannot possibly be far off. (I.xxi.71–72)

To remind us of the false promise of wholeness or completion inherent in our various divisions of knowledge (for example, the assumption that the various departments of a university divide all knowledge between them), I have echoed Sterne's play on *-ical,* dividing the 18 essays in this collection under the headings "Intertextual," "Skeptical," "Erotical," and "Ethical." In doing so, I thought to call attention to several issues central both to the present enterprise—gathering in one convenient volume the "best" that has been written about Sterne in the 15-year period between 1981 and 1996—and to Sterne's own perspective on knowledge and commentary and the relationship between them.

First, I will note the lack of a definite article in my introduction's title, "Four Faces of Sterne." I do not know how many "faces" Sterne may have, but surely it is more than four. Another editor, working with the same 18 essays gathered herein, could easily have found four different categories or, given the same four, have reassigned the essays differently among them. The categories and their contents, in other words, are not inherent to Sterne or to his work,

1

but derive from my reading of Sterne and of many essays about his work, most of which do not, and could not, appear in this relatively thin volume.

I selected the previously published essays in this collection because I found them the most interesting freestanding essays among perhaps 250 published in the last 15 years, all of which I confess to having read. I say "freestanding" because in a collection of "essays" I prefer not to include book chapters, a fastidiousness that limits my choices to some extent but preserves both the integrity of book-length studies and the unique perfections of the literary essay. In the face of a literary marketplace in which the number of books published annually may soon surpass the number of essays, it seems useful to preserve a dying art, especially if the *essay* proves true to its name and is, indeed, an attempt, a trial, an experiment, rather than a conclusion; we might well profit from fewer conclusions and more tentativeness in our literary commentary. The four essays and one translation written specifically for this collection are by authors—Anne Bandry, Tom Keymer, Elizabeth Kraft, Donald Wehrs, and Madeleine Descargues—whose previous fine work on Sterne attracted my interest; I am especially grateful for their contributions.

If our categories are simply the result of our "interests," it is always a careless manner of speaking to suggest a book or an author or a subject is "interesting." Sterne's own word for "interest" is, often enough, "hobby-horse," and if we believe there is a distinction between the two, Sterne invites us to demarcate it as best we can with as straight a line across the page as we can muster. One difficulty is that neither *Tristram Shandy* nor names nor fortifications are, in themselves, hobby-horses; rather, they are the indifferent occasions for "hobby-horsicalness," our interest in them being the return on our investment of intellectual or emotional capital.

Moreover, as is true of the hobby-horsical careers of Tristram, Walter, and Toby, my interest in Sterne is manifested primarily by attempts, in this collection and in 30 years of writing about him, to impose shape and order on materials that could just as readily be presented alphabetically or chronologically by a less interested reader, or in yet another shape and order by a reader with different interests. We order the occasions of our interests almost always with an eye toward Truth or Significance (two words closely akin to Interest), investing the data with our sense of some higher ordering principle, some movement toward the "acme" of knowledge that Sterne mocks. Hence, my four divisions move toward the revelation of Sterne's "ethical" face, attesting to my interest in a Sterne who transcends (I use that word fully conscious that it is under philosophical suspicion in many quarters today) textuality, skepticism, and sexuality in fictions that confirm finally the presence of measure and judgment in all his work. It is *my* arrangement of the essays, *my* own sequencing of them, that creates this reading of Sterne, and I have chosen essays that seem to me to move naturally in—and not to gainsay—the direction toward which I have pointed them. It is quite possible, however, that some of the essayists will not see their own work as contributing to my arrangement; some may even feel violated by it. A far different Sterne might emerge, for example, had I started with the "Ethical Sterne" and ended with the "Intertextual Sterne," thus creating the impression, much more in keeping with modernity, that for Sterne inherited transcendence (the Word) is overwhelmed by the inheritance of the many words that would seem to constitute our only reality.

The second point worth calling to attention about the organization of these essays is that "Intertextual" does not end in -*ical* and that I had to invent "Erot*ical*" to help my scheme. Systems of knowledge—in the Shandy world and in our own—always tend to break down in the details: a misdelivered child, a mistransmitted name, a misunderstood distinction between a ravelin and a horn-work. Here my little system breaks down due, simply, to my lack of wit: I could not think of a way to make the concept of "intertextuality" end in -*ical,* though I suspect Sterne would have found one. Of course the point of Sterne's remark has far more to do with the "end" of knowledge than with "endings," for behind the passage quoted earlier is the "skeptical" face of Sterne, the Sterne who shares with Rabelais, Erasmus, Montaigne, Swift, and many others at the beginnings of modernism grave doubts concerning the hopeful possibilities for knowledge (both scientific and spiritual) that swept through Europe in the early modern era. Sterne's sentence comes very close to several of Swift's observations concerning the perfection of humankind just around the corner; as with Swift, Sterne's irony is informed by an insistent belief in permanently flawed human nature and a concomitant belief in the infinite distance between this pervasive imperfection and the perfectness of the divine.

Thus, my seemingly teleological arrangement of the essays should be taken *cum grano salis* (with a grain of salt). To suggest that literary criticism moves closer and closer to the "truth" of a literary work, that the work of earlier generations prepares the way for a truth that emerges finally in our own time, is a self-indulgent luxury of belief challenged by almost all modern philosophy and literary theory—not to mention history and human experience. Before one accepts the validity of these challenges, however, one must ask whether it is possible, then, for modern philosophy and literary theory, for history and our own experience, to be themselves on a teleological track toward the revelation of this truth that there is no truth. Here, ultimately, is the great value of Sterne's writings—and of much else that endures in the European Renaissance tradition: Sterne teaches us that no discovery of another person's hobby-horse is valid if we have not discovered that we are also mounted and agallop. Swift's and Sterne's certainty in the *permanent* impairment of the human faculties must be carried forward to our own thoughts and systems, just as surely as we must also put into question whatever they considered certain and permanent. Hence, while I do not naively believe we are moving inexorably toward *the* truth about Sterne's writings, I

nevertheless selected and arranged the essays in this collection with some purpose about Sterne and his work directing my efforts, a purpose I believe is the
coherent result of our increased knowledge and sophistication about the past
and about literature. When one begins to confront the human paradox of
knowing that truth is unreachable but thinking and speaking and acting as
though knowledge moves us toward our goals, one has begun to understand
what I believe is the primary crux of Sterne's great fictions.

My final observation about the four categories I have created is that,
although they are arbitrary in relation to Sterne, they do seem to me to mirror accurately some, though not all, of the literary community's dominant
concerns in recent years. It is useful to recall that these concerns are in continual flux, that what "interests" one generation about a literary work quite possibly is of no interest to the next. Significantly, however, while these shifting
concerns would seem to argue for shifting objects as well, that proves only
rarely to be the case. Perhaps one can define a "classic," that much-maligned
concept in our time, as a work that remains the object of our varying concerns, that continues to be the measure by which we explore, evaluate, and
exercise our present interests. One mark of very bad literary criticism, I
believe, is that it sets out to destroy the objects of past interest in order to put
new objects (proletarian literature? soap operas? comic books? *Gilligan's
Island*?) in their place. The practice of denigrating past authors on the basis of
present popular demands—which too often in our century has resulted in
book burnings—is not excused if it is labeled "cultural criticism." If we truly
want to test the worthiness of our thinking on any subject, of our system for
organizing knowledge, our explanations of the world, it still seems best, to
my mind, to measure ourselves against what has long endured and been often
praised; doing so is, however, almost always a humbling experience, as Tristram ironically recognizes in pointing his own moral: "☞ A dwarf who brings
a standard along with him to measure his own size—take my word, is a dwarf
in more articles than one" (*TS,* IV.xxv.375).

The first section, "The Intertextual Sterne," contains essays that participate in
a very long history, for from the beginning readers have recognized Sterne's
penchant for embedding or incorporating other writers within his text. In the
beginning the work of identifying sources was often linked with moral condemnation; the first indefatigable searcher after Sterne's borrowings, John
Ferriar, raised the specter of plagiarism in his *Illustrations of Sterne* (1798), and
throughout the nineteenth century Sterne's sexual indiscretions were somehow seen as typical of a literary thief—or perhaps it was the other way round.
Today we are more tolerant of plagiarisms, certainly of those intended as self-
conscious signals alerting attentive readers to the authors and works that
have helped create the work in our hands; indeed, I would suggest that when
we do not recognize these signals, when we fail to discover a source, we fall
short of reading the entire work, just as surely as if we decide to skip chapters

or stop 50 pages short of the end. The *Florida Notes to Tristram Shandy* (1984) contains 550 pages of annotations, a good many of which are citations of sources, but not a word appears in that work to condemn Sterne's practice. To the contrary, the more we discover about Sterne's sources (and the process continues in contributions to the "Scholia" column reserved for that purpose in the *Scriblerian,* as well as in many essays and notes published since 1984), the more convincingly we will acknowledge, as we must, that an "entire" text is the phantom dream of critics who awaken when ("for I hate your *ifs,*" as Tristram remarks) they become annotators.

But of course our modern term *intertextuality* covers more ground than what were previously called "sources and analogues," and the essays in "Intertextual Sterne" demonstrate various facets of this broadened concept of how authors construct their texts from the textual worlds available to them. Hence, Jonathan Lamb extends his interest from Sterne's borrowings to the methodology of borrowing in those from whom Sterne borrowed, and he explores the notion that intertextuality is the way we construct not only our writings but our lives (and the lives of our characters) as well. Working with the large fund of borrowings identified prior to the publication of the *Florida Notes* by Ferriar, James A. Work (the Odyssey edition of *Tristram Shandy,* 1940), and others, Lamb asks us to consider the purposes to which Sterne puts his purloined texts, purposes that range from the construction of Walter's false erudition to Toby's sentimentalism (via Longinus).[1]

Conversely, Anne Bandry, in her essay written especially for this volume, gives us an account of the textual world created by Sterne's work (rather than of the one he used to create it), though ultimately she suspects that Sterne stood ready to profit from his imitators by imitating them. She even suggests he may have had a hand in creating at least one of the imitations of his own work! This suggestion of an intricate maze created by an original work not only constructed from previous writings but depending as well on the works it generates, either as a source of hints for future direction or for devices and formulas previously untried, connects Bandry's essay with Stephen Soud's exploration of Sterne's emblematic use of the labyrinth. Importantly, the clue of the maze does *not* unravel *Tristram Shandy,* but further reveals something about how its intricacies are constructed, in both Sterne's mind and the reader's. The texts Soud brings to bear, the contemporary literatures of warfare and gardening, suggest how broad the sweep of literary study can be when a scholar attempts to understand the world created by a single text; indeed, one might suggest that good literary criticism has always been splendidly eclectic, while much in cultural studies today is comparatively narrow minded, politics (whether of the unthinking left or the unthinking right) being always the enemy of free exploration. Significantly, Soud's essay, although rooted in what appears to be an old-fashioned historical study of sources, ends with a discussion of sexuality that coincides nicely with the essays gathered under "The Erotical Sterne." One quality I looked for in selecting essays for this collection was the author's refusal to rest secure in the pigeonhole of a single critical approach or to reflect merely one of Sterne's faces.

Broad-mindedness was not the only quality I looked for, however, as is evident in Tom Keymer's essay, also written especially for this collection. Because the essay has many of the characteristics of an old-fashioned influence study, its comparison of *Tristram Shandy* and *The Poems of Ossian* fits comfortably enough into the category of "The Intertextual Sterne." Old fashions are not necessarily unproductive or unperceptive, however, and Keymer convincingly exhibits the surprising ways, concrete and abstract, that these two contemporaries, Sterne and Macpherson, share a single text between them. By avoiding the well-worn umbrellas of sentimentalism or preromanticism as the single shared property of Macpherson and Sterne, and by exploring their relationship as texts in both traditional and modern ways (for example, Keymer carefully traces their artifacts within the world of publishers and booksellers), Keymer is able to read both works as centered on the postheroic. Macpherson offers a tragic reading, Sterne, obviously a comic one, but both share a strong sense of loss over the irretrievable past, a world more and more to be understood and communicated by obsessions and fragments—perhaps, most pertinently, an obsessiveness about the fragmented. This is an essay that informs its own text: one reads it with a sense of appreciation for a lost depth of scholarly investigation, increasingly fragmented today on the shallow rocks of bad politics and undigested theories—not to mention mixed metaphors.

One of the most often discussed intertextual questions of Sterne's canon is the role John Locke's *Essay Concerning Human Understanding* plays in it. Significantly, however, Peter Briggs's reexamination of the relationship opens for this volume a new category, "The Skeptical Sterne," for dwelling on "particular and easily identifiable instances" of Locke's appearance in *Tristram Shandy* risks "overlooking Sterne's more general exploitation of the grounding assumptions of Locke's system." To be sure, the definition of Locke's "assumptions" is itself a vexed problem for philosophers and literary scholars alike, but the essay's emphasis on Sterne's skeptical attitude toward the possibilities of knowledge opens a vein of inquiry into Sterne that is valuable both in itself and because it helps explain why Sterne, of all eighteenth-century authors, seems—at first glance—most amenable to postmodernism's own suspicion of intellectual systems. Whether Locke had a rosier view, as Briggs suggests, or whether he, too, partakes of the skeptical tradition remains a question needing further exploration; it is perhaps worth noting in this regard (and as an example of the always receding "entire" text of Sterne's work) that the key "riddles and mysteries" passage (*TS,* IV.xvii.350), which Briggs believes is a borrowing from Locke, is actually taken verbatim from Locke's first opponent in England, John Norris (1657–1711).[2] Interestingly, this discovery does not invalidate, perhaps even enriches, the point Briggs makes; whatever the mind's limitations, it constantly seeks to overcome, undercut, evade, or deceive them: "in this aspect, as in many others in *Tristram Shandy,* the search for understanding is a balancing act, a weighing of interpretive options, all of which have some claim to credibility."

Everett Zimmerman shares with Briggs the modern obsession with knowledge and its discontents, but his argument shifts from philosophical to historical inquiry, beginning with scholarly challenges to scriptural history in Sterne's day. If Locke (or Norris) was teaching Sterne to doubt the truth of his understanding of his present surroundings, the writing of history in Sterne's day taught him to exercise similar caution concerning the past. Between the two essays, Sterne might seem to more closely resemble a twentieth-century postmodernist than an eighteenth-century clergyman, and there is indeed a strong likelihood that whenever we read the past we will find our own present concerns in it, our "interests." Hence, when Zimmerman argues that Sterne's characters question "the usual valorization of object over subject, history over fiction, turning history into an appendage of the personal," he seems to thrust Sterne squarely into an ongoing quarrel between Derrida and formalists, between new and traditional historicists.

A particularly pleasing aspect of both essays, however, is their demonstration that the insights and doubts we think uniquely our own were already the intellectual meat of the eighteenth century—and, as we recognize if we study philosophy and history and literature carefully enough, of the Greek community centuries before the birth of Christ; the questions we ask today remain framed by the philosophical language of the Greeks, a discourse we seem unable to evade, much less escape. Sterne's sense of our inescapable past reveals itself somewhere between his intertextual and skeptical faces: he lovingly celebrates the past by inviting it again and again into his own world, but the voices of the past he most favors are those affirming the vanity of human wisdom, past and present.

Between Briggs and Zimmerman and the final three essays in this section, Sterne's skepticism was further explored in a most valuable essay by Donald R. Wehrs, "Sterne, Cervantes, Montaigne: Fideistic Skepticism and the Rhetoric of Desire,"[3] an essay I would certainly have included in this volume had he not provided an equally valuable new essay for it. In his earlier study, Wehrs examines Sterne's relationship to Pyrrhonism (classical skepticism) with one eye on modern deconstructive strategies, the other on those sixteenth- and seventeenth-century responses to celebrations of individual sufficiency, intellectual or spiritual, that came to be known collectively as fideism. When we use the word *skeptical* today, we are most likely thinking of a doubting attitude toward all religious faith, all transcendence—certainly a commonplace modern usage. During the Reformation, however, Pyrrhonism was revived in large part as a weapon not against religion's claims, but, quite the contrary, against the claims of reason and individual (as opposed to communal) revelation. Sterne is one of the last proponents of this mode of skepticism, following hard on the heels of his fellow countryman Swift. If skepticism throws the past and present into doubt, then the future as revealed to

Christians, the promise that repentant sinners would gain eternal life through Christ's redeeming sacrifice, becomes the only certainty of existence, creating the horizon of comprehension within which every other aspect of life can be understood: "One does not escape victimization by the unpredictable and the equivocal, or even transposition into digressive narrative series and linguistic projections terminating in death, but at least mortal life offers a joy that may, through faith, be experienced as a partial anticipation of a fulfillment that will not be partial" (Wehrs, 151).

Wehrs's 1988 essay forms a useful third leg to Briggs's argument from philosophy and Zimmerman's from history writing, for Sterne was an active cleric of the Anglican church from his 25th year to the end of his life, leaving behind 45 sermons that may serve as important glosses to his fictions. In my own essay in "The Skeptical Sterne," I use Wehrs's valuable argument about Sterne's religious faith to confront recent readings of Sterne that insist he share modernism's secular commitment to undecidable, indeterminate, disruptive, open, inconclusive narratives. I suggest instead that his satire of pretensions to knowledge, his skepticism, encompasses not only those who build and maintain intellectual systems, but also those who think they are immune from system building. That is to say, Sterne implicates himself and his readers in recognizing, as many modern critics fail to do, that the desire to clarify and explain *exactly* what we are thinking about overwhelms contrary assertions that language cannot clarify and explain the world. I also make the suggestion that Sterne would not have human beings acting otherwise, for the community celebrated in *Tristram Shandy* is not that of the Shandy brothers, but rather the ingathering of authors and books, documents and artifacts, indeed the commentary that surrounds Sterne's own work, commentary he richly anticipates even as he mocks it. Sterne celebrates this community of writers (creators) by filling his work with multiple illustrations of the human desire to learn, to communicate that learning to others, and most significantly, to commune with whatever transcends the human mind.[4]

In "Swift, Sterne, and the Skeptical Tradition," J. T. Parnell continues to probe this vein of skepticism and fideism, primarily to reopen the question of Swift's role in Sterne's canon. One of the consistent strategies of Sterne criticism throughout this century has been to describe Swift as a depraved and glum hater and then insist that the smiling (or smirking) Sterne is not at all like Swift. That Sterne himself seems to think otherwise, that he wants *Tristram Shandy* to swim down the gutter of time with *Tale of a Tub* (*TS,* IX.viii.754), has not hampered the flourishing of this distorting view, which John Traugott rigorously promulgated in *Tristram Shandy's World: Sterne's Philosophical Rhetoric* and which Martin Battestin embraced in *The Providence of Wit: Aspects of Form in Augustan Literature and the Arts*.[5] Parnell's essay sets itself directly against this tradition by way of a highly intertextual reexamination of the presence of Erasmus and Montaigne in particular, the high Renaissance in general, in the intellectual maps of Swift's and Sterne's worlds.

Michael Rosenblum takes his own unique route to arrive at a conclusion similar to that of the four preceding essays. Despite my having read his essay carefully and with full sympathy for its main point, in correspondence I several times misnamed it "Why What Happens in Shandy Hall Is 'A Matter for the Police,'" an error caused, I believe, by the fact that in modern theory everything is indeed a police matter, a site for suspicion. It is therefore a disorienting divergence from the commonplace for Rosenblum to assert that narratives do indeed exist wherein the usual suspects need not be interrogated: "If the old orthodoxy [that "realism" has aesthetic and semiotic purposes divorced from politics] now seems blandly optimistic, I would argue that the radical suspicion of the novel which is fast becoming the new orthodoxy is too reductive, too willing to assimilate all representation within the period to a forensic model of narrative." Sterne's particularism, or circumstantial exactitude, he argues, is not thrust into the service of state regulation but, to the contrary, opens to the reader a subjectivity that is neither illusion nor part of a repressive plot.

I hope it is not unfair to Rosenblum's argument to suggest that the subjectivity it affirms is akin to the skepticism adduced in the previous essays: Sterne's subjectivity, as does Montaigne's, reinforces a tradition of "unknowingness," a tradition under dire challenge in Sterne's century and our own, the challenge of rationalism. For the rationalist, the possibility that one can encounter a problem or contradiction and fail to resolve it is most unsettling; reason, logic, human progress, and mental well-being all suggest the need to resolve contradictions, make determinations, reconcile all conflicts as part of some larger and better design. Significantly, the notion that all aspects of human society should be made a "matter for the police" is a manifestation of our urge to contain every aspect of society within a rational system; but equally "rationalistic" is the pervasive suggestion today that every text of the past can (and must) be reduced to its role in this systematic repression or containment. One side celebrates the possibility of order, the other seems to deplore it, but insofar as both engage in sweeping generalizations, reductive readings, and final solutions, the two sides share the same certitude: the aesthetic must come under the authority of the political. It is, of course, a formula for a police state, whether belonging to the right or to the left.

Sterne's writings, on the contrary, keep alive an opposing viewpoint, a stubborn way of looking at contradiction and difference and freedom within a context (Christian and skeptical, as each sought reinforcement from the other) of human limitations and worldly complexities. Resolution and certitude are the tempting and inevitable vices of Sterne's worldview (and of critical reading, I might add), suspension and doubt, its difficult, if not impossible, virtues. It is not, however, the contradictions and puzzlements in character or subject matter alone that Sterne's fictions illustrate; indeed, far more important is the contradiction of Sterne's art, the carefully crafted impression of carelessness, incompleteness, inadequacy. Sterne is the eminently sane writer pretending to be mad (or at the very least, fragmented and capricious), one of the primary aesthetic defenses of modern art and artists against an insane world. In a world gone mad with the infinite hypocrisies of problem solving (which Sterne characterizes as *gravity,* Swift as *hypocrisy,* but fascists as *final solutions*), the artist must insist, in John Keats's famous formula, on the vast energies and joys found in the infinite contradictions of "negative capability": "At once it struck me, what quality went to form a Man of Achievement especially in Literature & which Shakespeare possessed so enormously—I mean *Negative Capability,* that is when man is capable of being in uncertainties, Mysteries, doubts, without any irritable reaching after fact & reason." Because every fiber of our being cries out to resolve the painful and threatening "Mysteries" surrounding us—especially in a secular age that insists on desanctifying the mysterious—the artist whose work embodies a countervailing tendency has something to teach us.

That the mystery of things is embedded in our sexual natures is an idea one finds on almost every page of Sterne's favorite authors: Rabelais, Montaigne, Burton, and Swift—and probably Cervantes as well, given Dulcinea del Toboso's inspiriting presence in almost every one of Don Quixote's adventures. Certainly in the past decade's criticism of Sterne, no subject has held more sway; impelled in recent years by a franker discourse in general (one is embarrassed to observe the embarrassment of critics even as late as the 1960s when discussing sexual aspects of Sterne's fictions), and by a spate of gender and feminist discourses more specifically, critics have found in Sterne's canon rich repositories of twentieth-century thinking about sexual matters.

The anachronism of that formulation is the reason behind the strange title of my contribution to the third section, "The Erotical Sterne." The point is simple enough: assuming we are readers, we come to Sterne with expectations and values inevitably shaped by the most important books of our own time, and hence modern authors do indeed influence our reading of Sterne. In noting several resemblances between Proust's description of Marcel in *The Captive* and Sterne's description of Yorick's quest for a justified eroticism in *A Sentimental Journey,* for example, I found a way I had not previously recognized to think about Sterne's work. One must always be concerned, however, that "justified eroticism" is a subject in Sterne only because we view him through the filter that Proust—or more generally, the modern era—provides; great literature has a way of echoing whatever is uppermost in our minds. For this reason I attempt throughout my essay to create an oscillation between a Sterne who appears uncannily coterminous with us and a Sterne who invokes Divine Judgment. All the essays in the last two sections, concerning Sterne's erotic and ethical faces, oscillate in a similar manner, keeping us aware, in a variety of ways, that the writer who seems to fit so comfortably and convincingly into our own world and time is actually separated from us by enormous changes and commitments. I confess to a predilection for critics who are alert to—even while aware that we cannot prevent—our tendency to read ourselves in others, and who make concerted efforts to counterbalance their reading with conflicting voices. Bakhtin's vaunted notion of a dialogized heteroglossia in the novel should find an even more fertile ground in literary commentary.

Nowhere is this valuable spirit of counterbalance more entertainingly displayed than in Juliet McMaster's refusal to dismiss *Tristram Shandy* as sexist exploitation, the reading of a number of recent critics of Sterne. To find an author "one of us" no longer means, as it once did, that the writing is congenial to our own tastes; on the contrary, given equal doses of suspicion concerning whatever is already past and whatever is called literature, "one of us" has come to mean, for many writing literary criticism today, that we place authors in an ill-conceived adversarial relationship with our own virtues and truths so that we can belittle theirs. The sole desire of these neo-Victorians seems to be to demonstrate the ethical failure of the author or work under study when compared to the far more ethical concerns of the commentator. The humorously satiric, deflationary tone of McMaster's essay, as with Sterne's own satiric humor, has a most serious target and purpose: to suggest that our *present* knowledge is just that, limited in time and place, and not as absolutely justifiable as we often seem to think. The other side of the coin is equally serious: writers of the past (and Sterne, significantly, seems to favor seventeenth-century sources) are not as intellectually, morally, or socially obtuse as we sometimes want to believe.

In the highly charged politicized world of present-day literary commentary, my comments in the previous paragraph would define me as a reactionary among the more kindly inclined polemicists, brain-dead among those for whom canonized authors are the sole obstacle between modern readers and a perfect world. To my own satisfaction, however, nothing in the paragraph indicates that I would fail to appreciate (and feel myself and Sterne enriched by) a skillful application of new models or approaches to Sterne's fictions. This is surely the case with Calvin Thomas's application of the psychoanalytical theories of Jacques Lacan to Tristram's sexual "history." Anyone who has studied Sterne for many years will certainly appreciate his precise reading of the text and his model's capacity to account for something we have passed over countless times without commentary: in the opening chapter, the omitted indefinite article before "*woman*" resonates with Walter's attitude toward women as property without autonomy and stands in sharp juxtaposition with the presence of the article in "*a man*": "*Did ever woman, since the creation of the world, interrupt a man with such a silly question?*" Or, a page later, how can we help but admire the suppleness of reading that recognizes in the prefix *inter-* not only the "*entre* and enter, union and penetration" of *inter*course, but Sterne's interest as well in *inter*ruption ("a 'coming between,' a severance of the self from its discourse, the opening of a rupture") and, finally, the prefix-turned-verb "to inter"? Other readers of Sterne have recognized the intricate pattern of potency, impotency, and death that hovers over both

Shandy Hall and its author, but Thomas forces us to recognize as well that Sterne's comic book is about the most profound concerns of humanity, concerns buried deep within the resources of its language.

What is of particular interest in the essays by McMaster and Thomas, and the essay following by Paula Loscocco, is that three totally different approaches support a very similar reading of the male-female relationship projected in *Tristram Shandy:* "the physical triad of the family romance is renounced while a wholly masculine 'spiritual' dyad of father and son is privileged." Following a path first suggested by Leigh Ehlers and Helen Ostovich, all three find Walter Shandy rather than Sterne the culpable misogynist of Shandy Hall.[6]

Even the most careless reading of Sterne, I think, would suggest that Walter's dream of a world without women is the nightmare out of which Yorick, Sterne's most persistent alter ego, negotiates his escape in both *Journal to Eliza* and *A Sentimental Journey*. With these works in mind, we can reenter the world of Shandy Hall with less hostility, perhaps, toward its author, more willingness to accept the abundant clues that signal Sterne's ironic dismissals of the Shandy brothers for their misplaced and shared erotic yearning for singleness, for clear demonstration and accurate reproduction, for triumphant victory. Again Thomas seems to speak to the thrust of all three essays and most eloquently, I believe, for Sterne himself: "*Tristram Shandy* is not . . . a misogynist text. Rather, the text undermines its own misogynistic gestures by exposing the male characters' projections onto women as precisely that—projections that spring from the male characters' own feelings of anxiety and lack." What Loscocco adds to the argument is a willingness to return to the deep origins of Western thought; Augustine does indeed have a bearing on Sterne, just as he does on Proust, on Lacan, on Loscocco, and on me. Loscocco's gesture of retrieval is echoed in the final group of essays, "The Ethical Sterne," in which Elizabeth Harries, Elizabeth Kraft, and Donald Wehrs (circuitously through the French phenomenologist and Jewish theologian Emmanuel Levinas) all return to the Bible as further required reading for those believing it important to know the works on which Sterne erected his own.

The final essay exploring the erotic Sterne returns us to *A Sentimental Journey,* to the section's opening essay, which compares Proust and Sterne, and to a question that penetrates every corner of Sterne commentary, the relationship between Sterne and his narrators. Madeleine Descargues's analysis of Yorick finds echoes in the earlier essays on Sterne's skepticism (among unknowable things, our own natures rank very high indeed) but fits more appropriately here because its primary concern is to recover Sterne's intent in exposing Yorick (and the reader) to the series of erotic challenges that constitute the episodic experience of the *Journey*. This essay originally appeared in French and has been translated by the author especially for this volume.

For many modern readers (not to mention Sterne's contemporaries), the notion of an "ethical Sterne" might seem ludicrous. Sterne has endured a long history of condemnation for indecency, "nasty trifling," in F. R. Leavis's huffy dismissal; more recently Sterne has been grouped by the neo-Victorians with other eighteenth-century writers as culpably unethical because of his sexist views or because his writings in the sentimental vein aid and abet the imperialist agenda of a colonizing power. He has also, of course, been celebrated as amoral, an author interested in playfulness (aestheticism) on the one hand, intricate questions of epistemology and narrative experimentation on the other—an author interested, in short, in anything but the ethical tradition he preached for an entire lifetime and the questions that tradition raises about the meaning of human conduct, one's own most pertinently.

My creation of a category for the "ethical face" of Sterne, and my affording it pride of place as the culmination of a gathering of recent studies, is in large part my response to this tendency among modernists to avoid the subject. Taking a cue from Emmanuel Levinas, whom Donald Wehrs invokes so effectively in the final essay, I have included in this section four essays that challenge us to consider ethics as "first philosophy," that is, ethics not as the product of existence but as its enabling possibility; one might similarly suggest that ethics is not the product of a literary work (these essays do not look for "messages" in Sterne) but the ground from which it springs. Criticism, too, might be considered ethically grounded, at least insofar as it restages the site of the ethical, our responsiveness to and responsibility for the otherness represented by the text we hold in our hands. I would hesitate to carry this ramshackle analogy much further, except to suggest that good reading tries not to reduce a work to the length and breadth of our own interests but rather makes every effort to allow our interests to be altered through the mediation of the work. To allow a book to revise our notions about ourselves and our reading is perhaps our best defense against the terrible destructiveness of narrowness and inflexibility—what Levinas calls totalization, the violent reduction of difference to sameness; it is also, as indicated by my sense that such good reading is the product of enormous efforts against powerful reductive inclinations, an ethical endeavor.

What is especially intriguing in Elizabeth Harries's essay is that a seemingly modernist obsession, the literary fragment, leads her further and further away from present interests to the roots of Sterne's fragmentations in scriptural notions, "the Biblical and even liturgical framework that was always a part of his life and thought." Similar in strategy, Elizabeth Kraft's "The Pentecostal Moment in *A Sentimental Journey*" also returns to scripture (and to the liturgical calendar) to provide context for Sterne's ideas on charity, love, and inspiration. Most significant, she also consults Sterne's sermons; no better source could exist for his thoughts on those three topics, the very heart of Christian theology. Harries's essay has recently been incorporated into a full-length study, *The Unfinished Manner: Essays on the Fragment in the Later Eighteenth Century;* Kraft's forms part of her *Laurence Sterne Revisited,* wherein Sterne's career as a prelate of the Anglican church is consistently brought to bear on readings of his literary work.[7]

Sandwiched between these two essays (the essays are ordered chronologically within each section) is a quite different sort of recovery of the past, Robert Markley's important revision of the Whig interpretation of the third earl of Shaftesbury's role in sentimentalism's rise in the early eighteenth century, a topic of vital importance to all readers of Sterne. Markley argues persuasively that Shaftesbury's new morality of feeling should not be separated from his "ideological project," the defense of "upper-class interests and privileges." The idea that Shaftesbury represents a progressive and enlightened mode of thought, similar to other claims that the century represented progress away from religion and toward "rational" constructs in all walks of life, is here counterbalanced by the exposure of Shaftesbury's quite reactionary purposes. This insight, in turn, leads to a reexamination of Sterne's sentimentalism, most particularly as embodied in charitable action, and the role played by eighteenth-century Christianity in service to Britain's emerging commercialism. There are moments in this essay when Markley comes very close to championing his own ethics over Sterne's ("Sterne's theatrics of bourgeois virtue, then, are devoted paradoxically to demonstrating the sensitivity of a culture that shies away from acknowledging its responsibility for inflicting upon its victims the very injuries that it mourns and pities but does little to alleviate"), a tendency of critics of all stripes that I have already addressed; when read alongside the other authors in this collection, however, and especially in conjunction with Kraft and Wehrs, one comes to understand the strength of Markley's argument, distinct from his own ethical stance.

Christianity, of course, is no stranger to the paradoxes inherent in its being a religion that redeems humanity within the fallen world and hence reconciles rather than separates the human and divine. Many of Jesus's parables address precisely the issue of how, in Christ, one uses the goods of this world to prepare for the next, and the advice given is often conflicted—as it continues to be in the eighteenth century. Or from a different perspective entirely, given the contradictory political agenda behind Shaftesbury's socially constructed charity, is it perhaps merely a continuation of that contradiction to consider ethics solely as a question of economic equality? Wehrs's use of Levinas's ethics of the face can be read possibly as a response to an ethics of socioeconomic equality; indeed, Levinas considered himself a respondent to Hegel.

Written especially for this volume, Wehrs's essay fully engages the criticism of recent years, while at the same time pointing us in a refreshingly new direction. This same duality marks the writings of Emmanuel Levinas, for he is completely engaged by the many facets of postmodern discourse (after all, he introduced phenomenology to the French), while at the same time remarkably detached from many of its conclusions—and almost all of its values. Wehrs provides one important clue to this Janus-like capacity:

Materialism, for Levinas as for Sterne, participates in the dehumanizing totalizations figured by war: "To place the Neuter dimension of Being above the existent which unbeknown to it this Being would determine in some way, to make the essential events unbeknown to the existents, is to profess materialism" (Levinas, *Totality and Infinity*, 298–99). By theorizing materiality in a radical way, Sterne and Levinas articulate vindications of transcendence consistent with, but not philosophically dependent on, the religious doctrines each writer elsewhere, within devotional genres, advocated and explicated—those of latitudinarian Anglicanism and Talmudic Judaism respectively.

After a century in which fashions in literary criticism replaced each other with often lightning speed, we find ourselves facing the new century locked in stagnant disputes that are marked on both sides by the materiality of which Levinas speaks and by their shared hostility to any concept of transcendence. The more heat, the less light.

The violence of this materiality, as Levinas affirms and as Walter's argumentativeness and Toby's bowling green embody, is in its proselytizing (warfare is simply the endgame for convincing the world of the desirability and rightness of one's own notions), its usurpation of all counterpositions. To be sure, in the world of literary criticism, where the stakes are relatively low—few if any lives have been lost over different readings of Sterne—one might well acquiesce to the conflictual state of affairs, particularly if one has a satiric bone and enjoys a good argument. Insofar as criticism turns against the work itself, however, arguing or attacking the work out of existence as a viable counterforce to our own ways of thinking (and our present discussions about canon formation echo well Trim's making of cannons from lead sash weights, with its disastrous results), one becomes suspicious indeed of our present direction.

We need not, of course, endorse either Sterne's Christianity or Levinas's Judaism in order to understand the value of transcendence within the literary realm, the ethical lesson that the work (and the author too, for authors are exiled by materialisms, returned by transcendence) we confront, face to face, is always more than the form and meaning we provide, always an overflowing beyond our containments. To reproduce ourselves over and over again in everything we read may be a natural instinct or, at the very least, a comfortable practice, but ultimately it will reduce us to the single book reflecting our own narrowness, masturbatory prefaces written in *desobligéants* with drawn curtains. Sterne urges us instead to open ourselves to the world beyond the self, an opening not manifested merely as toleration of the other's independence but, far more significantly, as a sharp, indeed painful desire to risk all in a dance at the ring of pleasure with otherness. We are called to answer the summons of Nannette in Languedoc, the peasant family outside Lyons, the book in our hands, to respect not merely their right to exist, but their right to have an existence beyond our own, more compelling than our own, a transcendence that does not worship abstract Being but rather draws us into homage (a startling word, I suspect, for today's critic) toward the face we meet and—I suggest—the book we read.

What ultimately ties together the 18 essays of this collection is not a uniform opinion about Sterne's works nor agreement about what is interesting or useful or meaningful in them but rather their authors' shared belief that Sterne calls us all to bear witness to his writings. Criticism that silences rather than witnesses is already everywhere apparent in our literary journals and university press booklists, more and more dedicated to whatever has *not* long endured, whatever does not call to us across time and difference. As we continue to reduce our world to its present moment, we can perhaps drop a single sentimental tear for Yorick and his unending openness to whatever is not himself, to the infinite space into which he—like the "Fair Youth" of Keats's Grecian urn—eternally casts himself:

So that when I stretch'd out my hand, I caught hold of the Fille de Chambre's

Notes

1.   An even richer sense of Lamb's insights into Sterne's intertextuality can be gained by reading this essay alongside two others he published at the same time, "Sterne's Use of Montaigne," *Comparative Literature* 32 (1980): 1–41, and "The Comic Sublime and Sterne's Fiction," *ELH* 48 (1981): 110–43.

2.   See my essay "The Odd Couple: Laurence Sterne and John Norris of Bemerton," *PQ* 75 (1996): 361–85.

3.   *Comparative Literature Studies* 25 (1988): 127–51.

4.   I explore this argument in more detail in my *"Tristram Shandy": A Book for Free Spirits* (New York: Twayne, 1994); the critical emphasis I am writing against may be found in Wolfgang Iser's *Laurence Sterne: "Tristram Shandy"* (Cambridge, England: Cambridge University Press, 1988) and Jonathan Lamb's *Sterne's Fiction and the Double Principle* (Cambridge, England: Cambridge University Press, 1989).

5.   John Traugott, *Tristram Shandy's World: Sterne's Philosophical Rhetoric* (Berkeley: California University Press, 1954); Martin Battestin, *The Providence of Wit: Aspects of Form in Augustan Literature and the Arts* (Oxford: Clarendon, 1974).

6.   Leigh Ehlers, "Mrs. Shandy's 'Lint and Basilicon': The Importance of Women in *Tristram Shandy*," *South Atlantic Review* 46 (1981): 61–75; Helen Ostovich, "Reader as Hobby-Horse in *Tristram Shandy*," *PQ* 68 (1989): 325–42.

7.   Elizabeth Harries, *The Unfinished Manner: Essays on the Fragment in the Later Eighteenth Century* (Charlottesville, Va.: University of Virginia Press, 1994); Elizabeth Kraft, *Laurence Sterne Revisited* (New York: Twayne, 1997).

THE INTERTEXTUAL STERNE

◆

Sterne's System of Imitation

JONATHAN LAMB

I continued to reason how much further one could proceed with this reflection
and multiplication of what is imitated: that is to say, whether one could not only
duplicate, but triplicate and quadruplicate it, and go as far as one liked, finally,
as it were one imitator imitating another imitator, and so on and so on . . .

—Alessandro Piccolomini

Ever since John Ferriar compiled a regular institute of Sterne's borrowings,
the novelist's reputation has been divided between praise for his spontaneity
and originality on the one hand, and an awed respect for the extent and subtlety of his thefts on the other. Sterne makes no bones about exhibiting these
two sides of his literary character and seems to see no need to reconcile them:
he is both the man who cautiously burned more wit than he published and
the "inconsiderate Soul . . . who never yet knew what it was to speak or write
one premeditated word,"[1] the man who in *Tristram Shandy* cleverly plagiarizes
Robert Burton's attack on plagiarism and the one who, in the same novel,
declares that he begins "with writing the first sentence———and trusting to
Almighty God for the second" (*TS,* V.i.408; VIII.ii.656). Like Tristram
Shandy, Sterne seems to alternate between discretion and carelessness,
between government of and by the pen, expressed as the difference between
writing fasting and writing full (VI.xvii.524–25). These days it is usual to
concentrate on his originality, his contempt for rules, his debunking of "conventions," his readiness to experiment with the novel-form, in short his modernism. By contrast, those critics who have studied the texts and methods he
used to supplement his originality have tended to conclude that he had an
old-fashioned taste for literature and wit and that what is odd about him is
what is out of date.[2] In this essay I want to strike a balance between these
two views by considering Sterne's way of writing as fairly typical of his time
and by showing that his most spontaneous and irregular production, *The
Journal to Eliza,* obeys the same laws as his more finished work.[3]

Although in his politics Sterne was a Whig, and invented in "uncle
Toby" a hero who has little in common with the Tory satirists on the subject

Reprinted from *Modern Language Review* 76 (1981): 794–810.

of the War of the Spanish Succession, in his writing he parodies the chiliastic visions of true-blue Moderns with as much vigour as Swift. Those who really believe that the arts and sciences are advancing towards their acme of perfection or who believe that wit and judgement will create between them an ultimate "effusion of light" (*TS,* I.xxi.72; III.xx.233) are mocked with paradoxes and with the facts of their own unredeemed nature. Sterne's view, like Fielding's, is that life is not going to change very much and that any attempt to transcend its imperfections and ambiguities, like Walter Shandy's systems or the Man of the Hill's delight in the nectar of infinity, is ridiculous. The "world" of *Tristram Shandy* is an Augustan one where "incorporated minds," in Johnson's phrase, try to find some tolerable room on the isthmus of a middle state, a place where trifles have their importance and where "small heroes" try to cope with destinies they never forged. That there is no amelioration of the human condition other than the light in which we choose to regard its discomforts and puzzles is the theme of most of Sterne's jokes. In the dedication he writes to a fellow-sufferer, Sterne offers laughter as a fence against infirmities, not as a cure of them. In many respects "Shandeism" is like the practical scepticism of *Rasselas, Tom Jones,* and *Humphry Clinker* in its determination to expect from life only what life will afford.

With an outlook similar to his Tory contemporaries it is not surprising that Sterne should share many of their literary tenets. He is not burlesquing Pope's rule:

> A perfect Judge will *read* each work of Wit
> With the same Spirit that its Author *writ*

when he asks "madam" to tame her curiosity or when he invites the reader to imagine, and even write, his or her own part of the narrative. In allowing the reader a dialectical share of the written product, he is asking for that sagacity which Fielding frequently demands from his reader (especially in his tender scenes), comprising sufficient experience, humanity, and sympathy to make the *poco meno* as detailed and believable as the *poco più.* Sterne is as opposed as Swift to that passive curiosity (so close to prurience in his opinion and Fielding's) which makes a beast of the "lazy grunting Reader."[4] Ideally author and reader occupy a common ground on which what is already known fruitfully intersects with what is written and read: "What oft was thought but ne'er so well exprest." Sterne's version of this precept is given in a letter to an American admirer where he says that the reader's ideas are "call'd forth by what he reads, and the vibrations within, so entirely correspond with those excited, 'tis like reading *himself* and not the *book*" (*Letters,* p. 411). It is a case of finding Pope's "something" which "gives us back the Image of our Mind."

In neo-Classical literary theory the author experiences an analogous intersection between his own ideas and a text, whether it is the Book of Human Nature which Fielding transcribes in writing *Tom Jones* and which

Johnson told Boswell diligently to read, or whether it is an actual text modelled on that great original. In the end the best literature and the Book of Human Nature are the same: Scaliger finds Virgil and Nature to be identical, while Virgil finds in Homer the same identity between what is and what is written. Classical literature forms a kind of institute of all human experience, hence Swift's horror at Bentley's officious attempts to lessen its authority and his mockery of the Moderns' assumption that contemporary experience will add to the stock. The dunce-narrator of *A Tale of a Tub* faces an embarrassing shortage of "new Matter" when he writes his book because he has not understood, in the words of the *Spectator,*

> that Wit and fine Writing doth not consist so much in advancing things that are new, as in giving things that are known an agreeable Turn. It is impossible for us who live in the later Ages of the World, to make Observations in Criticism, Morality, or in any Art or Science, which have not been touched upon by others. We have little else left us, but to represent the Common Sense of Mankind in more strong, more beautiful, or more uncommon Lights. (No. 253)

Joseph Warton, a critic skilled in tracing the genealogies of stories and ideas, concludes with Voltaire that "All is imitation . . . Boiardo has imitated Pulci, Ariosto has imitated Boiardo. The geniuses, apparently most original, borrow from each other."[5] For his own part, Sterne gestures freely at his models, noting the critical distances between himself, Swift, and Rabelais and drawing attention to what is "cervantic" in his sense of humour, not forgetting at the same time to emphasize "the air and originality" of his book (*Letters,* pp. 76–77). The nature of the originality and the imitation will become clearer by looking at *Tristram Shandy* and some of the books that have contributed to it.

Walter Shandy's career illustrates the problems a man of erudition faces when he has an ambition to be original. Although it is his axiom that "an ounce of a man's own wit, was worth a tun of other people's" and his belief that a man may pick up an opinion "as a man in a state of nature picks up an apple" (*TS,* II.xix.173; III.xxxiv.262–63) and show as inalienable a right to it, it is nevertheless the case that all his systems are cobbled together out of other men's books. No matter how exempt from the stream of vulgar ideas or the common road of thinking Walter thinks he is, and no matter how oddly he assembles his theories and applies them, it is evident from Chambers's *Cyclopaedia,* Burton's *Anatomy of Melancholy,* and Obadiah Walker's *Of Education* that his ideas once dwelt in other heads. He makes this point himself when he praises Ernulphus's anathema as a digest and institute of all possible modes of swearing and defies anyone "to swear *out* of it" (III.xii.215–16). Not that Ernulphus is original on this account: he merely provides the meeting point between all prior and all subsequent knowledge of oath-making (as Slawkenbergius does in the field of noses) to show that there is nothing new under the sun and that all is imitation. Walter's "singular and ingenious" hypothesis is no more than a theory of imitation that his son, with some minor provisos, espouses too. Even Tristram's most original inventions, the digressive-progressive system of writing and the life-writing paradox, are not as original as he claims they are: Longinus praises Thucydides's management of digressions so that "at length after a long Ramble, he very pertinently but unexpectedly returns to his Subject, and raises the Surprize and Admiration of all";[6] and Montaigne and Cervantes discuss the puzzles that arise when a life is being lived as well as written, not to mention Walter's frustrations with the *Tristrapaedia*.[7] Parodically, Tristram concedes the point when, amidst his father's energetic quotation of his grief for Bobby's death, he traces the course of Eleazer's sentiment from the Ganges to Yorkshire and comically refines upon Sir William Temple's theory of the geography of imitation.[8] And when he declares that he intercepts "many a thought which heaven intended for another man" (*TS*, VIII.ii.657) he outlines a potential community of ideas which is achieved whenever his interceptions are made, as they often are, at the level of libraries rather than the middle air.

At its most utilitarian, Sterne's borrowing on his hero's behalf is merely a way of finding convenient sources of recondite information with which to ornament a theme like love, education, or death. So Burton's partition on Love-Melancholy is used heavily during the Amours, just as Walker is used extensively for the *Tristrapaedia*. As an act of vanity borrowing can be the means to claiming prestigious friends: Rabelais, Montaigne, Cervantes, Locke, Shakespeare. But whatever Sterne's first motives are in borrowing, he often develops secondary ones which make the discovery of a theft his triumph and not the detective's, or which give an added allusive strength to a professed imitation. Consistent with his intention not to exert a false authority over the reader's imagination, Tristram advises us to "Read, read, read, read, my unlearned reader! read" (*TS*, III.xxxvi.268); and it is only by reading that we will appreciate his plagiarism of Burton's attack on plagiarism, or be aware of the careful distinctions being drawn between sense and nonsense in Walter's definition of a good tutor, or find the sequel to his interrupted definition of "analogy" (VI.v.496–99; II.vii.118–19).[9] Likewise it is by reading that we can piece together the clues about his intentions or opinions that Sterne is dropping for our benefit. Slop's arrival is keyed to a couple of allusions to *The Dunciad* ("majesty of mud" and "obstetric hand") that, combined with the simile of Hamlet's ghost, suggest a Smedley-cum-Douglas-cum-apparition emerging dirtily from below with just the sort of exaggerated theatricality that marks the dunces' performances in Pope's satire. Sterne has also wrapped this sequence in three allusions to Hogarth's *Analysis of Beauty* (II.vi.115; ix.121; xvii.141) which refer to the line of beauty and to the greater or less amount of detail needed in the composition of a figure, "the insensible more or less"; and they form a pictorial bridge between Slop's sesquipedality of belly and the natural grace of Trim's sermon-reading.[10] More than that they were consciously intended by Sterne "mutually [to] illustrate [Hogarth's] System & mine," a system of careful alternation between tact and circumstantiality that he had already called "the happiness of the Cervantic humour" (*Letters,* pp. 99, 77) and that Pope had praised as "the *true Sublime* of *Don Quixote* . . . the perfection of the Mock-Epick."[11] Clearly, Sterne was using and thinking of his Cervantic-Hogarthian system in two different but related ways, as a satirical weapon of deflation and as a humorous tool of enlargement. The one is signalled by his allusion to *The Dunciad,* where exaggeration is reductively mock-epic, and the other by his allusions to Hogarth, where exaggeration serves to highlight and cherish the comedy of average human behaviour. That the sermon Trim reads is Sterne's own, printed at York in 1750, and that Slop's overthrow is a version of the one Montaigne describes in his essay "Use makes Perfectness" serves to show that Sterne's faculty for allusive imitation is almost boundless.

Sometimes a borrowing is made in order to mock the author borrowed from. Sterne's respect for Locke did not exclude witty revenge being taken on the philosopher for his attacks on figurative language, and this is done mostly at the expense of Locke's occasional metaphors. When he calls the name of complex ideas "as it were the knot that ties them fast together" and stresses the importance of that knot in keeping the parts of the idea united, he allows Sterne the opportunity of making the name the very opposite of a neat bond.[12] Although Obadiah's knots are "good, honest, devilish tight, hard knots, made *bona fide*" (*TS,* III.x.198), they are untied into all sorts of puns: "knots" of speed, "knot" as noose, "knot" as life's obstacle, marriage "knot," and even the umbilical "knot" which Slop will have to tie when he has undone the other ones. Depending on names rather than on the natural associations of the mind is shown to be a risky business. Contrariwise Locke's idea of a dictionary, where the meaning of "words standing for things" might be fixed by "little draughts and prints made of them" (III, 11, 25), is borrowed by Tristram as a metaphor for facial expressions: "There are some trains of certain ideas which leave prints of themselves about our eyes and eye-brows . . . we see, spell, and put them together without a dictionary" (*TS,* V.i.413).

The associative habit of mind that Sterne defends from Locke's nominalism is closely related to the borrowing habit. A true imitator does much more than simply spatchcock other texts into his own, or dutifully give a foreign idea an "agreeable turn": other men's thoughts are not a supplement to his own but the very means by which his own thought takes place. His commonplace-book and his memory are to all intents and purposes identical, and every passing idea in his head, which will inevitably have a literary reference if not a literary origin, instantly assembles associated literary ideas around it. This is what Walter is doing in his oration on death, taming his grief by fettering it in the sentiments of ancient and neoteric stoics between which his mind moves with an almost natural associative agility. Just as fluidly, Tristram's mind can shift from one borrowed sentiment to another as if they were decreeing the development of his thought and the pressure of his feelings. A sentiment from

Montaigne leads naturally into one from Rabelais, and a quotation from Rabelais leads to an oath fetched not from Ernulphus but from *Don Quixote*.[13] The process is like Trim's knowledge of the fifth commandment, which is reached by going through the previous four: Tristram finds what he believes and feels very often by travelling through texts, *reading* himself in them and writing down the result. It is a sort of travelling commonly found in the eighteenth-century and early nineteenth-century comic novel: Parson Adams, Charlotte Lennox's Arabella, Catherine Morland, and Edward Waverley all try to find a path through life by books; yet the burlesque or pedantic elements of this imitative heroism are greatly outweighed by the freshness and vigour of minds that are formed by literary experiences or sharpened by literary expectation. This is a paradox that Sterne is well aware of and his favourite sources, as well as his characters, reveal his deep interest in the phenomenon of bookish naivety which accompanies true sincerity, and imitation which manifests an original integrity.

Montaigne and Burton are the two contemplative models, as it were, and Don Quixote the active one. Between them they represent the two sides of imitation: responding to literature as pure experience on the one hand, and converting experience into literary analogue on the other. All three confront the business of imitation in the spirit of classical criticism. When he decides to imitate the mad antics of Beltenebros, Quixote justifies his decision according to the rule of imitation that is observed in painting and "in all other arts and sciences that serve for the ornament of well-regulated commonwealths." Choosing to season his imitation with one or two of Orlando's frenzied actions, he carefully determines on those "most essential and worthy imitation" (I, 181–82). Montaigne and Burton both make the point that borrowing is no theft, provided the imitation measures up to the source (as Quixote's certainly does): Burton calls it "assimilating what he has swallowed," and Montaigne says it would be indigestion to do otherwise.[14] They stress how different the borrowed thing becomes in its new setting, "theirs . . . and yet mine," says Burton, and Montaigne: "a Work that shall be absolutely his own"; while Quixote declares the singular perfection of his imitation consists in running "mad without a cause, without the least constraint or necessity" (*DQ*, I, 183). Their originality lies in the manner of doing it, "the composition and method," and Montaigne warns his reader to regard not "the Matter I write, but my Method in writing. . . . For I make others say for me, what, either for want of Language, or want of Sense, I cannot myself well express" (*Essays*, II, 115). What seems to be a considered and highly self-conscious procedure of imitation is transformed into an extraordinarily intimate exhibition by means of the method of assimilation. "I expose myself entire," Montaigne confesses, and Burton says, "I have laid myself open (I know it) in this treatise, turned mine inside outward" (*Essays*, II, 72; *AM*, I, 27). In his Beltenebrosing, Quixote reveals parts so private, "such rarities, that Sancho even made haste to turn his horse's head, that he might no longer see them" (*DQ*, I, 194).

Of the three methods of imitation, Burton's shows most vividly how an odd individual can inhabit a book world and use its contents to reveal himself. His experience does not extend beyond the shelves of his college's well-stocked library; all his travelling is done by map, but because his theme is melancholy, a *disorder* afflicting the whole world as well as himself, he can never find an appropriate or standard response to the information of books. Although texts are exclusively his source for estimations of reality, they offer him neither order nor a coherent body of symptoms. So Burton is constantly expatiating, "ranging in and out," his moods constantly shifting between despair and optimism, anger and helpless laughter, all stimulated by the books he is endlessly traversing. His sentences have a loose subordinate structure designed for the instant incorporation of diverse material, and they present a constant temptation to elaborate ideas and heighten moods: the word "sermon" (*AM,* I, 35) or the simple proposition "I am contented with my fortunes" (II, 188) tends to spawn examples, synonyms, modifications, and quotations in such profusion that Burton often leaps the gap and begins to impersonate his subject. The proposition "He loves her, she hates him" is gone into so thoroughly that Burton is transformed into the forlorn "he": "I give her all attendance, all observance, I pray and entreat" (III, 231). When he cannot stop his words or the feeling they are intensifying, he commits what he calls "overshooting," as in "Democritus Junior to the Reader" where he becomes Democritus in earnest in spite of the reader. He moves towards his emotional declaration by quotation and allusion (Erasmus, Horace, Martial, Terence) then, suddenly realizing what he has done, he retreats in the same manner, by way of Tasso, Tacitus, Bacon, saying finally "in Medea's words I will crave pardon" (I, 122–23). Literature is the means both to promoting and excusing his decision to write satire; it is the vehicle for feelings of temerity and shame that Burton partly experiences and partly performs. It contributes to the larger performance in which he writes about melancholy in a melancholy manner, exhibiting in his treatise all the contradictions and irregularities that belong to the disease. Burton's real melancholy is both excited and controlled by books and his imitations of them, just as Quixote's imitation of Beltenebros is both the effect and the representation of madness. In both cases the otherwise unframeable contexture of a peculiar self finds an addition to its experience and a method of self-expression by an act of imitation.

In his essay "Upon Some Verses of Virgil," Montaigne addresses himself to the subject of eroticism in life and literature, old as he is, in order to discover the true principle of excitement. He does not find it in Martial's overnaked verse, but in Lucretius and Virgil, whose "words of flesh and bone" are the result of seeing "farther and more clearly into things" and finding in them a "Sense [which] illuminates and produces the Words" (*Essays,* III, 120–21). Discretion and obliquity are the keys to good love-poetry, an artful modesty of language in which "words signifie more than they express." This is what makes Virgil's Venus more beautifully alive than the original, and it is the same obliquity which makes the practice as well as the literature of love truly exciting. This is "naturalized art," bringing actions and words as close to their objects as possible, and it is Montaigne's too: his "Torrent of Babble" is exactly his, and yet not his; his "apish imitating Quality" (III, 124) has ensured that what seems carelessness is really the obliquity and discretion he has learned from the poets and from Plutarch. He has warmed his old blood with their words of flesh and bone, and used his own to "represent my self to the Life." They are the words that make the book consubstantial with its author, known in him and he in it; and the representation of himself in such a book discovers experiences he would never have had, as giving ear to whimsies "because I am to Record them" and studying books not to make his book but because "I had made it" (II, 509–10).

When Sterne invests Tristram with his knowledge of Montaigne's *Essays,* the *Anatomy of Melancholy,* and *Don Quixote* he gives him room to experiment with all aspects of imitation: the discovery of life in literature, literature in life; the conversion of what is read into what is acted, the translation of what is lived into what is read. The Shandy family are chiefly concerned to convert literature into action, like Quixote: Toby's bowling green is analogous to the infant Tristram in so far as they are both used to realize texts upon (the *Flanders Gazette* and the fruits of Walter's study). Disasters occur when the text is removed (the Treaty of Utrecht), or when the realization goes wrong and ceases to conform to the model, or when something happens for which there is no textual authority (the circumcision until it is redeemed by the advent of a book). But when things go wrong, literature comes unconsciously into the minds of those who think they are bereft of it. In his Apologetical Oration, Toby quotes consciously from Yorick's sermon a sentiment borrowed from Burton, having already unconsciously borrowed from the same source himself (*TS*, VI.xxxii.557; *AM*, I, 57, 60). When Walter lifts himself off the bed to exclaim against his ill luck and to offer himself some consolation, he starts quoting the beginning of Yorick's sermon "Trust in God" (*TS*, IV.vii.332).[15] Similarly, when he apologizes to Toby for having been rude about his hobby-horse he insensibly uses Cassius's words to Brutus: "forgive, I pray thee, this rash humour which my mother gave me" (II.xii.133),[16] prompting Tristram to make the comparison explicit in the next chapter but one. When Trim makes his speech on death equipped with no deeper reading than his muster-roll, he nevertheless manages to quote from the same essay of Montaigne that Walter is using (V.x.436).[17] It is as if the mind, faced with painful or unexpected circumstances, naturally forms a sentiment out of them and makes an accidental discovery of life's literary qualities; or at least it is as if Tristram wishes us to think so. Certainly in his own case he is moved, rather than simply inclined, to find an authority for his feelings when they reach a higher pitch by overshooting in Burton's or Cid Hamet Benengeli's words. Whether a character is being natural or studied, an imitation and therefore something of a performance takes place: texts control the emotions, as in Walter's discourse on death, and release them, as in Trim's. Either way, imitation guarantees a mode of expression for sentiments that otherwise might have none, so that in the heat of anger or the coolness of consideration oaths are made (as Montaigne says his are) by imitation and according to Ernulphian necessity. The imitative component in hobbyhorses is what makes them such apt instruments for character-drawing because it exhibits what the character wishes to present of himself (the "personate actor" in Burton's phrase [*AM*, I, 15]) and it also is the means of turning his inside outward. Nature as art and art as nature meet at the point of imitation: Quixote promises himself real pain in his impersonation of Beltenebros ("the blows which I must give myself on the head, ought to be real, substantial, sound ones, without any trick, or mental reservation" [*DQ*, I, 187]), while the real pain Walter feels at the attacks on his son's virility forces him to turn at once to books for solace and utterance.

Tristram organizes his narrative according to a system of double imitation; that is, he borrows both the structure and the matter of his situations, sometimes from different sources. Walter's letter of instructions to Toby, for instance, is based on Quixote's to Sancho but consists of advice out of Burton. Toby's oration is *like* Quixote's defences of arms against learning but is also pieced out with the *Anatomy of Melancholy,* in the same way that Walter's quotation of Yorick forms a scene that recalls Quixote's complaint after he has been trampled by the bulls (*DQ*, II, 383). The arrangement can be even more complex, as during the reading of Ernulphus when Tristram makes a Burtonian oath and a Benengelian wager to affirm the Cervantic contrast between Slop's reading and Toby's whistling. This is like Yorick's death, which in its situation is like Quixote's (a beating followed by the loss of illusions and then life), but which is accomplished in Sancho's words and recorded in Shakespeare's. At its most subtle, the technique can exactly reproduce the effects of the original: Trim's unconscious imitation of Montaigne imitates Sancho's unconscious imitation of Plutarch (*TS*, V.x.436; compare *DQ*, II, 440), and Sancho's speech is imitated again by Tristram when he wants to say something about sleep that is entirely natural and therefore better than "the dissertations squeez'd out of the heads of the learned" (*TS*, IV.xv.347). It is a clever irony and illustrates, as all these examples do, the inescapability of imitation.

Turning his own life into literature through the medium of literature, Tristram unites the methods of Burton and Montaigne. As well as a fund of erudition, Burton offers him the warmth and suddenness of imitative practice, and it is his overshootings that he concentrates on. The Lady Baussière rides on to the rhythm of Burton's callous rich man; Tristram pulls himself back from the brink of a vision of carnal bliss with the words Burton uses to extricate himself from nuns' and widows' melancholy;[18] and on his own account Tristram will overshoot himself into a warm contempt for rules (*TS*, IV.x.337) or into a devil of a chapter where the readers are advised to look to themselves (V.iii.418). And sometimes the habit of saying too much will suit the form of a Benengelian apostrophe, where Tristram will launch himself towards the object of his feelings, as Burton so often does, by inhabiting his text and speaking in it; and sometimes he will ring the changes on a word like "cant" or "nose" as Burton does on "sermon" or "mad." It is in Burton's manner that Tristram makes his most poignant declaration: he is "sick! sick! sick! sick!" (VII.ii.578) as scholars' labours are "mad, mad, mad" (AM, I, 47). Montaigne, on the other hand, does not supply a model of imitative emotion; rather he shows what sorts of unions can take place between the mind and its object after that emotion has been raised. Constantly studying his relation to experience he ends up dreaming that he dreams, liking the "deadest deaths" and finding a paradoxical completeness in writing a book that is its own subject, consubstantial with its sources and its author, because "this Form is, in me, turn'd into Substance."[19] When Tristram is fully aware of his life and book as the same thing, his imitations have the "ambitious subtilty" of Montaigne's associations: attacking plagiarism by plagiarizing Burton's equally plagiarized attack has the reflexive density of his borrowing Montaigne on the subject of borrowing (IV.xxv.375) or his invocation of Benengeli's invocation (IX.xxix.780; compare DQ, II, 285). His mind is so attuned to the business of imitation that there is no difference between writing and action, and he produces the very thing he is imitating.

That the emotions must be stimulated in the reading, assimilation, and production of literature is, of course, a sentimental axiom widely embraced by Sterne's contemporaries, but only he has investigated its implications for imitation far enough to find an appropriate critical theory. The process begins with his contempt for anything that is written in a straight line, emerging from the head as a cold unmetaphorical, "sententious parade of wisdom." Prose which separates itself from its subject, "tall, opake words, one before another, in a right line, betwixt your own and your readers conception" (TS, III.xx.235), will smother any fire in the person using it and utterly inhibit any vibratory response from the audience. In their sermons, Sterne and Yorick have avoided preaching that is designed merely "to shew the extent of our reading, or the subtleties of our wit—to parade it in the eyes of the vulgar with the beggarly accounts of a little learning, tinseled over with a few words which glitter, but convey little light and less warmth" (TS, IV.xxvi.377). Sterne's earliest attempt to discuss the difference between this bad sort of imitation and warmer performances of flesh and bone is in his Fragment in the Manner of Rabelais where, in two short chapters, a sympathetic churchman called Longinus Rabelaicus ("one of the greatest Critick's in the western World, and as Rabelaic a Fellow as ever piss'd") is proposing to write a "Kerukopaedia" or system and institute of sermon-making; meanwhile in the next room Homenas (the dwarfish borrower of Tristram Shandy) is making his sermon by transcribing some of Samuel Clarke's choice paragraphs and thoughts "all of a Row."[20] Homenas's tears of shame at being discovered in his theft completely refrigerate his borrowed sublimity; on the other hand Longinus Rabelaicus's scheme, for all its pedantic sound, is an art to combine the making and the giving of sermons, "a Way to do this to some *Tune*," suggesting the harmony of Tristram's fiddler "whose talents lie in making what he fiddles to be felt,—who . . . puts the most hidden springs of my heart into motion" (*TS*, V.xv.444). At the same time it is a plan to do for sermons what Ernulphus does for oaths, to create a pool of all possible sentiments so that no one can preach out of it.

In his important sermon "Search the Scriptures" Sterne turns again to the difference between language that is essentially moving and that which is coldly elegant and nice, and once again he mentions Longinus's name. Using translation as a standard, he undertakes to defend the scriptural or oriental sublime against critics (and Addison was one) whose delicacy prevents them from seeing its beauties. He begins by making the distinction Yorick makes in *Tristram Shandy* between eloquence which consists in "an over-curious and artificial arrangement of figures, tinsel'd over with a gaudy embellishment of words, which glitter, but convey little or no light to the understanding" and the language of the heart, in this case the biblical eloquence, which consists "more in the greatness of the things themselves, than in the words and expressions."[21] In translation the classical sublime suffers because it lies in the expression, whereas the lofty ideas of the scriptural sublime survive the "most simple and literal translations . . . and break forth with as much force and vehemence as in the original." Longinus's praise of the sublime in Genesis is instanced, and he is paid a version of the compliment paid to Longinus Rabelaicus: "the best critic the eastern world ever produced." Sterne joins a debate here that had much to contribute towards the development of the English sublime in "The Age of Sensibility,"[22] and it seems likely that some of his illustrations were prompted by reading Longinus in William Smith's translation. Not only does he take some of Longinus's examples of the classical sublime to show how poorly they translate (Neptune shaking the earth and the description of Pallas's horses), he also shares Smith's enthusiasm for the scriptural sublime, particularly the description of the war-horse in *Job*, and no doubt read the discussion of that passage in the *Guardian*, 86, to which Smith alludes (*OS*, p. 171, n. 3). The distinction which the *Guardian* critic, Smith, and Sterne all enforce is of course Longinus's. In the famous seventh section of *On the Sublime* (pp. 14–15) he recommends that poetry and prose be carefully scrutinized to see "whether it be not only Appearance":

> We must divest it of all superficial Pomp and Garnish. If it cannot stand this Trial, without doubt it is only swell'd and puff'd up, and it will be more for our Honour to contemn than to admire it . . . Whatever pierces no deeper than the Ears, can never be the true Sublime. That on the contrary is grand and lofty,

which the more we consider, the greater Ideas we conceive of it; whose Force we cannot possibly withstand; which immediately sinks deep, and makes such Impressions on the Mind as cannot be easily worn out or effaced.

It is the same distinction Tristram and Yorick use to mock the French, whose sublime consists in mere words ("*more* in the *word;* and *less* in the *thing*" [*ASJ,* 159]) and who believe that "*talking of love, is making it*" (*TS,* IX.xxv.787). On the other hand, when the expression is a function of a real idea operating on the whole man (Trim's dropping of the hat, Slawkenbergius's "lambent pupilability of slow, low, dry chat," or uncle Toby's *Lillabulero*), it "leaves something more inexpressible upon the fancy, than words can either convey—or sometimes get rid of" (V.vii.432). When words are used, they must be endowed with the expressive power of action or gesture and exert sufficient force to ensure a feeling response in the audience. This is the rhetorical and moral basis of Sterne's sermons and novels, for empty expression is not only bad in itself, it is also used to hide imperfections of the heart.

Sterne's use of the translation-test in establishing the superiority of the scriptural sublime points out one of the ways that Longinus contributes to his system of imitation. As a preacher Sterne felt it his duty to be the energetic medium between the force of scriptural language and the hearts of his congregation, so his "dramatic" sermons are translations of the primitive and sublime ideas of the holy text into expressions that are made as forceful and immediate as possible by concrete language and a variety of rhetorical devices. The sermons are not simply elaborations or explanations of the text but enactments or imitations of the divine original, the fruits of a mind "naturally elevated by the true Sublime, and so sensibly affected with its lively Strokes, that it swells in Transport and an inward Pride, as if what was only heard had been the Product of its own Invention" (*OS,* p. 14). Sterne was proud of his sermons in this way, despite their being filled with a good stock of Latitudinarian texts as well, because they testified to a necessary sympathetic power in him, which he could transfer to his parishioners or, to use his own coinage of Longinus, having "read" his own heart in the Bible text, his audience might then read theirs in his. In his novels, Sterne arranges a variety of literal and figurative translations, from Slawkenbergius's last tale to those prints and etchings in the countenance, all of which require that sixth sense of the heart to interpret rightly. In *A Sentimental Journey,* he fully develops the metaphor of translation to include all language, whether of the face, the body, the tongue, or an actual text, and this universal language provides the "volumes" of material that Yorick translates into his two volumes of book. But there is a technique of translation in *Tristram Shandy* that is related directly to the one he developed for his sermons, and that is to take a text not from the Bible but from proverbial wisdom like "*All is not gain that is got into the purse*" or "*Nothing in this world . . . is made to last for ever*" or "It is with LOVE as with CUCKOLDOM" (*TS,* III.xxx.256; VIII.xix.684; ii.656). No doubt Sterne shared

Quixote's opinion that proverbs are a non-systematic fund of truth, "all so many sentences and maxims drawn from experience, the universal mother of sciences" (*DQ,* I, 138), and he has Tristram dramatize them in the same way that his sermons dramatize a scriptural text. The text for Trim's speech on death ("Are we not here now—and gone in a moment?") is, as Tristram says, "one of your self-evident truths" (*TS,* V.vii.431–32), but when it is re-animated by Trim's rhetorical use of his hat "nothing could have expressed the sentiment of mortality . . . like it." Toby's gentleness, rendered in rather ornamental proverbial form by his nephew as having "scarce a heart to retalli-ate upon a fly" (II.xii.130), is illustrated in a dramatic realization of the proverb as Toby catches, apostrophizes, and liberates an actual fly.

There is a strong "Rabelaic" element in these restorations of proverbial truth to the human activity from which it derives. In almost every case the body participates with the tongue to give the borrowed text the force of an original sentiment, as often in *Gargantua and Pantagruel* Panurge will use body language to redeem words and ideas from abstraction. Toby's literal and metaphorical kindness to flies exactly resembles those situations where Panurge enacts the proverb that applies to him by eating his corn while it is green, having a flea in his ear, or sitting between two stools.[23] Whatever truth has been lost from the proverb by timeless repetition is renewed by an active or dramatic imitation which makes words once more conversant about *things.* Indeed this sort of rhetoric, or translation, tends to dissolve the differ-ence between text and example, word and thing, so that Trim, dramatically applying his body to the reading of Yorick's already dramatic sermon, be-comes so moved that he cannot distinguish between what is descriptive and what is real. There are Cervantine analogues for this state of affairs, for exam-ple Quixote's mistaking the representation of *Gayferos and Melisandra* for the real thing, but Sterne is concerned to stress the value of the sympathy that accomplishes these translations of the active meaning of a text into gesture, speech, and ultimately another text. He is also discovering, with or through Rabelais, a version of the comic sublime that has its origin in scripture. When Panurge prophesies victory over the Dipsodes by breaking a staff over two wineglasses, and when Tristram, in his Rabelaisian Preface, takes Pantagruel's advice about finding wisdom in ordinary things and comes to the crux of his argument by pointing to his cane chair, they are using a primitive figurative language called by Warburton, in his discussion of biblical examples of it, "the voice of the sign."[24] It is not a case of supplanting words with gestures, but of finding the complemental force of both that makes words, bodies, and things speak. This tendency carries both authors towards a kind of punning (also found in the Bible) that establishes an identity of action and naming: it is constantly to be found in Rabelais's etymologies of names and in his puns on *wine* ("Notez, amis, que de vin divin on devient"; *Cinquième Livre,* Ch. 45) where the deed and its verbal or liturgical signification become one; and Tris-tram is doing the same thing when he "drops" remarks and drops *Remarks*

(*TS*, VII.xxxvi.638–39). The same identity is established by Trim's hat, which does more than represent the sentiment of mortality: "It fell dead," and in doing so it returns the self-evidence of the truism to the much more powerful self-evidence of the voice of the sign.[25]

Sterne's choice of the name "Longinus Rabelaicus" indicates that he was aware of the potential connexion between the two before he thought of writing his first novel: in Smith's edition of Longinus he found the theory of eloquence that deals with things rather than words copiously illustrated, and in Rabelais he found it put into comic practice. But Longinus offers even more. When Tristram overshoots into a warm disregard for rules, and dispenses with the critical cant about chapters in the same phrase his Epistemon uses to cast doubt on the value of a Kerukopaedia ("a story of a roasted horse"), he adds, "O! but to understand this . . . you must read *Longinus*" (*TS*, IV.x.337). In Longinus's treatise we can find a rule for almost every one of Tristram's irregularities, and in this particular case Tristram, who is already imitating the performed warmth of Burton, is claiming a portion of the praise Longinus awards to Demosthenes when he says, "With him Order seems always disordered, and Disorder carries with it a surprizing Regularity" (*OS*, p. 56). Not only does Longinus stress the importance of imitation ("Let this, my Friend, be our Ambition; be this the fix'd and lasting Scope of all our Labours" [*OS*, p. 36]), he also discusses in great detail the art of seeming impulsiveness, the "brave Irregularities" that result from the deployment of rhetorical figures that are "then most dextrously applied" when they "cannot be discerned" (*OS*, p. 51). The use of sudden silence, circumstantiality, apostrophe, digression, and impersonation exhibits that "pliant Activity" of minds able to mark and transmit the flux and reflux of emotion so that "they alter their Thoughts, their Language, and their manner of Expression a thousand times" (*OS*, p. 58). The figures of *asyndeton* and *hyperbaton* are the ones Tristram is using when he seems oddest of all: his dashes, exclamations, and especially his "transposing Words or Thoughts out of their natural and grammatical Order" (*OS*, p. 57), which he carries to the point of transposing whole chapters, are his brave irregularities committed with Longinus's authority. These two figures also provide him with an official explanation of what Burton and Montaigne are doing. Montaigne is a past master in the art of giving "his Audience a kind of Anxiety, as if he had lost his Subject, and forgot what he was about" and then unexpectedly returning to his subject (*OS*, p. 60), while Burton is equally skilled at digressing with a warmth that "carries your Imagination along with him in this Excursion" by elaborating an image and often dramatizing it (*OS*, p. 64). What seems to be Tristram's odd originality is an art of performed feeling that has its rules in Longinus and its models in Montaigne's *Essays* and the *Anatomy of Melancholy*, and which contributes to his comic sublime of enacted language. It is the imitation of naturalized art, one that avoids the extreme of sheer disorder on the one hand and of cold correctness on the other.

Longinus teaches Sterne another lesson, not by precept but by example. Boileau spoke for many eighteenth-century critics when he said of the seventh section of *On the Sublime* that "this is a very fine Description of the Sublime, and finer still, because it is very Sublime itself" (*OS*, p. 115, n. 2). It was a compliment Addison sought to pay Pope's Longinian exercise, the *Essay on Criticism,* and which Warburton re-tuned in his high estimation of the *Essay on Man;*[26] and it is a compliment Sterne deserves too. Tristram's use of hyperbaton is often characterized by the production of the very thing he is talking about: writing about a digression he makes one (*TS,* IX.xv.767) and talking about gaps in his narrative he falls into one (VI.xxxiii.557–58). These comic sublimities arise from his decision never to separate the words he uses from the objects and feelings they name, so that they dwell *in* more than *about* their point of reference and, as the *Guardian* critic puts it, "flow from an inward principle" in the thing described. It is the same sublimity that is brought to those imitations of Burton, Montaigne, and Benengeli which contrive to be what they are also about, and they show that the best parts of Sterne's commonplace-book were not filled with well-worn sentiments that might be given an agreeable turn but with examples of irregularity that have the self-evident quality of "voices of the sign" or words of flesh and bone. These are the texts translated so directly and yet subtly from real experience of things or of other texts that they can be retranslated into *Tristram Shandy* with no loss of force. Tristram's imitations necessarily involve the expression as well as the sentiment because both his originality and his finest plagiarism depend on his seeing no difference between a live idea and its most appropriate form. With all the appearance of spontaneity lines are drawn and things "come out of themselves" because Tristram is master of the art of turning fortune and his library into nature and of perceiving in the result, with a Longinian eye, that it could not have been otherwise and that others have done it before him.

If *Tristram Shandy* were to be regarded as an institute or system of life-writing practice then it would partly explain why Sterne found that he could not live out of it. When his work burst upon the London literary scene he responded to the acclaim in the character of Tristram and, later, of Yorick. Having invented a character who translates his life into a book by "reading" his experiences and his texts and then transcribing them into his own, Sterne adopted the foible of Tristram's family by turning the book into his own life and talking shandean nonsense with the best. Not quite in the sense that Warburton uses the disparaging phrase, Sterne was "making himself" (*Letters,* p. 96) by imitating his imitations and fashioning a social style out of Tristram's asyndeton and hyperbaton. There can have been no sweeter triumph than his introduction to the Comte de Bissy when he "found him reading Tristram" (*Letters,* p. 151), an exquisite confusion that he re-translated into "The Passport. Versailles" in *A Sentimental Journey.* Really there is no contradiction between the imitative sincerity of Tristram, enacted in words on the page, and Sterne's, which "cut no figure, *but in the doing*" (*Letters,* p. 157):

both exhibit "that careless irregularity of a good and easy heart" (*Letters,* p. 117) that is formed on the principles of naturalized art. Sterne was able to explore Montaigne's paradox, of being known in his book and his book in him, while functioning like Quixote of the second part in being constantly aware of himself as a literary fact and as a real person, *and* in being pestered with false sequels to himself. As a result his next novel illustrates the theme of literature and life meeting in a rather different way from *Tristram Shandy,* where literature is seen as a fund of forms and ideas that life takes to express itself with. Although literature and life bump into one another in shandean ways in *A Sentimental Journey,* there is a constitutive as well as an expressive function to some of the incorporated texts. A paraphrase of Genesis about hands creates the circumstances of manual intimacy with Mme de L***, which in turn creates a metaphor of travelling by hand that is realized later in "The Fille de Chambre. Paris," when real hands meet once again over a text (Crebillon's two volumes of *Les Egarmens du Coeur et de l'Esprit*) whose title predicts the consequence of the meeting and whose story contains a scene in which the hero and his beloved exchange sentiments over a book.[27] In these related sequences texts are promoting the action and controlling its outcome as well as expressing the feelings of the participants; they are determining the course of the story by providing the occasions of feelings and the nature of their sequels. No doubt Sterne was trying to render some of the effects of the considerable alterations his first novel had produced in his own life.

While writing this novel Sterne was also writing his *Journal to Eliza,* and he compared the two manuscripts to the two front wheels of his chariot: "I cannot go on without them" (*Letters,* p. 364). What they have in common, and what distinguishes them quite markedly from *Tristram Shandy,* is a division between the body and the soul, action and sentiment, that is never properly bridged. At the upper level are sentimental feelings, often expressed in scriptural language, which are ethereal and disembodied; while at the lower level physical embarrassments take place that mock the spiritual aspirations. For example Yorick's physical ascent of Mt Taurira is outstripped by the spiritual rarefactions of "Maria," "The Supper," and "The Grace," only to be followed by the plunging bathos of "The Case of Delicacy." In the *Journal to Eliza* Yorick is forced to interrupt the poignancies of a heart "unsupported by aught but its own tenderness" to report that his doctors suspect him of having the pox. There are many more witty attempts to adjust these two levels in *A Sentimental Journey* than in the *Journal;* but what is interesting about the latter is that each level has its own imitative strategy that competes with the other.

When Eliza Draper sailed away to India aboard the *Earl of Chatham* Sterne built a dream-world out of literary artifice. The *Journal* is described as an English translation of a French manuscript containing the correspondence of two people represented "under the fictitious Names of Yorick & Draper" (*Letters,* p. 322). Very soon it is translated once more into the pages of its companion text, and the future editor of *A Sentimental Journey* is instructed how to write the footnote on "Eliza." In every respect this is a literary relationship conducted in pen and ink and vying with other famous literary love affairs such as those of Swift and Stella, Scarron and Maintenon, Waller and Saccharissa (*Letters,* p. 319). All the way from Lord Bathurst's table in London to the ghostly Cordelia's ruins at Byland, Yorick is introducing Eliza's name to literary company and literary archetypes, and she contributes her part by penning letters that exalt the art of writing "to a science" (*Letters,* p. 320). In this world, where "there wants only the *Dramatis Personae* for the performance" (*Letters,* p. 364), Yorick identifies himself as "a Dreamer of Dreams in the Scripture Language" (*Letters,* p. 366) and keys his highest moods to biblical phrases. Spiritual melancholy is linked to *King Lear* and especially to *Hamlet:* "Alas! poor Yorick!—remember thee! Pale Ghost—remember thee—whilst Memory holds a seat in this distracted World—Remember thee,—Yes, from the Table of her Memory, shall just Eliza wipe away all trivial men—& leave a throne for Yorick" (*Letters,* p. 346). By sentimental magic the jester is turned into the king's ghost and Eliza is turned into Hamlet, and this twice-dead Yorick finds a romantic and equally ghostly confidante in the dead Cordelia. Again and again Yorick refers to himself as a ghost or a spirit, "an etherial Substance" and a "gawsy Constitution" that lives scarcely conscious of its existence and that looks forward only to the purest mental pleasures from meeting the object of its love once more. Having retreated to reflection and books, Yorick feeds his mind and discards his body with fictions and performances that have nothing to do with action and which are tricked out in a false sublime drawn from Shakespeare and the Bible. Bathos is supplied from only one source, *Tristram Shandy.* Sterne's own book intrudes to name or characterize disasters that will not be sentimentalized. The symptoms of the pox arriving inopportunely to mock "Yorick's Spirit" are an embarrassment so comically disastrous that "Shandy's Nose—his name—his Sash-Window are fools to it"; hence it would "make no bad anecdote in T. Shandy's Life" (*Letters,* pp. 329–30). The same force of shandean prophecy is at work in the sequel, for the mercury treatment he is prescribed is taken from the authoritative work of Tristram's old enemy Kunastrokius (otherwise Dr Mead) and Yorick is obliged to submit to it "as my Uncle Toby did, in drinking Water . . . *Merely for quietness sake*" (*Letters,* p. 347). Similarly, when some of his nights are made restless by visions and hot blood that are less than sentimental, he believes they have been forecast by that "Prophetic Spirit wch dictated the Acc^t of Corp^l Trim's uneasy night when the fair Beguin ran in his head" (*Letters,* p. 326). The book has decreed what Yorick would prefer not to experience, accordingly he turns the prospect of his wife's imminent visit into shandean business and prose: "A Book to write—a Wife to receive & make Treaties with—an estate to sell—a Parish to superintend" (*Letters,* p. 376), aptly enough imitating Tristram's chapter of *things.* Mrs Sterne is no widow Wadman, but she represents the carnal antithesis to the shadowy Eliza since she is after nothing but cash and is suffering from "a weakness on her bowels ever since her paralitic Stroke" (*Letters*, p. 363). She will cause Yorick to sigh as many "Hey ho's" as Toby did after the Treaty of Utrecht, and a shandean finger points the moral (itself very shandean) of these trials and discomforts: "☞Every thing for the best!" (*Letters*, p. 347).

Longinus's metaphor for bad amplification, the multiplication of words that is unaccompanied by sublime meaning, is the separation "as it were of the Soul from the Body" (*OS*, p. 32) and it is as if Yorick has realized it in his *Journal to Eliza:* his upper half is sublimating itself amongst literary fragments and allusions while his lower one is collapsing into shandean predictions. That there seems to be no point of equilibrium is made comically plain in Sterne's letter to "Hannah" in which he promises to "give up the Business of senti-mental writing—& write to the Body" if his *Journey* does not make her cry as much as it has made him laugh (*Letters*, p. 401). Curiously Yorick uses the same metaphor as Longinus to describe the reason for writing the *Journal*, Eliza's departure: "'Twas the Separation of Soul & Body—& equal to nothing but what passes on that tremendous Moment" (*Letters*, p. 374). As a metaphor of his dissociated state made out of the literal separation that will take place at his death, it suggests both why the strategy of the sentimental sublime will fail and the reasons he had in using it. It is as if Yorick has planned to antedate his death by dying metaphorically into pure spirit, retaining his consciousness at the expense of everything else and converting all evidence of a real death yet to come into metaphors and tokens of one that has already occurred. His haemorrhages flow from a lover's bleeding heart and stain handkerchiefs which then become earnests of the absolute fidelity for which, as a ghost and a spectre, he waits to be rewarded. With all anchorage in things and bodies deliberately forsaken, the sentiment cannot help but attenuate and get lost in professions that have nothing but scraps of Shakespeare to perform with. Shandean bathos arrives with the reminder that there is still some real life left and also a real death yet to die; in fact it re-establishes the comic association of sex and death that is so common in *Tristram Shandy*. When Tristram breaks a blood vessel over Jenny he wryly acknowledges the dangers of going down to the centre as he goes off to get himself treated, whereas Yorick tries to evade them by making gruesome symbolism out of the disaster and turning himself into "Death alive," as Richard Griffith called him.

The *Journal to Eliza* ends with the contest between shandean imitations and sentimental ones unresolved, but in two last letters Sterne presents it once more. To Mrs Montagu he declares gallantly that he will laugh at disas-ters like Cervantes and Scarron and die in a joke. To Mrs James he writes a melancholy valediction acknowledging that his spirits are fled and asking pardon for his shandean follies; yet at the same time shandean imitation almost insensibly takes over as he recommends, Le Fever-like, his only child to the protection of an uncle Toby in the shape of Mr James. That is his last imitation and in it he fulfills the promise he made to Hall-Stevenson: "I shall leave you all at last by translation, and not by fair death" (*Letters,* p. 186).

Notes

1.   See *Letters of Laurence Sterne,* edited by Lewis Perry Curtis (Oxford, 1935), pp. 77, 117 (hereafter *Letters* with page references in text).

2.   See, for instance, D. W. Jefferson, "*Tristram Shandy* and the Tradition of Learned Wit," *Essays in Criticism,* 1 (1951), 225–48.

3.   I have found the following articles useful in compiling this one: C. J. Rawson, "Two Notes on Sterne," *N & Q,* 202, NS 4 (1957), 255–56; J. M. Stedmond, "Genre and *Tristram Shandy,*" *PQ,* 38 (1959), 37–51, and "Sterne as a Plagiarist," *ES,* 41 (1960), 308–12; Gardner D. Stout, "Some Borrowings in Sterne from Rabelais and Cervantes," *ELN,* 3 (1965), 111–17.

4.   *A Tale of a Tub,* edited by A. C. Guthkelch and D. Nichol Smith (Oxford, 1958), p. 203.

5.   Joseph Warton, *An Essay on the Genius and Writings of Pope,* 2 vols (London, 1782), II, 54.

6.   Dionysius Longinus, *On the Sublime* (London, 1739), p. 60. Reprinted in the translations of Nicholas Boileau-Despréaux and William Smith by Scholars' Facsimiles and Reprints (New York, 1975), hereafter *OS* with page references in text.

7.   Of his adding to but not correcting subsequent editions Montaigne says, "From thence however there will easily happen some transposition of Chronology; my Stories taking place according to their patness, and not always according to their Age"; and he goes on to draw the famous distinction between "I now, and I anon": *Essays of Michael Seigneur de Montaigne,* translated by Charles Cotton, 3 vols (London, 1711), III, 247 (hereafter, *Essays*). This seems very akin to Tristram's splitting himself up into two lives: "I perceive I shall lead a fine life of it out of this self-same life of mine" (*TS,* IV.xiii.342). When Don Quixote discovers that the first part of his adventures is already written and published he marvels that "there was such a history extant, while yet the blood of those enemies he had cut off, had scarce done reeking on the blade of his sword," and he asks Samson Carrasco if "the author promises a second part?" (*Don Quixote,* translated by Peter Motteux, Everyman edition, 2 vols [London, 1906; reprinted 1972], II, 19–20). This confrontation with his own experience as text begins all the life-literature paradoxes of the second part, culminating in the meeting with Don Alvaro Tarfe, a character from Avellaneda's spurious sequel (page references are to *DQ* hereafter).

8.   "Of Learning," noted by James A. Work, "The Indebtedness of *Tristram Shandy* to Certain English Authors, 1670–1740," unpublished dissertation (Yale University, 1934), p. 135.

9.   Compare Obadiah Walker, *Of Education* (Oxford, 1673; reprinted Scolar Press, 1970), pp. 46–47, 78–79. The definition is taken from Chambers's entry "Analogy."

10.   Compare William Hogarth, *Analysis of Beauty* (London, 1753; reprinted Scolar Press, 1971), pp. 62, 66, 135.

11.   "Postscript to the *Odyssey,*" *The Twickenham Edition of the Poems of Alexander Pope,* edited by John Butt and others, 11 vols (London, 1939–69), X, 388.

12.   *Essay Concerning Human Understanding,* ed. by A. Campbell Fraser, 2 vols (Oxford, 1894), II, 50 (III, 5.10).

13.   *TS,* V.xi.439. Compare the paragraph with Montaigne's distrust of his judgement: "Whoever shall call to memory how many, and how many times he has been mistaken in his own Judgment, is he not a great Fool if he does not ever after suspect it" (*Essays,* III, 403); and with Rabelais who maintains things "even unto the fire *exclusive*" (*Gargantua and Pantagruel,* translated by Sir Thomas Urquhart and Peter Motteux, Everyman edition, 2 vols (London,

1929; reprinted 1966), I, 138 (Prologue, *Pantagruel*). The quotation of Tickletoby's disaster and the advice to the reader which it introduces (*TS,* III.xxxvi.267–68) is confirmed with an oath "by St Paraleipomenon," formerly a knight with a shandean hatchment in *Don Quixote,* II, 254: "Sir Paralipomenon, Knight of the Three Stars."

14.   *Anatomy of Melancholy* (*AM* in subsequent references), Everyman edition, 3 vols (London, 1932; reprinted 1961), I, 25; Montaigne, *Essays,* I, 200.

15.   *Sermons,* 322.

16.   Compare *Julius Caesar,* IV.3.119: "When that rash humour which my mother gave me / Makes me forgetful."

17.   Compare "To Study Philosophy, is to learn to die," *Essays,* I, 89, 90.

18.   Compare *TS,* V.i.412–13: *AM,* II, 36; *TS,* VII.xiv.595: *AM,* I, 417.

19.   See *Essays,* I, 95; III, 125, 317, 397.

20.   See Melvyn New, "Sterne's Rabelaisian Fragment: A Text from the Holograph Manuscript," *PMLA,* 87 (1972), 1083–92 (p. 1088).

21.   *Sermons,* 392–93.

22.   See Northrop Frye, "Towards Defining an Age of Sensibility," *ELH,* 23 (1956), 144–52, where he discusses the influence of the translated Bible on the work of Smart, Macpherson, and Blake.

23.   *Gargantua and Pantagruel,* I, 265, 278; II, 355 (*Pantagruel,* Chs 2, 7; *Cinquième Livre,* Ch. 44).

24.   See William Warburton, *The Divine Legation of Moses Demonstrated,* 2 vols (London, 1837), II, 34–47. He gives examples from Jeremiah 35 and Ezekiel 31.

25.   Northrop Frye's discussion (cited above) of the "primitive" or "barbaric" metaphor that establishes identity rather than likeness bears a good deal on this one.

26.   *Spectator,* 253; *The Works of Alexander Pope, Esq,* edited by W. Warburton, third edition, 9 vols (London, 1753), III, 50–51, note.

27.   *The Wanderings of the Heart and Mind or Memoirs of Mr de Meilcour,* translated by Michael Clancy (London, 1751), p. 155. The bashful Meilcour manages to make conversation with Hortensia about the book she is reading, "the history of an unfortunate lover."

Imitations of *Tristram Shandy*

ANNE BANDRY

When the first "shilling pamphlet" reacting to *Tristram Shandy* appeared on 21 April 1760, Sterne was delighted: "I wish they would write a hundred such," he wrote to his friend Stephen Croft.[1] The two volumes he had published in York in mid-December 1759 had been reviewed, mostly favorably, and reprinted by Dodsley (3 April 1760); the "sketch of Yorick" had been excerpted in the *Gentleman's Magazine* (January) and reprinted in the *London Chronicle* (5 February). But it was the imitation that signaled the real success he had been craving: "I wrote not to be *fed* but to be *famous*" was the answer he had given to an attack on his improprieties (*Letters,* 90; 30 January 1760).[2] Approximately 40 reactions to *Tristram Shandy* appeared in print before Sterne's death in 1768: reviews, pamphlets, letters, and poems in the magazines, and imitative fiction. I will concentrate here on the texts closest to *Tristram* in order to sketch the reception of Sterne's volumes from a more literary viewpoint than that of Arthur Cash's biographical account or J. C. T. Oates's bibliographical account in *Shandyism and Sentiment: 1760–1800.* The imitators responded to Sterne's persona, but first and foremost they explored the possibilities opened up by the marks he had made on paper, the actual text of *Tristram Shandy*.[3]

The pamphlet that delighted Sterne, *Explanatory Remarks upon the Life and Opinions of Tristram Shandy; Wherein, the Morals and Politics of this Piece are clearly laid open, by Jeremiah Kunastrokius, M.D.,* provided a bantering comment on his text and paratext and participated in the elucidations of *Tristram* begun by some of the reviewers (mainly William Kenrick in the *Monthly Review,* appendix to volume XXI [July–December 1759]). By adopting the name Kunastrokius, the author put himself inside Sterne's text and set the tone for the 59 pages to come: in Sterne's first volume, Kunastrokius was one example of a man overruled by his hobby-horse (I.vii.12).[4] The narrator of *Explanatory Remarks* purports to be his son and refers his readers to passages in Sterne's text. The boldest stroke consists in completing one of Sterne's most famous lacunae: "My sister . . . does not care to let a man come so near her ****," which appears three times in *Tristram Shandy* (II.vi.115, II.vi.116,

This essay was written specifically for this volume and appears here for the first time.

II.vii.117; in the third instance, a dash replaces the asterisks). After one page of false leads that continue Sterne's own playful misdirections, "Kunastrokius" gets down to the "thing" itself:

> four *asterisms* are but four *asterisms*—and ever since asterisms have been in use, we have always been taught that their number should be supplied by a like number of letters to make out the sense.
>
> Curious, indefatigable, unblushing readers, consider what letters will properly supply the place, without infringing upon the sense.—Mind I have already exploded uncle *Toby*'s "backside" and "covered way."—What do you think of head? there are but four letters in this word—Ay, but it will not do, it is quite *opposite* to the author's meaning.—*Arm* and *leg* have but three letters, and be hanged to them.—*Thigh* comes near it, but then there is a letter too many.—I have it—the *third,* the *twentieth,* the *thirteenth,* and the *nineteenth* letters of the English alphabet certainly compose the word, though it is not to be found in any Lexicon extant—I hope. (*Remarks,* 27–28)

But blunt clarification is not enough; the logic of the pseudonym comes full circle when the asterisks are linked to the hobby-horse: "Mr. *Tristram Shandy*'s hobby-horse I take to be ****, . . . and his favourite argument the *argumentum ad rem*" (29).

This statement is quite in keeping with the pseudostraightforward definition given just before: "A hobby-horse is a machine which boys (ay, and girls too) frequently sit astride upon, and which going up and down affords them much amusement" (28). Textuality and sexuality unsurprisingly come together again:

> My *hobby-horse* is a *goose quill,* upon which I have rode through life to this period, and by which I hope to get *hobby-horsically* to my journey's end without much fatigue.
>
> N.B. My hobby-horse never goes on so briskly as upon a journey of prescriptions and receipts--for, instead of paying upon the first road, I receive toll; and the last excursion I seldom make but for the sale of some young *hobby,* the offspring of my goose quill. (29)

"Kunastrokius" takes on the role of a pimp, relying on the polysemy of "hobby." The quill that tickles Sterne's text enables the parasitic writer to make money at the expense of the newly fashionable author. "Exposing" Tristram Shandy is what he claims to be doing, especially by providing a translation of the "MEMOIRE presenté a Messieurs les Docteurs de SORBONNE." The precise parallels Sterne established in his editing of the Memoire and the shandean punctuation are left out, but those readers who did not "have a smattering of the Gallican tongue" (14) were provided with a good enough text.[5] In the section on Tristram's politics, Mr. Profound, who is made to declare that *"Tristram Shandy* is one compleat system of modern politics," suggests a "key" (but "the author . . . told [him] it was too dangerous" [44]). This section has lost much of its flavor over more than two centuries, but in both instances, "morals" and "politics," the pamphleteer is led to posit his text as a metatext. E. Cabe, the publisher, contributed as well: the advertisements state that "This Explanation is printed in the same letter and size as *Tristram Shandy,* to accommodate them who chuse to bind it with that work."[6] We have the case here of an imitated imitator, since Sterne had arranged for the York edition to be "of the size of Rasselas [published by Dodsley on 19 April 1759], and on the same paper and type" (*Letters,* 80).

In the last pages of *Remarks* the author plays on his knowledge of contemporary high society to ridicule the consequences of Sterne's success. Contrary to his model, for example, "Kunastrokius" cannot be given a *"living,* however lucrative . . . as [he is] not in orders" (58); on 29 March Lord Fauconberg had presented Sterne with the curacy of Coxwold (Cash, 28–29). David Garrick had paid him the rare compliment of "an Order for the Liberty of his Boxes, and of every part of his house for the whole Season" (*Letters,* 96–97; Cash, 8); "Kunastrokius" banters, "I am particularly obliged to the managers of both the houses, whose kind intentions I already anticipate, in favouring me with the freedom of their respective theatres" (*Remarks,* 58). Sterne's lionization was also mocked by the imitator's "ADVERTISEMENT. TO THE NOBILITY and GENTRY OF ALL EUROPE," in which "Kunastrokius" announces that he will "pay compliments to them, according to their different ranks; or, where upon a footing, according to their alphabetical succession" (57–58), just like "my Lord A, B, C, D, E . . . O, P, Q, and so on, all of a row, mounted upon their several horses" (*TS,* I.viii.13).

The paratext is also satirized, in a way that shows the author was well informed of rumors about the circumstances of *Tristram Shandy*'s publication: "and this is the dearest production to the bookseller, if *not* to the public, that has appeared for near half a centry [*sic*]" (*Remarks,* 56).[7] The imitator is here commenting on the first London edition, for which Sterne had secured a frontispiece by the aging Hogarth: "---Though he *ridicules* plates and cuts by a *ridiculous* stamp, may he not, with great propriety prefix a frontispiece to his second edition?" (53). He continues: "Again, with respect to dedications.— Though that in the middle of his first volume certainly means (if any thing) a burlesque upon dedications of what nature so ever, yet we find in his second edition, he has dedicated this moral-political (not *bawdy, ludicrous,* as some may imagine it) piece, to one of the most respectable characters in *England.*— But *who* can take offence at it?" (54). Burlesques of shandean pranks abound. The scribbler gives his readers the possibility of opting out, of skipping the translation of the Memoire; if they "fancy they comprehend the whole affair in the original, [they] have nothing to do but skip to chapter 9, and fancy there is no such thing as chapter 8 in this *whole* book" (14). Tristram suggested, "[T]o such, however, as do not choose to go so far back into these things, I can give no better advice, than that they skip over the remaining part of this Chapter," bidding them moreover to "——————Shut the door.——————" (*TS*, I.iv.5–6).

In its conclusion, *Remarks* blends pastiches of several passages. The political commentator of *Remarks* dies and is commemorated by the words "Alas, poor P R O F O U N D," equal to "Alas, poor Y O R I C K!" (*TS*, I.xii.35); the joke develops with "the mortifying news, that my printer has never a *black copper-plate* to subjoin; but I have desired him to borrow *Tristram*'s of his printer, and if he will but lend it, you may depend upon being as well *amused* and *enlightened* here, as you were in reading the *seventy third* and *seven fourth* [*sic*] pages of the 1st volume of *Tristram Shandy*" (48–49). And like Tristram, the scribbler makes the reader go backward: "if you think that there was only a single syllable that you did not attend to, I insist upon your returning back to the three preceding chapters, as you will swear, else, I have not fulfilled the promise of my title page, 'explaining the politics of *Tristram*'" (49–50). He then transfers a shandean jest from the sphere of the sexual to that of the mock-political: in *Tristram,* the female reader jumps when Tristram calls Jenny his "friend" (*TS*, II.xviii.56); in *Remarks,* Profound is the narrator's "deceased friend. Friend! did I say? Yes, I repeat it, a *great friend!* and what is more and difficult to believe, a *political friend!*" (50). Some few pranks of his own are also inserted—for example, his suggestion that the reader add Latin and Greek quotations in a "do-it-yourself" fashion (51–52).[8]

Thus, *Remarks* both makes some of Sterne's allusions and innuendos explicit and mimics Sterne's style, re-creating Tristram's prattling on the page with the due quantity and variety of dashes. "To own the truth," wrote the *Critical Review*, "we harbour some suspicions that the author himself is here giving breath to the trumpet of fame" (April 1760). This was the first of many semiserious attributions of derivative texts to Sterne. It shows that *Remarks* was perceived as a good echo chamber of *Tristram Shandy;* and, indeed, the reviews of the pamphlet were positive. The key to this success, perhaps, is that the author really did appreciate Sterne's comic text: his final judgment is that "*Tristram Shandy* is the most *excellent* (I was going to say— *est,* by way of a *superlative superlative,* suitable to the occasion) piece that has appeared for many years" (56).

A second benevolent text, Dr. John Hill's gossipy but fairly well informed biographical account, made Sterne even more a celebrity. It was published first in the *Royal Female Magazine* (April), then given a much larger audience when the *London Chronicle* reprinted it (6 May); in a third appearance, it was excerpted in *Tristram Shandy's Bon Mots* (published on 12 June). By the beginning of May 1760, then, it was common knowledge that "Tristram," alias "Yorick," alias Sterne, was a parson and that his culpability for indecency was great. John Hall-Stevenson's *Two Lyric Epistles,* printed by Dodsley (17 April), had helped Sterne's fame blow in that direction, as did critical letters in the

Universal Magazine of Knowledge and Pleasure and the *Grand Magazine*. Very soon the appreciation exhibited by the author of *Remarks* would turn to attacks—or in at least one instance, perhaps a mock-attack.

The suggestion in the *Critical Review* that Sterne, "under the form of explanatory notes," may have been "pointing the finger at some of those latent strokes of wit in Tristram's life and opinions, which may perchance have escaped the eye of the less discerning reader" may well be true—but not of *Remarks*. *The Clockmakers Outcry against the Author of The Life and Opinions of Tristram Shandy* was published on 9 May. Its argument is that "TRISTRAM the lewd has knock'd Clock-making up" (44), for clocks have become "obscene lumber, exciting to acts of carnality" (42). In many ways the *Outcry* is a companion to *Remarks*, another metatext, with a page-by-page commentary on Tristram's politics and morals and a character parallel to Mr. Profound: Ned Paradox. One main difference, however, is that there are four editions of the *Outcry*, each revised and improved.[9] The "clockmaker" focuses more than does "Kunastrokius" on details of the text, emphasizing such key phrases as "'Pray what was your father saying?—Nothing.' Why, for the obvious reason, because according to our author, He was a doing—Has ever a civilized people been so affronted with such a domestic scene of constupration?" (*Outcry*, 15). He also draws attention to the conclusion of the Memoire ("—*Before consummation!* O thou caitiff, as bawdy as ignorant!" [35]) and suggests illegitimacy much in the same way as does *Tristram*, not pushing it further than a mere suggestion—contrary to most other secondary texts (19). The author opposes (very) basic common sense to Sterne's "wickedness," thereby of course "pointing the finger" at the right passages.

A certain familiarity with details of Sterne's activities and intentions at this time may indeed narrow the authorship of the pamphlet to Sterne himself. For example, the "clockmaker" is using the York edition of *Tristram Shandy* (he comments on the bad French of "a le pere," important in Sterne's rewriting of the Memoire and maintained as such in the York edition with a cancel, but corrected in the London edition).[10] Some of the facts he includes were clearly public knowledge. Sterne's problematic relationship with Bishop William Warburton, for instance, had already been mentioned in (and not improved by) Hill's biographical account. Still, the obscene dedication to the bishop and another slap at him in the pamphlet are much in keeping with Sterne's thrusts in later volumes. Similarly, although Sterne's sittings for Sir Joshua Reynolds between 20 March and 21 April were no secret, the "clockmaker" condemns the writer for "hawk[ing] his face about . . . to all the portrait-painters in town, vainly begging to have his mazard multiplied" (*Outcry*, viii). There seems to have been no money involved between Sterne and Reynolds, probably because both were counting on E. Fisher's mezzotint engraving for financial returns; it was to serve as the frontispiece for the *Sermons*, published by Dodsley on 22 May, and hence was "multiplied" indeed. Although the creator of the "clockmaker" could have gathered his information concerning this "multiplication" from advertisements that appeared beginning on 22 April, he may have been more intimately informed.[11] Certainly he had an extraordinary knowledge of the different stages of advertising the *Sermons*. In March, just before leaving York, Sterne had inserted a call for subscribers in the *York Courant* for "The DRAMATICK SERMONS of Mr. YORICK. Published by TRISTRAM SHANDY, Gentleman." When the *Sermons* were advertised in the London papers (beginning 22 April), the title had been changed to "THE Sermons of Mr. YORICK. Published by the Rev. Mr. STERNE. Prebendary of York." The "clockmaker" comments on the omission of "dramatick" "in the late advertisements" (27). Who but Sterne (or a conniving friend) would have read the announcements so closely?

Some two years later, during his stay in Paris, Sterne wrote to Garrick about a new acquaintance:

> Crebillion has made a convention with me, which, if he is not too lazy, will be no bad *persiflage*—as soon as I get to Thoulouse [*sic*] he has agreed to write me an expostulat[o]ry letter upon the indecorums of T. Shandy—which is to be answered by recrimination upon the liberties in his own works—these are to be printed together—Crebillion against Sterne—Sterne against Crebillion—the copy to be sold, and the money equally divided—This is good Swiss-policy. (*Letters,* 162)

The proposed persiflage was probably never published, but the suggestion, added to the fact that Sterne was a masterly self-publicist who seized every opportunity to further his literary career, and to the circumstantial evidence given above, makes it very possible that he, like Pope and others before him, was "giving breath to the trumpet of fame."[12]

From mid-May to mid-July 1760, Tristram, Yorick, and the Reverend Mr. Sterne were everywhere, in the pages of every magazine, sometimes as "lyric epistles" or "admonitory epistles," but also as a new game of cards, a recipe for soup, and a letter from "a Methodist Preacher" that became "A letter from the Rev. George Whitfield" in a pirated version. There were also separate pamphlets—*Tristram Shandy's Bon Mots, Tristram Shandy at Ranelagh,* and *Tristram Shandy in a Reverie*—and the work was also the subject of several of Goldsmith's "Chinese Letters" in the *Public Ledger*.[13] *Yorick's Meditations* (published on 16 July) illustrated throughout its 110 pages the opportunities provided by an imitation of Sterne's use of digression, with due allusions to Swift.

Sterne's work calls for active reading, and some of the 1760 readers were so active that they initiated a flood of imitations, counterfeits, and variations on shandean themes. The *Monthly Review* turned this into a challenge in the beginning of July:

> Tristram Shandy's success has, of course, set all the writing mills a-going. Grind away, Gentlemen! and we will make all possible room for you, in our

Monthly Catalogues: but it will not be adviseable for you, like Dr. Kuna-strokius, to affect Mr. Shandy's manner of writing; it must be an excellent joke, indeed, that will bear repeating. (Appendix to volume XXII [January–June 1760])

After the metatexts and the various pieces in the magazines came volumes of imitative fiction, among which were obvious fakes as well as spurious contin-uations. Fakes were *The Life and Opinions of Miss Sukey Shandy,* which purloins Sterne's title (and format) but uses the epistolary form to distort the themes of generation into amorous intrigues, and *The Life and Opinions of Bertram Montfichet,* which claims to "outdo" *Tristram* by going even further back than the hero's conception and thereby results in two painfully unshandean vol-umes: *over*doing is the consequence of *out*doing. The compact pages of *Mont-fichet* make the reader long for the little excursions of the model, more often than not marked on each page by the profusion of dashes that provide breath-ing space both for the writer and the reader. The *Critical Review* (May 1761) called the *Montfichet* volumes "a dead letter without spirit"; their author was not in the least able to adopt a shandean manner. The only scribbler who did seem capable of capitalizing successfully on the interaction between the two components of the title he had appropriated was the author of *The Life and Opinions of Jeremiah Kunastrokius.* His insights into shandean writing are the logical continuation of *Explanatory Remarks,* and his conclusion is as astute as the rest of his text: after 156 pages the narrator announces a forthcoming vol-ume, which of course will never appear, by declaring, "I have not yet said any Thing that is *really* Part of my Life, or indeed my Opinions" (156).[14] A com-parable ending was used in *The Life and Amours of Hafen Slawkenbergius,* a witty 38-page pamphlet "in the size and manner of Tristram Shandy" (*London Chronicle,* 17–19 December 1761). The *Critical Review* halfheartedly sug-gested Sterne might be the author (January 1762).

The spurious volumes were another way to outdo Sterne—chronologi-cally. A spurious volume III was advertised in the *Public Advertiser* on 25 Sep-tember 1760 and has been attributed to John Carr.[15] Dodsley counteracted immediately with announcements (from 26 September to 4 October, when the advertisements for the spurious volume stopped) in the same paper "THAT the THIRD and FOURTH Volumes of TRISTRAM SHANDY, by the author of the TWO FIRST VOLUMES, will be published about Christ-mas next." This may explain why Sterne's disclaimer did not appear in the *York Courant* until 7 October. The *Critical Review* reacted quickly as well, for one can read in the September issue that "Tristram Shandy is at length born; but so unequal to the hopes conceived of him in the womb, that we appre-hend the public will cry out upon him as an abortion, or perhaps a spurious brat, palmed upon the fond parent for his own legitimate offspring." The rest of the review opposes "this stupid, unmeaning and senseless performance" to the original.[16] The *Monthly* was one month late and could only repeat that the volume was a forgery.

Spurious volume IX, published on 13 February 1766, one year before the genuine one appeared, shows that even though the interest in Sterne had declined after 1761, enough remained in 1766 to make such an enterprise worthwhile. Quite a few readers were taken in, among whom was the first German translator of *Tristram Shandy*. Only one disclaimer appeared, written by Dodsley, who was no longer Sterne's publisher; Sterne was in Italy and may not have worried, perhaps because he had taken the trouble to authenticate the third and fourth installments by signing the first pages of text in volumes V and VII, thus creating the expectation of an authenticating signature for the next installment as well. The reviewers of the spurious volume were uncommonly mild: "Not *genuine*," wrote the *Monthly Review*, "but not so ill counterfeited, as were some of the former imitations of Mr. Sterne's truly original manner" (February 1766). The *Critical Review* was even more enthusiastic: "We learn from the news-papers, that this is not the production of the Rev. Mr. S——: However, we may venture to assert, that the author has deprived that gentleman of the epithet of *inimitable*" (February 1766). Stylometric analysis shows that this work does imitate the writing of Sterne in a much more accurate manner than did Carr—but the later forger had more volumes on which to base his production.[17]

In order to pass for Sterne, the forgers had to fulfill the readers' expectations to a reasonable degree. Sterne had announced at the end of volume II that "a series of things will be laid open which [the reader] little expects" (*TS*, II.xix.181), creating a wide range of possibilities but making surprise a sine qua non. The "tolerable bargain with my bookseller" (*TS*, I.xiv.42) having been reached and made public by "Kunastrokius," among others, readers may have wondered why volume III was published alone; but the title page, reset during printing, was made to look like those of the first two volumes.[18] What the reader expected in volume III was Tristram's birth, of course, along with his maiming ("the loss of my nose by marriage articles") and his naming ("in opposition to my father's hypothesis, and the wish of the whole family" [II.xix.180]). The forger's opening is undeniably "unequal to the hopes conceived of him in the womb":

> If ever I grow poor (and I am already an author) I will never apply myself to an old man for relief. For I have experienced that my own heart grows harder and harder every year. This makes me think with such extravagant pleasure on my infant days, when I was benevolence and good humour all over; I dare say my intentions before I was born (if I had any then) were to be the kindest man in ——shire. Bless your dear soul! cries my old nurse when she reads this chapter, you were the sweetest little dear that ever woman bore, the man was happy that begot you, and the bed was blest you were begotten in.—Yes, good mother, that is all very true; but I must go on with my history. (Carr, 3–4)

The nurse also appears briefly in the genuine third and fourth volumes (III.xiii.216; IV.xv.345), but Sterne obviously preferred midwives, both male and female, as well as the *nursery* with its sash-window. The forger prepares Tristram's birth by establishing links with the first two volumes. The Shandy brothers talk of generation, in which "the woman is but little different from being entirely passive"; books are mentioned that belong to Toby's library; and the trick of the sermon serves again: "—Ah! *Toby,* you have never read a book, entitled, *Conjugal Love.*---Yes, but I have, said *Toby.* At least I have read the title of it; for I found it in the middle of my *Stevinus;* and when I had read a page or two, finding there was bawdy in it, I tore the leaves in halves down from the top to the bottom, and pasted them without order on the decayed cover of my *Mons. Blondel*" (Carr, 12–13). For the birth itself Carr uses Sterne's very phrases, transforming the pregnant metaphor of "as notable and curious a dissertation as ever was engendered in the womb of speculation" (*TS,* II.vii.118) into a rather heavy, if efficient, parallel: "But before he [my father] got himself safely delivered of his sentence, my mother was safely delivered of me" (Carr, 17). Such recycling is often the best Carr can achieve, and it occurs successfully several times in the volume's 224 pages.

Carr's play on naming is far more laborious and rests on an eccentric derivation: "----The midwife's grandfather had been a schoolmaster, who, on meeting with provocation, (whether from bad *Latin* or bad liquor) used to cry out, quoting *Ovid, Tristium! Tristium!* This exclamation descended to his first-born daughter, but underwent a little alteration into *Tristam;* which, for the greater disagreeableness of sound, her daughter the midwife changed into *Tristram. Tristram! Tristram!* says she, here he comes!----" (Carr, 17–18). The name disappears when baptism is called for, however, one of Carr's many inconsistencies. Another inelegant link with the first installment is created when we are told that "about an hour after my [i.e., Tristram's] birth, I grew so exceedingly ill, that my mother was very impatient to have me baptized. [Turn back to Vol. I, chap. 20]" (Carr, 30). The act of baptism itself ("a bason of water was every drop of it dashed most unmercifully, by the hands of the enraged *Lucina,* full in the face of poor me" [33]) provides an opportunity to refer to Sterne's reputation as established by the texts from the previous spring and summer: "Here it is likely Mr. What-d'ye-call-him will cry out, what stuff is this! if he be a parson!——Oh! what indignity! if he be a prebendary of *York!*----" (33–34). This could pass for one of the genuine Tristram's tricks, whereas another metatextual comment looks more like the forger pointing to his deed: "My Father and uncle talk as though they were not my father and uncle" (93). Little doubt is left by the last words of the text: "Rise not up, ah! rise not up to rival me!---or expect to be written down again by *Tristram Shandy,* Gentleman" (224).

With even more effrontery the second forger precedes his text with an "ADVERTISEMENT": "THE Manuscript, of which this is a faithful Copy, was dropt at the Publisher's Door, early one Sunday morning, wrapt in clean linen. Having more Children of his own than he could well maintain, he sent it to the FOUNDLING to be taken care of at the expence of the publick. If ever it comes to be of age, he hopes it will prove grateful to its benefactors" (spurious vol. IX, i–ii). Moreover, the last chapter maintains, "—No body knows me, and I know no body" (143), which could hardly apply to Sterne in 1766.

The forger complied with the expectations created at the end of volume VIII by narrating Toby's amours. New characters appear and were praised by the reviewers. Both forgers created far more new characters than Sterne ever did. In Carr, moreover, secondary characters from the genuine volumes become fully developed (Obadiah and Aunt Dinah, for example, become central characters with their own stories), leading to lengthy digressions that fail to make the work "digressive and . . . progressive too,—and at the same time" (*TS*, I.xxii.81). The new characters in volume IX help build a coherent story that offers some intriguing points of confluence with the genuine final volume. For example, in the spurious volume, chapters 17, 18, and 19 are taken as a pretext to send the reader backward (39); in Sterne's displaced chapters (xviii and xix), Toby proposes to the widow, then takes refuge in the Bible, "and popping, dear soul! upon a passage in it, of all others the most interesting to him—which was the siege of Jericho—he set himself to read it over—" (*TS*, IX.xxv.789). In the spurious volume Toby trades his love of fortifications for that of the widow, but still mounts his hobby-horse when provoked:

> The walls of *Jericho*, quoth my uncle, were certainly blown up by gunpowder.——It is absurd to suppose that they were thrown down by the sound of trumpets. They were at least thirty feet thick, and take my word for it, *Trim*, the mining work must have gone on very slowly. I think, replied *Trim*, that there must have been some error in the translation. I verily believe so, answered my uncle, and the *Hebrew* word ought to have been rendered gunpowder, and not trumpet. (115)

Coincidence *is* possible: Toby's interest in the siege of Jericho, quite logical for a character fascinated by fortifications, was suggested in volume V (*TS*, V.xxxvii.476). Finding a way to introduce the Bible into the story may have been sufficient to activate the suggestion anew.

More interesting, perhaps, is another echo: in both texts, Mrs. Shandy reminds her husband of "little family concernments" (*TS*, I.iv.6), with a reference to the fact that it is "sacrament day," that is, the first Sunday of the month. In the genuine volume the day is signaled by "Yorick's congregation coming out of church" (IX.xi.760); in the spurious one the instrument is the clock (the widow has become a regular visitor to Shandy Hall):

> This being a dull Sunday evening, my uncle was entertaining the widow in a corner of the room with an account of the battle of *Malplaquet*, while my father and mother were set close by the fire. . . .

> My dear Mr. *Shandy,* says my mother, laying her hand upon my father's right knee, how do you find yourself this evening? I think I never saw you look better in my life. Pray is it on the first or second Sunday of the month that I give widow *Boss* a shilling? It is on the first, replied my father, and by the same token, I must go and wind up the clock. Then go, jewel, and do not be long about it.——Crick, crick, cr, r, r, r, rick.——Pray sister, says my uncle *Toby,* were not my first regimentals faced with yellow? My dear jewel, let me unbuckle your stock, answered Mrs. *Shandy*——Crick, rick, cr, r, r, r, rick.——Pray sister, were not my first regimentals faced with yellow? "Come lovey."——Sure my sister is talking in her sleep. Sister, sister, were not my first regimentals faced with yellow? I know nothing about the matter, answered my mother peevishly.—This crick, crick, disturbed the widow's fancy full as much as my mother's, but my foolish uncle knew nothing about the matter, and it was not yet time to let him into the secret. (136–38)

Spurious volume IX is not the first text in which the clock is put to good use; there was *The Clockmakers Outcry,* of course, but also the *Supplement,* in which it is assigned an important role at the moment of Tristram's birth.[19]

To a certain extent the points in common in the two volumes IX reflect the forger's accurate perception of Sterne's narrative logic. But other similarities exist between derivative texts and the installment of *Tristram Shandy* that came after them. Sterne was working on volume IV when Carr published his volume. In the forgery there is no chapter 28, but the omission gives rise to no comment whatsoever; the chapter numbering may well be a simple error. However, it is not the only oddity to go without comment, the most striking one being bars of music (6). Volume IV is where Sterne uses the trick of a missing chapter (*TS,* IV.xxv.372). A missing chapter also plays a part in *The Life and Opinions of Jeremiah Kunastrokius,* which had been published in July. Moreover, IV.v consists of a single sentence: "Is this a fit time, said my father to himself, to talk of PENSIONS and GRENADIERS?" (330). The source for this may be the sentence "and! interrupted my mother, is this a time, my dear, for ands?" (Carr, 31) along with the use of very short chapters in *Explanatory Remarks.* It seems, in brief, that Sterne may have taken for his own use some of the ideas and devices of his imitators, just as he drew from numerous authors writing prior to his own work and recycled things he had written himself. There is a strong likelihood, in other words, that Melvyn New's comment that "Sterne seems almost incapable of any sustained writing that does not have recourse (or digression) to the work of others" should be extended to texts derived from his own; and this in turn adds a new dimension to Jonathan Lamb's observation that "Sterne was 'making himself' . . . by imitating his imitations."[20]

Sterne never filches from his imitators as they do from him, his possible borrowings always being incorporated within a new idea, a new context. But the line between Sterne, the original author, and his imitators is rather indistinct. By sending him an echo, often a caricature, of his writing, some of his

imitators inspired him. The resonance between Sterne's texts and the forg-
eries was amplified when the reviewers suggested that Sterne had perhaps
written the best derivative texts himself. The imitators were writing to be fed,
Sterne was writing to be famous; he could well permit them to feed on his
fame, as he was probably nibbling from their texts, even while "the swarm of
filthy pamphleteers" (*London Magazine,* June 1760) were making him ever
more famous.

Notes

1. *Letters of Laurence Sterne,* ed. Lewis Perry Curtis (Oxford: Clarendon Press, 1935),
107. The advertisement in the *Public Ledger* on 21 April, repeated on 22 April, predates the
one from the *Public Advertiser* quoted by Curtis, 108 n. 6. Most of the texts examined in this
paper can be found in *Sterneiana* (New York: Garland Reprints, 1974). Some extracts are provided by Alan B. Howes in *The Critical Heritage* (London: Routledge and Kegan Paul, 1974).

2. This is a reversal of Colley Cibber's "I wrote more to be Fed, than to be Famous" in
A Letter from Mr. Cibber to Mr. Pope (1742). Sterne had given a copy of this pamphlet to Mar-
maduke Fothergill, one of his "closest friends during the pre-shandy days" (*Letters,* 53, 92 n.
13). The phrase reappears twice in *Tristram Shandy,* somewhat transformed in the Preface
(III.xx.237) and verbatim in V.xvi.446.

3. Arthur Cash, *Laurence Sterne: The Later Years* (London: Methuen, 1986), 32–37 and
passim; J. C. T. Oates (Cambridge: Cambridge Bibliographical Society, 1968). In *Yorick and the
Critics: Sterne's Reputation in England, 1760–1868* (New Haven: Yale University Press, 1958),
Alan B. Howes mentions the derivative texts but does not analyze the links with Sterne's writing. And Peter M. Briggs concentrates on literary celebrity as a social phenomenon in "Laurence Sterne and Literary Celebrity in 1760," *The Age of Johnson* 4 (1992): 251–80.

4. In *Yorick and the Critics,* Howes writes that the "pamphlet, although it has a certain
amount of genuine humor, spends a good deal of time in capitalizing in a vulgar way on the
bawdy sections of Sterne's book" (8 n. 1). "Kunastrokius" represented Dr. Richard Mead
(1673–1754), famous for his "very voluptuous foibles" (*Letters,* 91 n. 7); his private life had
been the "subject of public comment" (*TS, Notes,* 57). In his "biography" of Sterne published in
May 1760, John Hill states: "I am afraid Mr. Yorick has indeed been merry with the
respectable character of Dr. Mead, under a name which I don't know how to write to a lady"
("First Biography of Sterne," in *The Complete Works and Life of Laurence Sterne: Letters,* 12 vols.,
ed. Wilbur Cross [New York: J. F. Taylor, 1904], 1:42).

5. "What immorality can there be in giving the substance of a *theological* dispute,
especially when every thing that can possibly give offence is expressed in a foreign tongue?"
(*Remarks,* 23). For details on Sterne's editing of the Memoire, see *TS,* Appendix 6, 939–51.

6. This was not an unusual practice. On the title page of *An Examen of the History of
Tom Jones* (1750) was proclaimed, "Proper to be bound with the *Foundling*" (Frederic T. Blan-
chard, *Fielding the Novelist: A Study in Historical Criticism* [New Haven: Yale University Press,
1926], 39–42). Several other examples of Sterneiana aping, or attempting to ape Sterne in this
respect, are given later in this essay.

7. Dodsley had refused Sterne's first two volumes in the spring of 1759, but then
bought the copyright to volumes I and II and committed himself for the unwritten volumes III
and IV (*Letters,* 98 n. 3). Sterne is reported to have come "skipping into [Croft's] room and said
he was the richest man in Europe" (Cash, 10).

8. "But if any of my readers should be desirous to divert themselves with a Greek or
Latin quotation, I would advise them to read me with *Homer, Herodotus, Virgil, Horace,* and a

few more of the classics by their sides, and if they understand them *not else,*—they have nothing to do, but now and then dip into one or other of them, and please themselves, and save me a great deal of unnecessary trouble" (*Remarks,* 51–52).

9.   The three London editions were published on 9 May, 14 May, and 20 June 1760 by J. Burd, who occasionally advertised in the *York Courant* (he did so on 8 July for the *Outcry*). The third edition was published in Dublin (and advertised on 10 June) by D. Chamberlaine, the printer of the first two Irish editions of the first installment of *Tristram Shandy;* according to Kenneth Monkman, Chamberlaine "obtained the York text in proof as part of a commission from Sterne" ("Tristram in Dublin," *TCBS* 7 [1979]: 347). The Dublin edition of volume III of *Tristram* includes an advertisement for "Explanatory REMARKS . . . and Supplemental REMARKS: Being the Clockmakers Outcry . . ." with the recommendation that the two pamphlets "be bound up with *Tristram Shandy*" (Monkman, "Dublin," 363); the size of all four editions of the *Outcry* made this impossible, contrary to *Explanatory Remarks.* Geoffrey Day and I published a text of the fourth edition of *The Clockmakers Outcry* with notes (Winchester, 1991), putting forth our theory of Sterne's authorship. Reactions were mixed: Jim McCue in the *TLS* (17 May 1991) finds the evidence "conclusive," whereas Melvyn New is more skeptical (*Scriblerian* 24.2 [1992]: 241 and 26.2 [1994]: 186).

10.   See *Tristram Shandy,* 943 n. 12, and Monkman, "Dublin," 346–47.

11.   See Kenneth Monkman, "Towards a Bibliography of Sterne's Sermons," *Shandean* 5 (1993): 42.

12.   Cf. *Letters,* 105, where Sterne writes to Catherine Fourmantel, apropos of the print: "I shall make the most of myself, & sell both inside & out." Pope, among many such activities, had published *A Key to the Lock* in 1715. Sterne used a similar device in his *Political Romance* in 1759; the form is also used in the *Outcry.*

13.   The letters alluding to *Tristram Shandy* all date from late June 1760. Letter 53 (as it was later numbered in the collected *Citizen of the World*) is specifically aimed at Sterne's volumes, whereas letter 51 is somewhat broader in its attack: "Do you see any thing good now-a-days that is not filled with strokes——and dashes?——Sir, a well-placed dash makes half the wit of our writers of modern humour."

14.   I have no doubt that the authors of the two "Kunastrokius" works are one and the same person. Any scribbler could have established links between the two texts, but the other imitations of *Tristram Shandy* are pedestrian enough to prove that not just any writer-for-hire had the talent to produce a clever derivative text, let alone two. *Explanatory Remarks upon the Third and Fourth Volumes of Tristram Shandy* was advertised on 25 February 1761, but no copy seems to have survived. The same hand may have compiled the jest book *Tristram Shandy's Bon Mots,* also published by Cabe (12 June 1760).

15.   Cash, 87; Monkman, "The Bibliography of the Early Editions of *Tristram Shandy,*" *The Library* 25 (1971): 23; Cross, *The Life and Times of Laurence Sterne,* 3d ed. (New Haven: Yale University Press, 1929), 231. Cross's evidence for this attribution is not recorded, nor has anyone since produced an argument for it; thus my reference to "Carr" in citing the spurious volume III is merely for convenience.

16.   This modifies substantially Cash's remarks (87–88). For additional details, see Anne Bandry, "The Publication of the Spurious Volumes of *Tristram Shandy,*" *Shandean* 3 (1991): 126–27, and "Early Advertisements," *Shandean* 4 (1992): 244.

17.   Unlike Carr, the forger of volume IX respects Sterne's tics, with a marked preference, for example, for *upon* over *on* and *amongst* over *among* (see Monkman, "More of Sterne's Politicks 1741–1742," *Shandean* 1 [1989]: 60). In Carr, far fewer *and*s are used than in the genuine volumes; I take *and* in conjunction with the dash to be a characteristic of Sterne's syntax. Spurious volume IX, on the other hand, does not differ from Sterne in this regard. To write more like Sterne, Carr would have needed to use *the* 50 percent more often than he did, which probably implies that he was using fewer nouns; again, the later forger does not differ from Sterne in this respect. Neither does he differ in the frequency of his use of *to be* (lemmatized),

whereas Carr used 40 percent more forms of the most common of English verbs; I take this to indicate that Carr had a much poorer vocabulary than did Sterne or the author of spurious volume IX. See Anne Bandry, "Une Etude stylostatistique de Sterne: Méthodologie," in *Gestion électronique de documents et nouvelles technologies en sciences humaines (France et Grande-Bretagne)* (Paris: Presses de l'Université Paris-Sorbonne, 1995), 79–99, esp. 84–94.

18.   The ornament on the title page was replaced by "VOL. III." The name of the printer, J. Scott, is given in the advertisement but not on the title page. See Bandry, "Spurious Volumes."

19.   "---To deal plainly, I came into the world just as other men do;---the old woman dextrously took me by the head, and was just going to bring me into this strange unaccountable world, when unluckily, the clock, which I have already mentioned, was wound up by one of the servants. . . . My mother, hearing the clock wound up, gave a sudden start, and cry'd out, *Once more, my dear*.---The old woman was just performing her office, but this loco-motive trick of my mother had such an effect, that my whole system was discomposed" (*A Supplement to The Life and Opinions of Tristram Shandy, Gent. Serving to elucidate that Work. By the Author of Yorick's Meditations,* 12–13). Notwithstanding its title, it also purported to be a volume III; publication on 17 December 1760 made it fit with the date Dodsley had announced when countering Carr, "about Christmas next." In *The Life and Opinions of Miss Sukey Shandy* (1760), the young woman is "led . . . not to a clock, . . . [but] to a c——ch, a thing of much more consequence to the intercourse of lovers" (57).

20.   New, "Some Sterne Borrowings from Four Renaissance Authors," *PQ* 71 (1992): 301; Lamb, "Sterne's System of Imitation," *MLR* 76 (1981): 807 (reprinted in this volume).

"Weavers, Gardeners, and Gladiators": Labyrinths in *Tristram Shandy*

STEPHEN SOUD

Why weavers, gardeners, and gladiators—or a man with a pined leg (proceeding from some ailment in the *foot*)

—*Tristram Shandy,* VIII.v

Many authors describing inextricable labyrinths write as if from a privileged perspective: they see where the ambiguous circlings lead, and they warn against labyrinthine perils.

—Penelope Reed Doob, *The Idea of the Labyrinth*

In Volume II, Chapter iii of *Tristram Shandy,* Tristram describes the beginning of Uncle Toby's encyclopedic reading of books on military science and tells us that Toby applies himself to the project "with the utmost diligence" because recovery from his wound depends "upon the passions and affections of his mind." But as Toby becomes increasingly entwined in the thread of his reading, Tristram must beseech him to

————stop! my dear uncle *Toby,*—stop!—go not one foot further into this thorny and bewilder'd track,—intricate are the steps! intricate are the mases of this labyrinth! intricate are the troubles which the pursuit of this bewitching phantom, KNOWLEDGE, will bring upon thee.—O my uncle! fly--fly--fly from it as from a serpent. (103)[1]

Although for Sterne the labyrinth does not seem to have the explicit, mythic overtones it often has in twentieth-century fiction, it is nevertheless part of the web of *Tristram Shandy.* The shandean world is labyrinthine in more ways than one, whether one considers Trim and Toby's elaborate fortifications on the bowling green, Walter's abstruse philosophical musings in the parlor, the Widow Wadman's romantic machinations, or the book's convoluted maze of interpolated texts. Above all, Tristram appears caught in a textual and chronological maze as he attempts to record the ins and outs of his family history.

Reprinted from *Eighteenth-Century Studies* 28 (1995): 397–411.

Tristram Shandy embodies Sterne's most fundamental insight into human nature: as temporal, mundane beings we are compelled to impose upon a labyrinthine world our self-made labyrinths that work, albeit unsuccessfully, to satisfy our urge for coherence amidst chaos. Toby discovers in his labyrinth that the "desire of knowledge, like the thirst of riches, increases ever with the acquisition of it" (II.iii.102), and ultimately Tristram must declare of his uncle, "Endless is the Search of Truth!" But Tristram's warning to Toby specifically raises the question of the significance of the maze in Sterne's world. Toby's "thorny and bewilder'd track," for example, probably alludes to the many spiral turf mazes found in the English countryside, especially in Sterne's Yorkshire. Interestingly, many of these mazes had names identified with Troy—and therefore with sieges.[2] These mazes were also associated with a ritual of running through the spiralling pathways called "treading the maze," and thus may lie behind Sterne's description of the very first maze in *Tristram Shandy,* the path of the homunculi, who, "by treading the same steps over and over again, . . . presently make a road of it, as plain and as smooth as a garden-walk" (I.i.2).[3] The idea of the labyrinth probably had two other important connotations for Sterne, both of which help to weave the subtle fabric of its meaning in the work. First, in Sterne's day the word "maze" had a second definition: "a winding movement, especially in a dance" (*OED;* in use as late as 1742). As we shall see, this meaning links Toby's entry into the maze with the dance at the end of Volume VII. Second, the labyrinth was a part of contemporary homiletics, which used the metaphor of the pilgrim caught in a spiritual labyrinth seeking the "right path" to salvation.[4]

Undoubtedly, however, the notion of the labyrinth that would have had the greatest currency for Sterne was the garden maze, which is demonstrably linked to Toby and his fortifications.[5] Late seventeenth- and early eighteenth-century culture in Europe harbored an urge for symmetry that was especially expressed in two areas, fortification and gardening, which represent, in contrasting ways, the desire to impose order on the world. During the sixteenth century, in the beginning of what has been termed the "Age of Symmetry" in gardens, English gardeners first began to use floral knots, which were designed along precise, intricate geometrical patterns. On a symbolic level, these patterns of unbroken, interlacing bands were emblematic of infinitude. But, for the eighteenth century, the knot was both evolutionally and etymologically related to the maze. Knots were historically the direct precursors of the garden labyrinth, which flourished in England from about 1650–1740, a period that includes the years in which Toby was staging his battles upon the bowling green. To the classically trained mind, moreover, "knot" was etymologically related to the Latin *nodus,* or node, the junction of paths in a maze. As we shall see, this relation between knot and labyrinth has significant bearing upon *Tristram Shandy.*

In the science of fortification, the other area of pervasive symmetry, one figure towered over all others—the French Marshal Sébastien LePrestre de

Vauban (1633–1707). Recall that immediately prior to Tristram's admonition, Toby is reading Vauban, among others, and becoming particularly absorbed in the geometry of warfare. Vauban singlehandedly raised the craft of military architecture to such heights that people considered his fortress designs impregnable; Louis XIV even kept scale models of them in the Louvre as works of art to show off to the court elite. With Vauban, Louis "walked through the sites of projected sieges, as Vauban explained his projects *in situ*. They quite literally walked (and rode) through entire campaigns together."[6] Surely Sterne, steeped in military history as he was, knew of Louis's miniatures, and it is worth considering to what degree Trim and Toby work as a satire of Vauban and Louis. At the very least, Louis's practice throws additional light on Walter's comment that "if any mortal in the whole universe had done such a thing [as the bowling green], except his brother *Toby*, it would have been looked upon by the world as one of the most refined satyrs upon the parade and prancing manner, in which *Lewis* XIV. from the beginning of the war . . . had taken the field" (VI.xxii.538).[7]

If calculus and nuclear physics are the sciences of modern warfare, geometry was the military science of Vauban's—and Sterne's—day. Vauban's works are fraught with an almost obsessive symmetry of bastions, glacises, firing trajectories, and trench-works. For Vauban, as one subsequent military tactician would remark, a fortress "grew to be treated somewhat as a geometrical puzzle, a species of maze."[8] But the fortifications were more than fearful symmetry; camouflaged and blending aesthetically into the surrounding landscape, they were not unlike gardens. Modern aerial photographs of many Dutch towns fortified during the era suggest this pastoral sense of the battlements merging smoothly into the countryside.[9] Not surprisingly, when Louis set about building the gardens at Versailles, he called upon Vauban's engineers to design the waterworks that would run the vast fountain system. Louis's fascination with both warfare and gardens did not go unnoticed by English gardeners: "The *French* King," one landscape architect would write, "like several other Great Personages, join[ed] the *peaceable Love of Agriculture* to the *tumultuous Passions of War*."[10]

There are other correlations between fortifications and gardening that suggest Sterne may have been connecting the two. It is especially interesting that the language of siegecraft bears striking resemblance to that of gardening. Here, for instance, are Vauban's instructions to the field officer for laying out the perpendicular of a trench:

> Inscribe this prolongation on the map as a sort of baseline, what I call the line of direction, extending it as far as necessary; from the rear of the trench and from each point where the separate segments of the trench (ab, bc, cd) meet to form angles, draw lines perpendicular to the line of direction [be, cf, dg], noting the length of each perpendicular and the distance between points where they intersect the line of direction.[11]

Compare this passage with Batty Langley's "Problem VI" in his *New Principles of Gardening* (1728), wherein he gives instructions to the gardener for drawing a perpendicular:

> *From a given point* (a *or* h) *to let fall or raise a perpendicular* (a h.)
> PRACTICE. With any interval make *a c* equal to *a b,* and with the Distance *b c* on *b* describe the Arch *e e,* and on *c* the Arch *f f,* crossing at *h,* join *h a,* and 'twill be the Perpendicular required; for *h b* is equal to *h c,* and *a b* to *a c,* and *h a* common. Therefore the Angles at *a* are equal and right-angled, and *a h* perpendicular.[12]

The early eighteenth-century gardener had a rage for mathematical regularity akin to that of the fortress-builder. Indeed the entire first section of Langley's book is dedicated to the geometry of gardening (as are sections in many gardening manuals of the period), with sub-headings such as "To draw a Tangent from a Point given," and "To describe a Serpentine Line about an Ellipsis."[13] Langley's extensive set of illustrations includes a design that unites fortress and arbor (fig. 1).[14] Even the vernacular of garden labyrinths resembled that of fortification: "The Walks of a Labyrinth ought to be kept roll'd . . . in the Shape of Half-moons."[15] Or again: "This Outside . . . is by the *French* called *la Fossé* [with] . . . two Foot and a half the Height of the Parapet-Wall."[16] The interchange went in both directions—there was a segment of skilled laborers in Vauban's trenches called "terrace-makers."[17]

This link between the symmetry and design of the garden maze and that of the fortress suggests that Toby's bowling-green fortifications are a form—a parody, perhaps—of the garden labyrinth. Comparing illustrations of eighteenth-century gardens and fortresses underscores their many similarities in design: their carefully plotted symmetry, zigzag arrangements, terraces, returning and salient angles. More specifically, garden and fortress are neatly conflated in two well-known designs completed during the reign of William III, the "Plan de Troy" at Hampton Court and "The Siege of Troy" at Kensington Palace, both of which Sterne may have had in mind when he created Uncle Toby.[18] In his "Essay on Modern Gardening" (1771), Horace Walpole describes the garden fortifications at Kensington:

> [C]ut yew and variegated holly hedges were taught (as the royal ideas were all military) to imitate the lines, angles, bastions, scarps and counter-scarps of regular fortifications. This curious upper garden, known as the "Siege of Troy," was long the admiration of every lover of that kind of horticultural embellishment and vegetable pedantry.[19]

At least one other gardener, Stephen Switzer, recognized the militaristic character of William's avocation, calling Hampton Court the "noblest work of that kind in *Europe*. . . . done in the Reign (too short) of a Prince always at War in Defence of the Liberties of Europe; yet in the least Interval of Ease,

Gard'ning took up a great part of his Time."[20] Switzer lacked, of course, our own psychoanalytic terminology, but it seems rather clear that William's gardening (like Toby's) was a sublimation of his more bellicose instincts.

William's chief gardener, Henry Wise, continued to incorporate fortress designs into his garden layouts even after the King's death. The original gardens at Marlborough's Blenheim Palace, for instance, included eight large bastions two hundred feet wide.[21] In one of his own designs (at Paston Manor), Switzer, a Wise protégé, included as a center-piece a verdant citadel (fig. 2). In *Ichnographia Rustica* (1718) Switzer describes the plan:

> [T]he Boundary of the interior Part of our Garden, which is easily discover'd to be an Hexagone in Fortification Work, for digging of the Ditch makes the Terrace in the Inside, and helps to raise the Banks on the outside; so as to admit other Slopes, being what they call [in] Fortification the cover'd way.[22]

Other garden designs probably followed suit, with Bridgeman's military-influenced work at Stowe an instrumental example of the new English garden. For Sterne, it would have been an easy transition from the labyrinthine fortress-gardens like those of Hampton Court and Paston Manor to Uncle Toby's fortifications on the bowling green.

FIGURE 1. "An Arbor in a Fortified Island." Plate 18 of Batty Langley's *New Principles of Gardening* (1728) depicts a plan for merging the jagged lines and geometrical symmetry common to both fortress and garden designs of the early eighteenth century.

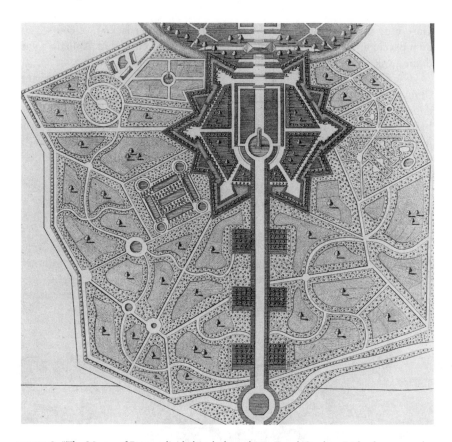

FIGURE 2. "The Manor of Paston divided and planted into Rural Gardens." The fortress at the center of Stephen Switzer's layout incorporates bastions, ravelins, and a "cover'd way," and the central axis includes battery positions—details which demonstrate his extensive knowledge of contemporary fortification science. Note also the meandering labyrinth adjacent to the fort (*right*), and the many nodes scattered throughout the design. (From *Ichnographia Rustica,* 1718.)

If it is Toby's wound that forces him to enter the labyrinth on the bowl-ing green, we must remember that the trench-works in which he incurred the wound were themselves a labyrinth. The battlefield at Namur "was cut and cross-cut with such a multitude of dykes, drains, rivulets, and sluices, on all sides,—and he would get so sadly bewilder'd and set fast amongst them, that frequently he could neither get backwards or forwards to save his life" (II.i.94–95). At Namur, Toby is lost and "bewilder'd" (the word echoes the passage in II.iii and may also suggest the section of landscape gardens called the wilderness); like a wanderer in a well-designed maze, he must move "backwards and forwards," toward and away from the center, to make any sort of progress. But Toby's recurrent entry into labyrinths raises a basic ques-tion: what, for him, is their lure?

That Toby desires the honor and glory of battle is too facile an answer—
and, given the paradoxes of his "Apologetical Oration" (VI.xxxii), an incomplete one from Sterne's viewpoint. Rather, to understand Toby's hobby-horse,
we must turn, I think, to the moment he and Trim decide to enact battles on
the bowling green. Expelled from the womb-like trench-works of Flanders ("I
had rather march up to the very edge of a trench —— — A woman is quite a
different thing—said the corporal" [VIII.xxx.715]), Toby is born into the
world with much of a child's helplessness and impotence. This impotence is
rendered in sexual terms by the wound on his groin, but even more significantly by the inadequacy of his language to define and order the world
around him. Thus Toby must reject language for pictograms (his maps), and,
finally, for the object, the unmediated "thing itself." All formal gardening,
which manipulates nature through the exercise of art, expresses the human
will to control one's environment, and Toby seems determined to reestablish
his lost control, at least upon the miniature world of his bowling green. His
fortress gardening is especially suffused with the vestiges of his lost sexuality:
"Never did lover post down to a belov'd mistress with more heat and expectation, than my uncle *Toby* did, to enjoy this self-same thing [the bowling
green] in private" (II.v.113). Thus the labyrinth in Yorkshire supplants the
labyrinth in Flanders, as Toby attempts to regain his lost potency in the garden maze.

Quite possibly, Toby's bowling green represents an implicit commentary
on Sterne's notion of the origin of warfare—a sublimation of the sex drive
forced by the delicate balance between human weakness and a longing for
empowerment. Historically, this opposition has been related to and borne out
in the garden: "If a sense of human powerlessness before nature was first
superseded by a sense that humans could coexist with, or even direct, that
power, there eventually came a time when the original relationship became
inverted. The garden became a symbol of human dominance over nature. We
think of Versailles as its exemplar."[23] By juxtaposing these two seemingly different occupations, gardening and warfare (suggestive as well of Louis and
William), Sterne delivers an ironic commentary upon a particular (masculine)
mode of expressing the human drive for empowerment and the traces of
depravity (the Garden behind the garden) in human endeavors. Sterne may
even have had in mind a 1746 statement by John Muller, Professor of Fortification at the Royal Military Academy: "The origin and rise of fortification, is
undoubtedly owing to the degeneracy of mankind."[24]

Toby's play with mazes has a further significance. Twice Tristram uses the
word "bewilder'd" to indicate Toby's mental state in the labyrinth. His bewilderment obviously suggests the distressful feelings of someone caught in a
labyrinth, and yet Toby's entanglement in mazes seems essential to his sense of
well-being. If building a maze represents a masculine will to power, the maze
itself has feminine connotations. The contours of early ritual labyrinths, for
example, were probably designed to duplicate the form of sacred labyrinthine

caves, symbolically placing the labyrinth in the traditionally feminine earth.[25] Sterne may even have known that many maze dances had included a rope, symbolizing the umbilical cord.[26] Thus Toby's desire to re-enter the labyrinth may be understood as an unconscious desire for the feminine, or at least an acknowledgement of his own loss and incompleteness. If the "male owner's 'penetration' into the 'inner spaces' of his garden was," as Carole Fabricant has suggested, "a journey into and through a variety of enclosures and structures deliberately designed as part of a feminine landscape,"[27] then this desire is quite literally played out upon the bowling green, where Toby attempts to penetrate ("breach," also connoting a wound) the walls of his miniature citadels. I do not wish to pursue a psychoanalytic reading, but rather to suggest that Sterne recognized (as did Robert Burton, among others, before him) that human aggression has a great deal to do with human weakness, and that human love may be the only path, however labyrinthine, away from both.

When the Treaty of Utrecht is signed, however, Toby again finds himself momentarily denied the control he so desperately seeks. Significantly, when romantic love offers itself in place of the bowling green, it does so again as a feminine labyrinth, or rather as a woman objectified as a labyrinth—the Widow Wadman. Tristram describes the situation in terms that clearly call the maze (and sieges) to mind:

> There was, Madam, in my uncle *Toby,* a singleness of heart which misled him so far out of the little serpentine tracks in which things of this nature usually go on; you can—you can have no conception of it: with this, there was a plainness and simplicity of thinking, with such an unmistrusting ignorance of the plies and foldings of the heart of woman;——and so naked and defenceless did he stand before you, (when a siege was out of his head) that you might have stood behind any one of your serpentine walks, and shot my uncle *Toby* ten times in a day, through his liver, if nine times in a day, Madam, had not served your purpose. (VI.xxix.550)

That Toby's "singleness of heart" *mis*leads him out of his labyrinth implies, ironically, that a sense of bewilderment is somehow necessary to him. Thus he ventures to re-enter a labyrinth, the maze-like "plies and foldings" of the Widow's "heart."[28] Once again expelled from his labyrinthine, womb-like trenches, Toby is a "naked and defenceless" newborn who seeks security by standing before the "serpentine walks" of a woman. In addition to its normal connotations with landscape gardens, "serpentine" not only echoes the passage in II.iii ("fly--fly--fly from it as from a serpent"), but also complements Elizabeth W. Harries's assertion that the "image of woman as Eve, the eternal temptress and source of evil, is always latent" in *Tristram Shandy*—and especially for Toby.[29] The labyrinth that the Widow represents is, however, one of an altogether different order from that on the bowling green. Unlike the besieged miniatures, the Widow can "shoot" back if it serves her purpose ("She has left a ball here—added my uncle Toby—pointing to his breast" [VIII.xxviii.712]). At last the center of the labyrinth is tangibly feminine and can no longer be dealt with through displacement. Desirous of personal warmth and love, Toby again struggles to communicate with pictures: "You shall see the very place, Madam," he tells the curious widow as he prepares to show her a map (IX.xx.772). Toby, however, is unable to negotiate the sexual implications of the Widow's interest in his wound; he returns instead to Shandy Hall, where he is once again relatively safe within the bastion provided by his brother's war on women and language and anything else that threatens his own labyrinthine systematizing.

Where Toby's labyrinth is physical and concrete, Walter's is metaphysical and abstract, a symmetrical maze of language and speculative systems. If "metaphysics is rooted in an implicit geometry which—whether we will or no—confers spatiality upon thought,"[30] then Walter can certainly be said to have created symmetrical philosophies via his beds of justice, his theory of names, and the egregious theory of auxiliary verbs. Like "all systematick reasoners," Walter "would move both heaven and earth, and twist and torture every thing in nature [like a landscape gardener] to support his hypothesis" (I.xix.61).[31] More directly linking Walter's philosophies with Toby's siegeworks, Tristram tells us his father "would intrench and fortify [one of his opinions] round with as many circumvallations and breast-works, as my uncle *Toby* would a citadel" (III.xxxiv.264). But if Toby builds labyrinths, Walter weaves them; his labyrinth is not so much the fortress as a twisted and tortured knot.

We have seen that Toby's descent into the labyrinth begins with his quest for a totalizing knowledge as a means of regaining the order lost in the trenches before Namur. Walter has his own encyclopedic attempt to encapsulate knowledge, the *Tristrapædia,* and it is "tied" to the knot: "My father spun his [knowledge], every thread of it, out of his own brain,—or reeled and cross-twisted what all other spinners and spinsters had spun before him" (V.xvi.445). Walter's efforts are doomed, because through delay, "the first part of the work, upon which my father had spent the most of his pains, was rendered entirely useless,——every day a page or two became of no consequence" (448). Hence, as Walter tries to weave his labyrinth of knowledge, the backward and forward motions associated with maze wandering are at work, creating a Swiftian misdirection by which progress is regress. The Swiftian satire is directed at the "chief mirage" of the early encyclopedists, "the belief that it was possible to compile a work that would supersede all books and render them unnecessary"; that is, that the world's knowledge was progressing teleologically.[32] Sterne's skepticism about the encyclopedic goal, so similar to Swift's (a point which the Florida editors establish),[33] is reflected in the fate of Walter's *Tristrapædia.* Walter's goal, ironically, is to bring his work "into so small a compass, that when it was finished and bound, it might be rolled up in my mother's hussive" (445–46). Like the symbology of the garden knot, the futility of Walter's project is revealed in this cyclical, interminable image: weaving a thread that ends up in the hussif where it started.

Walter's efforts to condense the totality of life into a single philosophic system end up in inextricable knots that can only be cut. The obvious image is of the Gordian knot, but cutting the knot may also signify cutting the umbilical cord (the "umbilical knot" [I.xxiii.83]), and hence of leaving one labyrinth to enter another. Both meanings may be at play in the debate in Volume IV between Walter and Toby, in which Toby rests his case on the authority of God. "That is cutting the knot," Walter responds, "instead of untying it" (IV.vii.332).[34] As Walter sees it, Toby is unwilling to cope with the vagaries of his secular philosophy. Walter, however, also seeks to cut through rather than untie the knots of life with his dreams of systematic order, especially his theory of auxiliary verbs, which he celebrates as a "North west passage to the intellectual world" (V.xlii.484). Indeed, all of Walter's theories are similar "passages" that aim to evade or deny (and are therefore hopeless impositions upon) the labyrinth of the world. Paradoxically, however, his attempts to cut the knot become labyrinthine knots themselves. In describing the theory of auxiliary verbs to Yorick, Walter presents it as twisted around a core with millions of branching offshoots: "Now the use of the *Auxiliaries* is, at once to set the soul a going by herself upon the materials as they are brought her; and by the versability of this great engine, round which they are twisted, to open new tracks of enquiry, and make every idea engender millions" (485). Using the theory properly, even a child may draw a "magazine of conceptions and conclusions" from it (V.xliii.486). The language here is telling. As Trim suggests, certain troops are called auxiliaries; at the heart of a fortress is a magazine (which, quite literally, fuels the "engines" of war); the use of "conception" links the image to the umbilical knot; all the paths ("tracks") ramify outward and lead to other paths, the ultimate sense of one caught in a maze.

In providing his particular example for the "great engine," Walter chooses the white bear, which may echo—in some shandean manner—the white bull that fathered the Minotaur of Daedalus's Cretan labyrinth. In thus ridiculing Walter, Sterne once again implies his fundamental skepticism about the possibilities of human knowledge and the notion that the world's labyrinth can be circumvented. It is almost certainly not accidental that when the Widow confronts Toby Shandy about his wound, she puts into action Walter's auxiliary verbs (IX.xx), his "white bear" becoming Toby's "it." By the end of this, the final volume, the "it" has metamorphosed into the impotent Shandy bull, which "might have done for Europa herself in purer times" (IX.xxxiii.808). Europa: mother of Minos, whose wife Pasiphae gave birth to the labyrinth-locked Minotaur.

The image of the labyrinth is also important to Sterne's conception of Tristram, who at the end of Volume VI offers his readers the most deceptive labyrinth of all, that of the single straight line. Mocking expectations of a standard narrative with the Aristotelian unities, and hence a direct route to the center of the maze, Tristram provides several labyrinth-like diagrams that outline the digressive nature of his writing in the first volumes. (In "Slawkenbergius's Tale" the unfolding of Aristotle's stages of narrative is called "unwinding the labyrinth" [IV.ST.317].) Visually, these diagrams delineate the various twists and turns of his narrative, but more importantly, the letters he includes to demarcate the last of them resemble the diagrams of fortifications found in the contemporaneous literature about military architecture.[35] Tristram, however, informs us he will mend his ways and "may arrive hereafter at the excellency of going on even thus;

---

which is a line drawn as straight as I could draw it. . . . This *right line,*—the path-way for Christians to walk in! say divines——" (VI.xl.571–72).[36] There is a parallel passage at the end of Volume VII: "I danced myself into Perdrillo's pavillion, where pulling a paper of black lines, that I might go on straight forwards [as opposed to backward and forward], without digression or parenthesis, in my uncle Toby's amours——" (xliii.651). The dance is itself a form of maze (as noted above), but the image of the straight line in both cases is a variation on the theme of cutting the knot—striking directly through to the heart of the labyrinth, only to discover another in its place.

If Tristram is having a joke at our expense—and he usually is—this one turns upon himself as well. In weaving a labyrinth, he is paradoxically entrapped by it. There are several suggestions in the early portions of the book that Tristram is himself a-mazed. *Tristram Shandy* begins with Tristram's *ab ovo* narration in the "knotted" labyrinth of the mother's womb, moves through Dr. Slop's attempts to cut Obadiah's maze of knots ("with such a multiplicity of round-abouts and intricate cross turns, with a hard knot at every intersection or point where the strings met" [III.viii.196]) to release his "instruments of delivery," to Tristram's misnaming, which calls forth one of Sterne's most poignant allusions to the labyrinth of human life: "But mark, madam, we live amongst riddles and mysteries—the most obvious things, which come in our way, have dark sides, which the quickest sight cannot penetrate into; and even the clearest and most exalted understandings amongst us find ourselves puzzled and at a loss in almost every cranny of nature's works" (IV.xvii.350).[37] Eventually, however, it is Tristram, the author, who is most significantly implicated in the labyrinth. Increasingly entangled in his maze-like narrative, attempting to construct his own account of his life and opinions and impose it upon reality, he inevitably creates a labyrinth to which—with equal inevitability—he becomes susceptible himself.[38]

Toward the end of Volume VI, just prior to introducing his diagrammatic labyrinths, Tristram confesses that "when a man is telling a story in the strange way I do mine, he is obliged continually to be going backwards and forwards . . . and now, you see, I am lost myself!" (VI.xxxiii.557–58). A few pages later he discovers "I can get on no further,—and find myself entangled on all sides of this mystick labyrinth" (xxxvii.565). On the one hand, we are asked to feel sympathy for the hapless Tristram who has never had control over the key events of his life: his conception, birth, naming, and education. He elicits this sort of sympathy from us in Volume VIII: "What! are not the unavoidable distresses with which, as an author and a man, thou art hemm'd in on every side of thee——are they, Tristram, not sufficient, but thou must entangle thyself still more?" (VII.vi.663). On the other hand, we know that human beings do not control these events in their lives, that Tristram the jester has reveled in sending us down the false paths and dead ends of his "mystick labyrinth":

> I tell you before-hand, you had better throw down the book at once; for with-out *much reading,* by which your reverence knows, I mean *much knowledge,* you will no more be able to penetrate the moral of the next marbled page (motly emblem of my work!) than the world with all its sagacity has been able to unraval the many opinions, transactions and truths which still lie mystically hid under the dark veil of the black one. (III.xxxvi.268)

Tristram here warns us in a passage that is reminiscent of his warning to Uncle Toby (II.iii), that if we wish to leave the labyrinth of knowledge, we must either put down the book(s), or—cognizant of our own finitude—realize that the quest for truth is itself infinite. There is no Northwest passage to knowledge, and any compartmentalization of truth yields only a fallible, human labyrinth. "Endless is the Search of Truth!" indeed, and the ultimate maze of *Tristram Shandy* may well be the marbled page, with its mystic truth obscured by the carefully designed swirls of color calculated to resist our systematizing, a "motly emblem" of both the labyrinth and of *Tristram Shandy.*

Notes

I am indebted to Melvyn New for his thoughtful advice on this article. Thanks are also due to Patricia Craddock and Alistair Duckworth.

    1.   The linkage between knowledge and the serpent surely is meant to invoke the Garden foremost in the minds of eighteenth-century readers. Sterne's choice of wording in the passage also suggests the Greek etymology of "ichnography": "track" and "footstep." Cf. II.v.110: "As summer is coming on, continued *Trim,* your Honour might sit out of doors, and give me the nography——(call it ichnography, quoth my uncle)."

    2.   W. H. Matthews, *Mazes and Labyrinths: A General Account of Their History and Developments* (1922; rpt. Detroit: Singing Tree Press, 1969), 77, 92. See also Penelope Reed Doob: "there may be a connection between the *lusus Troiae* [Trojan Ride] . . . and the abundant turf-mazes and stone circles of northern Europe known as 'Troy-Town' " (*The Idea of the Labyrinth*

from Classical Antiquity through the Middle Ages [Ithaca: Cornell Univ. Press, 1990], 28). Doob reprints a photograph of a turf maze (114).

3.   Sterne's customary punning comes into play here as well: "to tread" is also a fowling term for "to copulate."

4.   Doob, 213ff. Doob points out that specific homiletic usages of the labyrinth originated in Augustine, who suggested that a good sermon should be like a labyrinth.

5.   Two brief articles linking Toby's bowling green to garden layouts appeared while this article was awaiting publication. See James Fenton, "War in the Garden," *New York Review of Books,* 24 (June 1993): 23–26 and Pat Rogers, "Ziggerzagger Shandy: Sterne and the Aesthetics of the Crooked Line," *English* 42 (1993): 97–107.

6.   Joan DeJean, *Literary Fortifications: Rousseau, Laclos, Sade* (Princeton: Princeton Univ. Press, 1984), 21, 30.

7.   Cf. David McNeil, *The Grotesque Depiction of War and the Military in Eighteenth-Century English Fiction* (Newark: Univ. of Delaware Press, 1990). In addition to making a similar assertion regarding Toby and Vauban, McNeil has noted that "toy soldiers and artillery" were being "mass-produced for the public about the same time Sterne was writing *Tristram Shandy*" (154–55).

8.   Major George Sydenham Clarke (1848–1933) as quoted in Ian V. Hogg, *Fortress: A History of Military Defense* (New York: St. Martin's, 1975), 49.

9.   See, for example, the view of Naarden, Holland, in Hogg, 42–43.

10.   Stephen Switzer, *Ichnographia Rustica: Or, the Nobleman, Gentleman, and Gardener's Recreation,* 3 vols. (London: D. Browne et al., 1718), I:43.

11.   Sébastien LePrestre de Vauban, *A Manual of Siegecraft and Fortification,* trans. George A. Rothrock (Ann Arbor: Univ. of Michigan Press, 1968), 44.

12.   Batty Langley, *New Principles of Gardening* (1728; rpt. Westmead: Gregg International, 1971), 4.

13.   While the serpentine line might evoke the picturesque to some readers, it is worth keeping in mind that for Hogarth and others it was a "precise" line of beauty, the figure that, with mathematical regularity, produced the most beautiful form. Sterne parodies this precision in his figure of Trim reading the sermon (II.xvii.140), a figure he asked Hogarth to draw in order to illustrate their "systems." As he wrote Richard Berenger on ?8 March 1760, "The loosest sketch [of Hogarth's] . . . [would] mutually illustrate his System and mine" (*The Letters of Laurence Sterne,* ed. Lewis Perry Curtis [Oxford: Clarendon Press, 1935], 99). In any case, I wish to highlight a fairly consistent linking of garden, labyrinth, and serpent.

14.   Without straying too far from my argument, it is worth pointing out that Charles Bridgeman's pioneering work at Stowe (ca. 1713) on the English ha-ha, the sunken wall that enabled the formal garden and countryside to blend visually together and that usually is seen as the innovation leading away from the formal geometrical style to the planned spontaneity of the latter portion of the century, was influenced by military architecture. See G. B. Clarke, "The History of Stowe—VIII: Military Gardening: Bridgeman and the Ha-Ha," *The Stoic* 24 (1969): 11–15; and Christopher Thacker, *The History of Gardens* (Berkeley and Los Angeles: Univ. of California Press, 1979), 182–84.

15.   François Gentil, *The Retir'd Gard'ner,* trans. George London and Henry Wise, 2 vols., ed. John Dixon Hunt (1706; rpt. New York: Garland, 1982), 743.

16.   Switzer, II:164. "Half-moon," "fossé," and of course "parapet" were terms used in fortification; see the Glossary in the *Notes* to *Tristram Shandy.*

17.   Vauban, 51. See also Yi-Fu Tuan, "Gardens of Power and Caprice" in *Dominance and Affection: The Making of Pets* (New Haven: Yale University Press, 1984): "The [gardening] skills needed to move earth, build retaining walls, terraces, pools, and avenues were also those needed in the military constructions of the period." Hence many architects "worked on both military fortifications and princely gardens" (28).

18.   Matthews suggests that the Hampton Court maze "in all probability displaced an older maze, a relic of [Cardinal] Wolsey's time. . . . The circular Troy-town . . . formerly coex-

isted with the present maze" (129). See also David Jacques and Arend Jan van der Horst, *The Gardens of William and Mary* (London: Christopher Helm, 1988): "There was a Troy Town in the wilderness at Hampton Court, and the [gravel] pit at Kensington . . . was referred to as the 'Siege of Troy' " (164). *Spectator* #477 refers to this pit, but not as the "Siege": "*Wise* and *London* [the garden's designers] are our Heroick Poets, and if, as a Critick, I may single out any Passage of their Works to commend, I shall take Notice of that Part in the upper Garden at *Kensington,* which was at first nothing but a Gravel-Pitt. It must have been a fine Genius for Gardening, that could have thought of forming such an unsightly hollow into so beautiful an Area" (*The Spectator,* ed. Donald F. Bond, 5 vols. [Oxford: Clarendon Press, 1965], IV:190).

19.   Horace Walpole, "On Modern Gardening" in *The History of the Modern Taste in Gardening,* ed. John Dixon Hunt (1828; rpt. New York: Garland, 1982), 256n. Interestingly enough, Hunt believes the essay was written in the decade prior to its publication, the same years that Sterne was publishing *Tristram Shandy.*

20.   Switzer, I:76–77.

21.   David Green, *Blenheim Palace* (London: Country Life, 1951), 68–69.

22.   Switzer, III:84. We know that Sterne had at least a passing interest in gardening (Arthur H. Cash, *Laurence Sterne: The Later Years* [London and New York: Methuen, 1986], 67–68). And while the catalogue of books attributed to Sterne's library (*A Facsimile Reproduction of a Unique Catalogue of Laurence Sterne's Library* [New York: AMS Press, 1973]) is sometimes misleading (see W. G. Day, "Sterne's Books," *Library,* 5th series, 31 [1976]: 245–48), it is interesting to note that it includes a copy of "Switzer's *General System of Hydrostaticks and Hydraulicks*" (entry #574). Switzer's volume contains a diagram of a landscape design with a slope of greensward labeled "glacis" (*An Introduction to a General System of Hydrostaticks and Hydraulicks, Philosophical and Practical,* 2 vols., ed. John Dixon Hunt [1729; rpt. New York: Garland, 1982], plate 3, opp. I:130), leaving us to conjecture if Sterne initially made the connection between gardens and fortifications through Switzer's work.

23.   Robert B. Riley, "Flowers, Power, and Sex" in *The Meaning of Gardens: Idea, Place, and Action,* ed. Mark Francis and Randolph T. Hester, Jr. (Cambridge: MIT Press, 1990), 61. See also Ian Donaldson, "Weavers, Gardeners, Gladiators, and the Lame: *Tristram Shandy,* viii.5," *Notes and Queries* 228 (1983): 61–63, who explores some classical and Renaissance sources that link physical disability with sexuality.

24.   John Muller, *A Treatise Concerning the Elementary Part of Fortification* (1746; rpt. Ottawa: Museum Restoration Service, 1968), 19. In the *Notes* to *Tristram Shandy,* the editors refer to Muller's comment in their note to a passage (467.1–4) that brings together archetypal gardens, fortification, and procreative power. In the passage (in V.xxxi), Uncle Toby opines, "For when the ground was tilled . . . and made worth inclosing, then they began to secure it by walls and ditches, which was the origin of fortification." Significantly, this is Toby's riposte to Walter's borrowed theorizing on the "original of society," which he misremembers as "a man,—a woman—and a bull" (466). That Sterne should associate these ideas—the garden, fortification, the bull, and procreation—in a single chapter is, in light of my argument here, fortuitous. I discuss below the relation between the Shandy bull and the labyrinth, but surely to Western readers the labyrinth and the Minotaur are inextricably intertwined.

25.   Wendy B. Faris, *Labyrinths of Language: Symbolic Landscape and Narrative Design in Modern Fiction* (Baltimore: Johns Hopkins Univ. Press, 1988), 6.

26.   Janet Bord, *Mazes and Labyrinths of the World* (New York: Grove Press, 1962), 12.

27.   Carole Fabricant, "Binding and Dressing Nature's Loose Tresses: The Ideology of Augustan Landscape Design," *Studies in Eighteenth-Century Culture* 8 (1979): 122. In addition to her trenchant analysis of Stephen Switzer on these grounds, Fabricant reminds us that the "overriding conception" behind eighteenth-century gardens was the "myth of restoration" (127), a point that certainly applies to Toby.

28.   The language in this passage recalls the serpentine furrows of an English turf maze; the sexual implications of "plies and foldings" cannot be avoided. The association of a woman's heart (or at least that of the coquette) with the labyrinth seems to have been a popular notion

in the early eighteenth century, as in *Spectator* #281: "Our operator, before he engaged in this Visionary Dissection, told us, that there was nothing in his Art more difficult, than to lay open the Heart of a Coquet, by reason of the many Labyrinths and Recesses which are to be found in it, and which do not appear in the Heart of any other Animal" (II:594).

29. "The Sorrows and Confessions of a Cross-Eyed 'Female Reader' of Sterne," in *Approaches to Teaching Sterne's "Tristram Shandy,"* ed. Melvyn New (New York: MLA, 1989), 113. In Volume VIII, Tristram actually does dismiss the Widow as "A daughter of Eve, for such was widow Wadman, and 'tis all the character I intend to give of her" (viii.664).

30. Gaston Bachelard, *The Poetics of Space,* trans. Maria Jolas (New York: Orion, 1964), 212.

31. Denis Cosgrove has demonstrated the connection between symmetrical landscapes and mystical philosophies in "The Geometry of Landscape: Practical and Speculative Arts in Sixteenth-Century Venetian Land Territories" in *The Iconography of Landscape,* ed. Denis Cosgrove and Stephen Daniels (Cambridge: Cambridge Univ. Press, 1988), 254–76.

32. Robert Collison, *Encyclopaedias: Their History Throughout the Ages* (New York: Hafner, 1966), 2.

33. There is a parallel passage in I.xxi.72: "When that happens [the pinnacle of knowledge attained] . . . it will put an end to all kind of writings whatsoever;—the want of all kind of writing will put an end to all kind of reading;---and that in time, *As war begets poverty, poverty peace,——* . . . we shall have all to begin over again; or, in other words, be exactly where we started." The Florida *Notes* establish a link between Sterne's thought in this passage and Swift's *A Tale of a Tub.* It is worth noting at this juncture that one of the most prominent early encyclopedists, Charles Perrault, was the designer of the labyrinths at Versailles.

34. Cf. Leigh A. Ehlers, "Mrs. Shandy's 'Lint and Basilicon': The Importance of Women in *Tristram Shandy,*" *South Atlantic Review* 46 (1981): 71–72. Ehlers suggests that the "knot represents the accidents and misfortunes of life, like Tristram's crushed nose or his misnaming; faith and trust in God enable the Christian to cope with these afflictions, to cut through the illusions and obstructions of earthly existence" (72). Ehlers's language here recalls the homiletic rhetoric of the labyrinth noted earlier; interestingly, the Florida editors trace Sterne's phrasing in this passage to two of his sermons (see n. to 332.22–23).

35. See, for example, Plate III in the *Notes* of the *Florida Edition.* The plate, taken from *Chambers' Cyclopædia,* is particularly noteworthy for the top center diagram, which looks surprisingly like the narrative diagrams at the end of Volume VI.

36. Again, this passage reflects the homiletic labyrinth that Doob mentions.

37. Although two of Sterne's sermons make use of the language here (see n. to 350.11–19 in the Florida *Notes*), the phrasing is ultimately derived from Locke's *Essay Concerning Human Understanding,* IV.3.22. See the scholium to this passage in *The Scriblerian* 19.1 (1986):93.

38. Faris writes: "The writer's exploration of the labyrinth of the world leads him to create a mirroring labyrinth—the work of art" (167).

Narratives of Loss:
Tristram Shandy and *The Poems of Ossian*

TOM KEYMER

Surveying Calais in volume VII (1765) of *Tristram Shandy,* Tristram prepares to transcribe a lengthy account of the siege of the town from the historian Rapin de Thoyras. Then he relents: "No——! by that all powerful fire which warms the visionary brain, and lights the spirits through unworldly tracts! ere I would . . . make thee pay, poor soul! for fifty pages which I have no right to sell thee,—naked as I am, I would browse upon the mountains, and smile that the north wind brought me neither my tent or my supper" (*TS,* VII. vi.584). In the context of a work that famously makes plagiarism an art, this is an odd enough declaration. What most struck Ralph Griffiths of the *Monthly Review,* however, was its strange grandiloquence of style, which seemed to recall a work whose "bombast, extravagance, and absurdity" the *Monthly Review* had already censured on its appearance three years earlier.[1] "Nobly said!—that flight to the mountain's top was lofty indeed!" Griffiths sarcastically writes: "Perfectly Fingalian!"[2]

The passage is not, of course, perfectly Fingalian. Sterne may indeed have wished to bring Macpherson to mind as one very topical case of an author making his readers pay for just the commodity that Tristram here forswears— the work of another (in this case the work of Ossian, a supposed third-century bard). Perhaps he implies some wry acknowledgment that Macpherson and he have in a sense already changed fortunes and places: at a time when Tristram has "ten cart-loads of thy fifth and sixth volumes still—still unsold" (*TS,* VIII.vi.663), *Fingal* remains a best-selling success. Yet no real effort is made here to catch the distinctive measure of Macpherson's prose, while the vaguely Ossianic diction on which Tristram draws is mixed with concerns of far too decadent a kind (tents and suppers, to say nothing of smiling) to have much place in *Fingal*'s world. Whatever else Tristram has in mind to revive his flagging sales, a full-blown shift into the bardic sublime is clearly not in prospect. He fails to act on his later resolution to "go into Wales for six weeks, and drink goat's-whey" (VII.xxix.624), and no further trace of the Celtic vogue (fueled at

---

This essay was written in its present version specifically for this volume; a different version will appear in the proceedings of the Macpherson Bicentenary Conference held at Oxford in 1996.

the time not only by Ossian but also by such works as Evan Evans's *Specimens of the Poetry of the Ancient Welsh Bards,* 1764) is registered in the more than 500 pages of notes to the definitive Florida edition of *Tristram Shandy.*

Yet it remains the case that Ralph Griffiths in 1765 had ample reason to associate Sterne with Macpherson, just as Robert Burns was to do in a letter of 1783, and just as Malcolm Laing was to do in his "Historical and Critical Dissertation on the Supposed Authenticity of the Poems of Ossian" (1800).[3] If at first sight the ardent primitivism of *The Poems of Ossian* and the playful modernity of *Tristram Shandy* seem worlds apart, a closer look reveals affinities that run far beyond the more obvious differences of culture, language, and genre. This essay explores some of the many historical, formal, and thematic connections between these two great literary projects of the 1760s—connections that do much to highlight the distinctive emphases of each.

I

There are many ways in which Sterne's *Tristram Shandy* and the sequence of Ossianic texts on which Macpherson was simultaneously at work may justly be seen as parallel projects. Simply as publishing processes they share similar features, jointly highlighting the hunger for novelty, openness to experimentation, and sheer opportunist vigor that characterized the literary marketplace of the day. Both (from the point of view, at least, of the metropolitan literary culture for which the *Monthly Review* spoke) were texts from the margins, yet both made a rapid and forceful impact on the literary center to which their authors were simultaneously drawn. Both had protracted and strangely similar histories of production, *The Life and Opinions of Tristram Shandy* appearing in five installments between 1759 and 1767 and the body of work that would be known as *The Poems of Ossian* (its collected title of 1773) in three interconnected publications between 1760 and 1763. Both works developed, in effect, as long-running, improvised serials, creating and sustaining their own vogues, modeling and remodeling their own precedents, generating from each of their previous installments a potentially endless succession of future matter.[4] Both threw up in their wakes a mass of secondary writing—vindications and attacks, burlesques and imitations, bogus addenda and spurious sequels, *Clockmakers' Outcries* and *Staffs of Gisbal.* Hailed at first as unfettered productions of original genius, debunked in retrospect as plagiarism or hoax, both shared the fascinating aura of sensation, enigma, scandal.

By the end of the century, Malcolm Laing was trouncing *The Poems of Ossian* as some phony concoction from Milton, Young, and Pope's Homer, so (as he put it) "transferring them from the third to the eighteenth century," while John Ferriar was no less dogged in transferring *Tristram Shandy* from the eighteenth century to the seventeenth, as a tissue of thefts from Montaigne,

Rabelais, and Burton.[5] Both Macpherson and Sterne had by then been seen for decades as major literary names and were ripe for revisionist attack. Both emerged, however, in leaps from obscurity to instant fame, and from backgrounds that placed them at the very margins of the social, literary, and (in Macpherson's case) political worlds in which they later thrived. Macpherson began as a young highland schoolmaster, born and raised in a remote center of Jacobite allegiance where the Gaelic language remained firmly rooted; Sterne as a frustrated rural clergyman, born in Ireland and now marooned "in a bye corner of the kingdom, and in a retired thatch'd house" (*TS*, I, dedication), his career in the Church going nowhere. Setting aside a series of more or less fugitive early pieces, both made an inauspicious start with locally published damp squibs: in Macpherson's case *The Highlander*, an epic poem that "*disappeared*" (as Laing tartly put it) in Edinburgh in April 1758, ignored even by the two literary reviews managed by the poem's own publisher;[6] in Sterne's case *A Political Romance*, a clerical satire printed in York in January 1759, which more emphatically disappeared when all but a handful of copies were incinerated (apparently at the instigation of the satire's main targets).[7]

Setback, however, was only a spur to both writers, and both now embarked on the hugely successful literary projects that were to make their names, moving rapidly to London publishers when the success of a locally published sample of their distinctive material opened the way to a larger ongoing process of related production. The first installment of *Tristram Shandy* was published in York in December 1759 "merely to feel the pulse of the world," as Sterne told the London bookseller Robert Dodsley;[8] reissued by Dodsley the following month, the volumes themselves announced an open-ended process of annual publication that was sporadically fulfilled (and never unambiguously terminated) over the following seven years. Meanwhile Macpherson's *Fragments of Ancient Poetry*, published in Edinburgh in June 1760, played a similar role in testing the market and generating the audience for a possible large-scale sequel. Among other surviving remains of Gaelic antiquity, as the preface declares, "there is reason to hope that one work of considerable length, and which deserves to be styled an heroic poem, might be recovered and translated, if encouragement were given to such an undertaking" (*PO*, 6).

It is at this point that the careers of Sterne and Macpherson start to intersect in intriguing ways. Both were lionized by literary society during lengthy visits to London, and while their different political alignments to some extent confined them to different circles (*Tristram Shandy* is dedicated to Pitt, *Temora* to Bute), both are known to have been paraded during the same period by the influential patron Elizabeth Montagu (Sterne's cousin by marriage, and a generous early sponsor of Macpherson's research tours in the highlands).[9] More significant is their gravitation toward the same publishers and printers: first the brothers Dodsley, who brought out the first London editions of both *Tristram Shandy*, volumes I and II (January 1760), and *Frag-*

ments of Ancient Poetry (April 1761), as well as the first edition of *Tristram Shandy*, volumes III and IV (January 1761); then Thomas Becket, who published both *Fingal* and *Tristram Shandy*, volumes V and VI, within three weeks of one another in December 1761. For the printing of *Tristram Shandy*, volumes V and VI, and subsequent volumes, Sterne dealt directly with William Strahan, the Scottish printer and bookseller. Strahan was simultaneously at work on *Fingal*, having been asked by David Hume to assist Macpherson on the latter's arrival in London, and he continued to print and later publish for Macpherson well into the 1770s.[10]

In retrospect, the almost simultaneous appearance of *Fingal* and *Tristram Shandy*, volumes V and VI, marked the zenith of both literary projects. Sterne left London for the Continent in the early days of 1762, and although "very hard at Work" in May of that year (as he told Becket from Paris) he was unable to publish a fourth installment of *Tristram Shandy* before January 1765.[11] Macpherson retained his momentum with more success, and in March 1763 the tantalizing fragment *Temora*, first published as one of several brief makeweights to *Fingal*, was ready to reemerge in the new guise of a full-scale epic poem. Here was a technique of linked publication that Sterne would use when slipping into the final volume of *Tristram Shandy* a digressive chapter trailing his forthcoming *Sentimental Journey;* it was not for nothing that Malcolm Laing could scoff that "if we may judge from the subjects which [Macpherson] had provided, the pretended translator might have produced, each year, an epic poem like an annual novel, had the Temora been equally successful with Fingal."[12] As Laing's words suggest, however, Macpherson's project too was by this time beginning to burn out both itself and its audience. In the following years he contented himself with revising and reordering his material into the collected editions of 1765 and 1773, while *Tristram Shandy* capered to its abrupt halt of 1767 with the solitary volume IX.

Becket published—or, in the case of the collected Ossians of 1765 and 1773, copublished with Strahan—all these volumes. A staunch defender of Macpherson's integrity and an increasingly close friend of Sterne, he provides an important link between the two writers during the middle and later stages of their parallel projects. He was far from alone, however. Though Sterne would have been unable to inspect the *Fingal* manuscripts that Becket later claimed to have exhibited in London "for many months in the year 1762," he would not have been able to escape the ensuing controversy on arriving in Paris in January of that year.[13] There he became friendly with Jean-Baptiste-Antoine Suard and intimate with Denis Diderot and the Baron d'Holbach, three of the leading French enthusiasts for Ossian, shortly after the first of Diderot's Ossianic translations had appeared in Suard's *Journal étranger* for December 1761.[14] On returning to Paris in 1764 Sterne grew acquainted with Hume at a time when Hume remained preoccupied with the question of Ossian's authenticity and was actively promoting the poems in Parisian circles.

If all this left Sterne immune (as seems unlikely) to Macpherson's impact during the period when the final volumes of *Tristram Shandy* were in gestation, the same can hardly be said of his closer friendship in Paris with the brilliant young highlander whom Boswell dubbed "the *Marcellus* of Scotland." This was the Gaelic-speaking Etonian Sir James Macdonald of Sleat, a key witness in the authenticity controversy, who had quarreled with Macpherson but was prepared to attest that he had heard his Hebridean tenant John Mac-Codrum "repeat, for hours together, poems which seemed to me to be the same with Macpherson's translation."[15] Sterne and Macdonald met again at Turin in November 1765, traveled half the length of Italy in one another's company, and lodged together in Naples for a further two months.[16] The significance of this link between Sterne and one of the leading Ossianists of the day can hardly be overstated—although for sheer intimacy of connection Macdonald of Sleat is more than trumped by Elizabeth Draper, addressee of Sterne's *Journal to Eliza,* who rather bizarrely appears to have capped her sentimental liaison with the dying Sterne by becoming Macpherson's mistress a few years later.[17]

Sterne had no shortage of opportunity to consider Macpherson's writing, then, above all during the years in which the last three volumes of *Tristram Shandy* were planned and written. To talk in terms of these essentially biographical connections, however, is only to scratch the surface of a complex literary affinity. More important is the question of form, and the way in which both *Tristram Shandy* and *The Poems of Ossian* are linked by their conspicuous violation, or fragmentation, of the polite registers and elegant structures of neoclassical convention. It is no coincidence that both Macpherson and Sterne earned the hostility of the leading champion of established decorums, Samuel Johnson, for whom *Fingal* was "a mere unconnected rhapsody" that lacked "the *lucidus ordo*," while the dedication to *Tristram Shandy,* volume V (as he put it to Sterne's face), was simply "not English, sir."[18] It is tempting to see these objections as interchangeable, for by Johnson's criteria both works emphatically defied the norms of Horatian aesthetics, while neither was written in English. In Macpherson, the imitation of Gaelic verse creates an abrupt, disjointed, paratactical style, opaquely metaphorical, willfully irregular, devoid of orderly transition and explicit connection. And while Macpherson's prose swerves away from polite diction after the model (both real and imagined) of traditional ballad and recitation, so orality of a different kind is at work in Sterne, whose jerky mimicry of extempore utterance is similarly disruptive of the orotund, harmonious periods of Johnsonian English. Nor do the larger structures of literary form survive unbroken in either writer, Macpherson's emphasis on the irretrievability of intact sources and Sterne's frenetic ruptures of narrative coherence effecting a similar frustration of unity and completeness. It is for these reasons, and not simply due to the coincidences of printing history, that texts like *Temora* and the later volumes of *Tristram Shandy* can look so similar on the page, their ostentatious lacunae marked out by blocks of asterisks, their abrupt sentences chopped and set off by welters of shandean dashes.

To the extent that Macpherson and Sterne have been linked before, it has been in the sense that this common emphasis on fragmentation of style and form identifies them as fellow sentimentalists. When Burns named them together, he classed them approvingly as "authors of the sentim[l] kind"; when Laing did so, it was to allege the essential modernity of Macpherson's Ossian as a voguish participant in "the sentimental vein" of Sterne's fiction. More recently, John Dwyer has found in Macpherson's welding together of fragments "an uncanny resemblance to the literary techniques of sentimental writers" (he names Sterne in particular), so providing a way "to depict pathetic scenes without having to worry unduly about the potential distractions of plot."[19] It is certainly possible to find in this shared evasion of narrative logic a redirection of focus toward vignettes of feeling, and it is easy to juxtapose passages in which a comparably sentimental emphasis seems to be made. Consider "The War of Caros," when

> The king's soul was sad for Comala, and his eyes could not behold Hidallan.
> Lonely, sad, along the heath, he slowly moved with silent steps. His arms hang disordered on his side. His hair flies loose from his helmet. The tear is in his down-cast eyes; and the sigh half-silent in his breast. (*PO*, 111)

Here are the very hallmarks of sentimental excess—the gesture of lassitude, the single tear, the silence of grief beyond words. Sterne is less terse; but when Walter laments his own more mundane misfortunes in a volume of *Tristram Shandy* published 11 months earlier, we find an ironic elaboration of the same motifs: "he threw himself prostrate across his bed in the wildest disorder imaginable, but at the same time, in the most lamentable attitude of a man borne down with sorrows, that ever the eye of pity dropp'd a tear for.——
. . . his left arm hung insensible over the side of the bed, his knuckles reclining upon the handle of the chamber pot, which peep'd out beyond the valance. . . . A fix'd, inflexible sorrow took possession of every line of his face.—He sigh'd once,—heaved his breast often,—but utter'd not a word" (*TS*, III.xxix.254–55). Here Walter's grief is mocked as well as evoked, but in both texts a common interest in sentiment and sympathy produces not only shared gestures but a shared vocabulary of sorrow, disorder, silence.

Yet there is much more to fragmentation of literary form than some mere prioritization of interludes like these over the more dynamic plotting of continuous narrative; and it is here, not in a sentimentalism to which the relationship of each was at least equivocal, that we find the more profound and interesting affinities between Macpherson and Sterne. Fiona Stafford opens up more promising ground when she notes that Macpherson's "concentration on the isolated poet owed as much to the literature of the mid-eighteenth-century as to the classics," and when she finds in Sterne a comparable concern for the predicament of the modern memoirist "isolated within his own perceptions."[20] The emphasis on isolation is very apt, for both *The Poems of Ossian* and *Tristram Shandy* are works preoccupied with the loss of a remembered past, whether the idealized "other times" of Fingalian heroism or the fondly recalled experiences of Tristram's youth. Both review the periods they describe from the perspective of an imagined present that by comparison seems degenerate or empty, and both document the obsessive yet finally unavailing struggles of their presiding voices to recover and transmit, in memory and language, this otherwise fugitive past. Here fragmentation may incidentally provide a means of freezing narrative progress to highlight feeling, but it serves more centrally as a presiding metaphor for the sense of disintegration and loss so pervasive in both works.[21] At the level of form itself, fragmentation implies a view of human experience ("this Fragment of Life," as Tristram puts it in his first dedication) in which interruption, incoherence, and decay seem insuperable conditions, and in which the imperfect efforts of memory and language can only reaffirm the inevitability of separation from what is lost.

II

Locke's account of human psychology and language as vexed by obscurity and instability has long been recognized as an important context for *Tristram Shandy,* and persuasive moves have recently been made to read *The Poems of Ossian* in similar terms.[22] More is at stake in the case of the *Poems,* however, than some strictly philosophical loss of confidence, for the disintegration Macpherson laments is nothing less than that of a whole culture—the virtuous Celtic antiquity idealized in his *Introduction to the History of Great Britain and Ireland* (1771) and represented in his commentaries on Ossian as having long since retreated to its final stronghold of highland Scotland. For an Orcadian, Whiggish, and defiantly unromantic critic like Malcolm Laing, this is a culture marked only by "the vices of barbarians."[23] For Macpherson it is a locus of precommercial integrity, untouched by a debilitating modernity in which heroism is enfeebled and virtue corrupted by luxury and wealth. Such perfection belongs, however, to an irretrievable past. In his dissertations and annotations Macpherson constructs a history of internal decay barely less ancient than the Fianna itself, and he fails to suppress occasional disdain for such latter-day follies as "the ridiculous notion of the second sight, which prevailed in the highlands and isles" (*PO,* 433). More recent if shadowy components of his analysis are the military and social incursions of his childhood years: most obviously the post-Culloden suppression of the Jacobite clans and cultural-political measures like the Heritable Jurisdiction and Disarming Acts of 1746–1747, but also processes of longer duration and more lasting effect, like the engineering projects of General Wade (whose roads and bridges prised open the highlands in the 1730s) or the state-sponsored erosion of Gaelic and promotion of English (a process in train since well before the Union of 1707).[24]

Here, more even than military defeat, it is commercial modernity that lands the knockout punch—modernity of a kind that Macpherson deplored in theory as energetically as he embraced it in practice. In his analysis, a new mobility of people, goods, and values hastens the pace of centuries-old decline, teaching the highlanders "enough of foreign manners to despise the customs of their ancestors" (*PO*, 51), and leaving the culture as a whole fragmented in ways at once symbolized and compounded by the fate of its poetic productions. Just as the ancient culture itself is now in ruins, the implication is, so the epic verse in which its values had been most fully enshrined could no longer be found intact and entire: "The communication with the rest of the island is open, and the introduction of trade and manufactures has destroyed that leisure which was formerly dedicated to hearing and repeating the poems of ancient times" (51).

From this perspective Macpherson seems engaged, in his complex role as translator, restorer, and forger, in some rear-guard act of retrieval, salvaging the poems from "the obscurity of an almost lost language" (*PO*, 214) and from "a few old people in the north of Scotland" (448) in whose failing memories the verses survive in various and incomplete states. He gathers the fragments, pieces them together, fixes them for posterity in a medium, print, and a language, English, alien to the oral Gaelic culture that produced them but offering at least a residual afterlife in the dominant modes of the present. Nor is this revivification undertaken simply to give the ancient culture a new environment in which, if not to live, then to echo. It is also done to make the very processes of hybridization on which Macpherson blames the culture's demise cut other ways, promoting a new, Gaelic-inflected form of English that might in turn transform the nation's dominant language, however imperceptibly, into some more inclusively British tongue.

Conflicting impulses mark this ambitious project. On one side is Macpherson's impulse to fill out with confections of his own the space between fragments now known to bear at least a genuine relationship to authentic sources, while stabilizing in the form of a definitive text passages that have been "delivered down very differently by tradition" (*PO*, 433); on another, the impulse to represent in all their wreckage and instability sources that as such bear compelling witness to the loss of the world that produced them. Macpherson's literary career might well be seen in terms of a shift of emphasis from the latter to the former impulse, though both coexist throughout his works; the trajectory is nowhere better illustrated than in *Temora*'s transformation from the "imperfect and confused ... broken fragments" (479) described in *Fingal* into the elaborate display of epic unities pulled complete from the hat in 1763. It is at this end point that Macpherson talks of being able "to reduce the broken members of the piece into the order in which they now appear" (215); the image is of surgery, a restorative resetting of fractured limbs.[25]

That is not to speak, however, of a happy ending, of fragmentation euphorically repaired, for loss vexes not only the transmission of Ossianic verse but also its very content. "The fame of my former actions is ceased; and I sit forlorn at the tombs of my friends" (*PO,* 104); even when restored to some more or less plausible simulacrum of original wholeness, the poetry still bears witness to the disintegration of a culture and to the melancholy isolation of the poet from the departed heroes commemorated in his words. In its simplest form of 1760, the Ossianic fragment portrays the surviving poet, "the last of the race of Fingal" (18), as a sightless mourner, an aged leftover whose departed kin "return into my mind, and wound me with remembrance" (14). Later poems return with renewed obsessiveness to "the dim times of old" (296), yet their words are rarely more than gloomy acknowledgments of separation from what they describe, and in this sense the enterprise of Ossian himself, quite as much as his creator's, seems a desperate rear-guard attempt to mitigate loss. In "Oina-Morul" he likens his narratives to the flight of "the unconstant sun, over Larmon's grassy hill" and presents himself as one who "seize[s] the tales, as they pass." Such images of evanescence run throughout the poems, the mists, clouds, and waves of which are much more than mere scenery; it is as though the instability of language itself and "the shadowy thoughts, that fly across my soul" are endlessly at odds with the poet's struggles to "call back . . . the years that have rolled away" (323).

In a world where the hero's highest ambition is to be immortalized in the stones of a funerary mound or the lapidary language of a poem, and his greatest fear the obscurity of one who departs "like a beam that has shone; like a mist that fled away . . . till my footsteps cease to be seen" (*PO,* 88), Ossian's predicament is severe indeed. His commemorations rarely attain the pitch of confident celebration with which less accomplished bards "raise high the praise of heroes" (102); they retreat instead to a mode of gloomy retrospection in which to look back on the zenith of Fingalian heroism is only to be confronted by the irreversibility of its loss: "Often have I fought, and often won in battles of the spear. But blind, and tearful, and forlorn I now walk with little men. O Fingal, with thy race of battle I now behold thee not. The wild roes feed upon the green tomb of the mighty king of Morven" (79). Bereft of his race, Ossian can only sing into the wind, or into the ears of epigones; already he witnesses the onset of the degeneration to which Macpherson refers in the preface to *Temora,* degeneration that traces "the decay of that species of heroism, which subsisted in the days of Ossian" (211) through subsequent phases of social organization. Obsessed as it explicitly is with memorializing the fallen, his verse in fact suggests nothing so much as the absence of what it describes—the irrecoverability of a heroic past glimpsed only in the solitary incantations of an aged bard and entrusted thereafter to the vagaries of memorial transmission in a declining culture and language. The dilemma is most acutely felt at the close of "The Songs of Selma": "But age is now on my tongue; and my soul has failed. I hear, sometimes, the ghosts of bards, and learn their pleasant song. But memory fails in my mind; I hear the call of years. They say, as they pass along, why does Ossian sing? Soon shall he lie in the narrow house, and no bard shall raise his fame. . . . Let the tomb open to Ossian, for his strength has failed. The sons of song are gone to rest: my voice remains, like a blast, that roars, lonely, on a sea-surrounded rock, after the winds are laid" (170).

III

In one of his stranger footnotes, Macpherson praises "that melancholy air which distinguishes the remains of the works of Ossian," before adding a comment that hardly seems needed: "If ever he composed any thing of a merry turn it is long since lost. . . . Nor is it probable that Ossian dealt much in chearful composition" (PO, 472). Bardic comedy, to be sure, is hard to imagine. Yet if (like Malcolm Laing) we transfer Ossian from the third to the eighteenth century and from the hills of Morven to the vale of York, then *Tristram Shandy*—a work born of a sense "that every time a man smiles . . . it adds something to this Fragment of Life" (*TS*, I, dedication)—becomes just what he might have dreamed up.

It is not simply that the genre of Sterne's work is in Macpherson's eyes the characteristic production of a degenerate age, in which bardic epic has fallen away, via panegyric and mock panegyric, to satire and lampoon (*PO*, 519). Nor is it simply that the characters and environment of *Tristram Shandy*, when set against those of *Fingal*, so happily exemplify Macpherson's theories of latter-day decadence: that "quiet and retirement . . . weaken and debase the human mind"; that "in great and opulent states, when property and indolence are secured to individuals, we seldom meet with that strength of mind, which is so common in a nation, not far advanced in civilization"; that "as a state, we are much more powerful than our ancestors, but we would lose by comparing individuals with them" (500 501). Certainly Tristram's father and uncle, a retired Turkey merchant and a retired army officer, are former cogs in the great machines of commercial and military ascendancy whose mental enfeeblement and physical impotence are central to Sterne's comedy of post-heroic vulnerability. The circumscribed world of *Tristram Shandy* ("a small circle . . . of four *English* miles diameter," *TS*, I.vii.10) certainly resembles the mind-contracting environment that Macpherson deplores when contrasting the enlarged understanding of the roaming highlander with the immobility of the rural lowlander, whose knowledge and experience are "circumscribed within the compass of a few acres" (*PO*, 482). It would not be hard to see in

Tristram Shandy as a whole a comic exploration of something very close to Macpherson's conviction that "the powers of the human soul, without an opportunity of exerting them, lose their vigor" (205).

Yet the work is of course far more than some mock-heroic exemplification of the modern frivolity and degeneration that Macpherson's commentaries keep constantly in play as a foil to Fingalian heroism. It shares with *The Poems of Ossian* a pervasive and (as it progresses) a growing sense of loss, of detachment from a fondly remembered past to which the present experience of the solitary and increasingly sickly narrator stands in gloomy relation. It shares with the poems a sense of the overriding need to memorialize this past, to recover, fix, and transmit it in narrative language; and it shares too a sense that human memory and human language can never in fact fulfill such high ambitions, that the past never can be adequately brought back or textualized in all its fullness, that no matter how much it proliferates, writing can be in the end no more than some sorry trace of the absence of what it describes.

The past with which Tristram is concerned, of course, lacks the heroic aspect of Ossian's, and that indeed is Sterne's point. His characters inhabit a postheroic medium, a "scurvy and disasterous world" in which the high deeds of epic give way to "a set of as pitiful misadventures and cross accidents as ever small HERO sustained" (*TS,* I.v.8–9). It is a world of what Ossian would call little men, yet a world in which the remote chance of "performing any thing great or worth recording" (I.xix.63) seems only to intensify its inhabitants' need to record their lives all the same. Sterne's own version of the veteran warrior, Captain Tobias Shandy, is the perfect example. Where Fingal's campaigns in Ireland, and especially his battle at Temora with the Irish hero Cathmor, are marked by what Macpherson calls "instances of the greatest bravery, mixed with incomparably generous actions and sentiments" (*PO,* 456), Toby's participation in William of Orange's Irish campaign of 1690–1691 involves him in an inglorious past of mutual atrocities that (as Macpherson was to write as a historian of the campaign) "stain the annals of the times."[26] Where Fingal deals in heroic individual combat, Toby is entrenched in protracted, debilitating, and inconclusive wars of attrition that leave armies of tens of thousands, as he recalls, "scarce able to crawl out of our tents, at the time the siege of *Limerick* was raised" (*TS,* V.xxxvii.476). Where Fingal and his race withdraw in victory or finally fall in glory, Toby is ludicrously scarred, traumatized, and emasculated by a wound on the groin sustained from a chunk of falling masonry at the later siege of Namur in Flanders. Interestingly, it is only from volume V of *Tristram Shandy* onward that Sterne introduces the idea of Toby serving in Ireland as well as in Flanders, and apparently in a Scots regiment;[27] it is almost as though, at the very moment when *Fingal* is published, Toby's past is reinvented as some kind of mock-heroic travesty of Fingal's own.

For all the poverty of their modern achievements, however, Sterne's characters remain no less obsessively concerned than Macpherson's with the effort to recapture, relive, and reproduce their past experience. In the absence of bardic commemoration, Toby seeks to fix the scenes of his wartime afflictions—the flux at Limerick, the wound at Namur—on the ground of his garden in scale model, steadily encroaching from bowling green to kitchen garden as the need for further space makes him run "his first and second parallels betwixt two rows of his cabbages and his collyflowers" (*TS*, VI.xxi.535). Armed with a truly Ossianic ability to reconcile extravagant sentimentality with a relish for large-scale violence, he devotes his life and mind to an ongoing rehearsal of warfare. Yet even these material reenactments prove ludicrously vulnerable to loss and decay and fail to render permanent the past they seek to fix; at one point a cow breaks in on Toby's fortifications and partly eats them (III.xxxviii.278); the making of model mortars leads only to the loss of an older heroic memento, a pair of jackboots that had survived, as Walter protests, "ever since the civil wars;——Sir *Roger Shandy* wore them at the battle of *Marston-Moor*" (III.xxii.242). Trapped within his hobby-horse, Toby merely fritters away his days in the pointless and arid exercise of traumatized memory.

He is not alone in his absurdity, however, for in writing the history of these mock campaigns, and in the larger struggle to fix in print his own life and opinions, Tristram finds himself embroiled in a comparably futile endeavor. Where Toby seeks to fix a fugitive past experience in material form, Tristram models it in language, vainly attempting to recover, catch, and fix in words a past that perpetually shifts beyond reach. In his hands, the interruptions of language and fragmentations of form that most obviously link Sterne with Macpherson seem at once the result and the expression of conditions that make any linguistic recovery of the past, even in the relative stability of print as opposed to oral culture, a sadly impossible task. Setting out in all confidence to transmit to posterity his life and opinions, he sees the material to be commemorated perpetually sprawl out of control; anything about the past he chooses to say demands the inclusion of further context and explanation, so that "the more I write, the more I shall have to write" (*TS*, IV.xiii. 342). The work might swell to 80 volumes and still be incomplete. All the while, language fails in its office of conjuring in the reader's mind the ideas in the mind of its user, so that a page, famously, must remain blank for the reader to fill in himself the indescribable concupiscibility of Widow Wadman (VI.xxxviii.567). "Well might *Locke* write a chapter upon the imperfections of words" (V.vii.429): here is a distinctively modern and philosophically sophisticated version of the Ossianic dilemma, the dilemma of the aged and solitary bard whose words, far from bringing back the days of old, mark only separation and absence, and far from perpetuating fame must fade into the obscurity of an almost lost language.

It is a dilemma that Walter Shandy well understands, knowing as he does how the ruin of an ancient culture is intensified by the ensuing disintegration of its language: "What is become, brother *Toby,* of *Nineveh* and *Baby-*

lon, of *Cizicum* and *Mitylenæ?* The fairest towns that ever the sun rose upon, are now no more: the names only are left, and those (for many of them are wrong spelt) are falling themselves by piecemeals to decay, and in length of time will be forgotten, and involved with every thing in a perpetual night" (*TS,* V.iii.422). For the dying Tristram of the final volumes, the same dilemma assumes an intensely personal form. The installment of 1765 (the first Sterne wrote after Becket's almost simultaneous publication of *Fingal* and *Tristram Shandy* V–VI) opens with the consumptive Tristram desperately aware, as he addresses Eugenius, of his failure to immortalize a still-unwritten past as he flees from death: "for I have forty volumes to write, and forty thousand things to say and do, which no body in the world will say and do for me, except thyself; and as thou seest he has got me by the throat (for Eugenius could scarce hear me speak across the table)" (VII.i.576). He survives into the solitary volume of 1767 as some dandyish, latter-day bard of the age of prose; where Ossian describes "some gray warrior, half blind with age, sitting by night at the flaming oak of the hall, [who] tells now my actions" (*PO,* 174), Tristram becomes an avowedly "tragicomical" writer "sitting, this 12th day of August, 1766, in a purple jerkin and yellow pair of slippers, without either wig or cap on" (*TS,* IX.i.737). Yet he, like Ossian, is a memorialist similarly bereaved of those he remembers and trapped in a solitary present from which the past he seeks to bring back in language only slips further away. A few chapters later we find him looking toward his own end in truly Ossianic images of evanescence: "Time wastes too fast: every letter I trace tells me with what rapidity Life follows my pen; the days and hours of it . . . are flying over our heads like light clouds of a windy day, never to return more——— every thing presses on———whilst thou art twisting that lock,———see! it grows grey; and every time I kiss thy hand to bid adieu, and every absence which follows it, are preludes to that eternal separation which we are shortly to make" (IX.viii.754).

No doubt several factors influenced the change in tone discernible in the last three volumes of *Tristram Shandy,* where the robust exuberance with which Tristram at first confronts the impossibility of his task gives way to alternating gloom and panic as extinction approaches. One factor may have been the decline in Sterne's own health, which threatened to curtail his literary ambitions as much as those of his hero-narrator. Yet there is a distinctly Ossianic ring to his increasing emphasis here on the inevitability of separation from a fugitive past, and it is not impossible that another factor was the encounter with Macpherson's writing that must surely have followed the appearance of *Fingal* in December 1761. Given the insistence of their reference to the fragility of representation, *The Poems of Ossian* may well have alerted Sterne to some of the more melancholy possibilities inherent in what begins for Tristram as a strictly comic literary impasse. It is certainly in keeping with the poems that Tristram's early exultation over the need to keep his work "a-going these forty years" (*TS,* I.xxii.82) in order to fulfill its ambitions should modulate, with only 9 of his projected 80 volumes written, into an Ossianic sense of failure; he too is left alone as the last of his race, and as one whose imminent death will leave unperformed his increasingly desperate desire to fix in print a permanent record of all that is gone.

What is beyond question is that, whether by way of direct influence or the independent pursuit of shared concerns, Macpherson and Sterne have much more in common than some mere fashionable appeal to the conventions of sensibility. Both might be said, like Henry Mackenzie in their wake, to have formed their plans on "the Fragment Manner," and for both this fragmentation of form gives expression to a devastating loss of faith in wholeness or continuity as properties of the worlds they seek to describe.[28] Both share a common preoccupation with the weight of the past, with the decay and degeneration that separate past from present, and with the struggle of their hero-narrators to recover this fugitive past in memory and language. Both are preoccupied, moreover, by the ultimate futility of such ambitions; their texts are laden with a melancholy sense of the instability of language and the consequent ineffability of all experience, whether of an individual or a whole culture. "Language is only the instrument of science, and words are but the signs of ideas," as Johnson famously puts it in the preface to the *Dictionary*; he might almost have been writing on behalf of his twin adversaries as he wistfully goes on to wish "that the instrument might be less apt to decay, and that signs might be permanent, like the things which they denote."[29]

If either work escapes the pessimism toward which its efforts at representation so strongly tend, it does so in terms of a common appeal to the reader as one whose creative involvement in the production of meaning might somehow patch up the fragments or repair the breaches with which its text is necessarily riddled. "Writing . . . is but a different name for conversation," as Tristram insists in a well-known passage: "The truest respect which you can pay to the reader's understanding, is to halve this matter amicably, and leave him something to imagine, in his turn, as well as yourself" (*TS*, II.xi.125). It is in just this aesthetic of restorative readerly involvement that we find Macpherson at his most resolutely modern. In his *Critical Dissertation on the Poems of Ossian* (1763) Hugh Blair praises the poems for a narrative style "concise even to abruptness, and leaving several circumstances to be supplied by the reader's imagination" (*PO*, 354), and Macpherson himself makes the same emphasis: "Nothing new, nor adequate to our high idea of kings, could be said. Ossian, therefore, throws a *column of mist* over the whole, and leaves the combat to the imagination of the reader" (526). Indeed, Macpherson might almost be inviting the reader to draw his own Widow Wadman when he writes that "the human mind, free and fond of thinking for itself, is disgusted to find every thing done by the poet. It is, therefore, his business only to mark the most striking outlines; and to allow the imaginations of his readers to finish the figure for themselves" (543). Perhaps such gestures do no more than make a virtue of dire necessity, but in the absence of any truly stable, adequate, or permanent language, whether Gaelic or English, it is in imagination alone that the past must reside.

Notes

1. *Monthly Review* 26 (January 1762): 42. Coincidentally, this long review of *Fingal* (41–57) immediately follows a review of *Tristram Shandy* V–VI (31–41). Throughout this essay, references to *The Poems of Ossian* are cited in the text from *The Poems of Ossian and Related Works,* ed. Howard Gaskill, intro. Fiona Stafford (Edinburgh: Edinburgh University Press, 1996).
2. *Monthly Review* 32 (February 1765), in *Sterne: The Critical Heritage,* ed. Alan B. Howes (London: Routledge and Kegan Paul, 1974), 162.
3. Burns to John Murdoch, 15 January 1783, in *Sterne: Critical Heritage,* 260; Laing, *The History of Scotland, from the Union of the Crowns . . . to the Union of the Kingdoms in the Reign of Queen Anne,* 2 vols. (London, 1800), 2:407.
4. On this aspect of Sterne's work, see Keymer, "Dying by Numbers: *Tristram Shandy* and Serial Fiction," *Shandean* 8 (1996): 41–67.
5. Laing, 2:377; see also Ferriar, *Illustrations of Sterne* (London, 1798), especially chapters 2 and 3.
6. Laing, 2:407; Paul J. deGategno, *James Macpherson* (Boston: G. K. Hall, 1989), 15. (The journals are the *Scots Magazine* and the *Edinburgh Magazine,* and the publisher is Walter Ruddiman Jr.)
7. Arthur H. Cash, *Laurence Sterne: The Early and Middle Years* (London: Methuen, 1975), 276–77.
8. ? October 1759, in *Letters of Laurence Sterne,* ed. Lewis Perry Curtis (Oxford: Clarendon Press, 1935), 80.
9. Cash, *Laurence Sterne: The Later Years* (London: Methuen, 1986), 115–16, 24–25; deGategno, 80, 30.
10. J. A. Cochrane, *Dr Johnson's Printer: The Life of William Strahan* (London: Routledge and Kegan Paul, 1964), 159, 46, 51; Hume to Strahan, 9 February 1761, in Bailey Saunders, *The Life and Letters of James Macpherson,* 2d ed. (London: Swan Sonnenschein, 1895), 158–59. For the publishing history of *Tristram Shandy* see *TS,* II:814–31; for Macpherson, see George F. Black, "Macpherson's Ossian and the Ossianic Controversy: A Contribution Towards a Bibliography," *Bulletin of the New York Public Library* 30 (1926): 1:424–39; 2:508–24.
11. 16 May 1762, *Letters of Sterne,* 169.
12. *The Poems of Ossian,* ed. Malcolm Laing, 2 vols. (Edinburgh, 1805), 2:264; qtd. in *PO,* 529 n. On the relationship between "The Invocation" in *Tristram Shandy* IX and the Maria episode in *A Sentimental Journey,* see R. Putney, "The Evolution of *A Sentimental Journey,*" *Philological Quarterly* 19 (1940): 364–67.
13. 19 January 1775, qtd. in Saunders, 249.
14. Cash, *Later Years,* 136–39; Jacques Chouillet, "Diderot: Poet and Theorist of the Homer and Ossianist Revival," *British Journal of Eighteenth-Century Studies* 5 (1982): 228.
15. Cash, *Later Years,* 179–80, 187–88; David Raynor, "Ossian and Hume," in *Ossian Revisited,* ed. Howard Gaskill (Edinburgh: Edinburgh University Press, 1991), 150–59; Boswell, *Life of Johnson,* ed. R. W. Chapman, rev. J. D. Fleeman (Oxford: Oxford University Press, 1980), 1129 n.; Sir James Macdonald to Hugh Blair, 10 October 1763, in *Report of the Committee of the Highland Society of Scotland, Appointed to Inquire into the Nature and Authenticity of the Poems of Ossian,* ed. Henry Mackenzie (Edinburgh, 1805), Appendix, 4.
16. Cash, *Later Years,* 234–41.
17. J. N. M. Maclean, "The Early Political Careers of James 'Fingal' Macpherson (1736–1821) and Sir John Macpherson, Bart. (1744–1821)" (Ph.D. diss., University of Edinburgh, 1967), Appendix 3. I am grateful to Dr. Fiona Stafford for this information.

18. *Life of Johnson,* 443; *Sterne: Critical Heritage,* 138.

19. John Dwyer, "The Melancholy Savage," in *Ossian Revisited,* 184; for Burns and Laing see note 3.

20. Fiona Stafford, *The Sublime Savage: A Study of James Macpherson and the Poems of Ossian* (Edinburgh: Edinburgh University Press, 1988), 141, 142.

21. On fragmentation and its implications in the period's literature, see especially Elizabeth Wanning Harries, *The Unfinished Manner: Essays on the Fragment in the Later Eighteenth Century* (Charlottesville: University Press of Virginia, 1994); essay reprinted in this volume.

22. Stephen H. Clark, "The 'Failing Soul': Macpherson's Response to Locke," *Eighteenth-Century Life* 19 (1995): 39–56.

23. Laing, 1:44.

24. Stafford, 16–17.

25. "To restore (a dislocated, fractured, or ruptured part) to the proper position"; "To adjust, set (a dislocation or fracture)," *OED,* s.v. *Reduce,* 6 and 6b.

26. Macpherson, *The History of Great Britain, from the Restoration, to the Accession of the House of Hanover,* 2 vols. (London, 1775), 1: 667.

27. See the note to *TS,* V.vi.452 in III:368–70. Toby serves in the regiment of David Melville, third earl of Leven (1660–1728). This was originally raised among Scottish refugees in Holland and Germany, and accompanied William to England in 1688; the regiment then served against Jacobite forces in Scotland and Ireland and against the French in Flanders (*DNB*).

28. Mackenzie, *Letters to Elizabeth Rose of Kilravock,* ed. Horst W. Drescher (Edinburgh: Oliver and Boyd, 1967), 88 (18 May 1771); qtd. by Harries, 1.

29. Johnson, *Poetry and Prose,* ed. Mona Wilson (London: Rupert Hart-Davis, 1968), 304–5.

THE SKEPTICAL STERNE
◆

Locke's *Essay* and the Tentativeness
of *Tristram Shandy*

Peter M. Briggs

Truth may perhaps come to the price of a pearl, that showeth best by day; but it will not rise to the price of a diamond or carbuncle, that showeth best in varied lights.

—Francis Bacon[1]

Nearly all modern commentators on *Tristram Shandy* have agreed that Lockean ideas of human understanding figure importantly in the development of Sterne's novel. But they have differed considerably from one another in their attempts to assess the spirit in which Sterne wished to use Locke. Was Sterne engaged in a fictional translation and exposition of Lockean ideas? Or was he subverting Locke, using Locke as a straight man in the midst of a shandean comedy? Or is Sterne better understood simply as an artistic opportunist, capitalizing upon the public currency of Lockean ideas about the mind's various workings? And why invoke a philosopher in the first place? Most novelists do not appear to need philosophical assistance to complete their labors. There are no simple answers to these or related questions, as the great range of critical response amply demonstrates.[2] But the range of opinion itself suggests that Sterne may have used Lockean ideas in more than one way, in more than one spirit. It is possible to suppose, then, that Sterne adopted Lockean perspectives on experience, not because he believed or disbelieved particular tenets in Locke's systematic exposition of human understanding, but because Locke's analysis gave him *a set of options* which he could exploit and explore for his own novelistic purposes. (More than a philosopher, a novelist can be satisfied with a world of credible options for his characters and need not reach after the systematic, the definitive, the conclusive.) And if Sterne adopted Locke for the set of options that he provided, then examining Locke's presence in *Tristram Shandy* should help us to get beyond the obvious question, how is Sterne related to Locke, in order to address a subtler and ultimately more important question: how is Sterne related to Sterne? More specifically, how might the presence of Lockean ideas in *Tristram Shandy* help us to com-

Reprinted from *Studies in Philology* 82 (1985): 494–517.

prehend as parts of a coherent design the disparate and often apparently dissonant aspects of Sterne's hero and his novel?

I

When Locke first published *An Essay concerning Human Understanding* in 1690, he consolidated more than a century of speculation among skeptical philosophers and others as to how man comprehends his own experiences in the world. Urging his reader to examine analytically the processes of his own mind, Locke wrote to establish two central points: first, a recognition that man possesses no innate ideas; and second, a realization that all of the ideas that man does possess are derived from only two sources, sensations drawn from the experiential world and man's own reflections based upon those sensations. The individual mind works by finding patterns among the sensations it receives, by comparing new data and its earlier formulations of experience, by inferring connections among particular instances and general rules from them, by reflecting reasonably upon the design of its own experiences. Inevitably Locke's discussion of man's capacities for thinking and knowing involved a parallel discussion of man's incapacities, the things he could not know reliably either because of potential errors in the thinking process or because some phenomena were beyond the world reported by his senses and thus beyond his powers of reflection. But Locke's emphasis was primarily optimistic—"'Tis of great use to the Sailor to know the length of his Line, though he cannot with it fathom all the depths of the Ocean" (*Essay* I.i.6)[3]— for if man could not know everything, still he could manage his life in a reasonable way.

The impact of Locke's exposition of human understanding upon contemporary thought was considerable. In the first decades of the eighteenth century the *Essay* was widely read, frequently cited and quoted and debated, and adapted to various current uses by (among others) educators and journalists, satirists and divines.[4] But the pertinent fact to note here is that Laurence Sterne was *not* writing in those early decades and was *not* a party to the early celebration of the *Essay;* Sterne was born in 1713, twenty-three years after the publication of Locke's *Essay,* and most of *Tristram Shandy* was written in the early 1760's, a full seventy years after the appearance of Locke's work. Assuming, then, that Sterne adopted Lockean notions of understanding as the result of some degree of deliberate calculation, we might ask: what did Locke have to offer to an aspiring novelist? Of course, we have only the product of the experiment—*Tristram Shandy* itself—upon which to base an answer, but at least some advantages seem clear.

Tristram Shandy is quintessentially a book about man's attempt to give a reasonable and definitive form to his experience of the world—and about the inevitable tendency of experience to run counter to man's formulations. The basic post-Cartesian opposition between mind and world is the central fact not only in Tristram's life as he tries to assemble his memoirs, but in the lives of all the major characters whom he portrays as well. It is even the common denominator among many of the ostensibly "digressive" materials which he includes in his narrative—the contracts and curses, the travelogues and theological disquisitions and critical asides; these too represent man's genuine attempts, however misguided, to find an order in the world of experience or to impose one. Clearly these myriad instances imply a great deal of incidental satire directed against the particular and traditional follies of the learned professions—authors, lawyers, divines, physicians, and others—but in the special context of *Tristram Shandy,* they also signify something more unified and characteristic. In fact, all represent man's poor attempts to formalize and share an understanding of his experience of the world, to charm the inevitable powers of contingency with learning, with formulas, with reasonable methods, with words—and all fall short of the mark. Sterne's subject, then, is man's conscious and continual attempt to find or generate mental designs consonant with his experience; the basic strategies of his narrative are to explore the disparities among different mental formulations and the dissonance between all man's conceptions and the world at large; and his final goal is to assess what human attitudes are viable and constructive, should the splits between system and system and between mind and world prove irremediable, as they generally do. A peculiarly "modern" creation, *Tristram Shandy* is essentially an exploration of man's attempts to achieve a reasonable understanding of experience, written in the name of human awarenesses and attitudes, hopes and puzzlements, which are more complex and simultaneous and comprehensive than "mere" reasonable understanding.

When we see *Tristram Shandy* in this light, it is clear why Lockean ideas of cognition were particularly suited to Sterne's purposes. Tristram and his relatives repeatedly cite, quote, or burlesque ideas derived from Locke—notions of the relation of wit and judgment or of the association of ideas or of man's perception of duration—but to dwell upon such particular and easily identifiable instances is, I think, to risk overlooking Sterne's more general exploitation of the grounding assumptions of Locke's system. Some of those assumptions are so obvious as to require little elaboration: the notion that man has no choice but to perceive his experiences subjectively; the idea that cognition involves a logical series of mental steps which can be separated for the purposes of analytical examination; the belief that understanding is an ongoing *process,* not a fixed and final product; the realization that any comprehensive exploration of understanding must include the *expression* of understanding and therefore must explore the capacities and limitations of language; the conviction, central to Locke's rational empiricism, that understanding should be consonant with both reason and experience and thus answerable to both standards. What Sterne *did* with these assumptions was not simple and not necessarily Lockean, but for the most part he shared these principles in composing *Tristram Shandy* and to that extent his narrative is fundamentally Lockean.

In addition, there are two subtler points of similarity which do require elaboration. First, in his *Essay* Locke made a provisional separation between man's thinking processes and any notion of his overall character and worth, in order to devote more careful analytical attention to those habits of mind which, at least for the purposes of philosophy, can be abstracted from individuals. Sterne adopted this same provisional separation as a crucial part of his comic strategy for presenting his characters: the fact that a Walter Shandy or an Uncle Toby is laughably fallible as a thinker and a user of language does not necessarily impinge upon Sterne's attempts to assert their overall worth as people—mental fallibility and personal character imply two separable modes of evaluation. Second, Locke supposed that man is of necessity the *interpreter* of his own existence: he can have no idea of himself or of anything else unless he undertakes a long series of subjective interpretations which eventually yield a picture of himself and the world in which he has his being.[5] (Even Descartes' famous *cogito ergo sum* is not a simple statement of existence, but a personal interpretation of it.) And, of course, it is Sterne's realization that Tristram is both *free* and *compelled* to interpret his own existence and to shape his existence through personal interpretation that forms the enabling premise for all of *Tristram Shandy*.

Not surprisingly, Sterne altered Lockean assumptions even as he borrowed them—by treating them playfully, by personalizing them or refracting them through individual personalities, by particularizing general issues. Tristram speculates with mock-solemnity as to whether Uncle Toby's exceptional modesty was owing to nature or to nurture, and Locke's sober discussion of man's difficulties formulating simple ideas—he used the analogy of man's difficulty making a clear impression in sealing wax (II.xxix.3)—becomes in *Shandy* an absurd mini-drama with Dolly the chamber-maid trying hastily to seal a letter to Robin, a servant and presumably her lover, hurrying because her mistress is ringing the bell (II.ii.99).[6] In the same vein, Sterne characterized Walter Shandy's stubbornness in his eccentric opinions through a witty and extended double burlesque, Lockean psychology conflated with Locke's defense of private property in his *Second Treatise of Government* (sects. 27–28); by sweating over them, Walter—"as a man in a state of nature" does—acquired a property right in his own odd opinions (III.xxxiv.262–64).

Beyond such amusements and in spite of them, however, Sterne did imply a fairly consistent set of cognitive principles—basically Lockean principles—which substantially shape his novel. Shandean man has no choice but to see the world from within the confines of his own subjectivity, and Sterne followed the well-worn road marked out by Bacon, Descartes, and Locke from the subjectivity of individual perceptions to the relativity and provisionality of all particular interpretations of experience:

need I tell you, Sir, that the circumstances with which every thing in this world is begirt, give every thing in this world its size and shape;—and by tightening it, or relaxing it, this way or that, make the thing to be, what it is—great—little—good—bad—indifferent or not indifferent, just as the case happens. (III.ii.187)

In fact, Sterne continually made strategic use of Locke's insistence that all perceived particulars stand before a potentially infinite background of relationships and further considerations: "there is *no one thing . . . which is not capable of almost an infinite number of* considerations, in reference to other things: and therefore this makes no small part of Men's Thoughts and Words" (*Essay* II.xxv.7).[7] Subjective perspectives combined with notions of endless relativity help to explain the overall shape of Tristram's narrative. Tristram's life appears to him (and to us who follow his meanderings) as a series of experiential fragments to be reflected upon, parts of a potential mosaic of understanding; if his life is to have a definite shape, it will have one only by means of a continuing series of imaginative leaps and logical inferences.

The same considerations of subjectivity and relativity also qualify all particular observations in his story. Even spatial relationships in *Shandy* are shaped by the perspective of the observer, and it soon becomes clear that they provide no normative standards for accurate measurement. Seven miles on a dark night in the Shandy neighborhood are "almost equal to fourteen" (I.vii.11), and a midwife with "no small degree of reputation in the world" requires a personalized definition of the world in order to accommodate her: "by which word *world* . . . I would be understood to mean no more of it, than a small circle described upon the circle of the great world, of four *English* miles diameter, or thereabouts, of which the cottage where the good old woman lived, is supposed to be the centre" (I.vii.10–11). Tristram soon gives over his attempt to define the "world" altogether; whenever someone is described as being of importance in the world, "I desire [it] may be enlarged or contracted in your worship's fancy, in a compound-ratio of the station, profession, knowledge, abilities, height and depth (measuring both ways) of the personage brought before you" (I.xiii.39). In other words, the reader must supply the world, the normative context, which Tristram cannot—and that world is envisioned as an infinite regression of potential relationships; it is no wonder, then, that all relationships and proportions in the novel (and its relationship to *our* worlds) are slippery and to some degree ungrounded. Lockean wit, the capacity for finding out similarities in unlike objects, depends for effectiveness upon two constraints: the one always mentioned (for example, by Sterne) is its opposite faculty, the distinguishing power of judgment; the other, unnamed but assumed by Locke, is some realistic sense of context. Shandean wit is Lockean wit operating without a reliable sense of context; wit and judgment, too, are in effect licensed to be fanciful.

Shandean man's understanding of the world, like that of his Lockean ancestor, depends upon his interpretive and expressive powers, and Sterne showed himself an heir to Locke in another way by his continual sensitivity to the "accidents" which intervene between the mind and its objects. Man's senses are sometimes misleading, he often imposes upon himself (hobbyhorsically) through misconception, and his language seems a particularly slippery medium for fixing or sharing his thoughts. Walter Shandy lives in a world of inapplicable learning, ungrounded hypotheses, and words without objects; Toby's penchant for military metaphors leads him away from the real world, not into it; and Tristram's own gropings after appropriate words and conceptions are continually betraying him into digression, ambiguity, confusion, or bawdiness. Confused and obsessed protagonists had existed in literature long before Locke, but Sterne's Lockean awareness of the mind's systems for assembling understandings made it possible to characterize man's confusions more acutely and closer to their source.[8] That same Lockean awareness also allowed Sterne a deeper sense of what man's cognitive confusions might ultimately imply. Consider the case of Walter Shandy. A serious inquirer after truth, Walter adopts the empiricists' mistrust of received opinions and insists upon examining things for himself. He is independent-minded to a fault: "my father, Sir, would see nothing in the light in which others placed it;—he placed things in his own light;—he would weigh nothing in common scales;—no,—he was too refined a researcher to lay open to so gross an imposition" (II.xix.170). The man who sees *nothing* in the light in which others see it inevitably lives in a world entirely different from theirs, and, in his more speculative moments, at least, Walter represents a comic realization of one of Locke's greatest worries:

> if our Knowledge of our *Ideas* terminate in them, and reach no farther, where there is something farther intended, our most serious Thoughts will be of little more use, than the Reveries of a crazy Brain; and the Truths built thereon of no more weight, than the Discourses of a Man, who sees Things clearly in a Dream, and with great assurance utters them. (*Essay* IV.iv.2)

Thought conducted without reference to existing realities is in fact Locke's definition of madness.

The strategic advantages which flow from Sterne's carefully contrived perceptual relativism are many; it justifies and necessitates the free-floating relationship among objects and ideas and words in *Tristram Shandy* and makes possible the odd and ironical conjunctions (and non-conjunctions) where much of the novel's significance and ambiguity lies; it is the foundation of a novelistic world where no meanings are final except for those individuals who choose to take them for final. Consider, for example, the famous scene of Tristram's conception, when Mrs. Shandy interrupts Walter's love-making by suddenly recalling that the thirty-day clock needs winding (I.i.2). The implications of this unfortunate conjunction are multiple. How *are* love-making and clock-winding related? In an obvious sense they are not, save in the Shandy family where both occur at thirty-day intervals (if then), and that of course is the joke, a joke which combines humor and pathos. But in this special shandean world where proportions are unfixed and relationships are mostly mind-forged, all facts are potentially figurative ("noses" are not simply noses, after all), and the love-making, clock-winding association raises serious possibilities which radiate out through the rest of the novel: love is perhaps a merely mechanical phenomenon, perhaps impotent; the difficulties of the Shandy household are reflected in the two partners' inability to fix their minds upon a single object; love and time, or love and death, are inherently at odds, and the inexorable progress of time will inevitably disrupt human loves. Here and everywhere in the novel, possibilities for meaning are multiple and simultaneous, particular and figurative, straightforward and ironical.

The initial advantage of Sterne's strategy of counterpoising different subjective versions of experience is narrative flexibility—the dimensions of experience and its meanings are as various as its interpreters. But the final advantage occurs through the involvement of the reader: in a world without reliable normative contexts, things take on different meanings by virtue of the different standards we supply, we are *forced* to supply, in trying to comprehend the text. A "nose" is a nose or something else, depending upon the context to which we refer it. Uncle Toby's famous gesture of generosity toward a fly ("go poor Devil . . .----This world surely is wide enough to hold both thee and me"), which Tristram pronounces more valuable than a university education as a cornerstone of his moral outlook (II.xii.131), is either noble or absurd, depending upon the context in which *we* interpret it. Again and again, we must supply perspectives, definitions, proportions, inferences, even facts, which the text fails to provide. A novel that explores through partial views man's cognitive capacities would be remiss if it did not challenge our own abilities to grasp the things that enter our awareness. Tristram insists that writing, properly conducted, can be a "conversation" with the reader, and Sterne worked artfully to force us to keep up our end of that conversation.[9]

II

Beyond Sterne's particular amusements with Lockean materials and the strategic advantages which Lockean perspectives offered him as an author, there is a subtle and important "debate" between Locke and Sterne going on just beneath the whimsical surface of *Tristram Shandy*. Sterne quite consistently adopted Lockean notions of the mind's *mechanisms* for understanding, but with equal consistency he reserved for himself the right to interpret the *value* of those mechanisms and the overall structure of the mind in which they operate. In other words, Lockean notions of the mind often appear transformed and transvalued as they become parts of a shandean view of experience.

One particular section in Locke's epistemology evidently attracted Sterne's special attention, for he cribbed from the same passage at least five times in his own writings. The passage in question occurs in Locke's discussion of the inevitable limits of human knowledge. Locke urged that a reasonable and inquiring man can learn enough from experience to know his own good; still, a thoughtful man will be continually surrounded by reminders of the narrowness of his understanding.

> He that knows any thing, knows this in the first place, that he need not seek long for Instances of his Ignorance. The meanest, and most obvious Things that come in our way, have dark sides, that the quickest Sight cannot penetrate into. The clearest, and most enlarged Understandings of thinking Men find themselves puzzled, and at a loss, in every Particle of Matter. (*Essay* IV.iii.22)

Sterne borrowed from this passage in two of his published sermons,[10] and Tristram echoes some of its phrasing in his digression upon the "unsteady uses of words" (II.ii.100). However, Sterne's most interesting appropriation of it occurs when Tristram moralizes, rather grandiloquently, upon the obscurity of the goddess Nature:

> —But mark, madam, we live amongst riddles and mysteries—the most obvious things, which come in our way, have dark sides, which the quickest sight cannot penetrate into; and even the clearest and most exalted understandings amongst us find ourselves puzzled and at a loss in almost every cranny of nature's works; so that this, like a thousand other things, falls out for us in a way, which tho' we cannot reason upon it,—yet we find the good of it . . . and that's enough for us. (IV.xvii.350; compare also IX.xxii.776)

Here Sterne was in effect using Locke to some very unLockean ends: he borrowed Locke's exposition of man's inevitable limitations, then added a conclusion which offers an implicit denial of Locke's formulation of the mind's workings. Locke urged that any substantial good for man must come from reasoning upon known materials from the real world. Through Tristram, Sterne in effect responded that, though we cannot reason upon those things of which we have only partial awareness, still we can find some good in them: if this is so, then the mind must have some other ways of knowing and appreciating than "reasonable" ones, and the world may offer goods which transcend the precincts of reason. "We *find* the good of it" also has implications worth teasing out: Sterne implies that the mind, by a combination of attitude and will, can reshape experience, discovering some good which was not there before; rather than conforming itself to circumstance, the mind may profit by ignoring circumstance or seeking to rise above it. This requires further explanation, however.

The major endeavor of Locke's *Essay* is to sketch out a reasonable and reliable connection between the individual mind and the external world which confronts it. The mind must learn a judicious receptivity to materials from the external world and conform its own operations to the realities of that world; the mind is a relatively passive student, one to be stimulated, schooled, and disciplined by real experience. Locke mistrusted the mind's potential independence from external circumstances, and his discussion of free will offers a useful perspective on that problem. Locke argued that traditional debates over free will misstated the problem: the real question was not whether the will is free, but whether *man* is free, free to pursue his desires or to restrain himself from pursuit by a wise consideration (*Essay* II.xxi.21 ff.). In Locke's formulation, then, man's freedom is the ability to be reasonable and to implement his reasonableness in the world; man can work thoughtfully toward his own happiness, and any other notion of freedom is foolishness.

> Is it worth the Name of *Freedom* to be at liberty to play the Fool, and draw Shame and Misery upon a Man's self? If to break loose from the conduct of Reason, and to want that restraint of Examination and Judgment, which keeps us from chusing or doing the worse, be *Liberty*, true Liberty, mad Men and Fools are the only Freemen: But yet, I think, no Body would chuse to be mad for the sake of such *Liberty*, but he that is mad already.

The necessity of pursuing one's happiness in a reasonable and practical way is not a restraint of human freedom, "or at least [not] an abridgment of *Liberty* to be complain'd of " (*Essay* II.xxi.50). Freedom *from* reasonable consideration was a liberty beyond Locke's ken, and he systematically bound the mind's potential independence from external circumstance into a sane and sensible working relationship with circumstance.

Shandean freedom is of a wholly different sort. While Sterne did not denounce rational consideration of circumstance unconditionally, he consistently satirized particular attempts to encompass circumstances by reasonable means; the products of rational "liberty" in *Tristram Shandy* most often are narrow, self-contained, self-delusive, or simply foolish. Moreover, in the process of casting so much satiric doubt upon man's ability to achieve a consistent and reasonable grasp of his world, Sterne also cast considerable doubt upon the question whether man really *needs* such an understanding. (Here, of course, Sterne parted company with Locke, and the issue between them was not simply the capacities of reason, but a more comprehensive question, the true nature of "understanding.") Perhaps man might be better served by consenting to unreason and inconsistency. Sterne in effect used his fictions to propose alternative kinds of "understanding," ones which work by intuition, sentiment, facetiousness and whimsy, fantasy, and the wry celebration of incongruity. If man cannot pretend to know the world of objects as surely and reasonably as Locke expected that he might, perhaps he can make a virtue of the mind's detachment from that alien and elusive world.

As Tristram flees across France in the seventh volume of his *Life and Opinions,* trying to keep ahead of Death who stalks him, he expresses the view that "rolling about" is better than being at rest: "so much of motion, is so much of life, and so much of joy——and . . . to stand still, or get on but slowly, is death and the devil——" (VII.xiii.592–93). Tristram's remark clearly refers to physical motion, travelling, but in the larger context of *Tristram Shandy,* it might be taken to apply to the motions of the mind as well: mental motion is life and joy, and the stillness of the mind is death.[11] Consider a second instance. When Tristram describes his father's obscure researches concerning noses, he characterizes Walter as having a penchant for "that speculative subtilty or ambidexterity of argumentation . . . which heaven had bestow'd upon man on purpose to investigate truth and fight for her on all sides." Offered a plain statement of fact, Walter cannot rest until he has explored the "mystic" and "allegoric" significances of that statement: "here is some room to turn a man's self in" (III.xxxvii.271). Obviously, these remarks are meant as a joke, and Walter's overingenuity at interpretation is a source of satiric humor throughout the novel. However, a serious implication lies behind the joke: in a world defined by subjective perspectives, truth does have more than one side, and finding "some room to turn a man's self in" is a significant enterprise in *Tristram Shandy,* however misguided Walter's specific inquiries may be. The initial epigraph of Sterne's novel, drawn from Epictetus, contains a similar implication: "It is not actions, but opinions concerning actions, which disturb men" (title page).[12] Actions, circumstances, facts are neutral, still, and final, but opinions, the motions of the mind, are various, indeterminate, both disturbing *and* joyous—in short, life-giving.

Sterne's celebration of the ever-various motions of the mind has many implications, but one of the clearest is a transvaluation of Lockean psychology and epistemology; he had little argument with Locke as to how cognitive processes worked, but placed different values on those workings.[13] Locke rated the powers of the mind in a hierarchy stretching from reason at the top downward to include lesser powers—will, emotion, imagination, humor, and others—which ought by rights to be subordinate to reason; the different powers take their value from their proximity to or distance from reason. Sterne's implicit design for the mind's powers is more appositive, more counterpoised; all the powers of the mind have something to contribute to understanding, and all have limitations. So he satirized the pretensions of reason, while simultaneously exploring the other components of understanding, properly conceived; in practice, then, Sterne tended to celebrate the powers of the mind which Locke deprecated.

Consider, for example, the mind's capacity to create fantasies. Locke found little good in this power and dealt with it in the *Essay* only to warn against its seductions. Sterne agreed with Locke as to what a fantasy was, but he saw in fantasy a real potential for human good; military fantasies cure Uncle Toby's wound when the reasonable measures urged by doctors fail, and imagined battles on the bowling-green add life and color to an otherwise drab and frustrated retirement. The Peace of Utrecht is a tragedy in Toby's life—as Tristram remarks of Walter (III.xxx.256), the mind accustomed to odd and whimsical ways of thinking is vulnerable to odd and whimsical distresses—because it necessitates finding a new fantasy to structure his life (he promptly "falls in love" with Widow Wadman). Sterne's celebration of fantasy is not unequivocal—he charted a thousand ways in which Toby's fantasies are delusive, limiting, and self-isolating—but the central fact remains that Toby's fantasies are life-sustaining, and things that are life-sustaining ought not to be wholly removed from "understanding." The same might be said of humor; Sterne sought to restore humor (which Locke damned by faint praise as harmless "pleasantry") to the realm of understanding, again because of its life-giving powers: "I live in a constant endeavour to fence against the infirmities of ill health, and other evils of life, by mirth; being firmly persuaded that every time a man smiles,—but much more so, when he laughs, that it adds something to this Fragment of Life" (dedication).

Sterne's adaptations of associationism imply a similar transvaluation of Lockean understanding. Locke stood as "father" to associationism insofar as he defined the mind's propensity to form anomalous and illogical associations among different parts of its experiences—

> *Ideas* that in themselves are not at all of kin, come to be so united in some Mens Minds, that 'tis very hard to separate them, they always keep in company, and the one no sooner at any time comes into the Understanding but its Associate appears with it; and if they are more than two which are thus united, the whole gang always inseparable shew themselves together (*Essay* II.xxxiii.5)[14]

—but Locke described the phenomenon only to warn against it. Idiosyncratic mental associations are not a reflection of understanding, but a kind of madness ("opposition to Reason deserves that name, and is really Madness") which must continually be guarded against, if man is to make progress toward reasonable understanding. Here again, Sterne accepted Locke's definition of the cognitive mechanism while in effect denying Locke's estimate of the consequences. Both Tristram's style of telling his story and the modes of thought of his various characters stand as comic realizations of Locke's worst fears, embodiments of cognitive eccentricity and arbitrariness. Tristram cannot reconstruct his memories in a sequential way, and he is borne along by the stream of his own associations; Corporal Trim cannot recall the Ten Commandments without going through the manual-at-arms at the same time (V.xxxii.468–69); whenever Uncle Toby hears a military metaphor the "whole gang" of his military lore rushes to the fore, whether related or not to the topic at hand. From the point of view of reason, this is all "madness" and perhaps a kind of slavery, too, for these characters (except Tristram) are seldom able to step beyond the associative habits which shape their understandings.

Of course, Sterne was well aware that such "unreasonable" habits of mind can mislead and isolate people. However, this is not the *only* potential consequence of giving personal mental associations free rein, as Locke had supposed; there may also be "unreasonable" compensations to balance the disorientations of reason. When Walter Shandy hears of his son Bobby's death, he launches into an associative train of classical *sententiae* concerning death and nearly forgets the sad occasion of his eloquent allusions (V.iii.418–25); his mind's excursions help to protect Walter from the unbearable in a way that a more "reasonable" approach could not. And Tristram himself knows that the mind freed from reason and circumstance can expand both the dimensions and the qualities of real life, which is *mental* life: "I . . . must be cut short in the midst of my days, and taste no more of 'em than what I borrow from my imagination" (VII.xiv.595). The "unreasonable" mind can soften the harsh power of circumstances over men and thereby serve life,[15] and Sterne uses his power to manipulate "random" associations to suggest that associationism which is indeed a fallibility of reasonable consciousness can also serve as a creative principle, a generative mechanism, for discovering the unreasonable, often extra-reasonable relationships among phenomena. As Sterne's art everywhere suggests, we live in a world not easily reduced to reasonable principles, but this does not mean that it is wholly incomprehensible. Walter Shandy and Uncle Toby do not have and can never have a reasonable relationship, but they do possess one that is loving, sympathetic, highly eccentric, but also enduring; they "know" one another on terms which stand outside Lockean understanding.

In *Tristram Shandy* the world of experience seems significantly less fathomable than Locke had said it should be. Tristram speaks of the world as an "inextricable labyrinth" (VI.xiv.520), and individuals seem to participate in his world not so much as inquirers after truth but rather as victims of perverse circumstance: windows fall, brothers die, messages miscarry, love is unconsummated, preferment passes to others, battlements topple on people, horses become broken-winded, noses are crushed, Death knocks at the door. But there are potential compensations even amidst a train of disasters seemingly without end. In essence, Sterne shifted the realm of man's knowledge and of his freedom inward from where Locke had placed it; external circumstances are not so much the objects of knowledge as they are the catalysts of a more inward kind of knowing. If shandean man cannot encompass or control the world of circumstance, whatever freedom he can have is not in that world, but in his own attitudes, his posture toward experience; he cannot master the contingencies of the world, but he can try to control their impact upon his life and cares. Locke urged man to tie his mind by reasonable bonds to the external world; Sterne in effect recommends untying the mind both from a narrow bondage to reason and from a close conformity to external circumstance. In practical terms, this means multiplying attitudes toward the world of experience, for it is in the choice of attitudes where man's freedom finally lies. Reasonableness is a perfectly acceptable attitude, *if* it is balanced and qualified by a multitude of others: humor, sentimentality, whimsy, stoicism, irony, enthusiasm, fantasy, charity, self-consciousness, and a hundred others—Tristram and his relatives eventually touch them all.

The human tendency to indulge in posturing—melodramatic posturing, intellectual posturing, sentimental posturing, many other kinds—is one of the central jokes of *Tristram Shandy,* and Tristram himself is beyond doubt the worst offender.[16] But this is a *serious* joke, and it is difficult to define exactly where the "offense" really lies. Reality is not objects, but the play of the mind over objects, and mental amplitude, a variety of attitudes or postures toward those elusive objects, is the fullness of life. *All* the faculties of a man's mind have a role in this kind of understanding, his feelings and imaginings and hopes and humor. If external realities cannot be fixed and known, then let them be teased into shapes to suit the individual fancy.[17] If language will not stand still for rational discourse, then let man play at language as a provocative and witty game, while the unrestrained motions of the mind explore and celebrate its connotative, idiosyncratic, and figurative aspects. Soon enough, Tristram knows, reality will make claims which cannot be denied. Until then, however, why not let the mind negotiate a reprieve, why not borrow from imagination what need not be repaid, why not savor those privileged moments of sentiment or humor or whimsy or sincerity when the mind *feels* exempt from circumstance? Why not, just for a moment, live in a world consonant with the *full* range of man's faculties? Here, then, there is room for posturing and play, room to graze a hobbyhorse, room for a man to turn around in. Life is motion, stillness is death.

Half-seriously, half-ironically, Tristram invokes the spirit which inspired Cervantes and Don Quixote specifically as a power of imaginative grace strong enough to suspend circumstance: "GENTLE Spirit of sweetest humour, who erst didst sit upon the easy pen of my beloved CERVANTES; Thou who . . . turned'st the twilight of his prison into noon-day brightness by thy presence . . .——Turn in hither, I beseech thee!" (IX.xxiv.780). Tristram qualifies his effusion with self-conscious irony ("behold these breeches!——they are all I have in the world"), but the central assertion of his prayer is clear. A Quixotic mind has the power to rise above the austerities imposed by Lockean reasonableness, practicality, and passivity in the face of circumstance; it possesses the power to reshape the world by its imaginings, by its attitudes, by its willful appropriation of circumstance for its own purposes. Humor and imagination can transform the world of hostile circumstance into something sweet, gentle, and life-sustaining. Life—the mind's life—can be touched by grace.[18]

III

The mind's grace is an inconstant and unreliable one, to be sure, in a world where even a prayer for imaginative grace is qualified by irony. The ruling principle of Tristram's mind and of the world as he interprets it is neither grace nor confusion and despair but rather apposition, the uneasy coexistence of simultaneous possibilities. In this sad and vexing world, Tristram asks, "What is the life of man! Is it not to shift from side to side?" (IV.xxxi.399). So one prays for grace and at the same time feels self-conscious doing so. Understanding Sterne's strategies of apposition is central to grasping the strain and ambivalence in Tristram's vision of experience and in our own often divided responses to the novel.

Apposition is everywhere apparent in *Tristram Shandy,* from the initial yoking of love-making and clock-winding through to the final juxtaposition of Uncle Toby's amours and the symptoms of Tristram's fatal illness. Moreover, the principle of apposition seems to apply at every level of the narrative. Obviously it is crucial to the paratactic temporal structure of the novel; Tristram's adult opinions and circumstances are set side by side with the fragmented account of his conception, birth, and childhood, and all the free-floating pieces of his life can be brought into unobtrusive apposition with one another. Stylistic apposition seems omnipresent as well: Tristram commands (or borrows) many styles, and he often sets divergent styles in close conjunction; here the graceful energy of the sermon on conscience broken up by audience interruptions and a mechanically precise account of Trim's posture for reading it might serve as an example. The characters who inhabit Tristram's world also appear in apposition: Toby and Walter, Walter and Dr. Slop, Trim and Susannah the maid, Toby and Widow Wadman—all see the world and their particular affairs differently, and Tristram faithfully records their divergent perspectives, side by side. Tristram's breathless and eccentric prose implies apposition, too, as he skips from idea to idea, dropping out the syntactical and logical connections between them: "wit and judgment in this world never go together; inasmuch as they are two operations differing from each other as wide as east is from west.—So, says *Locke,*—so are farting and hickuping, say I" (III.xx.227).

The novel further offers a broad field for interpretive apposition. "Innocent" and "naughty" readings of a given word or passage stand in ironical suspension, waiting for the reader to be trapped in their apposition. Is Toby's bowling-green "service to the nation" noble, pathetic, generous, or absurd: the various possibilities stand in apposition to one another. Or consider Walter's ruminations upon the sexual waywardness of the Shandys' Aunt Dinah:

———My father . . . was a philosopher in grain,—speculative,—systematical;— and my aunt *Dinah*'s affair was a matter of as much consequence to him, as the retrogradation of the planets to *Copernicus:*—The backslidings of *Venus* in her

orbit fortified the *Copernican* system, call'd so after his name; and the backslidings of my aunt *Dinah* in her orbit, did the same service in establishing my
father's system, which, I trust, will for ever hereafter be call'd the *Shandean System,* after his. (I.xxi.76)

Tristram's comparison, the shandean equivalent of an epic simile, holds two
objects of disproportionate size and doubtful relationship in ironical suspension. Clearly the effect is humorously absurd—all "backslidings" are not of a
kind, and Aunt Dinah was presumably no Venus—but what exactly is the
focus of the absurdity? Walter Shandy, who thinks so systematically? Or Tristram, who makes the absurd comparison? Or system-making in general, in
which case Copernicus is a victim, too? Or comparison-making in general?
These readings may not be equally probable, but the real point is that the
terms of Tristram's comparison are so incomparable that the effect of his comparison is more appositive than comparative. Unlike simple comparisons (or
simple oppositions), shandean appositions refuse to fix a single principle of
similarity or difference and thereby to delimit and focus possible implications.
Like Homeric similes or Miltonic ones, they open up a far broader range of
interpretive possibilities, a simultaneous and unsettling awareness of whole
worlds of similarities *and* differences to be explored. (It is worth recalling that
Tristram's only specific criticism of Locke is for treating wit, the power to recognize similarities, and judgment, the power to discriminate differences, as
two separable faculties of the mind [III.xx.236–37]: Tristram insists that the
two must continually operate together, that each one, in fact, implies the
countervailing necessity of the other, that the two faculties are *equal* partners
meant "to answer one another." Shandean man is predisposed, then, to see all
things ambivalently or appositively.[19])

Sterne's many techniques of apposition go hand in hand with complementary arts of narrative suspension. Some sorts of suspension are immediately evident in *Tristram Shandy:* the story that never quite gets told; the conversation which somehow miscarries; the author interrupting a character's
speech to describe in minute detail the speaker's attitude or pausing to comment upon the artistry of his story even as he tells it. But there are subtler
kinds of suspension which deserve attention. Consider, for example, the marvellous story of Phutatorius and the hot chestnut which falls into his breeches
at Didius' visitation dinner. The story opens with Phutatorius' exclamation,
"Zounds!" (IV.xxvii.377) and his expression of pained astonishment. Tristram
first analyzes the musical qualities of this "Zounds!," then records the various
private opinions of Didius' guests as to its significance, then digresses to tell
of Phutatorius' liking for hot chestnuts, then debates whether so-called accidents are really accidental, then traces the course of the fatal hot chestnut,
then of Phutatorius' animal spirits feeling pain, then of the churchman's pan-
icked imaginings about the source of his pain (perhaps he is being bitten, not
burned)—and finally we arrive back at "Zounds!" (383). What we are wit-

nessing here is not simply narrative suspension but interpretive suspension; Sterne deliberately withheld those facts which would allow us to interpret Phutatorius' exclamation quickly and correctly, and instead, leads us a merry chase through erroneous opinions, irrelevant inquiries, digressive backgrounds, melodramatic psychologies, and so on. This is good comic technique, of course; it serves to insulate us from Phutatorius' pain and prepares us to laugh at him. But Sterne was also playing with our anxiousness to interpret what is happening, deliberately frustrating and misleading us, causing us to cast and recast our notions of what transpired.

Later in the narrative, Tristram describes explicitly the same state of interpretive suspension. Walter is waiting in eager anticipation for Toby to launch his romantic expedition against Widow Wadman; Toby and Trim are mired in digressions. Tristram observes, "When issues of events like these my father is waiting for, are hanging in the scales of fate, the mind has the advantage of changing the principle of expectation three times, without which it would not have power to see it out" (IX.x.756–57). Three is an arbitrary number; it could as easily be ten or a dozen. Whatever the number, the general point remains the same: the mind possesses many "principles of expectation" and is continually formulating and reformulating an order among its experiences in the light of those principles; no particular ordering can be assumed to be final, and even events which are finished can be reformulated indefinitely, as Tristram's memoirs themselves tend to demonstrate.

This idea of the mind reviewing its experiences and adjusting its expectations *sounds* very Lockean, and in some ways Locke's discussion of the mind's workings provides a good handle to grasp Sterne's strategies of apposition and interpretive suspension. Basically, the Lockean mind does work through processes of apposition: it receives disparate sensations which it must endeavor to combine into unified perceptions, and it must compare current perceptions with its previous formulations of experience to arrive through reflection at true understandings in the light of new information. All of this seems consonant with Sterne's practices. But unlike Sterne, Locke believed that man could get *beyond* apposition; apposition is the means but not the end of understanding. Their difference on this point requires careful explanation.

Locke's notion of understanding is fundamentally an incremental one: new information forces a man to refine or revise his previous formulation of experience, and the revised formulation eventually supplants its predecessor. When Walter Shandy "chang[es] the principle of expectation three times," there is no indication that principles of expectation supplant one another, merely that they exist as alternatives. By the same token, Tristram's earnestness does not supplant his humor, Toby's follies do not supplant his goodness, and "naughty" noses do not supplant "innocent" ones—instead, the alternative possibilities continue together in uneasy coexistence. What is the difference between Locke and Sterne on this point? In spite of the roles of apposition and reflective suspension in Locke's paradigm of understanding, the standard of *comprehension* in Locke is finally single, not appositive: man can and must attain a reasonable grasp of his experiences and of the world which he shares with others. Empirical reason—reason conjoined with available facts—stands as the final arbiter, both in the management of one's own mind and in the conduct of the shared world. There is *no* final arbiter in Sterne, which is why the world will continue to appear to the mind in terms of appositions. If reason is only a part of understanding and must share as an equal with man's other faculties in the work of understanding, then the powers of man's mind are themselves in apposition and everything which the mind considers will appear appositively.[20] Reason will always interpret experience in a different light than sympathetic feelings, comic whimsy, or creative imagination do, and all of these faculties have a legitimate though partial claim to interpret experience. Toby will forever be unreasonable, noble, touching, and absurd in about equal measure, and there will always be as much ambivalence in describing his character as in assessing the nature and implications of the undefined wound in his groin; he will be Nature's gentleman, even as he is Walter's frustration, England's patriot, Sentiment's favorite, and Reason's fool.

Sterne's good-humored ease at playing partial perspectives against one another finally signifies something more than strategic virtuosity, something more deeply ironical, indeterminate, and unsettling. Sterne created a fictional world in which the various facets of experience and the mind's equally various interpretations of those facets are held permanently in appositive suspension; the mind and the world that it addresses both appear as the sum of their appositions, and to possess "understanding" in the shandean sense is to possess interpretive *options*.[21] The story which does not quite begin or end at any specific place also implies an evaluative structure, a mode of understanding, which does not begin or end at any specific place either. Appositions are referred for resolution not to any shared or established standard but to further appositions. Judgments are neither impossible nor useless in a world defined by appositions; Tristram makes them all the time, even if he implies very disparate criteria, and Sterne often forces us to draw our own conclusions. But such judgments possess an oddly double aspect: all acts of interpretation under the sign of Shandy are continually ironical, partly because they are at best partial and provisional orderings of experience, also because they tend to reflect so clearly the mind and character of the interpreter.[22] The limitations of man's interpretive abilities are simultaneous with his capacities. This double aspect is implicit in Yorick's affectionate scolding of Fancy in *A Sentimental Journey:*

> thou art a seduced, and a seducing slut; and albeit thou cheatest us seven times a day with thy pictures and images, yet with so many charms dost thou do it, and thou deckest out thy pictures in the shapes of so many angels of light, 'tis a shame to break with thee. (*ASJ,* 92)

Fancy—or any faculty of interpretation—gives us both more and less than the object itself: more, in the sense that interpretation can lend variety, coherence, or embellishment to its objects (ultimately it gives to us our selves); less, because it misrepresents objects in order to grasp and organize them, because it cannot finally capture "things in themselves." Man's freedom and happiness lie in his ability to preside over his experiences in the world by interpreting them, to cultivate personal perspectives and attitudes which allow him to rise above mere circumstance. Man's sadness is that he will always stand at a distance from the world of circumstance and find it to some extent impenetrable. It is no accident that Tristram admires Don Quixote—"with all his follies"—more than the greatest hero of antiquity (I.x.23).

IV

The main business of this essay has been to establish two points about *Tristram Shandy:* first, to demonstrate that Sterne implied a broad range of attitudes toward the Lockean perspectives which he borrowed; second, to suggest that Sterne deliberately used the interplay of subjective and variable viewpoints to create a fictional world of appositions in which there is a great deal of interpretive latitude—"room to turn a man's self in."[23] It is in this open space amongst conflicting impressions and interpretations of events that the various characters find room to live, to become themselves and to enjoy the selves that they become.[24] It is the same open space that allows us as readers to make of the novel what we can, what we will—so long as we recognize that our views are likely to stand in apposition with the equally probable views of others. But there are some generally applicable consequences (and *non*-consequences) to this view of *Tristram Shandy* that are worth elaborating.

First, concerning the moral fabric of Sterne's novel. It is important to note that the perceptual relativism and consequent skepticism implicit in Sterne's methods are not necessarily bound up with moral relativism. Certainly Sterne used his appositive strategies to explore the relativity of moral perceptions (for example, in juxtaposing Uncle Toby's innocence with his defense of the usefulness of war) and he continually toyed with libidinous energies generally ignored by polite society which lie half-hidden in received language and metaphors. Still, the general accumulation of moral perspectives throughout *Tristram Shandy* seems in the end to argue more powerfully for moral toleration than for simple relativism. *Because* man lives in this world amongst riddles and mysteries, *because* he cannot gain a consistent grasp upon his own experiences and upon the values and perceptions of others, he should be generous, patient, honest, and good-humored; the more inscrutable or divided the world seems, the more necessary the Golden Rule is in the conduct of human affairs.[25]

Second, concerning whatever formal qualities we are tempted to ascribe to *Tristram Shandy*. Shandean aesthetics, with their thoroughgoing commitment to strategies of apposition, step willfully aside from some very traditional notions of literary coherence. Nearly any formalistic ideas of narrative rest ultimately upon assumptions so widely shared that they are seldom discussed: the notions that narrative action does indeed have a shape, that coherent meanings can be encompassed by such shapes, and that different readers can arrive at a common appreciation of such literary shapeliness and its implications. A shandean aesthetic founded upon the inevitability of unending appositions challenges all such assumptions: if the powers of the mind are themselves in apposition and understanding is finally only appositive, then the artistic forms which would express understanding must be similarly appositive, tentative, and forever unfinished. A well-formed work does not offer "conclusions" but coherent *options* for interpretation. The subjective mind which cannot formulate its own understandings may well reach for outside assistance—notions of genre, of convention and decorum, of received wisdom and audience expectation—yet all of these props meant to steady the subjective mind ultimately are implicated in its unsteadiness, for they are all subjectively perceived. If one would formalize a work that deliberately challenges our impulse to formalize our understanding, then one had better do so in jest—as Tristram repeatedly does. Tristram also suggests (cheerfully, appositively) that formal constraints are secondary to the pleasures of indulging one's imagination: "to write a book is for all the world like humming a song—be but in tune with yourself, madam, 'tis no matter how high or how low you take it" (IV.xxv.374).

Third, concerning the historical situation of *Tristram Shandy*. Some modern critics have been tempted to assimilate Sterne's novel to more recent works in philosophy and literature which emphasize the isolation of individual consciousness, to see Sterne as the prophet of that "modernity" which we associate with alienated antiheroes, self-conscious irony, and stoic comedy.[26] Others have sought to align *Shandy* with older, pre-Enlightenment traditions—Renaissance wit, humours comedy, menippean satire, philosophical rhetoric, and similar well-established conventions.[27] Both approaches can be justified textually, but to give either one predominance is perhaps to misrepresent Sterne's position. What the simultaneous presence of "modern" notions and more traditional ones in Sterne's novel really points to is the historical crossroads at which Sterne stood. *Tristram Shandy* is deeply traditional, at least insofar as it was consciously written against the background of and with continual reference to older kinds of literature; to be self-consciously unconventional is to depend fundamentally upon existing conventions. The novel is also significantly "modern" insofar as it is premised upon Descartes' reorientation of philosophy toward the subjective mind which must find its way in an elusive and substantially unknowable world (we overestimate the uniqueness of our "modernity"). But what is most important to point out, I think, is that Sterne possessed an appropriate strategy to dramatize the cross-roads at which he found himself: he could hold the old and the new in ever-varying patterns of apposition, lending credence to both but presumptive authority to neither. In this aspect, as in many others in *Tristram Shandy,* the search for understanding is a balancing act, a weighing of interpretive options, all of which have some claim to credibility.

It is important, by way of conclusion, to recall something very simple. *Tristram Shandy* is a book of fictional memoirs which center upon a person, not an idea—and persons are often rather contradictory creatures.[28] "Inconsistencies," as Johnson's Imlac reminds us, "cannot both be right, but imputed to man, they may both be true."[29] Tristram contains many inconsistencies, savors them in other people, and celebrates them as agents which keep the mind—and thus life—in motion. (Seen from this angle, Sterne seems closer in spirit to Montaigne than to Locke.[30]) And Tristram does his best to keep us off balance, to keep our minds in motion. He deserves our help. The ways that we can help him most are to surrender to the ambivalent processes of his book and to resist the urge to thrust upon *Tristram Shandy* any contrived consistency of ideas, however well-tempered, that represents a violation of its most basic impulse, which is motion, and its most basic structure, which is apposition. For books as well as for people, life is motion and stillness is death.

Notes

1.   From Bacon's grudging and ambivalent defense of the usefulness of fictions in "Of Truth," included in the 1625 edition of *The Essayes or Counsels, Civill and Morall.* Bacon went on to ask, "Doth any man doubt, that if there were taken out of men's minds vain opinions, flattering hopes, false valuations, imaginations as one would, and the like, but it would leave the minds of a number of men poor shrunken things, full of melancholy and indisposition, and unpleasing to themselves?"

2.   For particularly useful discussions of Locke's place in *Tristram Shandy,* see John Traugott, *Tristram Shandy's World: Sterne's Philosophical Rhetoric* (Berkeley, 1954), *passim* (deals primarily with Sterne's adaptations of Lockean notions of human communication); Ernest Lee Tuveson, "Locke and Sterne," in J. A. Mazzeo, ed., *Reason and the Imagination: Studies in the History of Ideas, 1600–1800* (New York, 1962), pp. 255–77 (Sterne follows the "liberating" lead of Lockean empiricism); Helene Moglen, *The Philosophical Irony of Laurence Sterne* (Gainesville, Fla., 1975), ch. 1 and *passim* (Lockean subjectivity offered Sterne the foundations for a far-reaching exploration of the ironies of human life, art, and awareness); and James E. Swearingen, *Reflexivity in "Tristram Shandy": An Essay in Phenomenological Criticism* (New Haven, 1977), *passim* (*Shandy* as a middle term between Locke and Husserl). Probably all attempts to stress the affinities between Locke and Sterne should be read in the light of Duke Maskell's skeptical and cautionary essay, "Locke and Sterne, or Can Philosophy Influence Literature," *EIC,* XXIII (1973), 22–40.

3.   Quoted from *An Essay Concerning Human Understanding,* ed. Peter H. Nidditch (Oxford, 1975). Future references to this edition will be cited in the text by book, chapter, and section numbers (I.i.6).

4. John W. Yolton offers an excellent account of the early reception of Lockean thought into divinity and philosophy in *John Locke and the Way of Ideas* (Oxford, 1956), *passim.* For Locke's reception into literature, see Kenneth Maclean, *John Locke and English Literature of the Eighteenth Century* (1936; rpt. New York, 1962), *passim.* Samuel F. Pickering, Jr., assesses the impact of Locke's ideas upon contemporary attitudes toward education in *John Locke and Children's Books in Eighteenth-Century England* (Knoxville, Tenn., 1981), pp. 5–12 and *passim.*

5. For thoughtful accounts of the difficulties of fabricating a self in a post-Cartesian, post-Humean world, see Patricia Meyer Spacks, *Imagining a Self: Autobiography and Novel in Eighteenth-Century England* (Cambridge, Mass., 1976), ch. 1, and John O. Lyons, *The Invention of the Self: The Hinge of Consciousness in the Eighteenth Century* (Carbondale, Ill., 1978), ch. 2.

6. Sigurd Burckhardt cites this same instance to argue that Sterne intended harsh criticism of Locke, that he meant to suggest that Lockean ideas do not exist, only words (and their attendant confusions) do. See *"Tristram Shandy*'s Law of Gravity," *ELH,* XXVIII (1961), 73.

7. W. B. C. Watkins, *Perilous Balance: The Tragic Genius of Swift, Johnson, and Sterne* (1939; rpt. Cambridge, Mass., 1960), p. 134.

8. For this reason Lockean perspectives on the mind's various workings were particularly valuable to contemporary satirists; see Peter M. Briggs, "Locke's *Essay* and the Strategies of Eighteenth-Century English Satire," *SECC,* X (1981), 135–51.

9. For a provocative discussion of the ways in which Tristram engages and "educates" his reader, see Howard Anderson, *"Tristram Shandy* and the Reader's Imagination," *PMLA,* LXXXVI (1971), 966–73.

10. See Sermons 19, "Felix's behaviour towards Paul, examined," and 44, "The ways of Providence justified to man" in *Sermons,* IV:177–85, 408–16.

11. Compare Tristram's characterization of "True *Shandeism"* as that which "opens the heart and lungs, and like all those affections which partake of its nature, it forces the blood and other vital fluids of the body to run freely thro' its channels, and makes the wheel of life run long and chearfully round" (IV.xxxii.401).

12. The usual translation "disturb" is perhaps too mild in its implications. The Greek verb in question, *tarassō,* ordinarily occurs in military contexts where it means "rout" or "throw into confusion."

13. For a provocative discussion of changing ideas of imagination and of the role of imagination in "understanding" during this period, see Ernest Lee Tuveson, *The Imagination as a Means of Grace: Locke and the Aesthetics of Romanticism* (Berkeley, 1960), chs. 1, 4–6.

14. Locke's famous chapter, "Of the Association of *Ideas*" (II.xxxiii), was not included in the *Essay* of 1690; it was added to the Fourth Edition in 1700. See the introduction to the Nidditch edition of the *Essay,* p. xxviii. For discussion of the supposition that Sterne was more influenced by Humean than Lockean theories of mental association, see Chinmoy Banerjee, *"Tristram Shandy* and the Association of Ideas," *TSLL,* XV (1973–1974), 693–706.

15. Even Walter Shandy recognizes that man possesses within himself a "secret spring" to balance the perversity of outward circumstances; he discourses to Toby on "that great and elastic power within us of counterbalancing evil, which like a secret spring in a well-ordered machine, though it can't prevent the shock—at least it imposes upon our sense of it" (IV.viii. 333–34).

16. Critics who approach *Tristram Shandy* from a rhetorical viewpoint, notably John Traugott, Melvyn New (*Laurence Sterne as Satirist* [Gainesville, Fla., 1969]), and Richard A. Lanham, have been particularly concerned to describe the place of role-playing in the novel. For a provocative discussion of this theme, see Lanham, *Tristram Shandy: The Games of Pleasure* (Berkeley, 1973), pp. 30–36.

17. In his *Journal to Eliza,* Sterne described himself "turning the world into a thousand Shapes to enjoy it" (*Letters of Laurence Sterne,* ed. L. P. Curtis [Oxford, 1935], p. 332). He elaborated a similar theme in *A Sentimental Journey:*

Sweet pliability of man's spirit, that can at once surrender itself to illusions, which cheat expectation and sorrow of their weary moments!—long—long since had ye number'd out my days, had I not trod so great a part of them upon this enchanted ground: when my way is too rough for my feet, or too steep for my strength, I get off it, to some smooth velvet path which fancy has scattered over with rose-buds of delights; and having taken a few turns in it, come back strengthen'd and refresh'd—When evils press sore upon me, and there is no retreat from them in this world, then I take a new course—I leave it—and as I have a clearer idea of the elysian fields than I have of heaven, I force myself, like Eneas, into them. (pp. 224–25)

The sentimental emphasis in such passages should not be allowed to obscure the more comprehensive psychological notions that they imply; whether a person teases the world into new shapes in accordance with sentimental impulses or humorous ones, the mind's ability to play freely with its objects implies a similar liberation from circumstance.

Seen in this light, Sterne seems to have anticipated in practice an argument developed by Friedrich Schiller a generation later. In his *Letters on the Aesthetic Education of Man* (1795) Schiller argued that man possesses a basic impulse toward aesthetic play which mediates between the sensual impulse which ties him to the material world and the formal impulse which leads him off into the world of abstractions; man makes fullest use of his faculties when he engages in aesthetic play, generating through play a humane world of "living forms." (See *Letters* xii–xv, and compare Lanham, *The Games of Pleasure, passim.*) Like Sterne, Schiller recognized that a work of art does not simply *represent* aesthetic play in itself or for its author but attempts to *induce* aesthetic play in its audience as well.

18.   For fuller discussion of the affinities between *Tristram Shandy* and *Don Quixote,* see Walter L. Reed, *An Exemplary History of the Novel: The Quixotic versus the Picaresque* (Chicago, 1981), pp. 139–46; Swearingen, *Reflexivity in "Tristram Shandy,"* pp. 1–6; Alexander Welsh, *Reflections on the Hero as Quixote* (Princeton, 1981), pp. 13–35, 102–5, 186–87; and Briggs, "Locke's *Essay* and the Strategies of Eighteenth-Century English Satire," 144–45, 150.

In general, Locke was mistrustful of the imagination and its works; at best, they offered man harmless "diversion," while at worst, they might seduce man away from those reasonable and practical concerns which led toward useful truths. However, it is ironical, at least from the point of view of my argument, to note that one of the few imaginative works which Locke *did* recommend was *Don Quixote*. In "Some Thoughts Concerning Reading and Study for a Gentleman, 1703" Locke wrote, "Of all the books of fiction I know none that equals Servantes his History of *Don Quixot* in usefulness, pleasantry, and a constant decorum. And indeed no writings can be pleasant which have not *Nature* at the bottom, and are not drawn after her copy" (*The Educational Writings of John Locke,* ed. James Axtell [Cambridge, 1968], p. 403). Locke owned a copy of *Don Quixote* at the time of his death.

19.   Compare Helene Moglen's argument in *Philosophical Irony,* ch. 3, that all of the major themes in *Tristram Shandy* are realized by being played against their negating opposites.

20.   Compare Coleridge's famous complaint against *Tristram Shandy,* that Sterne sought to play the white angel and the black angel in our minds off against one another: Alan B. Howes, ed., *Sterne: The Critical Heritage* (London, 1974), pp. 354–55.

21.   In *Tristram Shandy's World* (p. 26) John Traugott argues provocatively on very different grounds that "Sterne's capacity for doubt *is* his capacity for expression."

Several critics have argued that Tristram keeps his readers off balance without being off balance himself; for examples, see Lanham, *The Games of Pleasure,* pp. 97–98 (Tristram suffers only from a voluntary and self-imposed dizziness) and Benjamin H. Lehman, "Of Time, Personality, and the Author," included in John Traugott, ed., *Laurence Sterne: A Collection of Critical Essays* (Englewood Cliffs, N.J., 1968), pp. 30–32 (Tristram possesses "unity of consciousness"). But, as Locke insisted, all minds operate by means of the same basic mechanisms.

Tristram's advantage over his readers is not that he is self-balanced while they are not; it is that he can orchestrate the divisions in his mind and attitudes while we must try to follow his music. His mind, however, is finally no less divided than ours.

22. Compare Sterne's *Letters,* ed. Curtis, p. 411: "a true feeler always brings half the entertainment along with him. His own ideas are only call'd forth by what he reads, and the vibrations within, so entirely correspond with those excited, 'tis like reading *himself* and not the *book.*"

23. It is worthwhile to recall that the writers whom Sterne most admired—Rabelais and Cervantes, Montaigne and Burton, even Swift—shared with him the same impulse toward literary spaciousness, the impulse to establish an open-ended literary situation (whether an improbable voyage or a personal meditation) in which there would be room to try out a multitude of different, sometimes contradictory attitudes. Sterne might even be credited with seeking to use the new epistemology and psychology to provide new grounding for Renaissance notions of literary copiousness.

24. Compare Alexander Welsh's intriguing supposition (*Reflections on the Hero as Quixote,* p. 176) that, since man's various roles are thrust upon him by society and circumstance, he is most free to be and know himself in the privileged moments *between* roles. It might be argued in response to the rhetorical critics who have emphasized the importance of role-playing in *Tristram Shandy* (see note 16) that Sterne's true brilliance comes not from his virtuosity in manipulating traditional rhetorical roles, but rather from his ability to destabilize them, to allow characters to become themselves because the unstable fictional situation leaves them most of the time *between* roles.

25. Locke used basically the same argument in his various pleas for religious, civic, and intellectual toleration; see, for example, *Essay* IV.xvi.4.

26. For some interesting instances, see Hugh Kenner, *Flaubert, Joyce and Beckett: The Stoic Comedians* (Boston, 1962), pp. 48–49; Ernest H. Lockridge, "A Vision of the Sentimental Absurd: Sterne and Camus," *SR,* LXXII (1964), 652–76; Moglen, *Philosophical Irony,* ch. 4; and Swearingen, *Reflexivity in "Tristram Shandy," passim.*

27. Some well-known and useful examples would include: D. W. Jefferson, *"Tristram Shandy* and the Tradition of Learned Wit," *EIC,* I (1951), 225–48; New, *Laurence Sterne as Satirist,* ch. 3; Howard Anderson, "Associationism and Wit in *Tristram Shandy,*" *PQ,* XLVIII (1969), 27–41; and Lanham, *Tristram Shandy: The Games of Pleasure,* ch. 2. See also Melvyn New's intriguing essay on Sterne and the "burden of the past": "Sterne, Warburton, and the Burden of Exuberant Wit," *ECS,* XV (1981–1982), 245–74.

28. Ernest Tuveson has argued that a major consequence of the prevalence of Lockean epistemology in the eighteenth century was the "dissolution" of traditional notions of the stability of the individual personality. Locke in effect transferred the locus of stability in man's mind from his personality to his ideas, and was content to see personality as ever-shifting and ever-evolving. See "Locke and the 'Dissolution of the Ego,' " *MP,* LII (1955), 167–70.

29. Samuel Johnson, *The History of Rasselas, Prince of Abissinia,* ed. Geoffrey Tillotson and Brian Jenkins (London, 1971), p. 21 (ch. viii).

30. Jonathan Lamb explores this relationship sensitively and persuasively in "Sterne's Use of Montaigne," *CL,* XXXII (1980), 1–41.

Tristram Shandy and Narrative Representation

EVERETT ZIMMERMAN

Sterne's narrator Tristram attempts to found parts of his story on artifacts, models, and documents that promise to transcend individual life, fixing its instabilities and extending it into the past and future. But these extensions of self stubbornly retain their own opacities. *Tristram Shandy* thus undermines by implication not only the private history that is often claimed as a province of fiction, but also public history.[1] Sterne's novel engages eighteenth-century historical scholarship, including its eighteenth-century subdivision of biblical scholarship. Both kinds of historicism countered their suspicions of the subjectivity of interpretation by accruing information about the physical text.[2] The demand for presence succumbed to a demand for the documentation of a former presence, leading in some cases to a valuation of the artifact itself because of its supposed contiguity to a former presence.

Tristram Shandy alludes to a broad range of scholarly activities connected to textual criticism by incorporating into itself a multitude of seemingly digressive documents—Yorick's sermon, the consultation of the doctors at the Sorbonne, the curse of Ernulphus, Slawkenbergius's tale, for some examples—and evaluating the textual authority of these interpolations, commenting on the questions of provenience, transmission, and translation. Sterne's novel creates itself before our eyes, assembling itself as a book in the way that a textual editor might disassemble one. Tristram makes the process of composition part of his narration. He does not cover up the seams of the narration—the leaps in time, the alterations of voice, the digressiveness—but exposes them to scrutiny and comments on their weaknesses. As we are close to his consciousness, the book emphasizes presence and presentness, but this emphasis coexists with an equally strong concern with the recovery of a dead or dying past—the immediate past of his family and also the more distant historical past of some of the interpolated documents. These digressive insertions represent the documentary evidence on which the book is founded, but this evidence itself requires evaluation, thus leaving in question the validity of

Reprinted from *The Eighteenth Century: Theory and Interpretation* 28 (1987): 127–47 and *New Casebooks: Tristram Shandy,* ed. Melvyn New (London: Macmillan, 1992), 111–32.

the foundation. Sterne's novel self-consciously struggles to recover the past for a present moment and to extend its own presentness for a later reader; however, the attempt reveals both the private distortions of the consciousness that appropriates the past and the ultimate evanescence of the medium in which the past is represented. *Tristram Shandy* implies a bleak view of the possibilities of connecting a represented present with its contexts of past and future, that is, history.

Sterne's book displays a shift in focus from the "being" represented in a text to the "being" of the text, map, or model. In this it follows the lead of the satiric masterpiece that is one of its sources—Swift's *Tale of a Tub*.[3] Swift's attacks on the great textual scholar Richard Bentley and more generally on the "modern critic" derive some of their force from his persuasion that they separate medium from meaning, creating a specious material of the medium and infusing it with their own desires. Swift frequently satirizes the reduction of Scripture to an object, as when the brothers of the *Tale* manipulate the letters of their "father's will" or when Jack burns an inch of it under his nose to cure illness. Sterne's attitude toward the materiality of an intellectual production is somewhat less satiric and more rueful than Swift's. *Tristram Shandy*'s emphasis on the process of its own construction acknowledges the book as object. This conception appears too in smaller satiric details, reminiscent of the *Tale*. Nature having "sown the seeds of verbal criticism" in him, Walter Shandy uses his penknife to alter some letters in a dialogue by Erasmus, in order to arrive at a more satisfactory meaning than the "strict and literal interpretation" (III.xxxvii.271–72). Perhaps even more Swiftian is the incident in which Phutatorius, a hot chestnut having dropped into his breeches, is advised to wrap his burnt member in a "soft sheet of paper just come off the press . . . provided, quoth *Yorick,* there is no bawdry in it" (IV.xxviii.386–87).

The controversy between the deist Anthony Collins (*A Discourse of Free-Thinking,* 1713) and the Anglican Richard Bentley (*Remarks Upon a Late Discourse of Free-Thinking,* 1713) over the authority of Scripture provides a useful frame of reference for *Tristram Shandy.* Bentley and Collins differ sharply about the value of Christianity, but both are willing to rest their cases on the relative accuracy and, therefore, authority of the Bible. This controversy implies the movement toward the text as object that Swift had earlier so outrageously satirized in the *Tale* and that Sterne later reflects in *Tristram Shandy.* Anthony Collins argued that canon, text, and orthodox interpretation of Scripture are all without authority, impugned even by the scholarship of believers like the Catholic Richard Simon, who, in Collins' mischievous formulation, "labour'd so much to prove the Uncertainty of the Text of Scripture."[4] Despite their differing conclusions, Bentley and Collins agree in their perceptions of the Bible as a book subject to decay. Bentley argues, however, that textual scholarship has kept it alive: "since Time and Casualties must consume and devour All; the subsidiary Help is from the various Transcripts convey'd down to us, when compar'd and examin'd together."[5] The issue, as

Bentley defines it, is not whether errors have crept into the Bible but whether "Revelation" can "be communicated and convey'd to us in *Books*" (56). Collins' argument, Bentley suggests further, invalidates all ancient texts, not just the Bible.

The anxieties of Collins, Bentley, and many others in the eighteenth century about the biblical text are aroused by the heavy commitment of Protestant Christianity to biblical authority. The Reformation emphases on the grammatical, the historical, and the literal were intended to bring meaning within a perimeter of assent so unbreachable that it required no institutional affirmation. But the literal was multivalent, too, as complex as the allegory that is born from it (or that gives birth to it). Textual researches are a way to bring closer those ur-statements on which all depends, but the meaning of those statements recedes even as they are being uncovered. The text, however, remains. It is palpable evidence of the existence of the letter, even if uninterpreted, and it is contiguous to the history that is believed to justify faith. It retains authority as an object even if its meaning is questioned.

The process described here is one in which a text is substituted for a presence. More specifically, the pattern of development in the established church of England after the interregnum is away from conceptions of any direct communication of religious truths to individuals. The English had in a sense silenced their prophets, who had offended against political, social, and religious order.[6] The dissenters, justly accused both of bibliolatry and of claiming inspiration from God, insist on presence as well as on a book that claims contiguity with presence. Milton and Bunyan, for example, exhibit an attitude differing from that of Bentley and Collins. Although Milton takes Scripture as his authority in writing *The Christian Doctrine*, he subordinates the textual problems of the New Testament to spiritual insight: "It is difficult to conjecture the purpose of Providence in committing the writings of the New Testament to such uncertain and variable guardianship, unless it were to teach us by this very circumstance that the Spirit which is given to us is a more certain guide than Scripture, whom therefore it is our duty to follow."[7] The very extent and intensity of his claims to inspiration in *Paradise Lost* suggest that for him prophecy has not ceased. Bunyan too roots his subject matter and language in Scripture, but the Scripture is privately appropriated not publicly fixed. The Bible is for Bunyan and Milton the universal pattern into which all other experience is fitted, but that pattern is made private. Milton and Bunyan reconcile presence and text through an inward persuasion: Collins and Bentley use the norms provided by historical scholarship as their criteria for meaning and belief.

The interest aroused by textual scholarship (the Boyle–Bentley controversy as represented in *The Battle of the Books* is perhaps the best known example[8]) appears to be related as much to the *frisson* provoked by its potential subversiveness of authoritative texts as by its powers for patching up foundations. The triumphs of classical scholarship in recovering texts sometimes threaten in biblical scholarship to be converted into the defeats that mark a text's disintegration (as Anthony Collins eagerly argued). The destructive potentialities of textual criticism and analysis are apparent in the very work in which Bentley confutes Collins' attack on the authority of the biblical text. Bentley does to Homer what Collins wanted to do to the Bible: Homer "wrote a sequel of Songs and Rhapsodies, to be sung by himself for small earnings and good cheer, at Festivals and other days of Merriment; the *Ilias* he made for the Men, and the *Odysseis* for the other Sex. These loose Songs were not collected together in the form of an Epic Poem, till Pisistratus's time about 500 years after" (18).

The treatment of the sermon inexplicably found by Trim in the leaves of a book by Stevinus and read to the assembled Toby, Walter, and Dr. Slop by Trim is a parody of textual criticism and an example of the vanishing foundation in *Tristram Shandy*. On stylistic grounds Walter attributes the sermon to Yorick, a conjecture confirmed the next day when Yorick sends a servant to claim the sermon (II.xvii.165–66). But we are further teased by the question of how Yorick's sermon came to appear verbatim in the book we are now reading: "Ill-fated sermon! Thou wast lost, after this recovery of thee, a second time, dropp'd thro' an unsuspected fissure in thy master's pocket, down into a treacherous and a tatter'd lining,—trod deep into the dirt by the left hind foot of his Rosinante, inhumanly stepping upon thee as thou falledst;—buried ten days in the mire,—raised up out of it by a beggar, sold for a half-penny to a parish-clerk,—transferred to his parson,—lost for ever to thy own, the remainder of his days,—nor restored to his restless MANES till this very moment, that I tell the world the story" (II.xvii.166). So elaborately detailed and improbable an establishment of the provenience of the sermon *vexes* the very idea of provenience. Furthermore this sermon had already been preached and published by Sterne *in propria persona.*

The Yorick to whom the sermon is so definitively and yet ambiguously attributed is himself earlier given a precise lineage that gradually vanishes in indefinition and humor. From "a most antient account of the family, wrote upon strong vellum, and now in perfect preservation," Tristram learns that Yorick's name was spelled as it now is for nine hundred years. Drawing back from this assertion as an improbability, Tristram nevertheless finds that through the "religious preservation" of family records, he can trace Yorick's ancestry to Denmark's court. And because many of Shakespeare's plays "are founded upon authenticated facts" (I.xi.25–26), he concludes that the dead jester of *Hamlet* was Yorick's ancestor. Recognizing that this assertion still leaves Shakespeare's historical authenticity somewhat infirmly established, Tristram comically truncates the regression: "I have not the time to look into *Saxo-Grammaticus's Danish* history, to know the certainty of this;—but if you have leisure, and can easily get at the book, you may do it full as well yourself" (I.xi.26). We are left with a parody of historical method that does not yield even the appearance of the expected certainties.

The uncertainties of historical method as shown in *Tristram Shandy* are specifically linked to biblical criticism in Tristram's comparison of his father to Job, a figure whose very existence had been called into question: "*Now* my father had a way, a little like that of *Job's* (in case there ever was such a man——if not, there's an end of the matter)" (V.xiii.441). Although an interpretation of the fictional character is rather ineffectually bolstered by pursuing questions about the existence of his biblical prototype, Tristram decides not to abandon Job: ". . . because your learned men find some difficulty in fixing the precise æra in which so great a man lived;——whether, for instance, before or after the patriarchs, &c.———to vote, therefore, that he never lived *at all,* is a little cruel." The allusion here is to a specific controversy about the historicity of *Job,* in which William Warburton was a major participant.[9] Although Warburton specifically states that Job existed, his interpretation of the book is a dismissal of any literal view of its historicity. (One of the attackers of Warburton, Charles Peters, attributed to Jean LeClerc the view that the book of *Job* is only a parable.) Warburton and the controversy over Job appear to have occupied a more important place in Sterne's imagination than his almost casual remarks on Job might indicate. Walter Shandy is compared repeatedly to Job and, as Melvyn New has shown, Warburton's *The Divine Legation of Moses,* in which Job is discussed, appears in *Tristram Shandy* in repeated allusions.[10] In addition to these internal signs, a plausible, although secondhand, account of Sterne's early plan for *Tristram Shandy* suggests that it was to be a satire like *The Memoirs of Martinus Scriblerus,* with Dr. William Warburton as tutor to Tristram, and including an allegory on recent interpretations of *Job* in which Warburton was to be Satan and three attackers of his theories about Job—Richard Grey, Leonard Chappelow, and Charles Peters—were to be Job's comforters.[11] (Sterne also wrote two sermons on Job for the *Sermons of Mr. Yorick.*)

This controversy over *Job,* limited as it appears to be, expresses vividly the anxieties about Scripture that were generated by eighteenth-century historicism.[12] Warburton, constructing an allegorical interpretation to save the historical reference of a book whose literal statements he cannot accept, concludes that *Job* was probably written by Ezra and that it is an allegory of the difficulties of Judah after the return from the Babylonian captivity and the beginning of the rebuilding of the walls of Jerusalem. Job stands for the Jewish people, his wife is a heathen, and the three apparent friends are the covert enemies who tried to hinder the rebuilding, the Sanballet, Tobiah, and Gershom of the book of *Nehemiah* (*Divine Legation,* pp. 409–10).

This interpretation betrays a preference for the historical over the literary and a predilection for interpretation that links a book to a specific historical context. Confronted with a book like *Job,* which had the appearance of literature more than of history, Warburton allegorized it to make it allude immediately to the history of Israel. This allegorization, seemingly so foreign to Warburton's methods of interpretation elsewhere, is actually of a piece with them: a story needing interpretation is allegorized into the historical literal. Put another way, even allegory is preferable to the unhistorical.

This predilection for the historical is even more stridently exhibited by Warburton's opponent Charles Peters, whose *Critical Dissertation on the Book of Job* dismisses Warburton's arguments for allegory while insisting on a literal historicity for the book: "the Book, though a Poem, is in the main Historical, and probably *Job* himself the Writer of it."[13] *Job* is in "Order of Narration" like history: "is not a plain and orderly Relation of Facts, History?" (102). But taken as an "Allegoric Fiction . . . Times and Persons" in *Job* are jumbled and "the Truth of History is Destroyed" (47). The advantage of an older date than Warburton's is that even apart from its "Authority as an inspired Writing" a more ancient *Job* is "one of the most instructive, and most valuable Books that the World has ever seen" (38), giving "Evidence to the History and Doctrines of the most ancient Times" (80). The book has greater authority "the nearer it was written to the Times wherein the Events happened" (103); consequently, Job is the most satisfactory author, for then "all objections to the Historical Truth of it vanish at once" (125). In addition to believing in the historical circumstances conveyed by the book, Peters also uses it as a talisman. Its message, whatever its intrinsic value, is touched by and consequently touches us with a time long past, thereby extending our time (even if not our exact knowledge): "the oldest Writings, like the largest and best Diamond, are of a Worth superior to all Estimation" (81). The medium, which is conceived of as having once been touched by the being it no longer adequately represents, becomes the focus of attention and the repository of value.

Sterne's book is a compendium of arguments that may be used against Peters' conception of history. The notion of a "plain and literal meaning of common words" (8) that Peters relies on is obviously undermined by *Tristram Shandy:* not only can no conversation between Walter and Toby proceed on the basis of plainness or literality, but the reader in the book too is defined as a perverse punster, or allegorizer, who must be beseeched "to believe it of me, that in the story of my father and his christen-names—I had no thoughts of treading upon *Francis* the First—nor in the affair of the nose—upon *Francis* the Ninth—nor in the character of my uncle *Toby*—of characterizing the militiating spirits of my country" (IV.xxii.360). Peters' definition of history as an orderly relation of facts is persistently subverted by Tristram's demonstration that narrative is choice and order is exclusion: "O ye POWERS . . . which enable mortal man to tell a story worth the hearing. . . . I beg and beseech you, (in case you will do nothing better for us) that where-ever, in any part of your dominions it so falls out, that three several roads meet in one point, as they have done just here,—that at least you set up a guide-post, in the center of them, in mere charity to direct an uncertain devil, which of the three he is to take" (III.xxiii.244–45). Toby's difficulties in narrating his wounding question the authority that Peters grants to those who participate in the events they recount: Toby's view is limited and inarticulate until subsumed, distanced, and impersonalized by a map; then it becomes obsessive, leading him to disregard all other perspectives.

Tristram Shandy also dramatizes that veneration of an ancient object (such as Peters' *Job*) which seeks to transform it into a talisman. When interpreting the traces of the past that adhere to a document, Tristram often writes like a historian or editor, but his response then becomes not so much a matter of grounding his beliefs about the past as of stimulating his imagination of it:

> in a bundle of original papers and drawings which my father took care to roll up by themselves, there is a plan of Bouchain in perfect preservation (and shall be kept so, whilst I have power to preserve any thing) upon the lower corner of which, on the right hand side, there is still remaining the marks of a snuffy finger and thumb, which there is all the reason in the world to imagine, were Mrs. Wadman's; for the opposite side of the margin, which I suppose to have been my uncle Toby's, is absolutely clean: This seems an authenticated record of one of these attacks [of Mrs. Wadman on Toby]; for there are vestigia of the two punctures partly grown up, but still visible on the opposite corner of the map, which are unquestionably the very holes, through which it has been pricked up in the sentry-box.

Then acknowledging his apparent drift into religious and sexual imagination, Tristram concludes: "By all that is priestly! I value this precious relick, with it's *stigmata* and *pricks,* more than all the relicks of the *Romish* church" (VIII.xvii.678–79).

Tristram's implicit mockery of Catholicism presumably leaves the foundations of his own religion intact, yet his imagination requires the support of the same kind of legendary materials that he mocks. His account of his visit to the tomb of the two lovers reflects this desire for a relic to stimulate as well as verify imagination. He recounts the story of the two lovers in a severely reductionist form and states his intention of seeing their tomb, on which he wishes to drop a tear; however, "When I came—there was no tomb to drop it upon. What would I have given for my uncle Toby to have whistled, Lillo bullero" (VII.xl.643). The absent tomb, its absence visible only to the consciousness already engaged by it, is a suitable icon for *Tristram Shandy*'s view of history. The historical is brought into being by the consciousness that is able to create it, and it is lost when imagination fails. Not only is Locke's *Essay* a history "of what passes in a man's own mind" (II.ii.98), but so are all histories as well as all essays.

Nevertheless Sterne permits no easy access to his characters' inner beings. Tristram celebrates the humane feelings and behavior of characters like Toby and Trim, but his representations of them emphasize their imprisonment in their private worlds. Only through an act of interpretation can the meaning of their conduct be made accessible to a larger world. Trim's catechism, for example, is conducted by Toby, who requests each of the ten commandments in the form of a military drill. The moral goodness that Trim demonstrates is articulated through the process of connecting an ancient text to his and Toby's obsessions with their previous lives as soldiers. This rote behavior through which Trim's catechism is elicited causes Walter Shandy to be skeptical of the Corporal's understanding. "Prythee, *Trim,*" he asks, "What do'st thou mean, by *'honouring thy father and mother?'* " Trim answers: "Allowing them, an' please your honour, three halfpence a day out of my pay, when they grew old." After then ascertaining that Trim had indeed allowed his parents this sum, another listener, the parson Yorick, responds: "thou art the best commentator upon that part of the *Decalogue;* and I honour thee more for it, corporal *Trim,* than if thou hadst had a hand in the *Talmud* itself" (V.xxxii.470–71). Trim's remark is not, however, a comment on the biblical text but an absorption of it into the particulars of his life and society. Yet Yorick sees in Trim's too precisely specified response a desirable emphasis on the behavioral imperative of the text. He seizes on Trim's reduction of the commandment to the particular dimensions of his own conduct as an interpretable and thus generalizable emblem of the text's meaning. Trim's moral being is represented in the context of a rigidified form that causes it to be suspect; the truth of the text and of Trim's nature is elicited only through interrogation and interpretation.

In *The Presence of the Word,* Walter Ong attempts to reconcile the rigidities of a medium with the presence that it is designed to convey. Pointing out the textual intricacies of the biblical presentation of the Word that is Christ, he argues more generally that those media which produce in us a sense of separation from a presence have also "brought history into being and opened the past to us, making it possible to discover the word with new explicitness if less directness."[14] History is regarded as a way of recovering presence, its documentations forming a guide to the apprehension of religious and secular truth. Sterne is less optimistic about the possibility of recovering presence through representations. His novel often shows the process of representation taking on a life of its own, alienated from what it is intended to convey.

Take, for example, the play on the *where* of Toby's wound, which is exacerbated by Toby's difficulties in explaining in what part of Flanders it was received. The place of wounding is displaced from his groin to a "map of *Namur,*" enabling him to "give his visiters as distinct a history of each of their attacks, as of that . . . where he had the honour to receive his wound" (II.iii.101–2). When the mere map gives way to the models of the bowling green, Toby speedily recovers. But the Widow Wadman threatens to return the wound to his groin: "You shall lay your finger upon the place—said my uncle Toby.——I will not touch it, however, quoth Mrs. Wadman to herself" (IX.xx.773). Toby sends for his map, thus making his wound historical and documentable but not present.

Sterne's characters question the usual valorization of object over subject, history over fiction, turning history into an appendage of the personal. Early in the story Tristram writes that "The history of a soldier's wound beguiles the pain of it" (I.xxv.88), a statement that somewhat obliquely predicts the train of events by which the history of the War of the Spanish Succession is exfoliated from the history of Uncle Toby's wound in the groin during King William's war. While trying to narrate even the small part of the war that he saw as a participant at Namur, Toby discovers that "he could neither get backwards or forwards to save his life" (II.i.95). The expedient of a map then not only gives him relief by ordering his own history but also begins to substitute for his history, and in its eventual concretization as model becomes part of his history. Toby and Trim retire to the country "with plans . . . of almost every fortified town in *Italy* and *Flanders*" (VI.xxi.534) and reconstruct on the bowling green each of Marlborough's battles, "regulating their approaches and attacks, by the accounts my uncle *Toby* received from the daily papers" (VI.xxii.536). However, Toby takes his construction not as a representation of the daily papers' representations but as the very stuff of history. Warned by Walter that his modelling expenditures will ruin him, Toby replies: "What signifies it if they do, brother . . . so long as we know 'tis for the good of the nation" (III.xxii.242). For him the represented events are the presence that he denies in himself. Toby's mapping and modelling order and objectify experience, restraining its multiety and halting its process. But Toby is reduced to unintelligibility or silence in response to the demand that he be the representative of his own history: his words connect inadequately to the evanescence of event.

Sterne shows that writing about an event inevitably introduces the writer's time and the reader's time (see II.viii.119,120). The writer must "keep up the spirit and connection" of the narration (II.xix.169), narrating not only a sequence of events but also creating a nexus with the writer's and reader's times. As a consequence, event is redefined, its borders constantly shifting. Sterne parodies the periodizing that had been so important to Christian historiography; its fixations of time are incongruent with his fixation on the inseparable layerings of time. Within the seemingly fixed chronological schemes, he shows the human being on whose imagination all hinges. For example, in attempting to tell the story of the king of Bohemia, Trim identifies the time as shortly before "giants were beginning to leave off breeding" but, wanting a more specific time and encouraged by Toby to choose any date at all, he unfortunately specifies 1712. Tristram comments: ". . . of every century, and of every year of that century, from the first creation of the world down to Noah's flood; and from Noah's flood to the birth of Abraham; through all the pilgrimages of the patriarchs, to the departure of the Israelites out of Egypt——and throughout all the Dynasties, Olympiads, Urbecon-dita's, and other memorable epochas of the different nations of the world, down to the coming of Christ, and from thence to the very moment in which the corporal was telling his story . . . the corporal contented himself with the very *worst year* of the whole bunch" (VIII.xix.685). Sterne here summarizes the kind of periodization found in a multitude of religious historical treatises (he was perhaps most immediately motivated by Warburton's lengthy refutation of Newton's *Chronology*), and he comically exploits the incongruity between such epochal history and the seemingly more empirically definable contemporary history. Toby objects to the year both because it is one in which the English suffered a "sad stain upon our history" in Flanders and also because a story with giants needs "some seven or eight hundred years" to put it "out of harm's way, both of cricks and other people" (VIII.xix.686). Chronology either fades out of significance or merges with subjectivity.

One of Sterne's achievements is his extension of the critique of biblical and especially textual criticism to be found in Swift's *Tale of a Tub* to the whole range of historical studies.[15] Sterne, intensely conscious of the subjectivity of interpretation, sees the propensity for historical interpretation as a force for the dissolution of meaning as well as for validation. It is at least possible that he links *A Tale of a Tub* and *The Divine Legation of Moses* with *Tristram Shandy* not only to suggest Swift's work as a satiric commentary on Warburton's but also to acknowledge the subversiveness of all three: "for what has this book done more than the Legation of Moses, or the Tale of a Tub, that it may not swim down the gutter of Time along with them?" (IX.viii.754).

Like Swift, Sterne is impressed by the factitiousness of fact and artifact, but he conveys a keener sense of dependence on the artifact—whether manuscript or tomb—than does Swift.[16] His sense of the power of consciousness is balanced by an equally strong sense of its limits. It dies with us. Only his book, like Shakespeare's sonnet, is left to outlast marble tombs and outwit sluttish time. But Sterne's book systematically undercuts such confidence. The intertwining of book and life entangles both in mortality. His book is *himself dying* and his borrowings from other books often emphasize their deaths, too. Like the Bible revealed by textual criticism, the interpolated tales of *Tristram Shandy* disintegrate into damaged texts, poor translations, and dubious proveniences.

Tristram's accounts of his own writing point to the death implicit in the act of narration as much as to the continuance that it promises.[17] After narrating his own christening, Tristram (now author) sits awake alone: "all the curtains of the family are drawn—the candles put out—and no creature's eyes are open but a single one, for the other has been shut these twenty years, of my mother's nurse" (IV.xv.345). Tristram here has closed the gap between past and present, keeping the family alive in his consciousness. Only his waking authorial eye keeps them asleep: they too have by now joined the then waking nurse in death. The burdensome poignancy of Tristram's position as sole recollector and memorializer of the dead eventually makes him cry for relief from consciousness: "Leave we my mother. . . . Leave we *Slop* likewise. . . . Leave we poor *Le Fever*. . . . Let us leave, if possible, *myself:*——

But 'tis impossible,—I must go along with you to the end of the work" (VI.xx.533,534).

Writing, like Tristram, is the product of sin and death, increasingly assimilated to frustration and decay rather than to transcendence. Fleeing Death, that *"son of a whore,"* Tristram sets off for Europe, having "forty volumes to write, and forty thousand things to say and do." He imagines fleeing from Vesuvius to Joppa, Jonah's port of departure and later the site of Peter's dream that validates his preaching to Gentiles (VII.i.576–77).[18] The next chapter, describing Tristram's seasickness in a storm in the channel, apparently defines him as a Jonah, not a Peter. The allusion to the prophet who fled into storm to avoid speaking God's message points to Tristram's ambivalent sense of his fleeing and writing: *sic transit.*

Tristram's book, a monument to transience, is informed with the sense of the mutability of what he represents in it and the triviality of what is less transient. The reader of travels who wishes to know the "length, breadth, and perpendicular height" of a building is contemptuously dismissed, while Janatone, who "carriest the principles of change within thy frame," must be measured now (VII.ix.589). Tristram's very writing is a metaphor for mortality. While a building may represent itself for "fifty years to come" (not, incidentally, a very long historical frame), "every letter I trace tells me with what rapidity Life follows my pen" (IX.viii.754). The analogy of pen to life's frailty is elsewhere apparent. Having written about the crushing of his nose in childhood, Tristram remarks on his "sympathetic breast" that leads him to dip his pen with "sad composure and solemnity" while writing of his father's sorrows at his son's misadventure, contrasting this movement of the pen with his more usual one of "dropping thy pen,—spurting thy ink about thy table and thy books,——as if thy pen and thy ink, thy books and thy furniture cost thee nothing" (III.xxviii.254). The involvement here would appear to be with his own body as well as sympathetically with his father—nose, pen, and spurting ink suggest perhaps ejaculation but also bleeding, death counterpoised to generation, transience to creation.

Tristram's narrative becomes itself a figure of disintegration. Tristram finds it increasingly difficult to keep it "tight together" in anyone else's fancy, and he also admits to losing his own way (VI.xxxiii.557–58). Early in the book he promised an aid, "a map, now in the hands of the engraver . . . by way of commentary, scholium, illustration, and key to such passages, incidents, or inuendos as shall be thought to be either of private interpretation, or of dark or doubtful meaning after my life and my opinions shall have been read over" (I.xiii.40). Derived from Swift's *Tale,* this passage promises a critical apparatus to recover the book even before it is well underway, a testimony to the sense of mortality that is woven into it.

Poised in opposing tension to the disintegrating narrative of *Tristram Shandy* is the book as object. But while its palpability denies the metaphysical claims of its disintegration, its very bodily status allies it with the grave. The black page and the marbled page, a comment on the book as body, claim the richness of emblem, revelatory of meanings more complex than the linearity of narrative allows. However, both express the dead end of narrative rather than an escape from it. The mystery they reveal even as they conceal is chaos and night. The black page expresses the incomprehension arising from the absolute incommensurability of death, and the "motly" marbled page, which has been plausibly identified as an end paper, expresses the chaos of narrative and of the book, which can be concluded or continued by the arbitrary insertion or removal of such a page. Tristram's mocking remarks to the reader hint at the inarticulateness of these chosen emblems: "for without *much reading,* by which your reverence knows, I mean *much knowledge,* you will no more be able to penetrate the moral of the next marbled page (motly emblem of my work!) than the world with all its sagacity has been able to unravel the many opinions, transactions and truths which still lie mystically hid under the dark veil of the black one" (III.xxxvi.268).

References to mystical and allegorical meanings occur frequently in *Tristram Shandy,* allusions to the comprehensive interpretive scheme for the Bible that was devised by medieval Christianity and retained in part by Protestantism. This allegorical system connected Old and New Testaments as one unified narrative, beginning with creation and ending at the world's end. So comprehensive a scheme invites application to the human history that lies between the represented past and the forecasted future. It encompasses both the historical (in the sense of a particularized past and present subject to the vicissitudes of time) and the eternal (a pattern that is fixed and subsumes the historical). To embrace these realms it postulates two kinds of authorship, divine and human. The Bible then expands the private visions of its human authors, adding eternal to historical meaning.

Seventeenth-century Protestantism had kept and expanded one aspect of the allegorical tradition—typology, which had the function of connecting events and characters in the Old Testament to their fuller realization and more complete understanding in the New. This kind of typology was often extended to post-biblical history, and characters and events from the Bible represented a potential range of historical behavior that allowed all people to understand themselves in relation to biblical patterns.[19] But in eighteenth-century thought this expanded typology was persistently restricted. In *The Divine Legation of Moses,* for example, William Warburton finds both types and secondary senses only in the Old Testament, as their sole function is to prophesy Christ. Although the extension of the Bible to contemporary history had meaning to many in relation to apocalyptic thinking as found in the books of *Daniel* and *Revelation,* the easy personal connection between daily life and biblical pattern that one finds reflected in Bunyan and, to a lesser extent, in Defoe is suspect.

Walter Shandy's theory of names has an apparent affinity with typology. He sees names as passing on at least some of the powers of their own significance as acquired either from etymology or their former owners. This kind of typology has a hermeneutic as well as a prophetic function, for it connects a word to a tradition of language, history, or literature that implies a larger range of reference than the personal concerns of its author. It locates a book among other books, implying a meaningful structure in which private eccentricity may be corrected. This expansiveness, however, is frustrated in Sterne's book. Walter Shandy's theories about names are at best the object of a smile, and they are vulnerable even to the ridicule of Trim and Toby: "had my name been *Alexander,* I could have done no more at *Namur* than my duty" says Toby; "does a man think of his christian name when he goes upon the attack?" cries Trim (IV.xviii.352). Walter's own associations with Job are mired in historical questions about the personage who is, or might have been, his prototype.

Sterne's book, then, dissolves the public claims of allegory, showing it to have its roots in that small world which is measured early in *Tristram Shandy,* "a small circle described upon the circle of the great world, of four *English* miles diameter" (I.vii.10). Meanings are linked not to universal history but to "world" history. A direct quotation of the Bible may function appositely but not prophetically, for it is susceptible of as many meanings as are derivable from human psychology: " '*Make them like unto a wheel,*' is a bitter sarcasm, as all the learned know, against the *grand tour,* and that restless spirit for making it, which David prophetically foresaw would haunt the children of men in the latter days; and therefore, as thinketh the great bishop Hall, 'tis one of the severest imprecations which David ever utter'd against the enemies of the Lord. . . . Now, I (being very thin) think differently; and that so much of motion, is so much of life, and so much of joy——and that to stand still, or get on but slowly, is death and the devil" (VII.xiii.592–93).

Like allegory, *Tristram Shandy* is a testament to the fecundity of language, yet the irrepressible possibilities in language that it celebrates are mutable, subject to decay and death. Language may keep alive what would be otherwise irretrievably lost, yet the forms of linguistic life are themselves constantly changing in analogy to, but not identically with, what they purport to represent. As Walter remarks apropos of the death of his son Bobby, "The fairest towns that ever the sun rose upon, are now no more: the names only are left, and those (for many of them are wrong spelt) are falling themselves by piecemeals to decay, and in length of time will be forgotten, and involved with every thing in a perpetual night" (V.iii.422). Walter's reflections on mutability have sources in earlier literature, yet in this book, with its awareness of the materiality of the text, such traditional reflections take on a new force.

This novel, then, reflects for us that separation between presence and medium that was exacerbated by eighteenth-century historical and religious scholarship. Sterne exposes the processes of narrative representation, showing us that his story is the product of the interaction of the narrator Tristram with the limited possibilities of his medium, as well as with the reality or being that the story purports to represent. Sterne exhibits the narrator/author's struggle with a posited prior reality, producing a sense of an incomplete movement toward his chosen subject rather than a final representation of it. While enticing the reader sympathetically toward the subject matter, this treatment also undermines the moral vision that is overtly communicated. The represented process of representing goodness allows for no easy uncritical overflow of emotions in sympathy with the characters. The sympathetic imagination is checked by the difficulties of interpretation.[20] What is purported to occur is past, mediated by an observer who is himself dependent on documents and hearsay, and whose account is mired in the intransigence of his narrative medium. *Tristram Shandy* conveys to us the power of an admirable moral vision, and also the limitations of viewpoint, the deficiencies of documents, and the impediments of narrative that leave that moral vision obscured and problematic.[21]

Sterne's relentless exposure of the weak foundations for many of the putative facts of *Tristram Shandy* and of the evanescence of the medium as well as of its creator reveals the analogous entanglement with death of other eighteenth-century novels.[22] The new fiction's robust attempts to ally itself with contemporaneous life frequently take the form of claiming the authenticity of history and consequently emphasizing the pastness of any narrative representation. What Ian Watt names "formal realism" calls attention to the need to verify and thus resuscitate a life and condition that are mutable and perhaps extinct.[23] Defoe and Richardson use the figure of the editor to sustain the illusion of the novel as authentic document, but, as Sterne recognized, the editorial fiction actuates the search for an always receding ground. For example, *Robinson Crusoe* is cast into a retrospective autobiographical form, but the implicit claim of authenticity and presence of the first person narrator is insufficient and is supplemented by a journal putatively written during the isolation of the island and inserted into the text by an editorial operation of the narrator. This journal embedded in the larger narrative becomes one of the events of the island, a thing brought back to attest to the past or historical presence of the seemingly present narrator. Richardson's epistolary method, too, is an attempt, more systematic than Defoe's, to give both presence and historical contiguity to the narrator. "Writing to the moment" puts the narrator authentically close to the narrated event, and, more important, the narration itself thus becomes a significant part of the event. But having narrowed the gap between word and event, Richardson needs someone to textualize the words, to account for their order of presentation and their mode of transmission, in short, to authenticate them despite their acknowledged temporal separation from us. The editor is the collector and organizer of the letters, witness to their authenticity and also to their literariness, which

he orders as well as recognizes. He vouches for them, making them documents of a presence that is, nevertheless, past. The editor, to some extent,
replaces the seer.[24]

The understanding of textual criticism as a struggle with time and death
is not unusual in the eighteenth century. Swift's *Tale* of course plays unmercifully with the modern abrogation of the past, dedicated as the *Tale* is to
Prince Posterity but also giving grudging acknowledgement to "the Restorers
of Antient Learning from the Worms, and Graves, and Dust of Manuscripts."[25] Textual critics of the Bible such as Simon and Bentley recognize
the mortality even of Scripture, seeing it as subject to the same vicissitudes as
classical texts: according to Richard Simon, "the misfortune of Time and the
negligence of Transcribers have wrought changes in the holy Scriptures as
well as in prophane Authours."[26] Sterne's book is an even fuller recognition
of the great goddess Mutability. Commonly recognized as a complex parody
of conventional narrative procedures, *Tristram Shandy* is also an analysis of the
mortality of our very representations of the mortal. Sterne's novel shows that
by claiming the authenticity of history, the new fiction of the eighteenth century undermines the very claims of history on which it founds itself. In his
parody of narrative representation, Sterne discloses the skull that lies beneath
the flesh of history as well as of fiction.

Notes

1. J. Hillis Miller, "Narrative and History," *ELH,* 41 (1974), 455–73, discusses the
frequent claim of the novel to be history and the concomitant questioning of history when narrative is subverted by the novel. Leo Braudy, *Narrative Form in History and Fiction: Hume, Fielding, and Gibbon* (Princeton, 1970), discusses the efforts of both novelists and historians in the
eighteenth century "to form time, to discover its plot, and to give a compelling and convincing
narrative shape to the facts of human life" (p. 3). Of the novelists, Fielding alone is discussed
extensively. Hayden White analyzes the similar structures in fiction and history in several discussions, including "The Fictions of Factual Representation," where he asserts that "the techniques or strategies that historians and writers of fiction use in the composition of their discourses can be shown to be substantially the same, however different they may appear on a
purely surface, or dictional, level of their texts" (*Tropics of Discourse: Essays in Cultural Criticism*
[Baltimore, 1978], p. 121). The relationship of *Tristram Shandy* to historical writing is discussed by several critics. In "The Time Scheme of *Tristram Shandy* and a Source," *PMLA,* 51
(1936), 803–20, Theodore Baird finds that Rapin's *History of England* as continued by Tindal is
a major source for dates and allusions in *Tristram Shandy* and that historical events "exist in the
consciousness of Sterne's characters in the way that a contemporary historic event exists in our
minds today" (p. 804). In "Sterne and Late Eighteenth-Century Ideas of History," *Eighteenth-
Century Life,* 7 (1981), 25–53, Stuart Peterfreund argues that "Sterne felt the need to articulate
an idea of history in the dearth of any adequate idea available to him" (p. 26). He sees Sterne as
responding to concerns similar to those of Gibbon, Hume, and Kant, who "repudiated the
hope cherished previously by the 'scientific' historians, the hope of pursuing the study of history with total detachment and objectivity, and complete authority in meaning" (p. 33). In this

paper, I focus on questions of source, text, and transmission, as well as of interpretation, that are raised within *Tristram Shandy,* and I link Sterne's book to the development of eighteenth-century historical and religious scholarship.

2. Joseph M. Levine, *Dr. Woodward's Shield: History, Science, and Satire in Augustan England* (Berkeley, 1977), p. 210, summarizes in his chapter on Henry Dodwell some of the alterations of method in eighteenth-century historical scholarship:

> Indeed, Dodwell's criticism, like that of the best of his contemporaries, had advanced beyond the possibilities of Renaissance philology. Scholars of 1700 were no longer content to discover and to expose legend and forgery; they had begun the task of reconstruction as well. Thus they understood that it was not enough simply to accept or to reject the testimony of the Latin historians, but that their authorities and the sources of their authorities would have first to be reconstituted and as far as possible criticized. Every scrap of information from all of classical literature that might help to describe those lost works would have to be employed. Behind Livy lay annals; behind the annals, the *Libri lintei* and other possible authorities. Although almost all of this had disappeared, it might yet be painstakingly restored from the hints and fragments of later writers. The critical regression was infinite, but infinitely rewarding.

3. Ronald Paulson, *Satire and the Novel in Eighteenth-Century England* (New Haven, 1967), pp. 248–62, places *Tristram Shandy* in the context of eighteenth-century satire, pointing out changed directions in Sterne's work. Melvyn New, *Laurence Sterne as Satirist* (Gainesville, 1969), deals with *Tristram Shandy* as a variant of eighteenth-century satire, especially of *A Tale of a Tub.*

4. *A Discourse of Free-Thinking, Occasion'd by the Rise and Growth of a Sect Call'd Free-Thinkers* (London, 1713), p. 72. Subsequent references are in the text.

5. *Remarks Upon a late Discourse of Free-Thinking,* . . . , 6th edn. (Cambridge, 1725), p. 66. Subsequent references are in the text.

6. Richard Jacobson, "Absence, Authority, and the Text," *Glyph,* 3 (1976), 137–47, describes a similar situation after the final priestly redaction of the Pentateuch. Prophecy is antagonistic to the idea of the fixed text.

7. Ed. James Holly Hanford and Waldo Hilary Dunn, trans. Charles R. Sumner, *The Works of John Milton,* vol. 16 (New York, 1934), pp. 277, 279.

8. Rudolph Pfeiffer, *History of Classical Scholarship from 1300 to 1850* (Oxford, 1976), remarks that Bentley's writing of his *Dissertation Upon the Epistles of Phalaris* in English instead of Latin was "an innovation that marks an epoch in classical scholarship" (p. 150).

9. William Warburton, *The Divine Legation of Moses Demonstrated,* 2 vols. (1744; rpt London, 1837).

10. "Sterne, Warburton, and the Burden of Exuberant Wit," *Eighteenth-Century Studies,* 15 (1981–1982), 245–74.

11. See Arthur H. Cash, *Laurence Sterne: The Early and Middle Years* (London, 1975), pp. 278–80.

12. Hans W. Frei, *The Eclipse of Biblical Narrative: A Study of Eighteenth and Nineteenth Century Hermeneutics* (New Haven, 1974), gives an account of the impact of eighteenth-century historicism on biblical hermeneutics: "interpretation was a matter of fitting the biblical story into another world with another story rather than incorporating that world into the biblical story" (p. 130).

13. *A Critical Dissertation on the Book of Job* (London, 1751), p. 3. Subsequent references are in the text.

14. *The Presence of the Word* (New Haven, 1967), p. x.

15. Jay Arnold Levine, "The Design of *A Tale of a Tub* (with a Digression on a Mad Modern Critic)," *ELH*, 33 (1966), 198–227, discusses many parallels between *A Tale of a Tub* and the issues of biblical criticism that were current in Swift's time.

16. Elizabeth W. Harries, "Sterne's Novels: Gathering Up the Fragments," *ELH*, 49 (1982), sees connections between Sterne's fiction and the eighteenth-century awareness of "antique and 'Gothick' fragments," including the excavations at Herculanaeum and Pompeii (p. 36). (Reprinted in this volume.)

17. Jean-Claude Sallé, "A State of Warfare: Some Aspects of Time and Chance in *Tristram Shandy*," in *Quick Springs of Sense: Studies in the Eighteenth Century*, ed. Larry S. Champion (Athens, GA, 1974), argues that Sterne saw "The writer's creation making up, by its intensity, for the brevity of life" (p. 220).

18. *Florida Notes to Tristram Shandy* identifies the relevant biblical passages (p. 446).

19. J. Paul Hunter discusses this relationship of Puritans and dissenters to the Bible in *The Reluctant Pilgrim: Defoe's Emblematic Method and Quest for Form in Robinson Crusoe* (Baltimore, 1966), Ch. V, "Metaphor, Type, Emblem, and the Pilgrim Allegory." Barbara Lewalski, *Protestant Poetics and the Seventeenth-Century Religious Lyric* (Princeton, 1979), comments that Protestants generally were invited to see salvation history "recapitulated in their lives" (p. 131).

20. R. F. Brissenden, *Virtue in Distress: Studies in the Novel of Sentiment from Richardson to Sade* (London, 1974), suggests that "there appears to be a conflict between the inner life of the novel and its outer form"; "although Sterne's method of presenting the Shandys ultimately strengthens our sense of their reality it frustrates our attempt to involve ourselves with them" (pp. 190, 191).

21. Leo Braudy, "The Form of the Sentimental Novel," *Novel*, 7 (1973), 5–13, argues compellingly that the form of the sentimental novel derives from Richardson and Defoe and reflects the desire to make form adhere to feeling. What I suggest here is that Sterne understands a fragmentary form, needing an editor to provide coherence, as a form implying disintegration.

22. Robert Alter, *Partial Magic: The Novel as a Self-Conscious Genre* (Berkeley, 1975), remarks that the novel "concentrating on art and the artist" is "even in many of its characteristically comic embodiments, a long meditation on death" (p. 243). H. Porter Abbott, *Diary Fiction: Writing as Action* (Ithaca, NY, 1984), Ch. 10, "Samuel Beckett and the Death of the Book," discusses the paradoxical relationship of the material text and the spirit in Beckett, connecting his discussion to eighteenth-century fiction, especially Richardson. Garrett Stewart, *Death Sentences: Styles of Dying in British Fiction* (Cambridge, MA, 1984), analyzes the metaphoric implications of death scenes in fiction. Stewart's book deals primarily with later fiction but includes glances at Richardson and Sterne.

23. *The Rise of the Novel* (Berkeley, 1956), Ch. I.

24. The fiction of a recovered document presented by an editor long predates the eighteenth century. See, for example, *Don Quixote*, and examples in Percy G. Adams, *Travel Literature and the Evolution of the Novel* (Lexington, 1983), p. 98. I suggest, however, that in the eighteenth century this fiction engages the implications of a new historiography and more technical and critical editorial practices.

25. *A Tale of a Tub*, ed. A. C. Guthkelch and D. Nichol Smith, 2nd edn. (Oxford, 1958), p. 93.

26. *A Critical History of the Old Testament*, trans. Richard Hampden [?] (London, 1682), pp. 9–10.

Sterne and the Narrative of Determinateness

Melvyn New

> The reader who demands to know exactly what Sterne really thinks of a thing
> . . . must be given up for lost.[1]
>
> —Friedrich Nietzsche

I will begin with a seemingly non-controversial observation by a recent critic of *Tristram Shandy,* anonymous simply because it is the sort of comment any one of a hundred might write today: "Sterne's point," he asserts, "is clear enough: life is a confused muddle of intent and accident." It is the sort of generalization many have accepted at least since E.M. Forster in 1927 declared "muddle" to be the God ruling over the work.[2] However, a closer examination of this particular formulation, not a jot different from that of countless others, might suggest an interesting problem. Simply put, if the point of *Tristram Shandy* is *clear,* then the work must be significantly divorced from the life—defined as a "confused muddle of intent and accident"—it portrays. Or, from another perspective, critics who find Sterne's point "clear enough" are themselves divorced from a work they argue is a muddle—and from a life that also does not allow the *clarity* they believe it can have in *Tristram Shandy.* Can one reformulate the observation? Perhaps we might say that "Sterne's point is obscure and muddled; life is a confused muddle and so I, as a reflective reader, become muddled when I try to understand his imitation of that muddle; it is seemingly successful as an imitation, although I cannot be quite clear on that point either." Frankly, I do not foresee this becoming the new mode of critical discourse. In this essay I would like to suggest why not, drawing on what I believe to be Sterne's own encounter with the paradox of the indeterminate text in human hands.

Using *Tristram Shandy* as my model, I specifically want to explore a key means by which its narrative, while pretending to suspend judgment about itself (to remain muddle), simultaneously reminds us of the impossibility of reading without judgment; we are unable to refrain from seeking the definitive statement of what is *clear* about the work. Since the narrative of *Tristram Shandy* is nowadays taken as a prime illustration of disruptive, fragmented, open, disjunctive narrative,[3] it helps us at times to keep our attention not on

Reprinted from *Eighteenth-Century Fiction* 4 (1992): 315–29.

any particular interpretation, but more broadly on the contrasting "stories" people tell about the work, the narratives they initiate in order to organize or possess or subdue Sterne's mysterious text. In brief, while these modernist readers insist that *Tristram Shandy* is an open narrative, they all impose strategies of closure and *clarity* in their own writing upon it.[4]

Sterne had anticipated just such efforts in the characters of Walter and Toby Shandy, both of whom ride very hard the hobby-horse of explication and explanation. What Toby wants to do on the bowling green is to make very *clear* to the observer exactly what happened during the muddle of a real-life battle; what Walter wants to do with his theories, his consultations, his documents is to find very *clear* solutions to the muddle of a real life. In addition, the text of *Tristram* contains numerous interwoven narrative sub-texts that serve as commentaries upon the primary narrative—the marriage contract, the Memoire of the Sorbonne doctors, the sermon, Ernulphus's curse, passages from Burton and Rabelais, Montaigne and Chambers' *Cyclopædia,* and on and on.[5] These "narratives" restage the narrative strategies of the reader/critic, since they are almost always reifications, efforts to organize and control the flux of events and attitudes ("the life and opinions") by narrating them into a fixed (that is, a clear and explicable) order and arrangement. What Sterne shows us, I suggest, is that the instinct or desire to order the story is always more powerful than our capacity to rest in muddle, to celebrate disorder without a contrary urge to tidy up the place. Hence, for both character and reader, the interpolated narrative is almost always considered part of the larger narrative, a relevant commentary (limitation) upon it, rather than a further dislocation or random interference.

Sterne's technique is tied, I believe, to the classical doctrine associated with the sceptic Sextus Empiricus, concerning the inner suspension of judgment (ἐποχή) about the conformity of appearance to reality, that is, the meanings of narrative representations.[6] Like Hume, Sterne seems to suggest that such suspension, while highly desirable and useful, is not often within the human being's capacity—we cannot refrain from believing in the truth of our own perceptions, our own narratives.[7] As Terence Penelhum comments rather wryly in *God and Skepticism:* "Neither the plain man nor the philosopher can refrain from believing that they are veridical. We cannot make our own assertions *un*dogmatically."[8] *Tristram Shandy* explores the delusions of the undogmatic, indeterminate narrative, even while denying its possibility.

If Sterne embraces many strategies of indeterminacy as part of his general sceptical embrace of the mysteries and riddles of experience,[9] he is equally attracted to—indeed, fascinated by—the narrative instinct, the "art" of story-telling, as an emblem of that divine harmony to which he seems to have remained committed. Our narratives are "truths" in so far as they make life possible for us. The inner compulsion not to contradict these truths, the instinct to narrate our stories to some useful conclusion would seem inbred in our use of language; we *are* this instinct, since our being is our narrative. But where twentieth-century philosophy strives to keep our eye fixed always on the naïveté of assuming such narratives are true (the epistemological issue), Sterne's interest was at least equally focused on the comic and tragic impotence that results from insisting they are not—ultimately, an ontological issue. In particular, Sterne seems intent upon ridiculing those critics and nonbelievers *determined* to practise modes of *indeterminacy* and blind to the paradox of doing so.

Several years ago, in the course of a short essay on the process of annotating *Tristram Shandy*'s bawdy, I asked:

> Is there, then, nothing for the annotator to do with Sterne's game of sexual discovery? Is all such mediation an unwarrantable intrusion between the reader and the text, most especially so when the reader's capacity to "get" the text is the game being played? Sterne confronts the problem in the first volume . . . when he sends madam back to reread a chapter, punishment for having missed a clue concerning intrauterine baptism. Here the author plays his own annotator or mediator, forcing all his readers to "get" a text I am certain all will miss on first reading. Sterne's humour depends on requiring from his readers a knowledge they could not possibly be expected to have.[10]

Jonathan Lamb, a recent exuberant proponent of the indecipherable text of *Tristram Shandy* (as his recent book-length explication makes *absolutely clear*),[11] takes me to task for these comments in this manner: "The annotator [argues New] does his duty by 'forcing all his readers to "get" a text I am certain all will miss on first reading.' . . . [T]he absolute jostling [of] the reader in that sentence seems at odds with the relativising tone [New] adopted elsewhere" (p. 3). It is indeed at odds, since the "jostling" reflects Sterne's humorous "theory" of annotating, the "relativising" my serious response to its unacceptability. Lamb, however, is in no mood for such subtle distinctions: "I think it is a pity to strip initiatives from readers in this way, especially in view of the great lengths taken by Sterne to extend them," he laments (p. 3).

I present this exchange between Lamb and my own text not in order to defend the Florida volume of *Notes,* which proved quite useful to him in the course of his study despite his quarrel with its editor, but to argue against his fundamental premise, that Sterne goes to "great lengths" to extend the "initiatives" of the readers. Certainly that is not true in the present instance: Madam is given absolutely no choice but to read the text in one way—Mrs. Shandy was not a papist, and the documentation for that reasoned conclusion is provided—signed, sealed, and delivered—in French *and* English. Does the reader have a choice? Can it be somehow argued that the text (the Sorbonne's, Sterne's, Madam's) remains undetermined at this point? But the very issue being discussed by the Sorbonne is an emblem of absolute determinacy; not a scintilla of doubt will be able to survive the work of the doctors. Every question, every doubt, every possible avenue of uncertainty will be put to rest, brought to a satisfying conclusion, canonized into law; doubt will be turned into certainty before it is allowed to leave the womb.

The world that Sterne represents may be a muddle as has been suggested, but it is peopled by multitudes (inside the book *and* holding the book) with brooms and pens, *petites canulles* and swords, diagrams and models and paradigms, all intent on tidying up the place, making it neat and *clear*. There is, in short, no sufficient difference between the learned doctors of the Sorbonne and the learned doctors of today's academy: all work to establish the laws, the principles (the "double principle," in Lamb's case) that will make the muddle of life and its literature *clearer* and hence—no slight benefit— keep the proponents of such principles in positions of authority and acclaim. Sterne celebrates this tendency in Toby and Walter, in the doctors of the Sorbonne, in encyclopaedists, in classical and theological scholars, in men like Obadiah Walker[12] and Bishop Warburton.[13] His book celebrates them all, but the appreciation is tempered by his jealous rivalry with their seemingly boundless energies; and by his chastising reminders—satiric and Christian— that human wisdom is a constant dupe to its own aspirations.

The pattern of indeterminacy being put to rest by one means or another is, to my mind, as prevalent in *Tristram Shandy* as the opposing tendency, undeniably present, of shattering certainties into fragments of ambivalence and belief. The modern critical agenda, however, focuses all its interest on the second tendency. There is not a serious work of literature, from Homer to Dante, from Shakespeare to Joyce, that has not been shown to be indeterminate, a uniformity that alone might give wisdom pause, as might the absolute *sameness* with which the prevalence of *difference* is everywhere celebrated. Such paradoxes hover at the edges of Sterne's particular plan to confront us with our inability to remain in "uncertainties, Mysteries, doubts, without any irritable reaching after fact & reason."[14] And from the very beginning Sterne offers us a series of documents within *Tristram* that mimic—in their absoluteness and totality, their clarity, their principles of elucidation and discovery— the discourse of criticism that has accompanied Sterne's work from the beginning; the cant of criticism—a wonderful pun—he calls it at one important point.[15]

We are told, by Tristram and others, that this is the most cooperative book ever written, that we are joint sharers in its creation, half and half with its author.[16] But surely in the instance of the Sorbonne doctors, we have no such creative freedom. Even if we refuse to return with Madam to reread the passage, I do not think a similar option is available to deny Tristram's purpose in introducing the Memoire (I.xx.67–69), namely, to document certainty, not induce uncertainty. Such moves are seen everywhere in *Tristram,* beginning perhaps in chapter iv of the first volume, where Tristram consults a "memorandum in my father's pocket-book" concerning his whereabouts in the months prior to his son's conception. Then, in chapter xv, we are given, verbatim, the article in the marriage settlement that defines Mrs. Shandy's movements—and the codicil offered by Toby that slams shut the one slight evasion she might have exercised. Moreover, these documents do work: they confront issues that are undecided, and they decide them. Would we want to enter into a dispute with the Sorbonne doctors concerning the legitimacy of their findings? Are we invited to question the authorship of Walter's memorandum? Are we tempted to challenge the marriage settlement in court? Clearly Sterne is here not sharing his story-telling with the reader, but, quite the contrary, setting out one boundary at which language does serve human purposes—authorization, communication, control.

To be sure, these documents are parodies of the real things—or real documents in parodic situations, as is the case with the major interpolated document in volume II, the "Abuses of Conscience" sermon. For, ultimately, Sterne is not putting his faith in human language as the ultimate source of certitude; no one, not Locke in his much misunderstood (among Sterneans) *Essay Concerning Human Understanding,* or even Swift, with his maligned academy, believed in such a possibility, the eternal contradiction between "human" and "certitude" being essential to a religious construct all three accepted. But neither does Sterne put his faith in gesture, sentiment, or sympathy, the popular answers of the Shaftesburian "evasion," the fallacies of which the "Abuses" sermon directly addresses.[17]

Nor, finally, does he seem quite at home, this rural Anglican clergyman, in the indeterminate, existential, absurd, phenomenological, solipsistic universe where we nowadays seem to find him. Rather, the documents interpolated everywhere into the world of *Tristram Shandy* seem to me overt examples of one of Sterne's richest observations: the human being produces such texts, in one form or another, *endlessly, necessarily, inevitably.* The copy of *Tristram* we hold in our hands is one such document, Walter Shandy's *Tristrapædia* is another, Slawkenbergius's tome and this brief essay are also examples, and the works of Rabelais and Montaigne and Burton, whose texts reappear in *Tristram* as part of its "documentation," are all restagings of the instinct, the drive to order and comprehend through our language whatever is not yet our language. The urge not merely to begin but to *complete* the narrative of ourselves is evident everywhere in *Tristram Shandy.* That we fail to do so could easily be explained for Sterne within the Christian narrative of sin (human limitation) and death (its consequence). Why we nonetheless continue to *essay* to "tell all" (and it is Montaigne who most clearly literalizes this urge), to make absolutely, positively certain that we have found the fullest measure of explanation and definition, the ever-replenishing cornucopia of endless discourse, that is a question less easily answered and the one I believe particularly fascinated Sterne.[18]

I believe I could make my point with the "Abuses" sermon; or with Ernulphus's curse (a memorial to the urge for closure and the resourcefulness of language); or with "Slawkenbergius's Tale," perhaps Sterne's most extended analysis of the noise and dangers of endless commentary.[19] Indeed, almost all Sterne's interpolated documents respond to what I have defined as a quest for certainty and determinacy (documentation), perhaps because their received form as "supporting evidence" is the outcome of our own need to define, explain, and comprehend. Can we imagine, for example, a discussion of the "Abuses" sermon that suggests it has absolutely nothing to do with *Tristram Shandy*? Could we substitute another sermon in its place (perhaps by Sterne, perhaps by Donne) and argue that it would not matter? Such hypothetical silliness can often serve to test the more serious absurdities of our present critical environment.

I would like to focus attention, however, on two interpolated documents rarely commented upon among Sterneans, the first, Rubenius's *De Re Vestiaria Veterum,* which Walter is said to consult for the breeching of Tristram in volume VI; and the second, Spencer's *De Legibus Hebræorum Ritualibus,* which comes into play in chapter xxviii of volume V after Tristram's accident with the window sash.

Albert Rubens (1614–1657) catalogues the clothing of the ancients in a large quarto that wavers between the old style of learning and the new, between the universal citing of past authorities in the hope that truth would emerge from the welter of contrary opinions, and the beginnings of a more scientific orientation that accumulates and catalogues data as the foundation for further generalization. As such, *De Re Vestiaria Veterum, Præcipue de Lato Clavo (Of the Clothing of the Ancients, Particularly of the Latus Clavus,* 1665) is typical of late seventeenth-century learning, and Sterne seems brilliantly to have caught its genius in his reduction of Rubenius to lists, the cataloguing of knowledge in a manner that suggests above all the growing importance of distinction and difference. For example, Sterne lists eighteen different types of shoe, beginning with

> The open shoe.
> The close shoe.
> The slip shoe.
> The wooden shoe. . . . (VI.xix.531)

This listing, with its vertical presentation—an echo, perhaps, of similar lists in Rabelais—is of especial interest because Walter cannot find in it or in the various other lists of *De Re Vestiaria* the advice concerning breeches that he is looking for. What he does find is a wealth of argumentation, the concentration of energy into a single point upon which the learned of the world converge in their determination to settle a question—absolutely, definitively, and with the greatest clarity possible, namely, the identification of the *Latus Clavus:*

> *Rubenius* told him, that the point was still litigating amongst the learned:—
> That *Egnatius, Sigonius, Bossius Ticinensis, Bayfius, Budæus, Salmasius, Lipsius,*

Lazius, Isaac Causabon, and *Joseph Scaliger,* all differed from each other,—and he from them: That some took it to be the button,—some the coat itself,—others only the colour of it. (532)

Walter—and indeed Rubens before him—finds in this collection of data not a point of certainty but simply another list, this time of a community of scholars, a source of comfortable companionship that enables Walter to proceed with his life, whatever obstacles he encounters. Moreover, if the first list suggests to us the elusiveness, indeed impossibility, of the quest for "truth," for "the key," the second list just as certainly and dramatically indicates the refusal of the human mind to surrender to that impossibility.[20] The great satirists of scholastic learning who preceded Sterne—Rabelais and Swift— share with him an ambivalence towards learning that perhaps only the best ironists (and best sceptics) can have.

We must, however, qualify the list of authorities in two ways. In the first place, Sterne informs us that "the great *Bayfius,*" listed among the disputants, in reality "honestly said, he knew not what it was,—whether a fibula,—a stud,—a button,—a loop,—a buckle,—or clasps and keepers" (532). In a disputatious world of thesis and antithesis, statement and counterstatement, the admission of "ignorance," of "doubt," gives particular weight to the word "honestly." But Walter's response, typical of the learned world in general, indicates that "doubt" is simply not a satisfactory resting place for the restless mind: "———My father lost the horse, but not the saddle———They are *hooks and eyes,* said my father———and with hooks and eyes he ordered my breeches to be made" (533). The sceptical moment of ἐποχή, the suspension between equally interesting alternatives, is unsustainable because "interest," a word weighted with theological as well as moral meaning in the eighteenth century,[21] denies us the pleasure and satisfaction we might otherwise take in stasis. For Sterne, the idea is embodied most often in the concept of the hobbyhorse: to be thrown from one's horse, like Dr. Slop in volume III or Walter in this passage, is typical of the Shandy world; to dismount, as Bayfius appears to have done, is an heroic moment rarely encountered—except in the important normative actions of Yorick.

Second, and surely of no small significance to our present discussion, it is to be suspected that Sterne's discussion of clothing is indeed not from Rubens, that his citation is a false one. The Florida *Notes* suggests that while the list of authorities might have been gleaned from the first chapter of *De Re Vestiaria,* Sterne's other lists and the language of his discussion follow much more closely Lefèvre de Morsan's *The Manners and Customs of the Romans. Translated from the French* (1740). This is a handbook of Roman costume probably intended for schools; and precisely its commonplace nature suggests that Sterne may have used not it but a similar "textbook" as yet undiscovered.[22] In rather stark contrast to the "honesty" celebrated in Bayfius, we have here a seeming instance of basic scholarly dishonesty: deliberate miscitation. Walter's authorization to move forward collapses, the cited author and his text disappear, the determinations and absolutes of the learned prove to be indeterminate after all. Here, perhaps, is the muddle that Forster identified, the loss of "author(ity)" that makes *Tristram Shandy* seem so modern a work. I suggest, however, that the discovery upon which this collapse depends is not something Sterne could—or would—count upon. Indeed, quite the opposite. The annotator here creates an indeterminacy (two hundred years after the work's appearance) that Sterne made every effort to foreclose in a most time-honoured manner—by citing learned authority. It seems important to Sterne's conception of Walter that he participate in the community of scholars represented by Rubenius, that his researches be thorough and his consultations authentic; at the very least, there is nothing in the text that serves as a clue to the imposition of Rubenius upon unsuspecting readers.[23] One might argue, of course, that none of Sterne's citations is to be trusted, that the unreliability of Tristram as a narrator is constructed from the materials of false learning, but this is precisely to confuse the ontological question with the epistemological.

Sterne's point depends upon the reality of his documentation, the fact that the Sorbonne Memoire, the "Abuses" sermon, Ernulphus's curse, all actually exist; how true they are to the reality they attempt to define is a quite separate matter. But while it serves Sterne's purpose for the reader to recognize, for example, Tristram's attack on plagiary at the opening of volume V as a "steal" from Burton,[24] here his purpose seems best served by the sense of closure and determinateness produced in Walter after his consultation with "authority." Or again, where we are not asked to think of Slawkenbergius as anything other than a fabrication, here we are quite directed to the narrator's learning, not his invention, as a source of knowledge. Such distinctions are vital to our reading of Sterne because they indicate a more balanced perspective on, among other things, the documentation that is so inherent a part of the *Shandy* text itself. It is, indeed, no wonder that Tristram and his annotators should so often cross paths, since he, like them, expends much energy in the pursuit of authority, documentation, and closure; unfortunately in this instance, the annotator may have opened a door (extended an "initiative" in Lamb's terminology) that Sterne had gone to "great lengths" to close.

Unlike the other disasters that befall Walter and Tristram, the falling window sash finds the father quite prepared. He does not write about it, as we might assume—that response is reserved for Tristram, who *"completes"* (my emphasis) the *Tristrapædia* with his own chapter on sash-windows and chamber pots (V.xxvi.458–59). Rather, he turns to his library, to some heavy folios, while Mrs. Shandy runs for the "lint and basilicon." What is Walter looking for in these tomes, and specifically in John Spencer's *De Legibus Hebræorum Ritualibus (On the Ritual Laws of the Hebrews),* published twenty years after Rubenius on Roman costumes? Not simply consolation or curatives, for he has not proceeded very long before he is deep in controversy, a war of words, the futility and frustration of both history and language.

The parodic use of the documents we noted before is especially apparent here, both because of the subject matter and Yorick's guiding presence. Most important, Yorick knows the text beforehand, and the learning represented by four Greek footnotes is in response to his familiarity with Spencer's learned work. Hence, when Walter is about to let us know just what the theologians have debated, Yorick interrupts: "Theologically? said *Yorick,*—or speaking after the manner of apothecaries?—statesmen?—or washer-women?" (V.xxviii.461). The three groups are footnoted, Sterne (Yorick) responding to phrases he found in Spencer, one having to do with disease (anthrax), another with population, a third with cleanliness.[25] Yorick's position is significantly ambivalent, however; he knows the text (as did Sterne, obviously),[26] but he can wish he did not, and when Toby suggests it is all *Arabick to* him, Yorick chimes in, "I wish . . . 'twas so, to half the world." At this point, Walter's reading lapses quite into controversy. Having more or less ignored the opportunity to discuss whether the Jews or Egyptians practised circumcision first (which certainly occupies pages of Spencer and would occupy Bishop Warburton among many others),[27] he finds himself suddenly on the shoals of Ilus's identity and the controvertists' "two and twenty reasons" for his circumcising his entire army—a question which, significantly, immediately involves Toby's "determinate" nature as well: "Not without a court martial?" (462). Perhaps Spencer, perhaps Walter's obvious enjoyment of the controversy, leads Yorick to an attack on polemic divines: "I wish there was not a polemic divine . . . in the kingdom;—one ounce of practical divinity—is worth a painted ship load of all their reverences have imported these fifty years" (462); and in the next chapter, he reads Rabelais's description of Gymnast and Tripet's riding competition (another document!—and one that Yorick keeps in his coat pocket),[28] which serves to pin down in all our minds, exactly and definitely and determinately, Yorick's attitude towards the cavortings of the intellectual community. Yet Yorick's "familiarity" with Spencer suggests as well his community with that world of books and words. Significantly, it is the same community that Walter looks for when he seeks in *De Legibus* a consolation for the maiming of Tristram:

> Nay, said he, mentioning the name of a different great nation upon every step as he set his foot upon it—if the EGYPTIANS,—the SYRIANS,—the PHOENICIANS,—the ARABIANS,—the CAPADOCIANS,——if the COLCHI, and TROGLODYTES did it——if SOLON and PYTHAGORAS submitted,—what is TRISTRAM? ——Who am I, that I should fret or fume one moment about the matter? (V.xxvii.460)

Whether it is the link that Sterne forges with Rabelais at the end of this scene, the link with Shakespeare inherent in the naming of Yorick, or the link with a world of past scholars and churchmen, and the lost cultures of the past (and we must remember that volume V opens with a somewhat parallel passage, again an interpolated document, Cicero's consolatory letter to Sulpicius, by way of Burton's *Anatomy of Melancholy*),[29] one has here, I suggest, an answer to the question posed earlier: why do we continue to talk and write and exercise our language in the pursuit of knowledge, definition, unattainable clarity, and wisdom?

The real community of *Tristram Shandy* is not, as is so often said, simply that of the Shandy brothers; rather, it is represented by all the authors and books, all their documents and cultures and artifacts, all that illustrates to us what it means to live in a world written by God, and hence always approximated by the same human endeavour. At times the documents are necessarily ludicrous, as is so much human effort in the face of the infinite, but at other times they are useful and perhaps even profound, as human effort can also be. Sterne keeps us aware of both possibilities, and aware above all that while every attempt to create a world of certainty and truth will fail, the attempt is what ties us to the community of humanity, what offers us the equivalent of communion with our legacy, and, in the end, allows us to create, if not God's world, then our own world in imitation of His. Writing seems to have been an activity Sterne delighted in, not as an epistemological experience, but an ontological one. Sterne's "documents" suggest to me that the present emphasis in narrative theory on the epistemology of indeterminacy is a tendency he might have predicted but never have succumbed to. Sterne's fiction arises, to the contrary, in the ontology of the human urge to speak the truth.

That that urge so often takes the shape of fiction and folly is nothing that was not explained to him by his faith, and redeemed by it as well. Nietzsche is one of his few readers who seems fully to appreciate Sterne's ontological bent: "his antipathy to seriousness is united with a tendency to be unable to regard anything merely superficially. Thus he produces in the right reader a feeling of uncertainty as to whether one is walking, standing or lying: a feeling, that is, close to floating."[30] Classical scepticism might call it hovering between all possibilities, but I suspect Nietzsche, Sterne, and Sextus Empiricus each had a nicely muddled idea (*clarity* would not suffice) of approximately the same thing.

Notes

1.   Friedrich Nietzsche, *Human, All Too Human,* trans. R.J. Hollingdale (Cambridge: Cambridge University Press, 1986), pp. 238–39.
2.   "Obviously a god is hidden in *Tristram Shandy* and his name is Muddle, and some readers cannot accept him," *Aspects of the Novel* (New York: Harcourt, 1927), p. 146.
3.   See, for example, J. Hillis Miller, "Narrative Middles: A Preliminary Outline," *Genre* 11 (1978), 375–87; Ralph Flores, "Changeling Fathering: *Tristram Shandy,*" in *The Rhetoric of Doubtful Authority: Deconstructive Readings of Self-Questioning Narratives, St. Augustine to Faulkner* (Ithaca: Cornell University Press, 1984), pp. 116–44; and Jonathan Lamb, *Sterne's Fiction and the Double Principle* (Cambridge: Cambridge University Press, 1989).

4.　The most glaring instance is Wolfgang Iser's *Laurence Sterne: "Tristram Shandy"* (Cambridge: Cambridge University Press, 1988), where the reading of *Tristram* as an indeterminate text turns Sterne into both a forerunner and strict proponent of Iser's own critical theories. See also Robert Markley, *"Tristram Shandy* and 'Narrative Middles': Hillis Miller and the Style of Deconstructive Criticism," *Genre* 17 (1984), 179–90, an attempt to justify Miller's obfuscations while at the same time "translating" them into what might pass for a transparent (i.e., a *clear*) expository prose.

5.　This structure of borrowings is apparent on almost every page of *Tristram Shandy: The Notes;* one need only compare these notes with those required for Fielding's or Smollett's fictions (excepting *Adventures of an Atom*) in the Wesleyan and Georgia editions respectively to realize a fundamental difference between Sterne and the novelists with whom he is most often grouped.

6.　See the very fine essay by Donald R. Wehrs, "Sterne, Cervantes, Montaigne: Fideistic Skepticism and the Rhetoric of Desire," *Comparative Literature Studies* 25 (1988), 127–51.

7.　See David Hume, *An Enquiry concerning Human Understanding,* ed. Antony Flew (La Salle, Ill.: Open Court, 1988), pp. 189–90 (section 12, part 2): "For as, in common life, we reason every moment concerning fact and existence, and cannot possibly subsist, without continually employing this species of argument, any popular objections, derived from thence, must be insufficient to destroy that evidence. The great subverter of *Pyrrhonism* or the excessive principles of scepticism is action, and employment, and the occupations of common life. These principles may flourish and triumph in the schools; where it is, indeed, difficult, if not impossible, to refute them. But as soon as they leave the shade, and by the presence of the real objects, which actuate our passions and sentiments, are put in opposition to the more powerful principles of our nature, they vanish like smoke, and leave the most determined sceptic in the same condition as other mortals." Cf. the essays by M.F. Burnyeat ("Can the Skeptic Live His Skepticism?") and Robert J. Fogelin ("The Tendency of Hume's Skepticism") in *The Skeptical Tradition,* ed. Myles Burnyeat (Berkeley: University of California Press, 1983), especially pp. 118–21, 398–404.

8.　*God and Skepticism: A Study in Skepticism and Fideism* (Dodrecht: D. Reidel, 1983), p. 124.

9.　Sterne uses the phrase "riddles and mysteries" twice in *Tristram Shandy* and twice in his sermons (*TS,* IV.xvii.350 and IX.xxii.776; *Sermons,* 182; see also 414–15). Despite its religious context, critics have tended to follow Martin Battestin in asserting that the phrase indicates a secular worldview: the Shandy world is "inexplicable even when it appears most obvious, overwhelming in its multiplicity, unpredictable in its contingencies, it bewilders and eludes them all" (*The Providence of Wit: Aspects of Form in Augustan Literature and the Arts* [Oxford: Clarendon Press, 1974], p. 245). As Wehrs points out, however (esp. pp. 145–46), a fideistic Christian defines the mundane world in exactly the same fashion, human helplessness leading *to* faith and not *away* from it, as Battestin insists. That Sterne also has Locke in mind when using the phrase "riddles and mysteries" (see "Scholia" in *The Scriblerian* 19 [Autumn, 1986], 92–93) in no way negates this linkage between scepticism and faith; indeed, it helps explain Locke's own significant commitment to orthodoxy despite what Battestin calls "a distinctly 'modern' view of man based on Lockean epistemology."

10.　"'At the backside of the door of purgatory': A Note on Annotating *Tristram Shandy,"* in *Laurence Sterne: Riddles and Mysteries* (London and Totowa, N.J.: Vision Press and Barnes and Noble, 1984), p. 17.

11.　The title of Lamb's book, *Sterne's Fiction and the Double Principle,* contains its own statement of the problem I am exploring, namely, the human inability to confront "doubleness" without reducing it to a "principle"—to oneness. Only once, to my mind, does Lamb come close to recognizing this paradox (p. 104: "The lesson for the reader, you or me, comes unsettlingly close"); far more telling is the fact that not only Sterne but Cervantes and Montaigne as well are found to conform to Lamb's "double principle." Reductiveness, even in the pursuit of indeterminacy, is no virtue.

12.   The author of *Of Education,* from which Sterne borrowed, verbatim in many instances, his discussion of auxiliary verbs at the end of volume V; see *Notes,* pp. 392–94, n. to 484.11ff.

13.   See my "Sterne, Warburton, and the Burden of Exuberant Wit," *Eighteenth-Century Studies* 15 (1982), 245–74 for a full discussion not only of Sterne's borrowings from Warburton, but of his mixed response to Warburton's great (if hobby-horsical) learning.

14.   Herbert Read, an astute reader of Sterne, was perhaps the first to connect Sterne and Keats: "We know that Keats was familiar with *Tristram Shandy,* and it may be that his notion of *Negative Capability* ('which Shakespeare possessed so enormously') owes something to Sterne's character of Yorick—in any case, Sterne was certainly also 'a man . . . capable of being in uncertainties, Mysteries, doubts' " (*The Contrary Experience* [London: Faber and Faber, 1963], p. 330). Keats outlined his idea in a letter to his brothers dated 21 December 1817.

15.   *Tristram Shandy,* III.xii.214: "Of all the cants which are canted in this canting world,——though the cant of hypocrites may be the worst,—the cant of criticism is the most tormenting!"

16.   See, for example, *Tristram Shandy,* II.xi.125: "The truest respect which you can pay to the reader's understanding, is to halve this matter amicably, and leave him something to imagine, in his turn, as well as yourself." Perhaps the favourite incident for those critics who take such comments literally as the shaping spirit of the work is Tristram's invitation in volume VI, chapter xxxviii, to draw the widow Wadman in the blank page provided for our fancy. Yet surely, even here, Sterne's point is far more determinate than indeterminate, since his work depends not at all upon the reader actually taking pen and ink in hand (and I have never found a copy of *Tristram Shandy* in which the offer was accepted), but upon grasping the humour of Tristram's distinction between wife and mistress. That women might not find the passage humorous at all indicates precisely how overdetermined Sterne's joke is at this point.

17.   Interesting recent discussions of Sterne and Shaftesburian sensibility include Robert Markley, "Sentimentality as Performance: Shaftesbury, Sterne, and the Theatrics of Virtue," in *The New Eighteenth Century: Theory, Politics, English Literature,* ed. Felicity Nussbaum and Laura Brown (New York and London: Methuen, 1987), pp. 210–30 (reprinted in this volume); and John Mullan, *The Language of Feeling in the Eighteenth Century* (Oxford: Clarendon, 1988), pp. 147–200. See also, *Notes,* pp. 180–81, n. to 157.14ff.

18.   Montaigne's own embrace of Pyrrhonic scepticism, most especially in the "Apology for Raimond de Sebonde," leads I think to his often stated love of self-exploration. See, for example, "Of the Resemblance of Children to their Fathers": "I do not hate Opinions contrary to my own. I am so far from being angry to see a Disagreement betwixt mine and other Men's Judgments . . . that on the contrary . . . I find it much more rare to see our Humours and Designs jump and agree. And there never was in the World two Opinions alike, no more than two Hairs, or two Grains. The most universal Quality, is *Diversity*"; and "Of Repentance": "Could my Soul once take footing, I would not essay, but resolve; but it is always learning and making trial. Every Man carries the entire Form of [the] human Condition" (*Essays,* trans. Charles Cotton, 6th ed. [London, 1753], 2:521;3:20). In September 1760 Sterne confirmed a correspondent's guess that Montaigne was a favourite author: " 'for my conning Montaigne as much as my pray'r book'—there you are right again" (*Letters,* ed. Lewis Perry Curtis [Oxford: Clarendon Press, 1935], p. 122).

19.   I explore this aspect of *Tristram Shandy* in "Swift and Sterne: Two Tales, Several Sermons, and a Relationship Revisited," *Critical Essays on Jonathan Swift,* ed. Frank Palmeri (New York: G.K. Hall, 1993), pp. 164–86.

20.   An interesting confluence of Sterne's interest in the learned community and his life as an Anglican clergyman may be seen in a popular clerical manual like John Wilkins's *Ecclesiastes: or, A Discourse Concerning the Gift of Preaching,* which reached its ninth edition by 1718. Wilkins's efforts are primarily bibliographical, pages upon pages listing works to consult on such topics as "Scripture-Philosophy," "Scripture-Geography," "Scripture-Measures and Weights," then on individual books of the Bible, usually at least twenty sources for each, and finally on

topics such as "Independency" or "Communion and Schism," each list divided into "pro" and "con." This vast accumulation of learning, when thus catalogued, is at once an impressive commentary on human endeavour and human folly; perhaps Wilkins sensed the ambiguity when he warns the clergy in his introduction to "beware of that vain affectation of finding something new and strange in every text, though never so plain. It will not so much shew our *parts* . . . as our *pride* and wantonness of wit" (p. 16).

21. See, for example, Isabel Rivers, *Reason, Grace, and Sentiment: A Study of the Language of Religion and Ethics in England, 1660–1780* (Cambridge: Cambridge University Press, 1991), pp. 70–88.

22. See *Notes,* pp. 417–22, n. to 529.17ff.

23. There is good evidence, indeed, that Sterne wanted to pass as more learned than he really was; see my "Sterne, Warburton, and the Burden of Exuberant Wit" (cited above, n. 13), for one possible explanation. The single instance where he most successfully achieved an unearned reputation may be his borrowings from Locke; twentieth-century critics have often discovered in Sterne a profound commentator on the *Essay Concerning Human Understanding,* although they remain undecided as to whether Sterne supports or criticizes Locke. In fact, Sterne's citations of Locke repeat the most common notions associated with him and might easily derive from popular sources, for example, Chambers's *Cyclopædia.*

24. Sterne gives ample indication that Burton's *Anatomy of Melancholy* is on his mind, from the two mottoes on the title-page of the first edition of volume V to borrowings from Burton in both the Whiskers episode (see *Notes,* p. 342, n. to 412.5ff.) and Walter's funeral oration (*Notes,* p. 345, n. to 418.8–12, etc.).

25. See *Notes,* p. 374, n. to 461.16–17.

26. Spencer's *De Legibus Hebræorum Ritualibus* appears twice (items 303 and 810) in *A Facsimile Reproduction of a Unique Catalogue of Laurence Sterne's Library* (London: James Tregaskis, 1930); Rubenius appears as item 828. The catalogue is not an accurate representation of Sterne's library (other libraries were grouped in the sale), but the appearance of Rubenius and Spencer in a 1768 sale catalogue of private libraries helps to make one essential point of this essay: there was a community of learned lay readers (with a capacity for Latin, to be sure) in mid-eighteenth-century England whose libraries were well stocked with arcane learning from the seventeenth century.

27. See *Notes,* pp. 372–73, n. to 460.9–11.

28. Sterne borrows from Rabelais. See *The Works of Francis Rabelais, M.D.,* trans. Thomas Urquhart and Peter Motteux, with notes by John Ozell, 5 vols. (1750), 1:35; see *Notes,* pp. 376–78, n. to 463.1ff.

29. See *Notes,* pp. 348–50, n. to 421.17–422.28. That Warburton had used a similar parody of the letter by Scarron to attack the "wits" of the age (see the "Dedication to Free Thinkers" in his *Divine Legation of Moses*) was almost certainly on Sterne's mind; and perhaps, as well, a parody of Cicero's letter by Swift. To suggest that such a text, then, is somehow open and indeterminate and that the annotator who directs attention to these relationships limits the reader's freedom strikes me as absurd; indeed, I might suggest, instead, that the reader who does not hear Cicero, Burton, Scarron, Swift, and Warburton in this passage is exiled from the community of *Tristram Shandy,* much as Toby "frees" himself by this literal interpretation: "My uncle Toby had but two things for it; either to suppose his brother to be the wandering *Jew,* or that his misfortunes had disordered his brain" (V.iii.423). Toby is at this point a very poor reader of his brother's text.

30. Nietzsche, p. 239.

Swift, Sterne, and the Skeptical Tradition

J. T. PARNELL

In a recent essay Donald Wehrs suggests that the tradition of fideistic skepticism offers a meaningful context for Laurence Sterne's narrative and thematic concerns.[1] In so doing he highlights the most significant, and hitherto overlooked, legacy of the Renaissance humanists with whom Sterne's name is so frequently linked. It has long been a commonplace to see *Tristram Shandy* in the tradition of learned wit, but the late flowering of the tradition in Sterne's fiction has never been adequately explained. Similarly, the epithet "skeptic" occurs regularly in discussions of Sterne, from John Traugott's influential *Tristram Shandy's World* in the 1950s to Jonathan Lamb's recent *Sterne's Fiction and the Double Principle*. Until Wehrs' article, however, *skeptic* had been used in its modern sense, denoting at worst universal doubt, or at best the kind of philosophical—and, more or less, secular—skepticism associated with Locke and Hume. Awareness of the tradition of fideistic skepticism allows us, for the first time, to understand more fully Sterne's "skepticism" and his relationship to those writers to whom, in his fiction and correspondence, he consistently draws his readers' attention.

It is no coincidence that Erasmus, Rabelais, and Cervantes were as highly prized by Swift as by Sterne or that the Scriblerians and Sterne were equally familiar with the skeptical writings of Montaigne and Charron.[2] The Renaissance legacy was, of course, pervasive in the eighteenth century, but the far reaching influence of the skeptical branch of the Christian-humanist literary tradition on Sterne and Swift in particular has yet to be explored. For Swift and Sterne, as ministers of the Church of England during periods when Anglicanism was coming under increasing threat, Erasmus, Rabelais and Burton offered obvious role models. All five writers found a literary arena in which they could display their exuberant wit while attempting to sustain the belief system to which they adhered. It is too rarely stressed that the literary tradition represented by these writers is massively informed by their religious beliefs. In *The Praise of Folly, Gargantua and Pantagruel* and *The Anatomy of Melancholy* "belief" is apparent in more than the shadowy presence of religious norms behind the exuberance of discrete artistic creations. In these works and the fiction of Swift and Sterne, form and content reflect and enact

Reprinted from *Studies in Eighteenth-Century Culture* 23 (1994): 220–42.

a skepticism that is closely allied to a defence of hard-pressed Christian ideology. In their favorite writers Swift and Sterne found formal techniques that were seized upon as the best means of addressing epistemological issues that had far-reaching implications for Anglican hegemony. The issues may have been born in the Reformation crisis, but they were far from moribund in the eighteenth century. An investigation of Sterne's and Swift's relationship to Christian-humanist fideism helps us to understand Sterne's professed admiration for the Dean of St. Patrick's, and suggests that a reassessment of critical commonplaces about the relationship might be in order.[3] In particular, the notion—which has become a critical fiat since Traugott first pronounced it— that Sterne's "comic vision" diverges from Swift's in "an odd synthesis of the satiric method of the Scriblerians with Locke's philosophical skepticism,"[4] needs to be re-examined.

If *Tristram Shandy* remains an anachronism for many critics, it is because Sterne is too often viewed as a freak, a prophet of modernity, or even postmodernity. To be sure, if we look for evidence of "pre-Romanticism," existentialist angst, or postmodern relativity, *Tristram Shandy* will offer comforting glimmers of confirmation, but the more difficult task is to face a less congenial anachronism. If Sterne remains hard to place, it is surely because he shares so much with pre-Enlightenment traditions—traditions that inform his plan of "taking in . . . the Weak part of the Sciences . . . [and] every Thing else, which [he found] Laugh-at-able."[5] Blithely unaware of the alleged decline of satire and the conditions that produce it, Sterne discovered in Erasmus, Rabelais, Montaigne, and the Scriblerians not just formal techniques, but a credo fully in keeping with his role as a clergyman. The potential problems raised by exchanging one anachronism for another can be forestalled by a fuller understanding of why, as Wehrs puts it, "Sterne transposes into narrative the rhetorical techniques of classical skepticism."[6] Such an understanding will also enhance our awareness of the affinities between Swift and Sterne— affinities recent scholarship has mistakenly ignored in a rather narrow insistence on the perceived gap between the poisonous Augustan satirist and the amiable sentimentalist.

Without wishing to rehearse a full summary of the tenets of fideistic skepticism, it is necessary to outline the history of the tradition in order to understand its impact on Sterne and Swift. For our purposes it is essential to look at the philosophical underpinnings of classical skepticism *and* the remarkable uses to which such skepticism was put by Christian apologists from the sixteenth century onwards. The methods of the classical skeptics were employed in the sixteenth century, chiefly by Catholic writers, as a defence against the central arguments of the Protestant reformers. As Richard Popkin puts it in *The History of Scepticism from Erasmus to Spinoza,* "the dispute over the proper standard of religious knowledge . . . raised one of the classical problems of the Greek Pyrrhonists, the problem of the criterion of truth." Luther's assertion that conscience was an infallible guide to correct biblical exegesis led to doubt in the whole field of epistemology and hermeneutics. This was not a localised debate but one that, according to Popkin, "was to have the most far reaching consequences, not just in theology but throughout man's entire intellectual realm."[7] Indeed, for Pierre Bayle—whose *Dictionary* was a source for Sterne and the Scriblerians—the rediscovery of Sextus Empiricus' *Outlines of Pyrrhonism* was seen as the beginning of modern philosophy. From the rediscovery of classical skepticism in the sixteenth century, the skeptical stance became one of the key weapons of philosophical and theological debate. Having been employed in the battle against the reformers, skepticism was levelled next against Scholastic and Platonic modes of thought before evolving in the late seventeenth century as a foil to Cartesian rationalism. In fact skepticism was a philosophical system capable of countering any and every system, including its own—its end being suspense rather than certainty. It is worth remembering that the legacy of the Schoolmen was such that its influence on the English universities was still felt late in the eighteenth century. That the satire of Sterne and the Scriblerians is consistently anti-Scholastic confirms the pervasiveness of the legacy. That both should attack Cartesian rationalism with the very skeptical strategies Descartes had sought to discredit further suggests Swift's and Sterne's keen awareness of the epistemological debate. Descartes joins the Schoolmen as a builder of "edifices in the air."

It was Erasmus, whose influence on *A Tale of a Tub* and *Tristram Shandy* has long been acknowledged,[8] who in the *Praise of Folly* first exploited the possibilities of a union of the characteristic discursive strategies of philosophical skepticism with the literary discourse of the paradoxical encomium. Indeed, Erasmus and his heirs clearly demonstrate what such twentieth-century skeptics as Nietzsche and Derrida are so keen to stress—the untenable nature of neat distinctions between literary and philosophical discourse. But in the face of the burgeoning *crise pyrrhonienne,* Erasmus sought a solution to dogmatic wrangling and religious faction—behind which the faintest tones of the death knell of religious certainty could be heard. In the use of a form capable of demonstrating the complexity of sublunary truth, he sought to clear the way for an acceptance of God's even more vexed truths. While Erasmus did not have access to Sextus Empiricus' *Outlines of Pyrrhonism,* he was familiar with Cicero's less thorough accounts of Academic skepticism and Diogenes Laertes' summary of Pyrrhonian skepticism. In addition, the recent experience of translating Lucian's serio-comic dialogues offered Erasmus a literary form that, through its exploitation of the comic, its love of paradox, its extravagant foregrounding of intertextuality, and its "dialogue without closure,"[9] presented a perfect vehicle for satire on opposition voices that could at the same time endorse the wisdom of Christian "folly."

Just how close Erasmus is to Sterne and Swift can be seen from the passage where Folly aligns herself with a blend of stoic and skeptical thought: "But it's sad, people say, to be deceived. Not at all, it's far sadder *not* to be deceived. They're quite wrong if they think man's happiness depends on actual facts; it depends on his opinions. For human affairs are so complex and obscure that nothing can be known of them for certain, as has rightly been stated by my Academicians, the least assuming of the philosophers."[10]

Echoes of the *Praise of Folly* in the *Tale* have been well documented.[11] But the possibility that Swift's debt extends beyond a *general* concurrence of world views and shared rhetorical strategies to a fideism that informs narrative structure has never been articulated. Swift's much debated skepticism can, in fact, be better understood when the nature of the skeptical tradition is grasped. For readers of *Tristram Shandy*, Folly can be seen as anticipating Tristram's endorsement of the benefits of *philautia*, an endorsement that finds a parallel in *A Tale of a Tub* in the Hack's delight in the "sublime and refined point of felicity, called *the possession of being well deceived*."[12] More significantly, the passage contains the stoic maxim that Sterne chose as his epigraph to the first installment of *Tristram* and would have found in two texts central to his satire's intertextual fabric—Montaigne's *Essays* and Shakespeare's *Hamlet*.[13] Further, the final sentence not only encapsulates the skeptical stance, but parallels one of Sterne's most repeated borrowings from Locke:

> we live amongst riddles and mysteries—the most obvious things, which come in our way, have dark sides, which the quickest sight cannot penetrate into; and even the clearest and most exalted understandings amongst us find ourselves puzzled and at a loss in almost every cranny of nature's works; so that this, like a thousand other things, falls out for us in a way, which tho' we cannot reason upon it,—yet we find the good of it . . . and that's enough for us. (IV.xvii.350)

Given Sterne's familiarity with Erasmus, it is hard to imagine that he was unaware of the allusive resonance of his own use of Epictetus and Locke. In this light, the lifting of the phrasing from Locke seems less a confirmation of Sterne's much discussed debt to the *Essay Concerning Human Understanding,* and more an endorsement of a commonplace Christian sentiment.[14] The stress on the inadequacy of *reason* in the face of Nature's complexity is hardly new to the eighteenth century, but is rather typical of a fideistic view that is traceable to St. Paul and that came into particular prominence in the skeptical crisis precipitated by the Reformation. Folly's words confirm also, if confirmation were necessary, that Sterne did not need Locke, still less Hume, to direct him to the skeptical highroad.

The influence of Erasmus' thought and his use of the rhetoric of fideism was profound. The extent of the legacy is such that in the fiction of those who come after him it is sometimes difficult to ascertain whether the influence is direct or whether it has been picked up at second hand. Rabelais and Cervantes absorb much of Erasmus, but take his formal strategies much further by extending them into the realms of narrative satire.[15] But behind the marvellous complexities and skeptical nuances of *Gargantua and Pantagruel* and *Don Quixote* lies a fideism that is closer to the conservative skepticism of St. Paul than the "radical" skepticism of modernity. In this light we should beware of seizing upon Swift's and Sterne's seemingly radical skepticism as evidence of the crumbling of conservative Anglican ideology. Nor in Sterne's case should we be too quick to celebrate a modern voice that breaks out from the supposed shackles of an imagined neoclassicism. Valerie Grosvenor Myer's claim that we should consider Sterne "in relation to the dissolution of Augustan values into relativism and subjectivity in the wake of Locke,"[16] while typical of much criticism of *Tristram Shandy,* is quite untenable. In this account Locke's "wake" has washed over (or under?) Swift, Pope, and Addison and hit Sterne full in the face seventy years after the *Essay*'s publication. Without question, Locke's influence on eighteenth-century thought was profound, but he can hardly be held responsible for the dissolution of "Augustan values." Locke possibly had a greater influence on the Scriblerians than on Sterne, since they respond to his ideas while they are still fresh.[17] Furthermore, we have to be extremely wary of any simplistic conception of "Augustan values." The formulation may be comforting, but it too readily falsifies literary history because of its tendency to turn what is disparate into a forced whole. Sterne found numerous examples of subjectivity and relativism of a different order in a tradition that long predates Locke.

Too much of the criticism that has dealt with the Locke/Sterne nexus has privileged the philosopher's influence without a sufficient investigation of the history of skeptical thought. One result is that Locke's skepticism is seen as more radically modern than it actually is. The nature of fideism is that it is a mitigated form of skepticism so that, for all the signs of "modern" preoccupations in Erasmus, Rabelais, Cervantes, Swift, and Sterne, the underpinning certainty of belief in the Christian deity qualifies any celebration, such as Bakhtin's, of the writers' debt to the kind of joyful relativity exemplified in the carnivalesque.

That the skepticism of these writers is mitigated is crucial to our understanding of their texts. Far from embracing the conclusions of Pyrrhonian skepticism, they adopt its rhetoric for quite different ends. As Terence Penelhum has argued, Erasmus *uses* skepticism in defence "of one dogmatic solution—namely a middle-of-the-road theology."[18] Similarly, all of the writers under consideration use a bewildering range of weapons from the skeptic arsenal to serve satiric, and consequently dogmatic, ends. Erasmus is unrelenting in his satire on "false" learning, but is finally more interested in discrediting his religious opponents.

From Erasmus onwards, the alliance of fideism and Menippean form became almost exclusively associated with a skeptical interrogation of the human-based search for truth in the sciences and the arts and with satire on "abuses" in religion.[19] In the seventeenth century Anglican apologists usurped the form to counter both the Jesuits and the Puritans. Burton's

Anatomy—beloved of Swift and Sterne—and More's *Enthusiasmus Triumphatus* are the most enduring examples of the characteristic blend of satire on religious opponents and skeptical rhetoric in the service of Anglican fideism. Again Swift's and Sterne's acknowledged debt to Burton becomes more significant with a fuller historical overview of the skeptical tradition.[20]

Scriblerian and Sternean satire should be seen in the context of this tradition of skeptical, anti-dogmatic arguments of the sixteenth and seventeenth centuries. The satiric reduction of system-builders in Burton, Swift, and Sterne is more than a conflict between the comic and the scientific; it is a product of, and a response to, an intellectual movement that had its birth in the crisis of the Reformation. Swift and Sterne employ the rhetoric of fideism—at some risk of undermining the very ground they seek to preserve—and seize on narrative strategies calculated to deflect readers from the search for *rational* grounds for truth towards acceptance of Anglican orthodoxy. The skeptical method of perplexing the adversary with an exuberant heaping up of pros and cons at the extreme poles of debate on vexed issues gives their satire a seldom-rivaled edge.

Donald Wehrs has rightly noted the "interpretative 'suspense' " that Sterne brings about by breaking off the narrative of the Widow Wadman and Toby's amours at the very moment when the extent of Toby's wound is to be revealed. Expected resolution is denied and the reader is left in suspense. This strategy—typical of Sterne's narrative technique throughout *Tristram Shandy*—comes *close* to genuine skeptical suspense, but should not blind us to the fact of Sternean certainties, certainties central to a proper understanding of the skeptical tradition in which, paradoxically, skeptical rhetoric is made to serve dogmatic ends. For the reader, at least, the nature of Toby's wound does not "remain uncertain."[21] At the end of the preceding chapter, Tristram resolves this particular ambiguity in his discussion of Toby's "fitness for the married state." Nature had not only made Toby "gentle, generous and humane," but

> she had moreover considered the other causes for which matrimony was ordained——
> And   accordingly   *   *   *   *   *   *   *   *   *
> *   *   *   *   *   *   *   *   *   *   *   *
> *   *   *   *   *   *   *   *   *   *   *   *
> *   *   *   *.
> The DONATION was not defeated by my uncle Toby's wound. (*TS*, IX.xxii.777)

In spite of the preceding lacuna, the final sentence is unequivocal.[22] Within six short chapters, just to make certain that the *facts* are known, and in order to extract the greatest humor from his "choicest morsel," Sterne has Trim apprise Bridget of the same information. The Trim/Bridget scene of chapter xxviii beautifully parallels the Toby/Widow Wadman scene in chapter xxvi, in such a way as to recall the doubleness of truth that we may see as characteristic of Sterne's skeptical strategies. The contrast between master and man is stark. In response to the Widow's "whereabouts?" the hopelessly deluded Toby calls upon documentary evidence in the shape of a map of Namur. By contrast, Trim first responds to Bridget's enquiry by indicating, on his own body, the exact place where Toby received his wound, "*here*——In pronouncing which he slightly press'd the back of her hand towards the part he felt for——and let it fall" (IX.xxviii.796). Bridget's doubts cause Trim to denounce vehemently the rumours as "false as hell." The chapter ends in a mass of equivocal lacunae in which the one certainty is that whatever *is* happening is the "unfortunate" result of Bridget's having "begun the attack with her manual exercise" (797). Suspense here is not all that it might be. There is no doubt that Sterne exploits the skeptical form as a means of demonstrating the non-linear, labyrinthine nature of the paths to truth, but that does not prevent him, as a satirist, from demonstrating quite clearly that there *are* some truths.

In the second of his *Crazy Tales* ("My Cousin's Tale of a Cock and a Bull"), John Hall-Stevenson is insightful about Sterne's view of knowledge. Impersonating his friend's voice, Hall-Stevenson describes the quadrangle at Jesus College in which undergraduates were "taught to wrangle," under the shade of the "Tree of Knowledge":

> It overshadowed ev'ry room,
>> And consequently, more or less,
> Forc'd ev'ry brain, in such a gloom,
>> To grope its way, and go by guess.
>
> For ever going round about;
>> For that which lies before your nose,
> And when you come to find it out,
>> It is not like you suppose.[23]

Bereft of any other merit, the verses neatly encapsulate the basis of Sterne's skepticism with regard to knowledge. Toby, the seeker after the arcane "truths" of fortification, is so blinded by his hobby-horse and his sensibility that he is unable to *understand* the obvious denotation of the Widow's question. By contrast, Trim—whose artlessness is clearly approved of by Sterne in other contexts—understands completely the drift of the question and quickly turns Bridget's curiosity into another sexual encounter. As William J. Farrell has demonstrated, "Nature" and "Art" do constant battle in *Tristram Shandy,* and Sterne, like his skeptical forebears, consistently endorses the superior claims of nature.[24] Similarly, Charron in *Of Wisdom* (which is heavily dependent upon Montaigne's *Essays*) recommends that, given the impossibility of discovering truth other than by revelation, our moral lives should be guided by following nature. Hence, in the contrasting courtship scenes the "truths" of Nature are firmly set against the arid "truths" of the science of fortification. Here—their functions constantly shift—Trim and Toby are the means by which Sterne is able, quite clearly, to recommend an uncomplicated sexuality as against the naive confusions of a soldier/sentimentalist who has forgotten that war involves death and that marriage involves sexual pleasure.

Another of Tristram's favorite skeptical strategies is to offer two or more possible explanations for a given happening and to refuse to "determine" anything from the opposing possibilities. Tristram's comments on his father's response to Susannah's unhelpfully brief relation of Elizabeth Shandy's condition is fairly typical: "Pish! said my father, the button of his breeches slipping out of the button-hole—So that whether the interjection was levelled at *Susannah,* or the button-hole,—whether pish was an interjection of contempt or an interjection of modesty, is a doubt, and must be a doubt till I shall have time to write the three following favorite chapters . . ." (*TS,* IV.xiv.345).

The discourse is characteristically equivocal and is typical of many passages in which Tristram uses the device that classical rhetoric termed *aporia.*[25] On one level, Sterne is satirising the pointless human obsession with causality, but on another he is demonstrating the "riddles and mysteries" of interpretation at the most fundamental, and seemingly trivial level. In an earlier passage Tristram explains his strategy: "My way is ever to point out to the curious, different tracts of investigation, to come at the first springs of the events I tell;—not with a pedantic *Fescue,*—or in the decisive Manner of *Tacitus,* who outwits himself and his reader;—but with the officious humility of a heart devoted to the assistance merely of the inquisitive;—to them I write,——and by them I shall be read,——" (I.xxi.74). There is, of course, more than a hint of irony in Tristram's claim, but given Sterne's grasp of the post-Reformation tradition of Christian skepticism and its characteristic rhetoric, it can also be taken more seriously.

Interestingly, Tristram's skeptical method is defined in opposition to Tacitus' "decisive" manner. The Florida edition of Sterne's work notes Tacitus' reputation for "excessive subtlety," but "decisive" implies a conviction of certainty that, in human affairs at least, is anathema to Tristram and his creator. Furthermore, Bayle's entry on Tacitus in the *Dictionary* suggests another reason for Tristram's rejection of the historian's methods. Bayle endorses Tacitus' standing as a historian, but adds that "he may be censured for the affectation of his language, and for inquiring into the secret motives of actions, and construing them to be criminal."[26] It is precisely the dogmatic conclusions of the inquirer into the "secret motives of actions" that Tristram rejects in favor of a skeptical approach to human motivation.

Tristram's refusal to offer his readers the clarity afforded by "a pedantic *Fescue*" may seem something of a throwaway rejection of reductive didactic methods. Yet the image of the arrow-straight and inflexible certainty of the fescue clearly resonates with the other straight lines against which *Tristram Shandy* defines itself. Just as Tristram's digressive and unruly narrative lines mock the grave rectitude and certainties of writing masters and cabbage planters,[27] so the refusal to point directly to "first springs" is informed by a comparable skepticism. Such Christian skepticism seeks to preserve mysterious truths by discrediting the kind of mistaken convictions and excessive curiosity embodied by Sterne in the person of Walter Shandy.

Pierre Charron, to whom Sterne, notably, alludes in the first and last chapters of *Tristram Shandy,* offers a useful gloss on the fuller significance of Sterne's dismissal of misplaced and pedantic conviction. For Charron, the "Pedante" is the very antithesis of the wise man. "Pedantical Science," pictured in the emblematic frontispiece as one of Wisdom's four slaves, is described as having a "sullen visage, her eye-lids elevated reading in a Booke, where was written, *Yea, No.*"[28] The curious reader is freed from the mind-numbing choice between affirmation and denial that so plagues Walter. Thus, Tristram's constant use of the favorite device of *aporia*—at a local and structural level—represents a calculated foil to dogmatic assertion. Given the qualities Tristram defines his method against, the epithets applied to the ideal reader are doubly significant. Rather than dogmatists and pedants, Tristram hopes for "curious" and "inquisitive" readers. Not, of course, the curiosity of a Walter or a Hume, but the kind of humble questioning implicit in the Greek derivation of "skeptic," one who inquires and reflects rather than determines.[29]

Neither Sterne nor Swift needs to have been deeply read in esoteric works to have been familiar with skeptical methods of argumentation or the intellectual and theological debates in which they were employed. The intellectual map had itself been irreversibly changed by the Reformation and the *crise pyrrhonienne* it was to generate. Quite apart from the literary models, both writers were familiar with the philosophical tenets of fideistic skepticism from a number of sources. As well as the comic and somewhat reductive account of Pyrrhonian skepticism in Book 3 of *Gargantua and Pantagruel,* and Diogenes Laertes' "life" of Pyrrho, Swift and Sterne could have read the first English translation of Sextus Empiricus' *Outlines of Pyrrhonism* in Stanley's *History of Philosophy.*[30] But by far the most influential treatment of fideism is to be found in Montaigne's *Apology for Raimond de Sebonde.* Again, we would be ill advised simply to abstract philosophical "content" from Montaigne's discourse since, as in the essays of Sir Thomas Browne, form and rhetoric are inseparable from the skeptical ideas conveyed. Thus the acknowledged influence of the essayists on Sterne's narrative techniques also has a skeptical lineage. That said, it is worth reminding ourselves of Montaigne's defence of fideism in the *Apology* in order to correct our tendency to view him as something of a whimsical banterer, a view that profoundly affects our notion of his influence on Sterne and Swift. The *Apology* demonstrates how close Montaigne's fideism is to Swift's and Sterne's Anglican orthodoxy, and to their stance as satirists. Montaigne is important not just because of Swift's and

Sterne's familiarity with the *Essays,* but because of the immense impact of his articulation of the skeptical position for fideistic ends.[31]

Unlike Sterne, Swift may seem an odd bedfellow for Montaigne. Montaigne's supposed geniality has been seen to have more in common with Sterne's tone than the satiric rage of Swift. Here, as elsewhere, critical pigeon-holing can prevent us from understanding what these writers share. Montaigne's avowed purpose in the *Apology* suggests Sterne might have gleaned more from the *Essays* than what Fluchère has called "amused tolerance."[32] Montaigne aims to "crush and spurn under Foot Pride and human Fierceness; to make them sensible of the Inanity, Vanity and Vileness of Man: To wrest the wretched Arms of their Reason out of their Hands, to make them bow down and bite the Ground under the Authority and Reverence of the Divine *Majesty*" (*Essays,* 2:128–29).

The language and tone might seem closer to received readings of Swift than Sterne, but the purpose is surely one that all three share. It is also worth remembering that it is this assault on human self-sufficiency and the limitations of human reason that lies behind Montaigne's account of Pyrrhonian skepticism in the *Apology.* Skepticism itself is seen as a check to human pride. It cannot be overstressed that for the Christian, skepticism, far from undermining faith, becomes the key reason for relying on faith above everything else. The fact that such skepticism often results in negative dogmatism rather than the suspense that classical skepticism required, is one of the main reasons why the conclusions of the Christian differ radically from those of the secular skeptic. Humility in the face of God's "riddles and mysteries" leads, according to Montaigne, to "a peaceable condition of Life, temperate and exempt from the Agitations we receive by the Impression of Opinion and knowledge that we think we have of things" (*Essays,* 2:195).

It is evident from the *Apology* that Montaigne has moved further than Erasmus in his anti-intellectualism. The desire to put an end to religious sectarianism is common to both writers, but, as Penelhum argues, "by being as explicit . . . about the impotence of reason . . . [Montaigne] is shifting away from a strict Pyrrhonism toward the very sort of negative dogmatism he says he follows Sextus in rejecting."[33] A similar negative dogmatism is evident in the artfully dialogic satiric discourse of the *Tale* and *Tristram Shandy.* The undermining of faith in the sufficiency of human reason is, of course, continued by the Scriblerians and Sterne in such arid rationalists as Cornelius Scriblerus and Walter Shandy. The assault on blind faith in the reasoning faculty is relentless in *Gulliver's Travels,* and in *Tristram Shandy* the antithesis between "truths" of the head and heart constantly undermines the claims of the former. Anti-intellectualism and the satiric reduction of the *philosophus gloriosus* can, of course, be traced back to Aristophanes, but the employment of skeptical strategies and their intimate relationship with religious apologetics is peculiar to the skeptical tradition.[34]

Since Philip Harth has aligned Swift's religious thought with "Anglican rationalism"[35]—in direct opposition to the "heresy" of fideism—it may be well to remind ourselves of the nature of late seventeenth-century Anglican theology. South, Stillingfleet, Tillotson, and other major divines who did so much to form Anglican thought of the succeeding century were themselves forced into addressing the central problem raised by the Reformation crisis, the problem of the criterion of truth. Without, of course, adopting skeptical strategies, Anglican divines after the Restoration had to provide reliable grounds for scriptural interpretation in opposition to the perceived dangers of Puritan subjectivism. Thus they attempted to explain the Christian "mysteries" in an intellectually satisfying manner without having recourse to the potentially subversive escape clause of private conviction. Much has been made of the fact that the divines resolved the problem by calling upon the shining light of "Reason," but, as Gerard Reedy argues in *The Bible and Reason,* the "scriptural apologetics of the divines must rank very low in any hierarchy of rationalisms one might construct out of late seventeenth-century thought." In the end the gap between the theology of the seventeenth-century divines and the fideism of some of their Catholic predecessors may not be so great. As Reedy demonstrates, the divines were forced into a "wider" definition of reason: "Reason in this wider sense thus holds, in its core, an abiding affection for a source of truth that is not rationally verifiable in all its operations; such a commitment is not the result of persuasion but of some deeper human act that has always been called, in spite of the divines' attempt to broaden the category, specifically religious faith."[36]

There is no suggestion that Stillingfleet and Tillotson embraced Pyrrhonism, but it is important to see that rational proof was inadequate to the task of closing what Popkin has called the "Pandora's box that Luther had opened at Leipzig."[37] The skeptical strategies of Swift's and Sterne's fiction have the same *ends* in view as the more orthodox discourse of their sermons, sermons that owe much to Tillotson's careful negotiation of the boundaries between reason and faith. Rather than adopting a dangerous heresy, all three colonise skeptical positions for the Anglican cause.

It is hard to escape the conclusion that reason is used only selectively by the divines because of the risk of undermining religion itself. There is, therefore, a vested interest at stake in Swift's and Sterne's adoption of the rhetoric of fideism, and more than a hint of a contrary dogmatism in their satire on Catholics and Enthusiasts. Hence the Christian skeptics' attitude to much scientific and philosophical enquiry is deeply conservative, since faith in the incomprehensible makes such enquiry fruitless. Beyond the sure knowledge of God, man can have nothing but the will-o'-the-wisp of opinion. One of Montaigne's repeated arguments against the sufficiency of human reason is that, characteristically, it is incapable of achieving certainty: "it finds Appearance for divers Effects. 'Tis a Pot with two Ears, that a Man may take by the Right or Left" (*Essays,* 2:293). Interestingly the enquiry into the seat of the soul, and the debate between the ovists and animalculists are two of Montaigne's examples of the contradictory nature of scientific enquiry—debates which both the Scriblerians and Sterne were later to hold up to ridicule.

What is significant about the *Apology* for our purposes is that, as well as recommending skeptical suspense as an alternative to dogmatism, Montaigne offers a full and cogent manifesto for fideism. Not only does the *Apology* highlight the power of skeptical arguments to counter opponents, but it provides an intellectual foundation for satire on abuses in learning. For Montaigne, "whoever should bundle up a lusty Faggot of the Fooleries of human Wisdom, would produce Wonders" (*Essays*, 2:248), and Sterne, like the Scriblerians, devotes much comic energy to the bundling up and exposing of just such "Fooleries." The intimate relationship between satire on system builders and that on religious opponents in the *Tale* and *Tristram Shandy* becomes clearer in the context of Montaigne's arguments. By relentlessly ridiculing the inadequacies of human systems, Swift and Sterne are better placed to recommend the haven of Anglican certainty. Thus the satirists were not motivated simply by the fact that the eighteenth century offered more numerous examples of misguided theorists than previous ages. Although Sterne and the Scriblerians are concerned to attack what they perceive to be "of disservice to sound learning," their attitude towards *all* system builders is the same as Montaigne's. When Gulliver learns from Aristotle in Glubbdubdrib that all "new Systems of Nature were but new Fashions, which would vary in every Age,"[38] Swift treats Gassendi, Descartes, and Newton with the same skeptical contempt. The blending of satire on contemporary intellectual folly together with that on already outmoded thinking is yet one more way of demonstrating the limitations of human reason. What John Ferriar failed to see when he accused Sterne of attacking "forsaken fooleries"[39] was the satiric impact of yoking together ancient and modern searchers after the truth. John Burton and Archbishop Warburton join the Schoolmen, Descartes, Obadiah Walker, and many more, as dangerously misguided seekers after certainty. The point is clear; if reason demonstrably fails to elucidate the sublunary world, how much more inadequate is it likely to be in achieving certainty with regard to the deity. All human systems are flawed because, in Montaigne's words: "'Tis *Faith* alone, that livelily and certainly comprehends the deep Mysteries of our Religion." While we should strive to "accompany our faith with all the reason we have," we must beware of believing that "it is upon us that it depends . . . [or] that our arguments and Endeavours can arrive at so supernatural and Divine a knowledge" (*Essays*, 2:120).

The influence of Montaigne's *Apology* was far-reaching. Popkin summarises it thus: "throughout the 17th and 18th centuries, Montaigne was not seen as a transitional figure, or a man off the main roads of thought, but as a founder of an important intellectual movement that continued to plague philosophers in their quest for certainty."[40] While it would be quite wrong to ignore what distinguishes Sterne and Swift by subsuming them into a falsely homogenous category, the fideistic tradition influences their literary discourse to such an extent that what they share is more pronounced than their differences. Although Melvyn New's thoroughgoing attempt to demonstrate that "*Tristram Shandy* can best be understood by locating it in the mainstream of the conservative, moralistic Augustan tradition" has proved unpopular with some critics, its thesis still stands. By understanding the skeptical heritage that Sterne and Swift drew upon, the claim that "*Tristram Shandy* joins works like *A Tale of a Tub* and *The Dunciad* as one further effort to stem the eighteenth century's ever increasing enthusiasm for human self-sufficiency," can, in fact, be substantiated.[41] Many of the problems associated with accepting that *Tristram Shandy* is a satire recede when the alliance of skeptical strategies and Christian dogmatism is understood.

Of all the works of the Scriblerians, it is *A Tale of a Tub* that, for obvious reasons, has most invited comparison with Sterne's masterpiece. Critics, before emphasising the differences, have acknowledged the formal resemblances between the two works. Max Byrd's assessment is typical: "from a common starting-point they tend to go racing in utterly different directions." For Byrd, as for many commentators, the crucial difference is that "Swift is writing a satire, Sterne a novel." Ronald Paulson—who is prepared to go further than most in acknowledging the similarities between the Scriblerian project and Sterne's—distinguishes between the two writers' approach to the "chaotic" form. For Paulson, Sterne "does with the image of chaos almost the reverse of what Swift did, restoring the positive value it had for Rabelais and Erasmus."[42] Apart from the fact that Swift's and Sterne's use of form is anything but antithetical, Rabelais and Erasmus are clearly models for both. For all four writers the "image of chaos" is, in large part, a foil to the dogmatism that they seek to counter. Sterne, in fact, took more from Swift than a suggestion of the *comic* possibilities of the experimental form. Both *A Tale of a Tub* and *Tristram Shandy* engage in one of the central issues of post-Reformation intellectual enquiry—that of the proper criterion of *truth*. Both works are concerned with hermeneutics at textual and metaphysical levels, and both employ form as a rhetorical tool in order to endorse the arguments of skeptical fideism against secular dogmatists and abstruse system-building.

Everett Zimmerman has argued convincingly that Sterne extends "the critique of biblical and especially textual criticism to be found in Swift's *Tale of a Tub*," and that he is concerned to show the impossibility of certainty based upon the kind of textual scholarship practised by the likes of Bentley and Warburton. In the same essay he offers an insightful explanation of Sterne's linking of *A Tale* and *The Divine Legation of Moses* with *Tristram Shandy:* Sterne links them, according to Zimmerman, "not only to suggest Swift's work as an ironic commentary on Warburton's but also to acknowledge the subversiveness of all three."[43] While Zimmerman is right to note the potential subversiveness of the works, the common factor is surely a concern with epistemology and hermeneutics, and an exploitation of skeptical rhetoric to serve the

Anglican cause. Sterne's treatment of the Job controversy, like Swift's of textual scholarship, is skeptical and commonsensical. What Sterne makes clear in *Tristram Shandy* and his sermon "Search the Scriptures," is that questions of historical provenance or allegorical readings fly in the face of the "simplicity" of the Christian message. For Sterne, the Bible is quite simply "that grand charter of our eternal happiness" (*Sermons*, 396). In *Tristram Shandy*, for all of its formal complexity, Sterne endorses the "simple," Christian, "common sense" beliefs, expounded at critical moments by Toby, Trim, and Yorick.

Since, as we have seen, the methods of the classical skeptics were resurrected in the sixteenth century to deal with arguments over the proper standard of religious knowledge, it should come as no surprise to find Swift and Sterne countering the same problems with the rhetoric of fideism. Swift ingeniously links the allegory of the brothers—dealing explicitly with the Reformation crisis—with the attempts of the Hack and various system builders to explain away the "riddles and mysteries" of God's universe. Swift's commonsense endorsement of the Anglican *via media* is intimately linked with his satire on "new schemes in philosophy." The link is made not simply because an abuse at one level is symptomatic of a deeper malaise, but because they are all homocentric answers to epistemological and teleological issues. The Catholics, the Dissenters, and such textual scholars as Bentley are guilty of overrefining the simplicity of the Gospel in the same way as the philosophers who advance "new systems . . . in things impossible to be known" (*Tale*, 80). The allegory of the brothers treats the issue of biblical interpretation in deliberately reductive terms, warning of the dangers of the human propensity to distort Divine meaning. The *Tale* proper is also concerned with epistemology as it charts the attempts of the Hack, and more auspicious system builders, to achieve certainty by the most convoluted of means.

For Swift, as later for Sterne, these aberrations have a common source—the over-zealous desire of the prideful dogmatist to make the self the measure of all things. The Hack himself attempts to disguise the inane and the vacuous under a cloak of pseudo-scholarship and mystification, but this becomes the means by which Swift, paradoxically, recommends an uncomplicated "belief in things invisible" (*Tale*, 82). The form of *A Tale of a Tub* is much more than the result of Swift's desire to parody the methods and style of the Grub-Street hacks. While Swift is clearly concerned to highlight the shortcomings of the moderns, he did not need their digressive habits to shape the *Tale*. The writers of the skeptical tradition all employ non-linear and "open" form as part of their assault on dogmatism. The *Tale* is a vivid example of just how easily the human imagination, when it "is at cuffs with the senses" (*Tale*, 82), can construct an abstruse framework to disguise emptiness. Like that of *Tristram Shandy*, the form of the *Tale* graphically illustrates the vanity of human-based attempts to achieve certainty without reference to God. In both works, the skeptical form demonstrates the labyrinthine paths into which seekers after truth are led. At the same time—and here we are reminded of the dou-

bleness of truth in the *Praise of Folly*—the reader is being led into a comic celebration of skepticism in all matters *except* the divine "truths" of Anglicanism.
The range of Swift's and Sterne's satire should not blind us to the fact that all
of their targets are finally guilty of searching for truth everywhere but where
it is to be found, not in man but in divinely sanctioned "received wisdom."

The complexity of Swift's vehicle, like Sterne's, can prevent us from seeing the one pervasive and dogmatic blind spot that underpins them. Swift and
Sterne, like Rabelais before them, never tire of the joke that beneath the surface of their work lie hidden meanings and allegories, largely to check the
readers' propensity for over-reading. At the same time, we are constantly
being urged to seek the Christian truths within. The metaphor of the Sileni
central in Erasmus and Rabelais is quite deliberately echoed by Tristram and
the Hack. The Hack simultaneously recommends deep delving and surface
scratching just as Tristram insists that the marbled page ("motly emblem of
my work"), like the black one, mystically hides "opinions, transactions and
truths" (*TS,* III.xxxvi.268). On one level, all four writers are satirising the dangerous ingenuity of scriptural exegetes, but on another they are insisting upon
the opposing truth of the simplicity of the gospel message. As several critics
have noted, there are dangers inherent in viewing the Hack or Tristram as consistent satiric butts since part of their function is to endorse Pauline Christian
folly. Hence the narrators of the *Tale* and *Tristram Shandy* can at one moment
appear as despicable egotists and at another as spokesmen—albeit foolish
ones—for their authors. The effect is a quite deliberate perplexing of the
reader, which is further enhanced by the dialogic texture of the prose. Swift's
and Sterne's pleasure in exercising the exuberance of their wit cannot be
doubted, and yet their suspicion of rhetoric and intellectual obfuscation is so
pronounced as to validate their own methods only as a means to pious ends.
The writers of the skeptical tradition, for all their own erudition and mastery
of rhetoric, consistently derogate refinements in the arts and sciences because
they represent a perceived threat to the "illogical" message of the Gospels.

Behind the anti-intellectualism and praise of folly lies a favorite skeptical
text—St. Paul's defence of the indefensible in 1 Corinthians. St. Paul, in the
face of "contentions" amongst the church of Corinth makes a virtue of his
lack of eloquence in much the same way as Sterne recommends Trim's eloquent ineloquence in opposition to Walter's rhetoric. The eminently reasonable desire of the Jews for "a sign" and of the Greeks "to seek after wisdom" is
swept aside with a sleight of hand consistent with all Christian apologetics
and particularly prominent in the skeptical texts under consideration. For St.
Paul, since earthly wisdom provides no access to God, the flaw *must* be in
man: "God hath chosen the foolish things of the world to confound the wise"
(1 Cor. 1:27). If Paul's words lack persuasion, it is because his discourse is not
that of "the enticing words of man's wisdom" (1 Cor. 2:4). Finally, Paul
trumps his opponents with a claim that validates Erasmus', Rabelais', Montaigne's, Swift's, and Sterne's relentless satire on searchers after truth: "we

speak the wisdom of God in a mystery, *even* the hidden *wisdom,* which God ordained before the world to our glory" (1 Cor. 2:7). We may be inclined to feel Walter's exasperation—after years of delving into the mysteries of nose sizes—with Toby for providing Grangousier's unanswerable solution to the problem, but St. Paul, Toby, and Grangousier have much in common. It is, in part, the very weakness of the case for the defence that leads Swift and Sterne to adopt skeptical strategies to silence their opponents.

The butts of Swift's and Sterne's satire are the same as Montaigne's targets in the *Apology*—those, in the Hack's words, "whose converting imaginations dispose them to reduce all things into *types,* who can make *shadows,* no thanks to the sun, and then mould them into substances, no thanks to philosophy," who refine "what is literal into figure and mystery" (*Tale,* 92). Swift's association of the Dissenters with the Aeolists and the Hack's work with the empty tub has the same rhetorical effect as the images of wind and smoke that Montaigne employs in his arguments to undermine dogmatism.

Laughter is, of course, the primary means by which the Scriblerians and Sterne attempt to discredit the vast range of dogmas that they perceive as pernicious. Despite the wealth of criticism that has concentrated on the fundamental differences between Swift's mordant satire and Sterne's amiable humour, there is basically very little difference in attitude or tone. As is well known, both writers claim that their works are "writ against the spleen,"[44] emphasizing the importance of laughter as purge. While this belief in the medicinal value of laughter found support in Burton and such works as William Stukeley's *Of the Spleen,* its source may be older and of more particular significance than has previously been allowed. In the preface to the first modern translation of Sextus Empiricus' *Hypotyposes,* published in 1562, Henri Estienne explains how he discovered the work. Reading Sextus when he was sick made him laugh, and so helped bring about a cure. In Popkin's summary, Estienne "saw how inane all learning was, and this cured him of his antagonism to scholarly matters by allowing him to take them less seriously."[45] Estienne's claim was itself an extension of Sextus' own metaphor for the ends of skeptical philosophy: the medical metaphor of skepticism as laxative or diuretic, administered to cure the mental disquietude caused by dogmatic wrangling. If Sterne and Swift had not come across the metaphor in Sextus, they could have found it in Montaigne's *Apology.* Laughter, then, for Sterne and Swift is much more than Hobbes' "sudden glory." It is a liberating and happiness-inducing activity that is calculated to purge the mind as preparation for the reception of God's grace. Shandean and Swiftian laughter, like Pantagruelism, belongs properly to a fideistic response to the complexities of the world, a fideism that enables its adherent to "remain in Suspense [rather] than to entangle himself in the innumerable Errors that human Fancy has produc'd" (*Essays,* 2:196).

The relationship between Sterne and the Scriblerians needs to be looked at anew. If this is undertaken without the prejudice of received readings of

Swift and Sterne, our understanding of both writers can be enhanced. Of course, Sterne is much more than a latter-day Swift, but by tracing the fideistic line of descent from the Renaissance humanists through the Scriblerians to Sterne, we are, perhaps, better able to understand both writers. Swift's skepticism no longer seems incompatible with religious belief and *Tristram Shandy*'s much vaunted indeterminacy can be better understood when it is seen as part of a consistent satiric strategy. Some well-worn commonplaces of Sterne criticism may have to be put to rest, but that is all to the good. We may, for example, have to accept that Sterne's religious belief was no sham; that he may never have read the "novelists," let alone contemplated a devastating critique of the shortcomings of the emerging genre; and that Locke is no more the interpretative "open sesame" than the Doctors of the Sorbonne or Tobias Smollett.[46] Sterne wrote late enough in the eighteenth century for many of his readers to be unaware of the full implications of his explicit alignment with the writers of the learned-wit tradition. Consequently, then as now, *some* readers and critics considered the work original and impious, but many contemporaries, including Lord Bathurst, familiar with less fashionable writers like Burton and the Scriblerians, immediately understood the significance of family resemblances.

Notes

1. Donald R. Wehrs, "Sterne, Cervantes, Montaigne: Fideistic Skepticism and the Rhetoric of Desire," *Comparative Literature Studies* 25 (1988): 127–51.
2. For a discussion of Sterne and Charron see Françoise Pellan, "Laurence Sterne's Indebtedness to Charron," *Modern Language Review* 67 (1972): 752–55, and *Tristram Shandy: The Notes,* 39–40, 549–50. Pope refers to Montaigne and Charron with approbation in the *Epistle to Lord Cobham* (line 87). Swift owned copies of the *Essays* and *Of Wisdom. Dean Swift's Library,* ed. Harold Williams (Cambridge: Cambridge University Press, 1932), items 21, 648.
3. The most notable dissenting voice in discussions of the relationship between Swift and Sterne is Melvyn New. Since 1969 New has consistently and persuasively argued the shared Anglican and satiric basis of the Swift/Sterne nexus.
4. John Traugott, *Tristram Shandy's World: Sterne's Philosophical Rhetoric* (Berkeley: University of California Press, 1954), 17.
5. Laurence Sterne, *Letters,* ed. Lewis Perry Curtis (Oxford: Clarendon Press, 1935), 74.
6. Wehrs, "Sterne, Cervantes, Montaigne," 130.
7. Richard H. Popkin, *The History of Scepticism from Erasmus to Spinoza* (Berkeley: University of California Press, 1979), 1, 4.
8. The most thorough consideration of Swift and Erasmus is Eugene R. Hammond, "In Praise of Wisdom and the Will of God: Erasmus' *Praise of Folly* and Swift's *A Tale of a Tub,*" *Studies in Philology* 80 (1983): 253–76. Ronald Paulson also considers the relationship in *Theme and Structure in Swift's Tale of a Tub* (New Haven: Yale University Press, 1960). Sterne's relationship to Erasmus is discussed by John Traugott and John M. Stedmond, *The Comic Art of Laurence Sterne* (Toronto: University of Toronto Press, 1967) and Wehrs, "Sterne, Cervantes, Montaigne."

9.   P. H. Holland, "Robert Burton's 'Anatomy of Melancholy' and Menippean Satire" (Ph.D. diss., University of London, 1979), 362. Holland applies the phrase to Menippean satires in general, but considers the *Tale* and *Tristram Shandy* as examples of the genre.

10.   Erasmus, *Praise of Folly,* trans. Betty Radice (Harmondsworth: Penguin Books Ltd., 1971), 135.

11.   See Hammond, "In Praise of Wisdom," and Paulson, *Theme and Structure.*

12.   Jonathan Swift, *A Tale of a Tub,* ed. Angus Ross and David Woolley (Oxford: Oxford University Press, 1986), 84. Future references to this edition will be cited in the text.

13.   Montaigne, *Essays,* trans. Charles Cotton, 5th ed., 3 vols. (1738), 1:285. Future references to this edition will be cited in the text. Shakespeare, *Hamlet,* 2.2.249–50.

14.   This is also the conclusion of the editors of the *TS Notes,* 313.

15.   For a discussion of Erasmus' influence on Rabelais see Radice's annotations to *Praise of Folly.* The Erasmian elements of *Don Quixote* are considered at length by Alban K. Forcione in *Cervantes and the Humanist Vision: A Study of Four Exemplary Novels* (Princeton: Princeton University Press, 1982).

16.   Valerie Grosvenor Myer, ed. *Laurence Sterne: Riddles and Mysteries* (London and Totowa, NJ: Vision and Barnes and Noble, 1984), 9.

17.   For a stimulating discussion of Locke's impact on the Scriblerians see Christopher Fox, *Locke and the Scriblerians: Identity and Consciousness in Early Eighteenth-Century Britain* (Berkeley: University of California Press, 1988).

18.   Terence Penelhum, "Skepticism and Fideism" in *The Skeptical Tradition,* ed. Myles Burnyeat (Berkeley: University of California Press, 1983), 294.

19.   See Eugene Kirk, *Menippean Satire: An Annotated Catalogue of Texts and Criticism* (New York: Garland, 1980), especially ix–xxxiii.

20.   For an insightful treatment of Burton's links with Sterne see Holland, "Robert Burton's 'Anatomy of Melancholy'," 411–15.

21.   Wehrs, "Sterne, Cervantes, Montaigne," 143.

22.   For earlier discussions of the question of Toby's potency see Mark Sinfield, "Uncle Toby's Potency: Some Critical and Authorial Confusions in *Tristram Shandy,*" *Notes & Queries* 223 (1978): 54–55; and Arthur H. Cash, *Laurence Sterne: The Later Years* (London and New York: Methuen, 1986), 258 n. 16.

23.   John Hall-Stevenson, *Crazy Tales* (1762), 17.

24.   William J. Farrell, "Nature versus Art as a Comic Pattern in *Tristram Shandy,*" *ELH* 30 (1963): 16–35.

25.   See Richard Lanham, *A Handlist of Rhetorical Terms* (Berkeley: University of California Press, 1968), 126.

26.   See *TS Notes,* 110; Pierre Bayle, *The Dictionary Historical and Critical,* 5 vols. (1734–1738), s.v. Tacitus.

27.   See *TS,* VI.xl.570–72.

28.   Pierre Charron, *Of Wisdom,* trans. Lennard (1608), ix. For Sterne and Charron see note 2, above.

29.   For another possible implication of Tristram's construction of "curious" readers see *TS Notes,* 50.

30.   Thomas Stanley, *History of Philosophy: Containing the Lives, Opinions, Actions, and Discourses of Every Sect,* 3rd ed. (London, 1701).

31.   See Dominick Grundy, "Skepticism in Two Essays by Montaigne and Sir Thomas Browne," *Journal of the History of Ideas* 34 (1973): 530–42; Popkin, *History of Scepticism,* 42–86.

32.   Henri Fluchère, *Laurence Sterne: From Tristram to Yorick. An Interpretation of "Tristram Shandy,"* trans. and abridged by Barbara Bray (London: Oxford University Press, 1965), 178.

33.   Penelhum, "Skepticism and Fideism," 295.

34.   For a discussion of the relationship between Menippean satire and religious apologetics see Kirk's introduction to his *Menippean Satire.*

35.   Philip Harth, *Swift and Anglican Rationalism: The Religious Background of "A Tale of a Tub"* (Chicago and London: University of Chicago Press, 1961), especially 21ff. Harth's conception of Anglican rationalism is, in fact, consistent with Popkin's definition of fideism. However, Harth rejects Kathleen William's suggestion that Swift can be viewed as a fideist on the grounds that such a distinction suggests that reason and supernatural religion are incompatible, and that fideism itself was associated with Puritanism.

36.   Gerard Reedy, *The Bible and Reason: Anglicans and Scripture in Late Seventeenth-Century England* (Philadelphia: University of Pennsylvania Press, 1985), 62, 37.

37.   Popkin, *History of Scepticism,* 4.

38.   Sterne, *Letters,* 120. Jonathan Swift, *Gulliver's Travels,* ed. Paul Turner (Oxford: Oxford University Press, 1986), 198.

39.   John Ferriar, *Illustrations of Sterne with other Essays and Verses* (London: 1798), 182.

40.   Popkin, *History of Scepticism,* 54.

41.   Melvyn New, *Laurence Sterne as Satirist: A Reading of "Tristram Shandy"* (Gainesville: University of Florida Press, 1970), 1, 2.

42.   Max Byrd, *Tristram Shandy* (London: Unwin Hyman, 1988), 40; Ronald Paulson, *Satire and the Novel in Eighteenth-Century England* (New Haven, Conn.: Yale University Press, 1967), 256.

43.   Everett Zimmerman, "*Tristram Shandy* and Narrative Representation," *Eighteenth Century* 28 (1987): 127–47, 138; reprinted in this volume. For a different, but equally interesting, reading of the linkage see Melvyn New, "Sterne, Warburton, and the Burden of Exuberant Wit," *Eighteenth-Century Studies* 15 (1982): 245–74.

44.   *TS,* IV.xxii.360; Swift, "The Author Upon Himself," line 48.

45.   See Michael DePorte, *Nightmares and Hobbyhorses: Swift, Sterne, and Augustan Ideas of Madness* (San Marino, Calif.: Huntington Library, 1974), 136; Popkin, *History of Scepticism,* 33–34.

46.   For dissenting views of the Locke/Sterne relationship see Duke Maskell, "Locke and Sterne: Or Can Philosophy Influence Literature?" *Essays In Criticism* 23 (1973): 22–39, and W. G. Day, "*Tristram Shandy:* Locke May Not Be the Key," in Myer, *Laurence Sterne,* 75–83.

Why What Happens in Shandy Hall Is Not "A Matter for the Police"

MICHAEL ROSENBLUM

Critically speaking, we live in interesting times—as in the Chinese curse "may you live in interesting times." My title refers to Derrida's claim that all organized narration is a "matter for the police."[1] I am using this famous slogan as a shorthand for the radical critique of narrative and representation which surfaces in much contemporary theory and which makes these times so "interesting"—that is, both provocative and disturbing. In this view Narrative is a way of knowing that "tracks, tames, frames the world under the aegis of the Law (in its various incarnations as the Father, the Censor, the Institution, the State, and ultimately, the Word)."[2] "Shandy Hall" in my title is shorthand both for the realistic novel, a practice allegedly impelled by this motive to track and frame, and for the eighteenth-century culture in which the novel originates and flourishes. Thus, according to this view of the novel, it is no accident that a kind of narrative which tracks characters in a minutely discriminated temporal-spatial grid should arise in a culture discovering similar techniques for rationalizing time and space in the interests of productivity and surveillance—a sinister Enlightenment which, David Harvey tells us, the "core of Post-Modernists" would have us "abandon" in the interests of "human emancipation."[3]

Aside from his relation to Locke (which might make him amenable to being "situated" in relation to the Enlightenment), or his institutional affiliation as a clergyman, Sterne and his fictional surrogates, Tristram and Yorick, seem benign and marginal figures. Certainly they are less likely to be implicated in schemes of legitimation and surveillance than Fielding, the novelist-magistrate, or Defoe and Richardson, the entrepreneur-novelists. But I choose Sterne to stand for the novel because he is the most circumstantially exact of novelists, the one most given to "tracking" his characters on their various paths, and it is this very exactitude which has been connected with the policing function of narrative. Thus Derrida imagines as one possible scene of origin for narrative an "authoritarian demand" made by "a force of order or law" which asks "What exactly are you talking about?" The subject responds by

Reprinted from *Eighteenth-Century Fiction* 7 (1995): 147–64.

"recounting something, remembering an event or a historical sequence, knowing who he is, where he is, and what he is talking about."[4] Or, in a related formulation, the Law is not the interlocutor demanding narrative of the subject, but the voice of the omniscient narrator tracking the subject's movements.[5] In either case, whether the narrator is the subject accounting for himself to some authority, or an omniscient narrator identified with authority who is rendering an account of the subject, the narrative seeks exactitude, a precise and full notation of circumstances of time and place in order to maintain surveillance or establish guilt. Thus Tristram's precision in establishing chronologies, reconstructing the exact disposition of the family and servants within Shandy Hall, and promising to assemble auxiliary documents, could be seen as a literal response to the demands of an examining magistrate: "Tell us exactly what happened on the night of March 1/2 in 1718 and how did you come to know of these events? Why did Slop arrive on November 5th when he had not been summoned? Under what circumstances did Walter Shandy learn of the birth of one son and the death of another?"[6]

We do not have to take Shklovsky's hyperbole about the "typicality" of *Tristram Shandy* literally to connect this expansiveness, a response to the demand for exactitude, with the expansiveness of those later novelists who give increasingly circumstantial accounts of narrower stretches of time and space, a process of particularization which culminates in the tracking of a group of citizens through the streets of Dublin.[7] In less interesting times it might have seemed that Joyce (or Austen or Woolf) thought, with Blake, that "singular and Particular Detail was the Foundation of the Sublime," or that the precise notation of comings and goings was in the service of mobility rather than constraint. But we have come a long way from the relative cheerfulness of 1957 when Ian Watt could compare the novel's "mode of imitating reality" with the procedures of "another group of specialists in epistemology, the jury in a court of law," which also takes a "circumstantial view of life."[8] Implicit, but unexplored, was the darker side of the comparison: trials and novels both produce narratives which track somebody's movements in order to adjudicate guilt or innocence. What was witty in 1957, a proposed similarity between two such seemingly disparate enterprises as the Law and the Novel (both assumed to be truth-seeking endeavours), between credibility in the courtroom and verisimilitude in realism, now seems two aspects of the same phenomenon: D.A. Miller argues a "radical entanglement" between the practice of the police and the novel, John Bender a connection between the sentences of a novel and the Law.[9]

It makes matters worse that the very feature of the novel heretofore taken as liberating and innovative, the particularity of Watt's "formal realism" or the detailed time-spacing of the novelistic chronotope which Bakhtin claimed gives us the proximity that overcomes hierarchical distance and allows access to history, turns out to be the very feature that connects it with a repressive order. From the forensic perspective of the new narratology, the seeming exhaustiveness of realism is illusory because its wide range of data is winnowed down to those "telling details" which will figure in the indictment or the resolution of the plot. The circumstantiality of realism therefore becomes a mechanism for generating "circumstantial evidence," and as Alexander Welsh has recently argued, "the whole project and promise of circumstantial evidence in the eighteenth century acquired a prosecutorial bent."[10] Only those circumstances figuring in the ultimate indictment will turn out to be *really* relevant, because those details reveal the hidden order whose emergence has been the secret justification for the narrative all along.

In these "interesting times," much of the energy of recent serious scholarship of the eighteenth century derives from its sceptical (if not adversarial) stance towards the object of study, viewed, not as a remote past that has to be painstakingly recreated, but a still-persistent set of assumptions from which we can liberate ourselves only by the most strenuous endeavours.[11] And the most powerful and distinctive discourse of this culture is a realism which "enables the novel to participate in the containment, control, and reformation of social life."[12] In this essay I would like to comment on the arraignment of the circumstantial realism of the eighteenth-century novel, which in some of its melodramatic versions seems more curse than blessing. But like most provocations it does offer opportunities—in this case the opportunity to interpret "the rise of the novel" as something more than a dynamic redescription of the world which harnesses the energies of a new epistemological-technological economic order. I would concede that this traditional account of the motives for representation needs to be sharpened by a greater awareness of, in W.J.T. Mitchell's formulation, the relationship between "aesthetic or semiotic representation" and "political" representation. If the old orthodoxy now seems blandly optimistic, I would argue that the radical suspicion of the novel which is fast becoming the new orthodoxy is too reductive, too willing to assimilate all representation within the period to a forensic model of narrative. The eighteenth-century novelists might pursue an exactitude which seems to answer Derrida's question ("What exactly are you talking about?"), but each novelist has a personal version of exactitude, and not all exactitude is a matter for the police. Sterne's way of bounding his representational space suggests that the frames of realism do not necessarily "frame" us, track us in order to stop us in our tracks, or confine us to the familiar and false knowledge promulgated by an authoritarian order. On the contrary, Sterne's circumstantially dense representational space (and by extension, the density of all realistic notation) undoes a forensic exactitude in which circumstances become relevant only to the extent that they bear upon questions of legitimacy, guilt, and inheritance. In the course of this essay I will be playing Sterne off against Fielding, a novelist who does seem to fit the forensic model (though his connection with the techniques of realism is less clear). My point is not that what happens in Allworthy's Paradise Hall is any more a matter for the police than what happens in Shandy Hall, but that narrative framing and the circumstantiality of formal realism are trickier than the more polemical applications of the "matter for the police" slogan might suggest. Which is, I think, Derrida's point in the essay "Living On: Border Lines" from which the slogan is drawn, an attempt to pose and pursue borderline questions. Derrida's "problematic of judicial framing and of the jurisdiction of frames" encourages us to think through more carefully what is at stake in the framing of narrative fields and the relation of frames to the circumstances which figure within them. A more flexible approach to framing allows us to see that the most powerful narrative fields, realistic or otherwise, always point or can be made to point "beyond" their own borders to something else that might have been given representation. Thus Realism (to the extent that there is such an entity) does not have to be associated with closure, an illusory and misleading totalizing impulse, but, on the contrary, with a constant reminder of the contingency of any given narrative field.

I shall begin with Fielding because, as his prominence in Bender and Welsh might suggest, his way of framing seems to "fit" the forensic account of framing. The typical Fielding novel tracks its characters through seemingly random and far-ranging paths, but ends with a convergence of paths which establishes the final truth about who Joseph (or Tom, Jonathan Wild, Colonel Booth) really is, and what he has and has not done: the circumstances assembled by the omniscient narrator establish the protagonist's guilt or innocence, his legitimacy or illegitimacy, his inheritance or disinheritance. Exactitude is achieved and in that sense Fielding's narratives can be said to be matters for the police.

What is less clear is whether Fielding's way of framing the narrative has as much to do with the circumstantially exhaustive grid of the new realism as John Bender claims. Fielding is in fact notoriously casual in waiving away stretches of time or space which do not interest him; his most characteristic gesture as a narrator is to announce that he is skipping something that deserves to be skipped. Fielding preserves the "dignity" of his "history" by ruling something out of bounds: whether the world is seen as time or space to be traversed, there are vacant stretches, "the centuries of Monkish Dulness when the world seems to have been asleep," or "the gloomy and dull Plain" which must be hurried over. One narrates only when the coach is full, only when one has a prize to announce rather than the many more "blanks in the grand lottery of time," only when there is some "news," something "remarkable." Characters and incidents need not be "trite, common, or vulgar; such as happen in every Street, or in every House, or which may be met with in the home Articles of a News-paper."[13] Only the "painful and voluminous Historian" would imitate the newspaper and think "himself obliged to fill up as much Paper with the Detail of Months and Years in which nothing remarkable happened" (2, 1, 75). What always happens—copulation, marriage, births—or what the readers could figure out for themselves (the predictable scenes of courtship between Blifil and Bridget, or the course of Bridget's grief) is the least promising material for imitation. What *does* have "information value" for Fielding is the apparent break with the norm, what will surprise the reader because it does not happen in every street or every house.[14] The proper concern of narrative is therefore the extraordinary violation of the norm: "When any extraordinary Scene presents itself (as we trust will often be the Case) we shall spare no Pains nor Paper to open it at large to our Reader" (2, 1, 76). The mark of the extraordinary is the coincidence, a "falling together" in time or space. The more unlikely the "fit" in space and time, the more remarkable the event, the more narratable it is. As in Bakhtin's chronotope of adventure time, "X" marks the spot where the paths cross or do not cross and that makes all the difference.[15] What happens in Fielding's novel is therefore a function of a simple relation in time and space: "who is where" and "when," and for the purpose of the kind of narrative plotting very few of the attributes of "when" or "where" are relevant, the mere conjunction of these persons in this place at this time being enough to establish (and exhaust) their remarkability. Circumstances are important only to the extent that they figure in the tightly constructed causal chain which is the plot. Because he is a "judicious" historian, he knows the value of the "many little Circumstances too often omitted by injudicious Historians, from which Events of the utmost Importance arise. The World may indeed be considered as a vast Machine, in which the great Wheels are originally set in Motion by those which are very minute, and almost imperceptible to any but the strongest Eyes" (5, 4, 225). That Partridge just misses seeing Jenny Jones at Upton is one of those instances "we may frequently observe in Life, where the greatest Events are produced by a nice Train of little Circumstances; and more than one Example of this may be discovered by the accurate Eye, in this our History" (8, 2, 916). While the accurate eye of the reader will note and appreciate what the strong eye of the historian has spotted, neither will be overwhelmed by many such little circumstances. Only *some* circumstances need be noted, those that lead to great events, little wheels being important only in relation to big wheels.

In this kind of narrative, circumstances are crucial only in the sense that, had matters been otherwise, there would have been no "great Event." But there is no sense that the character of events is shaped by circumstances or that another set of circumstances could produce a different but equally remarkable set of events. A narrative's circumstantiality is measured not so much by the number of circumstances which figure within it as by the narrator's sense that each unforeseen contingent circumstance makes a claim upon his attention, establishing thereby a new and wider field of potential relevance for the rest of the narrative. When the accumulation of circumstances deflects the narrative from its original path it is impossible to distinguish between big and little wheels, great and small events. In Fielding's narrative machine the contingent aspect of circumstances, their very chanciness, is overshadowed by the sense that only the particular circumstances selected by the narrator will yield the exact truth about the hero.

Such a narrative is framed centripetally around the extraordinary event, the point of coincidence, which is the test and limit of relevance. If it is the fact of intersection (or non-intersection) which makes the event remarkable, then the circumstances, "the totality of surrounding things" or "condition or state of affairs surrounding and affecting an agent, especially the external conditions prevailing at the time," or "the logical surroundings or 'adjuncts' of an action; the time, place, manner, cause, occasion . . . amid which it takes place" will figure in the narrative in only a limited way (*OED*). Like Dr Johnson, who associates the circumstantial with "something adventitious, which may be taken away without the annihilation of the principal thing considered," Fielding always feels the secondariness and inessentiality of circumstance.[16]

In striking contrast, Sterne always makes circumstance "the principal thing considered." Tristram claims that circumstances "give everything its size and shape," and Yorick professes to be "governed by circumstances." Since for Sterne there are no blanks in the lottery of time, since all plains can be converted into cities, since it is impossible to imagine Tristram or Yorick saying (as Fielding's narrators always do) "nothing remarkable happened," Sterne's narrative journey is always deliberate and attentive to circumstances that turn up along the way. Each circumstance has a weightiness, a claim to relevance not circumscribed by its relation to a whole. Where Fielding's principle of framing is centripetal (only what is at the point of intersection need be given representation), Sterne's is centrifugal: more important than "X," the point of intersection, is everything that surrounds it.

Thus the most celebrated and extended narrative sequence in *Tristram Shandy*, Tristram's account of his birth, is characteristically circumstantial, a representation of what *surrounds* the event in time and space. The birth is not an event so much as an occasion to pursue "the totality of surrounding things": the causes and the effects, the time immediately before and the time immediately after. The stretch of time preceding the birth is notated: the hour and a half of silence downstairs during which Toby puffs his pipe and contemplates his new pair of black plush breeches. This is broken by the "noise of running backwards and forward . . . above-stairs" which signals the impending event; the two minutes and thirteen seconds between the ringing of the bell summoning Obadiah and the arrival of Slop; the subsequent two hours and ten minutes during which Tristram is still not born.

But we do not know the exact moment of his birth. We know the birth only as something that happens while, elsewhere, something else is happening: it happens while Toby and Walter doze belowstairs in the parlour, while Slop, the midwife, and Mrs Shandy labour abovestairs, and while, somewhere on the premises, Trim converts boots to mortars. And in yet another time and place, Tristram writes his preface. The birth itself, the great event, we find out about only incidentally, when Walter asks about the noise in the kitchen and Trim tells him that Dr Slop is building a bridge. When Walter learns the truth of the birth and disfiguration, he goes upstairs to collapse in bed. His collapse is minutely described, as are the motions of his body when, somewhat later, he rises from bed and gestures to Toby, who is sitting in the minutely described chair. Walter makes his way back to the stairs, descends to the landing, chats with Toby, and questions the maid Susannah, who appears briefly at the foot of the stairs with a large pincushion. In order to get Walter and Toby off the stairs and off to bed (except for the short nap, they have not slept since "nine hours before Slop's arrival"), Tristram drops the curtain. Walter had asked Susannah how the child was doing and where Slop was. She suddenly appears in Walter's bedroom to answer the questions: the child is doing badly and Slop is gone. And so is Yorick. We do not know when or why both have left, or when the curate named Tristram has come, their departures and arrivals being part of the general comings and goings of a complicated household. After the baptism everybody, the nurse included, goes back to sleep. In the morning Walter asks that Trismegistus be sent down to keep his father and uncle company at the breakfast table; he soon learns that Susannah has run upstairs crying and wringing her hands, and that her mistress is also having hysterics upstairs. As Walter makes his way to find consolation at the fishpond, Toby summons Trim from the bowling green. Another unlucky accident has occurred, coincidentally, more or less at the same time as the unfortunate baptism—not in the gallery as Toby thinks, but in the garden. Trim postpones telling Toby that the cow has broken into the fortifications, although Tristram has already, memorably, told us.

Narrative on this model is a matter of tracking comings and goings within and around the house, of shuttling between upstairs and downstairs, and even the landing between. The narrative field is decentred and dispersed: each event is preceded or followed by, and simultaneous with, other events which might also deserve representation, and each event takes place in a site that borders on a contiguous site where something else is happening. Nor is there a natural and inevitable scale by which to apportion the "proper" degree of representation. Tristram asks: "Is it not a shame to make two chapters of what passed in going down one pair of stairs? for we are got no farther yet than to the first landing, and there are fifteen more steps down to the bottom; and for aught I know, as my father and my uncle *Toby* are in a talking humour, there may be as many chapters as steps" (I.x.336). Sterne knows the normal narrative value of a conversation on the stairs, the customary relation of chapters to steps, but that does not prevent him from imagining another more exhaustive scale of representation. Neither Tristram nor his reader can predict the duration of the conversation. Tristram pretends to acquiesce in something that is out of his hands ("let that be as it will, Sir, I can no more help it than my destiny"), but then, obeying "a sudden impulse," he drops the curtain and rules a line to begin a new chapter, which becomes the promised chapter on chapters (I.x.337). The threatened "excess" of representation abruptly gives way to no further representation, and either alternative seems an equally possible framing of the field. Sterne's wilful inclusions and exclusions, his experiments in scales of representation, his lowering of the threshold of narration to include conversations on stairs, the description of rush chairs and the placement of chamberpots suggest the arbitrariness of any set of representational choices. At any point there is something more that the narrator might have felt as relevant and which therefore might have figured within the frame of the narrative. Instead of producing closure, such exactitude generates new circumstances and the need for new explanations. It may well be that after hundreds of pages, we still do not know the exact truth about Tristram's paternity.

By contrast, the sense of relevance for Fielding is relatively straightforward: for all the amplitude of his novels, the proper path of the narrative is clearly marked, the speed of the narrative brisk as it moves through a Nature that needs be sampled only selectively. There is no regret about alternate paths, or the terrain on the other side of the path, what Leo Braudy has called "the possibilities beyond the hedge."[17] In *The Journal of a Voyage to Lisbon* Fielding complains that "Nature is not, any more than a great genius, always admirable in her productions, and therefore a traveller, who may be called her commentator should not expect to find everywhere subjects worthy of his notice." It is better to set too little of the world before the reader than too much, "better to be hungry than surfeited, and to miss your dessert at the table of a man whose garden abounds with the choicest fruits than to have your taste affronted with every sort of trash that can be pick'd up at the greenstall, or the wheelbarrow."[18] This kind of pickiness is foreign to Sterne's narrator, who "interests his heart in every thing," and sees "what time and chance are perpetually holding out to him as he journeyeth on his way." The world is barren only to the man "who will not cultivate the fruits it offers" (*ASJ*, 114–15). These different ways of moving through the world reflect differences in temperament and situation—one dying man remembers and imagines a journey through which the other dying man is still suffering. But they are also the differences between an older and a newer model of "time-spacing" narrative.

In *Middlemarch* George Eliot observes that Fielding lived "when summer afternoons were spacious, and the clock ticked slowly in the winter evenings." Because she is a "belated historian," she feels she cannot linger: she "has so much to do in unravelling certain human lots, seeing how they were woven and interwoven, that all the light . . . [she] can command must be concentrated on this particular web, and not dispersed over that tempting range of relevancies called the universe."[19] Though misapplied (Sterne, not Fielding is the eighteenth-century novelist who lingers because he feels the universe is "a tempting range of relevancies"), Eliot's images make a suggestive opposition between two ways of framing/plotting/tracking. The light of representation which illuminates an otherwise dark world can be concentrated within the converging geometries of the classical web of plot with its secrets of birth, and secret crimes, or it can be dispersed to "cover" more time and more space of a universe which is seen as offering "a tempting range of relevancies." Eliot's "particular web" is like Fielding's "machine"—a construction for contracting representational space using the time-spacing of traditional plotting. Such constructions do achieve a forensic exactitude in that the subject is tracked until sufficient "telling details" are amassed to reveal the hidden secrets. But such constructions are not a new kind of narrative developed by an "Enlightenment" culture concerned with rationalizing time and space, but a continuation of the oldest models of plot-making descended from the most intricate web/machine of all, the story of Oedipus, a narrative built upon coincidences, all of *them* definitely a matter for the police. Although Eliot may weave her plots out of such webs in the interests of closure, like Sterne (or Defoe or Richardson) she is really drawn to the more leisurely time-spacing which construes the universe as a tempting range of relevance. In this sense the exactitude of realism undoes forensic exactitude: it is expansive, more concerned with opening up frames and the sense of relevance than in closing them down. As in Sterne, more representation is always a possibility because circumstances within the frame may imply circumstances beyond the frame.

Nicholas Boyle notes that Roland Barthes in speaking of a photograph of his mother refers to "the chance detail . . . in which the absolute singularity and contingency of the recorded moment leaps from the frame. In virtue of that one detail the otherwise unknown subject acquires 'a whole life outside her portrait.' " Boyle then goes on to argue that what Barthes says happens in a photograph also happens in the realistic novel: the chance detail leaps from the frame to imply a "hidden ground" beyond the frame:

> the realistic work of literature . . . suggests that beyond it, between its chapters and before and after, lies *more* of the world, its world and ours, than happens, contingently, to have been articulated. . . . we recognize that every picture has its frame, but our mind is projected beyond this particular frame into the one world which we share with the creatures of the writer's fiction and which we know in many modes and from many pictures and many different stories. "How many children had Lady Macbeth?" is a trivial question . . . but it is not meaningless.[20]

As with Sterne's provisional borders, there is always more of "the world" beyond the frame of the text. Boundaries can be extended in time and space, since there are potential narratable events as well as describable contiguous existents before, after, and beyond the actual margins of the narrative. Tristram's foregrounding of his representational choices (this site or this interval rather than the adjacent site or interval, and on this scale rather than another) is a reminder of the extent to which representation is always a matter of choice, of framing in or out a piece of "its world and ours."

Such framing, as contemporary criticism argues, is ideological in nature, since only some of the things that happen (or can be imagined as happening) will seem significant enough to be "narratable." Dr Johnson insists that the novelist "select objects, and . . . cull from the mass of mankind, those individuals upon which the attention ought most to be employ'd. . . . it is necessary to distinguish those parts of nature, which are most proper for imitation."[21] But *which* objects, *which* individuals, *which* parts of nature are most proper for imitation? Why will some things rather than others seem worthy of narration or description? And narration or description on what scale? In the past such choices might have been seen largely as a matter of the internal dynamics of narrative or the particular stylistic choices of an artist, but it is becoming clearer that the sense of what is "most proper for imitation" depends upon prior (and ideologically shaped) framing conventions. Thus Barthes imagines the realist author as needing to place an empty frame in front of objects: he can only describe them by first transforming "the 'real' into a depicted object (framed)."[22] Or in Michael Holquist's formulation: "Novels are not pictures but Frames. They are pictures of frames."[23]

Thus Fielding's concern that the rotten fruit be framed out and Sterne's that the abundant fruit of the world be framed in are matters of inclusion and exclusion that involve "radical social assumptions of causation and consequence."[24] Fielding's man of sense would rather miss dessert at the table of a gentleman than resort to the greenstall for nourishment. The social implications of the comparison of the parts of the world that are unworthy of representation with the trash of the greenstall are as difficult to ignore as they are in Sir Joshua Reynolds's assertion that "whatever is familiar, or in any way reminds us of what we see and hear every day, perhaps does not belong to the higher provinces of art, either in poetry or painting."[25] The unworthy parts of "Nature," the trash of the world, what we see and hear every day, must be denied representation; a properly militant framing must "cull" and "select" to avoid the plebian food/narrative or familiar sights and sounds offensive to the fastidious Augustan gentleman. Dr Johnson's celebrated warning about excessive representation in the novel makes the social issue clear:

> If the world be promiscuously described, I cannot see of what use it can be to read the account; or why it may not be as safe to turn the eye immediately upon mankind, as upon a mirror which shows all that presents itself without discrimination.[26]

Unlike the mirror, which promiscuously reflects all parts of the world, safe accounts of the world discriminate lest they be contaminated by pieces of the world unworthy of representation.

Johnson's uneasiness about narratives which promiscuously represent too much of the world and mix together what should be kept distinct reverses the current longing for a radically promiscuous narrative that fully mingles categories of high and low or calls those categories into question: a heterogeneity that confounds the hierarchies of class, race, and gender. The ideological preferences of contemporary criticism reverse Johnson's. In order to "rise" in the first place, the novel had to overcome neoclassical qualms about "minute particularity," representation for its own sake that descended to circumstances unworthy the dignity of narrative. In our own time, precisely because the possibility of representation for its own sake has been called into question, critics like Bender and Miller see the "telling detail" as more forensic than artistic. Where the contemporary critic wants a promiscuity of representation that he or she knows is illusory (narrative being "always already" in the service of what is being passed off as moral truth), Dr Johnson worries that too much representation will undermine the social order's "moral truths." The neoclassical critic worries that not enough of the world will get framed out while a modern critic like Barthes complains that what is allowed into the frame only replicates prior framing practice. One worries about the precariousness of frames, the other about their ubiquity. The neoclassical critic complains that frames might not do what the contemporary critic claims framing cannot help doing.

These converging and contrasting worries suggest that the current mistrust of representation is, as Christopher Prendergast has demonstrated in *The Order of Mimesis,* only the latest stage of a long-standing debate about the motive and purposes of representation. The present emphasis on the ideological basis of framing seems to me an interesting and legitimate contribution to that debate. Less helpful is the claim that the ideological basis of framing necessarily contaminates it and ultimately implicates *all* mimesis (the realistic novel is only the easiest target) in an "authoritarian gesture" that imprisons "us in a world which, by virtue of its familiarity, is closed to analysis and criticism."[27] I have been arguing that the frames of realistic representation are not as clearly demarcated or as predictably forensic in intent as Bender and Miller would claim. Rather, as Boyle argues, chance details within the frame can imply more of the world beyond the frame. Bakhtin insists upon the "sharp and categorical boundary between the actual world as source of representation and the world represented in the work," but he also warns that it is "impermissible to take this categorical boundary line as something absolute and impermeable."[28]

Thus Fielding's militant patrol of the borders of his text might lead some modern readers to feel that he has framed out what they most might have wished to see represented. When Tom Jones goes into George Seagrim's house in search of Molly, such readers might feel that Fielding has missed the opportunity to describe the circumstances of the rural poor, even though what we get instead is as amusing as the discovery of Square squatting behind the rug/blanket. But when John Richetti reads the passage it is reframed:

Square's ridiculous posture reminds the narrator of "the Attitude in which we often see Fellows in the public Streets of London, who are not suffering but deserving Punishment by so standing" (5, 5, 229). Richetti says that:

> we are violently transported from a Somersetshire transformed by comic invention to an actual London . . . to urban squalor unmodified and unmediated by comic artifice. . . . these squatting fellows point briefly to something like an actual urban disorder the novel pointedly avoids and consistently transforms.[29]

Richetti's reframing of the narrative field makes it "point" to something that Fielding "pointedly avoids," the urban disorder which E.P. Thompson has taught us to seek. Square's squatting points to the hidden ground of history in the same way that the wreath of smoke in "Tintern Abbey" points to the dispossessed workers camping just around the bend of the Wye. In this kind of criticism, the distinction between what is inside and outside the frame is tenuous, and interest shifts to what might have figured within the field.[30] What figures within a narrative is always less than the more that might have figured (and vice versa), narrative being an actual saying against the ground of a potential might-have-been said. Frames seem more ubiquitous in that everything turns out to be a matter of framing, but also a lot less solid in that frames can always be reframed.

Sterne's emphasis upon the arbitrariness of any representational space, of the world that is always beyond the frame, seems to me consonant with this understanding of the hypothetical nature of frames. Moreover, his novel does not need much reframing to get us from its represented world to the historical world "outside" the text. If Fielding (via the interventions of a reader like Richetti) can momentarily transport us to the urban squalor of eighteenth-century London, then Sterne far more directly and in an unprecedentedly sustained way takes us "inside" domestic space to render an account of the birth of a child to a Turkey merchant living in quiet retirement in an English village. From Walter's perspective all of the circumstances of Tristram's conception and birth are remarkable, instances of extraordinary and tragic coincidences, but all the hypotheses about noses, names, and undisturbed homunculi do not hide the fact that from another perspective—Toby's for example—Tristram's birth is entirely normal: a natural process that takes place against a background of such ordinary human activities as waiting, sleeping, having breakfast, or walking up and down the stairs.

With the exception of volume VII, almost everything that happens in *Tristram Shandy* happens within Shandy Hall or its immediate vicinity. For Sterne, as his phrase "domestic misadventures" suggests, the domestic is not incompatible with having a story worth telling. The reference to the traditional romance plot that underlies so much of Fielding's and Smollett's fiction (disinheritance, exile, return) is vestigial, surviving only in the news of Bobby's death and Tristram's subsequent status as heir to Shandy Hall. And if, as Robert Gorham Davis has suggested, the circumcision and subsequent breeching of Tristram refer to the rites of passage of the mythic hero, both the birth of Tristram and the death of Bobby are assimilated to a domestic context.[31] The news of Bobby's death comes on the day that Obadiah discovers that the household is out of yeast, and when he brings in the letter bearing that news, he follows his usual practice of making sure that the parlour door is ajar when anything interesting is in the air. The bad hinge that separates the kitchen and the parlour is thus associated with the news of Bobby's death just as it is with the news of Tristram's birth. The news revealed in the letter reaches Mrs Shandy as she bends at the door in the dark passageway, and becomes the subject of simultaneous and contrasting orations in the parlour and the kitchen in the same way that the news of Tristram's circumcision also traces a path through the household: as Susannah runs from the nursery she passes the cook, who gives the news (with commentary) to Jonathan, who gives it to Obadiah, who, summoned by the bell, gives an account to Walter, who goes upstairs to see for himself.

Although Bobby dies only once, and Tristram is born and circumcised only once, Tristram's emphasis is not on those extraordinary departures from the norm, but on the ordinary workings of the household, what is *always* the case with the Shandys: "was every day of my life to be as busy a day as this— And why not?—and the transactions and opinions of it to take up as much description—And for what reason should they be cut short?" (IV.xiii.341–42). "This day" is "busy" because it is Tristram's birthday, but Tristram sees every other day of his life as similarly eventful, full of "transactions" that merit telling. Unlike Fielding and Reynolds, Sterne sees that the quotidian is compatible with having a story worth the telling. Although the representation is not fully "promiscuous" in the sense that Johnson fears and contemporary critics admire (Mrs Shandy is usually out of the range of the narrative, the servants are *comic* servants, the narrator is an Augustan gentleman, and so forth), it nevertheless makes a contribution to the history of the everyday, a beginning at least in giving representation to what Lefebvre describes as "the immense wealth that the humblest facts of everyday life contain."[32] We are given a precise representation of how a husband and wife, a pair of brothers, servants and masters arrange themselves within domestic space. We are told how two sets of stairs connect upstairs and downstairs, how the gallery connects the bedrooms, how the dark passageway, the bellpull, and the bad hinge connect the parlour and kitchen. And beyond the house are the paths leading to and from the fishpond and the bowling green. Tristram gives us all the conduits along which the life of the family flows, making Sterne the first of the major novelists to be interested in exploring the narrative possibilities of intersections of paths within a household.[33]

This is tracking, as concentrated a circumstantial realism as it is possible to find in the eighteenth century and an obvious model for the later tracking and framing of Jane Austen and her successors, but it is not, I would argue, a matter for the police. The surveillance is innocent: nobody is watching Tristram but Tristram himself, or us watching ourselves watching Tristram. Moreover, the exactitude of the narrative is an exactitude that Tristram himself insists upon rather than an exactitude that has been enjoined upon him. Indeed, if there is an "authoritarian demand" anywhere in the transaction, it is Tristram's demand that the listener/reader submit to so much exactitude. Although exactitude might suit the purposes of the police, it also suits any teller who thinks he has a story worth the telling. And if the teller can justify his tale, make it seem "narratable," it suits the reader as well. This traditional view of the genesis of the narrative situation tells us at least as much about the "narrativity of narrativity" as Derrida's more provocative reconstruction of the scene of origin of narrative. Michael Holquist has claimed that the function of the novel is to "mitigate the laws that govern the 'proper' categories of biography, thus keeping open possibilities of individuation available nowhere else in society."[34] By contrast, John Bender argues that "the liberal state . . . aspires to record as many stories as it has citizens or subjects; its mode is realism of the most extremely particularized kind." But for Bender such narrative Particularity is ultimately in the service of bureaucratic Generality: these individual stories are organized "categorically so that they will be comprehensible, that is, so that their subjects can be identified as controllable, storable resources."[35] The contrast between Holquist's Bakhtinian spin on the novel and Bender's Foucauldian spin could not be clearer. In this essay I have been arguing that the linkage of circumstantial exactitude to forensic tracking is less persuasive than the traditional claim that the particularity of "formal realism" opens up rather than closes down possibilities of representation. Tristram's Exactitude (or Clarissa's or Moll's for that matter), far from homogenizing him and making him a "controllable, storable resource," allows us to know who he is in all his singularity: to know Tristram is to know his circumstances. At the same time, for all of Tristram's insistence upon the particulars of his account, his narrative is inescapably general in its thrust, appealing as it does to the history of the family, the routines and "scripts" drawn from a familiar social world. And this too is more than a mere recycling of official, authoritarian knowledge. Sterne draws upon and contributes to "a world intersubjectively known and held in common"[36] which is not (though the "matter-for-the-police" critics would say otherwise) an illusion or part of a plot against us.

Notes

1. Jacques Derrida, "Living On: Border Lines" in *Deconstruction and Criticism,* ed. Harold Bloom et al (New York: Seabury Press, 1979), p. 102.

2. This is Christopher Prendergast's gloss on Derrida's formulation in his brilliant account and critique of contemporary attacks on mimesis, *The Order of Mimesis* (Cambridge: Cambridge University Press, 1986), p. 217.

3. David Harvey, *The Condition of Postmodernity: An Inquiry into the Origins of Cultural Change* (Oxford: Blackwell, 1989), p. 14.

4. Derrida, pp. 104–5.

5. John Bender argues that the narrator in Fielding "personifies the conventions of transparency and objectivity implied in formal realism and, through the juridical analogy, links them with the rational but invisible order of the metropolitan bureaucracy." *Imagining the Penitentiary: Fiction and the Architecture of Mind in Eighteenth-Century England* (Chicago: University of Chicago Press, 1987), p. 179.

6. In *Sentimental Journey* Sterne tracks Yorick's erratic path from the exact notation of that hour and twenty minutes in Calais through the twists and turns of the itinerary in Paris and Versailles. Of course the fact that Yorick is travelling without a passport even gives us a literal crime.

7. Such particularity continues to be valued in contemporary culture: in the particularities of Updike, the inexhaustible chronicler of Brewer; in the penchant for "thick description" in cultural studies; in Frederick Wiseman's traversal in real time of the high school or the madhouse. To say nothing of the elaborations of ordinary lives in remote stretches of Alaska or Brooklyn offered by the *New Yorker.*

8. Ian Watt, *The Rise of the Novel* (Berkeley: University of California Press, 1957; reprinted 1964), p. 31.

9. D.A. Miller, *The Novel and the Police* (Berkeley: University of California Press, 1988), p. 20; Bender, p. 35.

10. Alexander Welsh, *Strong Representations: Narrative and Circumstantial Evidence in England* (Baltimore: Johns Hopkins University Press, 1992), p. 47.

11. Thus Nancy Armstrong's goal in *Desire and Domestic Fiction* (New York: Oxford University Press, 1987) is to "provide some understanding of our own status as products and agents of the hegemony I am describing" (p. 27). Similarly, John Bender emphasizes the need to avoid "a frame of reference—that fundamentally reproduced Enlightenment assumptions themselves." See "Eighteenth Century Studies" in *Redrawing the Boundaries: The Transformation of English and American Literary Studies,* ed. Stephen Greenblatt and Giles Gunn (New York: MLA, 1992), p. 79.

12. Bender, p. 257.

13. Henry Fielding, *The History of Tom Jones, A Foundling,* ed. Martin C. Battestin and Fredson Bowers (Middletown, Conn.: Wesleyan University Press, 1975), 8, 2, 407. References are by book, chapter, and page number of this edition.

14. I. Lotman points out that "an event is that which did occur, though it could also not have occurred. The less probability that a given event will take place (i.e., the greater the information conveyed by the message concerning the event), the higher the rank of that event on the plot scale." See *The Structure of the Artistic Text,* trans. Ronald Vroon (Ann Arbor: Department of Slavic Languages and Literature, University of Michigan, 1977), p. 234.

15. "What is important is to be able to escape, to catch up, to outstrip, to be or not to be in a given place at a given moment, to meet or not to meet and so forth." Mikhail Bakhtin, "Forms of Time and Chronotope in the Novel," *The Dialogic Imagination,* ed. Michael Holquist, trans. Caryl Emerson and Michael Holquist (Austin: University of Texas Press, 1981), p. 91. The various plots against Tom unravel when, at the end, all paths meet in London and the characters can figure out where and when their paths have crossed before. The original cause of many of Tom's difficulties is an incomplete coincidence: a brother and a sister fall ill at the same time, but not in the same place.

16. Samuel Johnson, *Dictionary of the English Language,* 4th edition (London, 1773).

17. Leo Braudy, *Narrative Form in History and Fiction: Hume, Fielding, and Gibbon* (Princeton: Princeton University Press, 1970), p. 164. I borrow the figure from Braudy, but I reverse his emphasis.

18. Henry Fielding, *Journal of a Voyage to Lisbon,* ed. Austin Dobson (London: Oxford University Press, 1907), p. 6.

19. George Eliot, *Middlemarch*, ed. W.J. Harvey (London: Penguin, 1964), p. 170.

20. Nicholas Boyle, "Nietzsche and the 'Middle Mode of Discourse,' " in *Realism in European Literature: Essays in Honour of J.P. Stern*, ed. Nicholas Boyle and Martin Swales (Cambridge: Cambridge University Press, 1986), p. 150.

21. Samuel Johnson, *The Rambler* 4 (31 March 1750), ed. W.J. Bate and Albrecht B. Strauss (New Haven: Yale University Press, 1969), p. 22.

22. Roland Barthes, *S/Z*, trans. Richard Miller (New York: Hill and Wang, 1974), p. 55.

23. Michael Holquist and Walter Reed, "Six Theses on the Novel—And Some Metaphors," *New Literary History* 11 (1980), 418.

24. Raymond Williams, *Marxism and Literature* (Oxford: Oxford University Press, 1972), p. 176.

25. Sir Joshua Reynolds, "Discourse 13" (1797), *Discourses on Art,* ed. Stephen Mitchell (Indianapolis: Bobbs-Merrill, 1965), p. 198.

26. Johnson, p. 22.

27. Prendergast, p. 6.

28. Bakhtin, p. 253.

29. John Richetti, "Representing an Under Class: Servants and Proletarians in Fielding and Smollett," in *The New Eighteenth Century: Theory, Politics, English Literature*, ed. Felicity Nussbaum and Laura Brown (New York: Methuen, 1987), pp. 93–94.

30. Stephen Greenblatt asserts that the "rigid distinction between that which is within the text and that which is outside" must "be opposed on principle." See "Culture" in *Critical Terms for Literary Study,* ed. Frank Lentricchia and Thomas McLaughlin (Chicago: University of Chicago Press, 1990), p. 227.

31. Robert Gorham Davis, "Sterne and the Delineation of the Modern Novel," in *The Winged Skull,* ed. A.H. Cash and John M. Stedmond (London: Methuen, 1971), p. 38.

32. Henri Lefebvre, *Critique of Everyday Life,* trans. John Moore (1947; reprinted London: Verso, 1991), 1:132.

33. Perhaps a similar claim could be made for Richardson. But although the positioning of the various family members within Harlowe Hall is carefully notated, the emphasis is more on their placement in an extraordinary crisis rather than on their place in the family's ordinary domestic routines.

34. Holquist, p. 423.

35. Bender, p. 155.

36. Prendergast, p. 22.

THE EROTICAL STERNE

◆

Proust's Influence on Sterne:
Remembrance of Things to Come

Melvyn New

In the opening pages of *La prisonnière*, Marcel looks from the window of his Paris apartment to the street below, hoping to "catch a glimpse of some laundress carrying her linen-basket, a baker-woman in a blue apron, a dairymaid with a tucker and white linen sleeves. . . . But if the access of joy brought me by the spectacle of women whom it was impossible to imagine *a priori* made the street, the town, the world, more desirable, more deserving of exploration, it set me longing, for that very reason, to recover my health, to go out of doors and, without Albertine, to be a free man. How often, at the moment when the unknown woman who was to haunt my dreams passed beneath the window, sometimes on foot, sometimes at full speed in a motor-car, did I not suffer from the fact that my body could not follow my gaze which kept pace with her, and falling upon her as though shot from the embrasure of my window by an arquebus, arrest the flight of the face that held out for me the offer of a happiness which, thus cloistered, I should never know!" (p. 20).[1] Some 150 years earlier, Sterne's alter-ego, Yorick, had also looked out his Paris window at the sexual energies in the street below, out of reach: "I own my first sensations, as soon as I was left solitary and alone in my own chamber in the hotel, were far from being so flattering as I had prefigured them. I walked up gravely to the window in my dusty black coat, and looking through the glass saw all the world in yellow, blue, and green, running at the ring of pleasure.—The old with broken lances, and in helmets which had lost their vizards—the young in armour bright. . . . Alas, poor Yorick! cried I, what art thou doing here?" (pp. 155–56). The passage is typical of Sterne's most mature writing—a virtuoso mingling of heretofore incompatible intentions, most obviously the pathetic and the bawdy. The sad redundancy of *solitary and alone*, the elevation of *prefigured*, the touching contrast that begins with *gravely*, moves to the *dusty black coat* (*grave*, *dust*, and *black* playing out another trope) and concludes with the prismatic colors through the glass—all this is the work of a masterly craftsman earning an emotional response. But then

Reprinted from *MLN* 103 (1988): 1031–55.

comes the ring of pleasure, a bawdy image borrowed from Rabelais, and a sudden series of jokes—"broken lances," "lost vizards" and the young "in armour," that is, in condoms, according to eighteenth-century usage. The accumulation of pathos is too rich to be unintentional, but so is the accumulation of bawdiness.

These two literary characters, Marcel and Yorick, so closely identifiable with their respective authors but *personae* nonetheless, are trapped behind glass, cut off from the rich sexuality of the world in the street below. Proust returns again and again to the contrast between this street and Marcel's prison-apartment in the fifth volume of *A la Recherche du Temps Perdu,* translated as *The Captive* by C. K. Scott Moncrieff. For Sterne, too, the separation between Yorick and the sexual world (of France, of health, of youth) dominates his *Sentimental Journey.* It is perhaps the final episode of Sterne's work that can best serve us as a paradigm for much that concerned both authors— and it would be well to remember that Proust's truly extraordinary wit would have delighted in the comedy of the scene. Traveling alone, Yorick finds himself required to share a room with a woman at the inn. For both, the sexual nature of the encounter is uppermost in mind, but the treaty they make puts Yorick on his honor to ignore desire; it is, as the chapter title has it, a "Case of Delicacy." But when in the course of a restless night Yorick exclaims "O my God," the treaty breaks down. The lady, who has also not slept, accuses him of breaking their agreement; Yorick, choosing an unfortunate word, protests it was only an "ejaculation," and reaches across the space between the beds just as madame's maid comes running into the room: "So that when I stretch'd out my hand, I caught hold of the Fille de Chambre's/END OF VOL. II" (p. 291). This final ambiguous gesture, along with the verbal ambiguity of *ejaculation,* and indeed of *case*—a longstanding pun for the pudendum—in the title encapsulate the persistence of desire in *A Sentimental Journey* and, as well, our persistent evasions of it as we communicate with one another—and indeed, with ourselves.

This persistent desire—which I would like to read as the desire of the death-burdened male to escape himself by reaching toward, connecting with, the death-defying female—manifests itself along the twin paths of language and silence, paths that alternately reveal and conceal—and finally always evade—the satisfaction that seems to be the goal. For Marcel, this evasiveness involves the play between hetero- and homo-sexual desire; just as he searches for the woman he does not possess, he also yearns for the man (or woman) who might possess his captive, Albertine, because his own possession destroys love: "to tell the truth, when I began to regard Albertine as an angel . . . whom I congratulated myself upon possessing, it was not long before I found her uninteresting; I soon became bored in her company; but these moments were of brief duration: one only loves that in which one pursues the inaccessible, one only loves what one does not possess, and very soon I began to realise once more that I did not possess Albertine" (pp. 390–91). Marcel's inability to touch—or be touched by—Albertine, despite the fact that she is a prisoner in his apartment, is imaged by a return to a separating glass: "I no more perceived [her joys] than does the spectator who has been refused admission to the theatre, and who, his face glued to the glass panes of the door, can take in nothing of what is happening on the stage" (p. 391). Yorick and Marcel, so vastly different in so many ways, share the perpetual gesture of reaching toward the feminine they shrink from possessing; and for both, sexual enjoyment is always on the other side of the door or window or curtain—barriers at once so ambiguous and yet so absolute.

A Sentimental Journey opens with an episode in which Yorick, newly arrived in France, writes his preface in a "desobligeant," which Sterne tellingly annotated himself as a "chaise, so called in France, from its holding but one person" (p. 76). This isolation is broken by contact with a woman, a delicately sexual conversation that takes place while they hold hands in front of the locked door of the inn's coach-house: "Monsieur *Dessein* had *diabled* the key above fifty times before he found out he had come with a wrong one in his hand: we were as impatient as himself to have it open'd; and so attentive to the obstacle, that I continued holding her hand almost without knowing it; so that Monsieur *Dessein* left us together with her hand in mine, and with our faces turned towards the door of the Remise . . ." (p. 90). As everywhere in the *Journey,* Yorick attempts to move outside himself, to connect with the feminine, always with a gesture covertly sexual. Hence, although sentimentality was a favorite eighteenth-century way to deny sexuality, in Yorick the two can never be distinguished. Neither Yorick nor the reader, for example, could possibly disentwine the strands of sentiment and sexuality in this simple declarative sentence: "The pulsations of the arteries along my fingers pressing across hers, told her what was passing within me . . ." (p. 97). And yet the door remains closed because Yorick, like Marcel, shrinks in the face of the barriers he imagines lie ahead, an imagining attributable perhaps to his black clerical garb, perhaps to his Englishness. As the woman remarks, Yorick destroys the connection in the very act of observing it:

> THIS certainly, fair lady! said I, raising her hand up a little lightly as I began, must be one of Fortune's whimsical doings: to take two utter strangers by their hands—of different sexes, and perhaps from different corners of the globe. . . .
> —And your reflection upon it, shews how much, Monsieur, she has embarassed you by the adventure.—
> —When the situation is, what we would wish, nothing is so ill-timed as to hint at the circumstances which make it so: you thank Fortune, continued she—you had reason—the heart knew it, and was satisfied; and who but an English philosopher would have sent notices of it to the brain to reverse the judgment?
> In saying this, she disengaged her hand with a look which I thought a sufficient commentary upon the text. (p. 96)

Yorick's inability to allow the situation its own life, his need to turn desire into the language of desire (that is, the language of seduction), bespeaks the failure he will address throughout his sentimental journey. The significance of Sterne's portrayal of human sexuality is his awareness, shared by Proust, although largely, I will urge, on different grounds, that male aggressiveness is internalized self-destructiveness, while female passivity is the powerful fuel of appetite, the energy by which we convert ourselves into another. It is an insight not too far removed from what Sterne would have preached from his Anglican pulpit concerning the true nature of Christian love—and significantly, by reading Sterne through Proust, we can perhaps draw closer to that insight because Proust allows us to understand that the gendering of aggressiveness and passivity is a convenient fiction and nothing more.

In one of the next episodes of the *Journey,* Yorick hires La Fleur primarily on the recommendation that he "is always in love" and then offers us a fragment about the conversion from enmity to love in the ancient town of Abdera: " 'O Cupid! prince of God and men'—in every street . . . in every house—'O Cupid! Cupid!'—in every mouth, like the natural notes of some sweet melody which drops from it whether it will or no. . . . The fire caught—and the whole city, like the heart of one man, open'd itself to Love. . . . 'Twas only in the power, says the Fragment, of the God whose empire extendeth from heaven to earth, and even to the depths of the sea, to have done this" (p. 131). On the one hand, the idea is commonplace; on the other, within the context of Yorick's journey, where desire is always covert and love always just beyond reach, there is a pathos here that emerges from man's inability to escape the demands of the self and the imperfection of all human response to the God of the "Fragment."

Never forgetting obvious and enormous differences, I would suggest that Sterne and Proust are fascinated by much the same human problem— human at least insofar as a certain tendency in male-female relationships manifested itself among mid-eighteenth-century humanity in western Europe and continued into the beginning of the twentieth. Here is Marcel addressing his own "Cupid! prince of God and men": "O girls, O successive rays in the swirling vortex wherein we throb with emotion on seeing you reappear while barely recognising you, in the dizzy velocity of light." And in his very next sentence, he confronts the destruction of the vision: "We might perhaps remain unaware of that velocity, and everything would seem to us motionless, did not a sexual attraction set us in pursuit of you, O drops of gold, always dissimilar and always surpassing our expectation!" (pp. 58–59). Attraction calls forth pursuit, which in turn changes the unfixed perfection of the object into one mode or another of fixed imperfection, not because the loved one is unobtainable but precisely because she can be—and will be—possessed. For Sterne and Proust both, the aggressive act of possession is simultaneously an act of loss; and for both, that loss has to do with the fact that desire has become an intellectual (verbal) pursuit rather than a sexual one, an act of memory rather than of presence.

Over and over again, Proust makes the point that language stands between Marcel and his capacity to love, nowhere more pathetically than when Marcel describes why Albertine sleeping is the only Albertine he can possess:

> her sleep realised to a certain extent the possibility of love: alone, I could think of her, but I missed her, I did not possess her; when she was present, I spoke to her, but was too absent from myself to be able to think of her; when she was asleep, I no longer had to talk, I knew that I was no longer observed by her, I no longer needed to live on the surface of myself.
>
> . . . She had called back into herself everything of her that lay outside, had withdrawn, enclosed, reabsorbed herself into her body. In keeping it in front of my eyes, in my hands, I had an impression of possessing her entirely which I never had when she was awake. (p. 64)

While she sleeps he possesses her completely "like an unconscious and unre-sisting object of dumb nature," while when she is awake and he listens to her, he cannot "penetrate" her. As we might suspect, Marcel's belief that he has penetrated the sleeping Albertine is a self-deception, one he comes to realize in the closing pages of *The Captive;* but his inability to possess her through language remains consistent and there are no words, early or late in the novel, that can open Albertine to his desire: "all the residuum of reality which we are obliged to keep to ourselves, which cannot be transmitted in talk, even from friend to friend, from master to disciple, from lover to mistress, that ineffable something which differentiates qualitatively what each of us has felt and what he is obliged to leave behind at the threshold of the phrases in which he can communicate with others only by limiting himself to externals . . ." (p. 259).

Sterne explores the interrelationship between love and language in Yorick's inability to write to Madame de L*** when they meet at Amiens; and more precisely in the neat turn of La Fleur's all-occasion love letter:

> L'amour n'est *rien* sans sentiment.
> Et le sentiment est encore *moins* sans amour.
> (p. 153)

Quite clearly, La Fleur's "amour" suggests physical love, while "sentiment" suggests an idealized love, which, like all idealizations, exists in language alone. In an age of moral certainties, the first sentence is obviously most apro-pos. But in a sentimental age, an era in which language is fundamentally altered in its perceived relationship with reality (and who is more "sentimen-tal" than Marcel?), when the "language of the heart" has become the measure of man, then the second sentence is the moralist's stern reminder: "le senti-ment est encore *moins* sans amour." As in *Tristram Shandy,* where Sterne brings Toby toward a reluctant realization of human sexuality in his encounter with Widow Wadman, so also in *A Sentimental Journey* he confronts his character with the reality of desire, glimpsed intermittently through a language that masks as often as it provides communication.

It is at this moment in the *Journey* that Yorick enters Paris and looks out his chamber window at the sensual life in the street below. The image that concludes his meditation is equally replete with the combination of pathos and bawdy commented upon earlier: "seek—seek some winding alley, with a tourniquet at the end of it, where chariot never rolled or flambeau shot its rays—there thou mayest solace thy soul in converse sweet with some kind *grisset* of a barber's wife . . ." (p. 157). That by "converse sweet" Yorick means a sexual union is rather apparent; but for Sterne, watching over Yorick's struggle to escape from language into desire and, conversely, from desire back into language, such union is an elusive peace that passes under-standing. Even when the union is achieved—and it is several times in *A Sen-timental Journey*—Yorick is unable or unwilling to sustain the moment and, like Tristram before him and Marcel after him, he moves away from the "cursed slit" in the petticoat (vol. VII, chap. 43 of *Tristram Shandy*). Herein lies the full pathos of the human being, whose fulfillment both begins and ends in language and hence, at the very moment of harmony and oneness, begins again to separate, divaricate.

Yorick meets his *grisset* in the next episode, and again the scene is of the utmost delicacy, the feeling of her pulse—and the utmost sexuality, insofar as the fitting of a glove is yet one more trope for sexual union. But this time, Sterne gives us a strong hint of completion, significantly one that sets lan-guage aside:

> There are certain combined looks of simple subtlety—where whim, and sense, and seriousness, and nonsense, are so blended, that all the languages of Babel set loose together could not express them—they are communicated and caught so instantaneously, that you can scarce say which party is the infecter.
> . . . she had a quick black eye, and shot through two such long and silken eye-lashes with such penetration, that she look'd into my very heart and reins. . . . (pp. 168–69)

The non-verbal gesture, which Sterne uses so successfully in *Tristram Shandy* to allow Walter and Toby to bridge their mental and emotional gaps, is here made a viable path between the baffling conflicts of the self and the elusive intentions of the other. Most significantly, this movement from self to other is imaged first as a silent sexual balance ("which party is the infecter"), followed by the male surrender of aggression (pursuit) to the female who "penetrates" his reins.

Perhaps Sterne's major insight into the nature of human desire is the idea that the most satisfying human union is achieved when the female penetrates and the male receives. I would prefer to believe that with the model of Christian love constantly before him, Sterne could perceive the genderless potentiality of this exchange; Christ the incarnate God could enter us, male and female both; and male and female both could receive Christ. It is, however, perhaps asking too much of Sterne by the middle of the eighteenth century; certainly a century and a half later the only model available to Proust to demonstrate the same genderless point was that of homosexual love. It is one measure of the tragedy of *Remembrance of Things Past,* especially when aligned against Sterne's ultimately comic vision, that Proust's model provides absolutely no escape from the imperfections of human love, while Sterne's seems to keep possible a model of perfection for ultimate validation—a perfection, to be sure, that Yorick moves toward (and away from) rather than possesses.

Marcel's compulsive interest in the shop-girls of Paris bears many similarities to Yorick's; his urge is to detain "for a few moments at close quarters one of those whom from the height" of his window he has seen: and in an image fraught with sexual overtones, just as Sterne's had been, he speaks of having to "intercept in the long unwinding of the animated frieze some damsel carrying her laundry or her milk, transfer her for a moment . . . into the proscenium arch of my bedroom door, and keep her there before my eyes for long enough to elicit some information about her which would enable me to find her again some day, like the identification discs which ornithologists . . . attach before setting them free to the legs . . . of the birds . . . whose migrations they are anxious to trace" (pp. 134–35). We will return to the image of the bird later, but surely we see here an anticipation of Yorick's later scene with the *fille de chambre* in his own bedroom. Marcel's meeting is, of course, a disaster because love has to do with the unknown, and the milkmaid, once in his presence, loses her mystery. "Indeed, if we wanted to embody in a formula the law of our amorous curiosities, we should have to seek it in the maximum divergence between a woman glimpsed and a woman approached and caressed" (p. 138). The disappointment is inevitable: "And so one spends one's life in anxious approaches, constantly renewed, to serious working girls whose calling seems to distance them from one. Once they are in one's arms, they are no longer what they were, the distance that one dreamed of bridging is abolished" (p. 139). It is insufficient to see this as only Marcel's inadequacy, and Yorick helps us achieve the necessarily broader outlook when we come to realize that he too perpetually yearns and is perpetually disappointed. Both works might well be seen to examine the same curious dilemma surrounding sexual union; and it might defy even an astute reader to decide whether it is Sterne or Proust who delivers this verdict: "How I suffered from that position to which we are reduced by the obliviousness of nature which, when instituting the division of bodies, never thought of making possible the interpenetration of souls!" (p. 393).

Sterne reinforces his insight that nonverbal communication and sexual exchange may be the means to bridge the Proustian dilemma in his next chapter, "The Translation," in which once again the sexual union begins with a nonverbal stasis, as Yorick and the Marquesina di F*** attempt to sidestep one another; here, however, the balance is beautifully, almost quantifiably, maintained, while again the aggressor and recipient roles are reversed:

> Upon my word, Madame . . . I made six different efforts to let you go out—And I made six efforts, replied she, to let you enter—I wish to heaven you would make a seventh, said I—With all my heart, said she, making room. . . .
>
> I will only add, that the connection which arose out of that translation, gave me more pleasure than any one I had the honour to make in Italy. (p. 173)

The passage seems to me bawdy, but unlike earlier passages where the bawdiness held sentiment in check, here it releases it. The "connection" is a moment of fulfillment, quite alone in the *Journey* in its implicit unfettered actualization. I think it noteworthy, therefore, that it takes place in the portion of Yorick's journey that remained unwritten, namely the journey to Italy. Perhaps Sterne intended a projection of the fulfillment to be achieved at journey's end, after all has been learned and experienced; or perhaps, more subtly, he intimates that "connection" must always be that portion of our journey that remains unverbalized, unwritten.

Certainly that is one of Proust's favorite devices, for throughout *The Captive*, it is not only the street that promises Marcel freedom, but also his dream of Venice, his often aborted trip toward which he leans as he does toward the young girls he does not know. The two often merge: for example, on an evening when he returns to his apartment where Albertine is waiting for him, he thinks of the pleasure "of unknown women, into whose life I should have attempted to penetrate, in Venice perhaps, or at least in some corner of nocturnal Paris" (p. 336). Most significantly, as he looks up at the lighted window of his apartment, he sees his own cage: "So that, as I raised my eyes for one last look from the outside at the window of the room in which I should presently find myself, I seemed to behold the luminous gates which were about to close behind me and of which I myself had forged, for an eternal slavery, the inflexible bars of gold" (p. 337). We have several images throughout this volume of Albertine as the trapped bird (and indeed a caged bird is used as an emblem on the title page of volume III of the Random House edition), but surely here we are given a clear indication that the situation is quite the reverse; Marcel will fly back into the cage—and ultimately Albertine will leave it—and indeed we are in on her secret that Marcel's hold upon her or control over her movements has been quite fabricated and is a tissue of self-deception. Only Marcel is captive.

The problem of entering into, penetrating, the other holds Sterne's attention throughout the middle of *A Sentimental Journey*. Each episode suggests the value of non-verbal communication and, at the same time, explores the failure of language in the search for "connection." Of particular significance for understanding Sterne's commentary on the Age of Sentimentality are the chapters concerned with a caged starling (one of which is serendipitously entitled "The Captive"), a bird the Sterne family used on its coat of arms (identifying its dialectical rendition *starn* with *Sterne*). Yorick "translates" the bird's song as "I can't get out," but for Sterne the exercise of translation, no matter how energetically pursued, is often nothing more than words, "sentiment . . . sans amour." (Compare Proust: "when two people part it is the one who is not in love who makes the tender speeches, since love does not express itself directly . . ." [p. 363]). Significantly, Yorick replays the encounter with the Marquesina; the bird cannot "get out" and Yorick, try as he might imaginatively to enter into the bird's captivity, cannot "get in": "I could not sustain the picture of confinement which my fancy had drawn" (p. 203). Indeed, the bird is passed from hand to hand, but is never freed, for the roles remain always the same: "all these [the owners] wanted to *get in*—and my bird wanted to *get out* . . ." (p. 205).

This failure is not merely a failure of the imagination. Insofar as Yorick's efforts to identify with the starling are conscious and aggressive (filled as they are with English francophobia), they are diametrically opposed to the reversal of roles that Sterne finds necessary for true penetration and connection. Until the bird is allowed to leave the cage and Yorick can enter it, Sterne sees no communication taking place, despite the emphasis his contemporaries placed on moral sensibility and empathic understanding. There are actions missing here—the freeing of the bird, the entering into captivity—that no intensity of sentiment, no virtuosity of language can replace. Sterne's interest is focused on the nature of that action, the paradoxical passivity that seems its necessary concomitant, and the transfer of (sexual) identity that is achieved at the moment of fulfillment.

On the night in which Marcel first becomes aware of the gold bars on his windows, a disagreement takes place that is never healed, and Marcel spends the last 100 pages of *The Captive* anticipating—fearing—Albertine's departure. It is at this time in particular that their language collapses altogether; again and again, Marcel stresses his insight that all people, but particularly lovers, work only to deceive in language when they are face to face (p. 350). And even to himself he cannot speak truth. Hence he acknowledges on the one hand that he has "clipped her wings, and she had ceased to be a winged Victory and become a burdensome slave of whom I would have liked to rid myself" (p. 378), while on the other hand, he knows fully (as does Albertine) that it is only her passivity in the cage that produces this attitude; the moment she begins to fly against the bars, Marcel's overwhelming belief that he is in love with Albertine revives.

As with Sterne, the caged bird is a vital image for Proust, one that begins several volumes earlier, when Marcel first observes Albertine's band of young girls on the beach at Balbec ("weird and shrill, like an assembly of birds before taking flight" [*Within a Budding Grove,* I: 850]), and arrives at one of Proust's most dramatic scenes, just a few days before Albertine's escape. Entering Marcel's bedroom in a Fortuny gown imprinted with images of both the Grand Canal and mating birds (symbols, Proust writes, "of death and resurrection"), Albertine, who has been quite cool to Marcel since their disagreement, now resists his suggestion that she remove her gown "for fear of crumpling that fine stuff, and there are those fateful birds between us. Undress, my darling" (pp. 406–407). Albertine does not, but they sit on the bed together, when suddenly they hear the "pigeons beginning to coo," announcing morning and Spring, and for Marcel an augury of death, "as though Albertine were about to die."

The birds on the other side of the window, redolent of the same sexual energies associated earlier with the young working girls in the street below, are death to Marcel, for his fears in these closing pages of the novel are clearly limited to keeping Albertine caged, himself "free." Hence it is with considerable irony that when Albertine leaves for her own room, he does not dare to call her back. "But my heart beat so violently that I could not lie down again. Like a bird flying from one end of its cage to the other I alternated between anxiety lest Albertine should leave me and a state of comparative calm," produced by arguing with himself that she could not leave without warning. And then, in one of Proust's most brilliant moments, just as Marcel falls fitfully asleep, he is startled "by a noise which, though apparently insignificant, filled me with terror, the noise of Albertine's window being violently opened" (pp. 408–409). Marcel spends the final pages of the work deceiving himself that the relationship is still in his hands, but Proust has beautifully told us, with this one pregnant image, reverberating through all the uses of doors and windows in *The Captive,* that Albertine has already left, has "*got out*" in Sterne's phrase. It is only many pages later, well into the sequel, *The Fugitive,* that Marcel acknowledges the final triumph of Albertine: "Set free once more, released from the cage in which, here at home, I used to leave her for days on end without letting her come to my room, Albertine had regained all her attraction in my eyes; she had become once more the girl whom everyone pursued, the marvellous bird of the earliest days" (p. 481).

Yorick's metaphor of a journey for his attempt to move from self to the other is effective, but also quite traditional; his use of the "passport" as a means of establishing the grounds of his own selfhood is, on the other hand, a splendid stroke. Yorick's quest for his passport suggests indeed not so much a search for identity as for connection with another, for only in communion with the other does the self fully emerge. For this reason his search begins in earnest when the conversation turns to women: "The Count [who is to secure the passport for him] led the discourse: we talk'd of indifferent things;—of books and politicks, and men—and then of women. . . ." Yorick proclaims his view: one must love womankind in order to love a particular woman, he "being firmly persuaded that a man who has not a sort of an affection for the whole sex, is incapable of ever loving a single one as he ought" (p. 216). Yorick returns to a similar equation a paragraph later when, in response to the Count's bawdy innuendo, he tells us that he "cannot bear the shock of the least indecent [i.e., sexual] insinuation." In a work filled with such insinuation, the assertion is clearly ironic. In this instance, however, Yorick acknowledges that his "modesty" is no particular virtue; indeed, trying to overcome it, he has "hazarded a thousand things [in conversation] to a dozen of the sex together—the least of which I could not venture to a single one, to gain heaven" (p. 217). One is reminded here of Swift's famous comment that he hated and detested "that animal called man, although I heartily love John, Peter, Thomas, and so forth." Yorick comes at the question of love from the other direction, loving all women, but unable to say to one woman what is required to "gain heaven."

It is no accident, given this admission that he "can't get in," that the Count's next question forces upon Yorick the problem of his own identity; or that Yorick's first response is that there "is not a more perplexing affair in life to me, than to set about telling any one who I am. . . ." His approach is to identify himself with someone else, in this case with Shakespeare's court jester, although he insists at the same time that the two Yoricks are distinct. Even more troublesome than identity, however, is what Yorick calls "bad" sensations, by which we can assume he means, among other things, his appetites and desires. Indeed, the problem of identity is the problem of these appetites, for Sterne's primary concern, here and in *Tristram Shandy,* is the human tendency to ignore, or mask, or argue down the riddles and mysteries of our nature—most particularly, our animal bodies and desires. Yorick's evasion, for example, is to counterbalance the "bad" with "some kindly and gentle sensation."

But just as we cannot identify ourselves by pointing to another, so we cannot understand the nature of desire by counterpoising sentimentality. The sentimental, Sterne seems to argue, is an evasion of desire, a refusal to acknowledge that, like the self, desire must be defined solely on its own terms, and its value acknowledged solely in its own right. In one of his finest passages, significantly in the final chapter of the "passport" section, Sterne has Yorick grasp a better definition:

> But there is nothing unmixt in this world; and some of the gravest of our divines have carried it so far as to affirm, that . . . the greatest [enjoyment] *they knew of,* terminated *in a general way,* in little better than a convulsion.

Yorick cites one such grave authority, Bevoriskius (a Dutch physician and author), who in his commentary "upon the generations from Adam" (and the

"procreative" text should be noted) breaks off to observe sparrows on his win-
dowledge:

> —'Tis strange! writes Bevoriskius; but the facts are certain . . . the cock-
> sparrow during the little time that I could have finished the other half this
> note, has actually interrupted me with the reiteration of his caresses three and
> twenty times and a half.
> How merciful, adds Bevoriskius, is heaven to his creatures! (pp. 228–29)

Here is Yorick's real identity, and his "passport" to connection, fulfillment,
"heaven": We are creatures born to the puzzlement of our sexual appetite and
our desperate need for connection with the other. To acknowledge ourselves
as such is to begin to unravel the puzzle; Yorick's response, however, suggests
his inability even to take this first step:

> Ill fated Yorick! that the gravest of thy brethren should be able to write that
> to the world, which stains thy face with crimson, to copy in even thy study.
> But this is nothing to my travels. . . . (p. 229)

On the contrary, Bevoriskius's sparrows embody the thematic core of *A Sentimental Journey*.

If anything, Proust plays an even more teasing game with the identity of
his protagonist than Sterne played with Yorick—who appears, of course, not
only in *A Sentimental Journey*, but in *Tristram Shandy* and as the "author" of
Sterne's published sermons as well—a particularly interesting fact in the
archaeology of Sterne's writings. In *Remembrance of Things Past*, Proust gives
the substance of a name to his narrator only twice in its 3,000 pages, both
times significantly in *The Captive*. The first occasion is as Albertine awakens
from one of her constantly observed sleeps and Marcel notes the pleasure he
takes in the fact that her initial thought of "Where am I?" must be answered
by "in *my* home": "In that first delicious moment of uncertainty, it seemed to
me that once again I was taking possession of her more completely, since . . .
it was my room that . . . was about to enclose, to contain her. . . ." It is at this
moment of awakening that Albertine would say " 'My darling——' followed
by my Christian name, which, if we give the narrator the same name as the
author of this book, would be . . . 'My darling Marcel' " (pp. 68–69). The
"possession" Marcel gains over the sleeping Albertine is a masturbatory fantasy; and his "possession" of the awake and living woman is equally sterile
and illusory, fed by the dual eroticisms of jealousy (masochism) and captivity
(sadism), and well illustrated by the self-deceiving joy Marcel takes in Albertine's second and far more direct mention (and iteration) of his name in her
hugely deceptive letter from the Trocadéro (pp. 153–54). But in that fuga-
cious moment between waking and sleeping, between consciousness and
unconsciousness perhaps, Albertine identifies Marcel, and he "locates" her—

answers her question "Where am I?," so similar to the Count's "Who are you?" This moment of union is made possible, I would suggest, because Albertine *penetrates* to the identity of Marcel, while he responds to her with an enclosing and containing gesture that is not the hostile act of captivity, but the feminine act of identification—the same loving moment depicted so brilliantly in the opening pages of *Swann's Way,* when Marcel catalogues the various bedrooms in which he has slept and awakened.

Indeed those opening pages of Proust's long novel are clearly in his mind at this point in *The Captive,* as we see when a few pages later Marcel once again envisions Albertine's penetration: "Incomparable as were those two kisses of peace, Albertine slipped into my mouth, in making me the gift of her tongue, as it were a gift of the Holy Ghost, conveyed to me a viaticum, left me with a provision of tranquillity almost as precious as when my mother in the evening at Combray used to lay her lips upon my forehead" (p. 72). But it is, of course, precisely that movement from mistress to mother that is so damaging to Marcel's search for the other, for as he acknowledges at this point, an Albertine who becomes one with him, who can assume his identity (by naming him?), who reflects not "a distant world, but desired nothing else . . . than to be with me, to be exactly like me, an Albertine who was the image precisely of what was mine and not of the unknown" (p. 70), is a woman he shrinks from and cannot love. We cannot pause at this point to explore all the many reasons for this failure, but certainly much of it has to do with Marcel's denial of his own sexuality, so closely tied as it is to the necessary mystery of his mother. Insofar as he thinks of love as a forceful, masculine act of penetration into that mystery, he is forever locked behind the window of his own guilt, cut off from the fullness of intercourse with the other. Almost eerily, given our earlier discussion of Bevoriskius's sparrows, Marcel concludes this particular memory of Albertine with the following conversation between them:

> "Tell me, by the way, when I came in this evening, you knew my step, you guessed at once who it was?"
>
> "Of course. Could I possibly be mistaken? Couldn't I tell my little sparrow's hop among a thousand? She must let me take her shoes off before she goes to bed, it will give me such pleasure. You're so nice and pink in all that white lace." (p. 72)

Here, in brief, is the question again of identity, but this time the answer returns Albertine to her cage, lovemaking is reduced to a fetishistic act, and as Marcel realizes about his entire response, "amid the sensual expressions, others will be recognised that were peculiar to my grandmother and my mother. . . ." It is no wonder, given the intricate intertwinings between male and female that are here so carefully explored, that Proust, in a rhetorical gambit far more familiar to the strategy of the eighteenth-century writer than the twentieth, turns to apostrophe: "O mighty attitudes of Man and Woman, in which there seeks to be united, in the innocence of the world's first days and with the humility of clay, what the Creation made separate, in which Eve is astonished and submissive before Man by whose side she awakens, as he himself, alone still, before God who has fashioned him!" (p. 74). I can think of no writer between Sterne and Proust who could have gotten away with—indeed triumphed in—such a passage.

Yorick's most memorable apostrophe in *A Sentimental Journey* (and it is well to remember Sterne's mastery of the device in his fiction) is delivered to "Dear sensibility . . . [the] great SENSORIUM of the world!" (pp. 277–78). Two centuries of readers have wrestled with Sterne's intentions regarding these two terms—and even more with the "sentimental" of his title, a word he is credited with having popularized throughout Europe in the late eighteenth century. Interestingly enough, Marcel's mother moves us close to one possibly important distinction: "[my mother was] always ready to explain to me that one ought not to confuse genuine sensibility ["la veritable sensibilité"] with sentimentality ["la sensiblerie"], what the Germans . . . called *Empfindung* and *Empfindelei*" (pp. 102–3). This distinction immediately precedes a long "digression" in *The Captive* concerning the sounds in the street to which Albertine and Marcel awaken, sounds that Marcel considers "the symbol of the atmosphere of the world outside, of the dangerous stirring life through the midst of which I did not allow her to move save under my tutelage . . ." (p. 122). And yet, as we know, Albertine is constantly outdoors, indeed constantly free, since she can so easily circumvent his "tutelage"; while Marcel lives "in a perpetual chill by her habit of leaving doors [and windows] open" (p. 127), a perpetual captive to his fear of the "dangerous stirring life" in the street below.

This danger, this clash of warmth and chill (*Empfindung* and *Empfindelei*, sensibility and sentiment) is magnificently imaged for us in one of Proust's most Shandean moments, during which, against the background of the street sounds, Albertine luxuriates in her imagined eating of ices: "whenever I eat them, temples, churches, obelisks, rocks, a sort of picturesque geography is what I see at first before converting its raspberry or vanilla monuments into coolness in my gullet. . . . They make raspberry obelisks too, which will rise up here and there in the burning desert of my thirst, and I shall make their pink granite crumble and melt deep down in my throat which they will refresh better than any oasis. . . . I can see quite clearly postillions, travellers [sentimental ones to be sure], post-chaises over which my tongue sets to work to roll down freezing avalanches that will swallow them up . . ." (pp.125–26). Throughout this wonderfully erotic monologue, Marcel's interruptions are woefully inadequate and comical; he listens to the language (*parole*) but fails to hear Albertine's potent, penetrating tongue (*langue*); and at the last her mention of Monjouvain is too painful for his jealousy and he cuts her short, to which she retorts, "I'm boring you, good-bye my darling" (pp. 125–26). One is reminded of Toby's dismal failure with the widow Wadman (volumes VIII and IX of *Tristram Shandy*) and, again, of Tristram's dancing away from Nannette and the "cursed slit" in her petticoat (volume VII), passages in *Tristram Shandy* that were written while *A Sentimental Journey* was already in gestation.

In this later work, however, Sterne presents a far more ambivalent picture of male-female relationships, nowhere more so than in Yorick's "conversation" with the fair *fille de chambre* in his bedroom. In their earlier meeting, Yorick had talked about "virtuous convention," a "kiss of charity," and the "fine-spun threads" that draw an affection—in short, in the language of sentimentalism he had dismissed the girl, much as Marcel dismisses the sensual overtures of Albertine and her ices. Now, however, Yorick admits to something in him "not in strict unison with the lesson of virtue I had given her the night before . . . the devil was in me." Earlier, despite the sentiment, Yorick's desires were clearly revealed by bawdy undercurrents in his language. In the second meeting, although the innuendoes remain (particularly with the play on the "green taffeta" purse in her lap, "just big enough to hold the crown" [p. 236]), Yorick confronts his desires not masked by the posturing of sentiment but with an open assault on the puzzle of the human constitution. When he and the *fille de chambre* tumble on the bed together, the chapter abruptly ends; and the next, ambivalently entitled "The Conquest," begins with a challenge to "clay-cold heads and luke-warm hearts" who are able to argue down or mask their passions:

> tell me, what trespass is it that man should have them? . . .
>
> If nature has so wove her web of kindness, that some threads of love and desire are entangled with the piece—must the whole web be rent in drawing them out? (p. 237)

Bevoriskius's sparrows suggest not, and Yorick's impassioned apostrophe and question seem to be leading us toward a frank avowal of desire and connection.

But Yorick retreats again from sexuality, choosing instead a "virtue," the ambivalence of which is in his language: "Wherever thy providence shall place me for the trials of my virtue . . . let me feel the movements which rise out of it, and which belong to me as a man—and if I govern them as a good one—I will trust the issues to thy justice . . ." (pp. 237–38). Yorick suggests a masculine victory, a triumph over desire by firm governance—a conquest over himself. The *Journey,* however, contains a search not for moral triumph, but for the far more difficult victory of self-understanding and human love. Yorick's ambivalence suggests he is still unable to reconcile his sexuality with his morality, his sensibility with his sentimentality; he remains isolated and unsuccessful in his search for connection and for love, an eighteenth-century prototype of Marcel and all those in the twentieth century for whom sexuality is "dangerous stirring life"; all those for whom desire is a threat to the post-

Christian era's need to define itself not through its bodily existence but through language alone, a language that we believe has no relationship with reality—but which is, conversely, our only reality. That this scene ends with Yorick's locking the door and putting the key in his pocket is not a very hopeful sign. Indeed, as mentioned earlier, the similarities between this episode of *A Sentimental Journey* and Marcel's encounter with the dairymaid in his room are startling; the underlying urges of each conversation—"amorous curiosities" (Proust, p. 138), the need to penetrate the mystery of the unknown, the drive to connect with the other—are basically identical. And the outcomes are also identical, not only in Marcel's dismissal of the girl, but in his conclusion that "one spends one's life in anxious approaches, constantly renewed . . ." (p. 139).

I find *A Sentimental Journey* a more hopeful work than Proust's, however, and Yorick's penultimate encounter with a woman, with the mad Maria, suggests to me a communion that may be within human reach. Indeed, nowhere in his writing does Sterne come closer to portraying a workable union of desire and language. As he weeps with Maria in mirrored, balanced actions ("Maria let me wipe them [her tears] away . . . with my handkerchief.—I then steep'd it in my own—and then in hers—and then in mine—and then I wip'd hers again"), he discovers in a convincing manner the strongest sense of identity, not simply with Maria, but with himself: he discovers the existence of his soul:

> I felt such undescribable emotions within me, as I am sure could not be accounted for from any combinations of matter and motion.
> I am positive I have a soul; nor can all the books with which materialists have pester'd the world ever convince me of the contrary. (p. 271)

The feeling, significantly, is not free from sexual desire. Yorick's description of Maria is really the first time he "sees" the woman he is with as a physical being rather than merely a sentimental construct:

> Maria, tho' not tall, was nevertheless of the first order of fine forms—affliction had touch'd her looks with something that was scarce earthly—still she was feminine—and so much was there about her of all that the heart wishes, or the eye looks for in woman, that could the traces be ever worn out of her brain . . . she should *not only eat of my bread and drink of my own cup,* but Maria should lay in my bosom, and be unto me as a daughter. (p. 275)

The last phrases paraphrase Nathan's parable of the poor man's ewe lamb (2 Samuel 12:3), which is cared for as Yorick vows to care for Maria; the source alerts us to the fact that not only should we not burden "as a daughter" with unnecessary interpretation, but also that it is a moment of legitimate insight on Yorick's part. Nathan uses the parable to recall to David his sin of taking

Bathsheba from Uriah, David being Sterne's favorite example of the stern moralist who is severe on other sinners but blind to his own transgressions. As such, the biblical allusion reminds us again of the question of identity; as David is forced to acknowledge his desire (and his sinfulness), so Yorick, finally, comes to an honest acceptance of his own desires—free from deception, from innuendo, from repression.

It is within this context of a hard-won embrace of the complexity of human nature that Yorick's famous apostrophe to sensibility in the next chapter should be understood. It has often marked Sterne as the foremost sentimentalist of a sentimental age, often been used to suggest Sterne's celebration of the "heart" over all else. But coming late as it does in *A Sentimental Journey,* its context is the exploration that has preceded it of sensibility's relation to desire and to language. In this context we understand "sensibility" as that particular capacity that makes love possible: the awareness of the wholeness of the human experience, including both the exchange of sexual roles (aggressor and recipient, active and passive) and the knowledge that sensibility is not limited to those stirrings we can accept with clean hands and uplifted hearts:

> —Dear sensibility! source inexhausted of all that's precious in our joys, or costly in our sorrows! thou chainest thy martyr down upon his bed of straw—and 'tis thou who lifts him up to HEAVEN—eternal fountain of our feelings! . . . all comes from thee, great—great SENSORIUM of the world! which vibrates, if a hair of our heads but falls upon the ground, in the remotest desert of thy creation. (pp. 277–78)

Yorick's prayer is an assertion of providence echoing Matthew 10:29–31, which promises God's continuing hand in human affairs despite the Fall, despite the intricate web of good and evil that human life has become. It is, in short, a statement of faith.

And faith is answered by "Grace," the penultimate chapter of *A Sentimental Journey.* Tristram had found a similar moment of communion in the peasant dance at the end of his tour through France, although the moment is tainted by repressed desire, Nannette's "cursed slit." Nothing interferes, however, with Yorick's appreciation of this moment. In harmony at last with himself, he is able to be in harmony with others. The beautiful assertion that he beholds "*Religion* mixing in the dance" (p. 284) is an insight gained through travel, and loneliness, and perhaps, we should add, glancing at Sterne's own biography, the impending threat of death, which renders the need for human connection all the more intense and necessary. Importantly, the "grace" is not spoken but acted out; but equally important, Yorick is able to find the words to express the joy of the dance without equivocation or innuendo. The distance between Tristram and Yorick (and between Marcel and Yorick) at this point is the measure of the spiritual content of *A Sentimental Journey,* Sterne's final effort to bring his readers to his own understanding of (and surrender to) the nature of language and of desire, of both human and—separating him from us—divine love. For Sterne's faith is ultimately an orthodox faith, built upon Christianity's acknowledgement of human desire and its capacity to deal with it. From the pulpit Sterne could argue, quite similarly, that "when the affections so kindly break loose, Joy, is another name for Religion" (*Sermons,* p. 190), which is not at all a moment of modernism, liberalism, or nominalism, but the fully conceived understanding of a religious faith that offered a sense of explanation and comfort to human beings not readily available in any of the systems we have tried to put in its place.

Yet, as Pope writes, "Man never Is, but always To be blest." The moment of "grace," of insight, is ultimately only a moment in the stream of life. Tristram flees from insight, Yorick is simply unable to sustain it, which, in a fallen world, is man's natural relationship to grace. And so the "Case of Delicacy" is the final chapter, reminding us that the quest is as long as life itself, that however else we may recall Yorick, he is also the man endlessly reaching across the void for the woman on the other side. Insight, love, wholeness, grace, all are possible for the human being in this model, but none permanently. What is permanent is desire and the language by which we conceal it from ourselves and reveal it to others. "Vive l'amour! et vive la bagatelle!"—was La Fleur's motto (p. 153) and might well have been—had he looked only forward and not backwards as well—Sterne's.

And Proust's! For while I do not find in Marcel's world the saving grace (in all its sundry meanings) that informs Yorick's, both characters do hold in common the insight that human desire and human language play an intricate—and destructive—game with one another. In the eighteenth-century world Sterne creates, the clergyman Yorick is able to unravel that intricacy by appeal to certain scriptural constructs that give presence to language, however mysteriously (and "Joy" is another name for mystery!), positing love as an obtainable (and bestowable) essence. In our own age, whose difference from its past is so minutely detailed by Proust, no way out seems to exist. Marcel cannot "love" what he possesses, can "love" only that which he has not yet experienced; obviously, the idea of "love" itself now eludes substance, unless "bagatelle" is the appropriate reality. Marcel's own correlatives are telling: "the words *midinettes, little shopgirls* . . . an unknown person who might perhaps come to love me . . . [creating] out of nothing desirable women . . ." (p. 154); or again, "the fusion of our shadows had a charm for me that was doubtless more insubstantial, but no less intimate, than the contiguity, the fusion of our bodies" (p. 173).

But it is finally Marcel's celebration of the lie that informs us of the absolute emptiness we are left with when desire and language are irretrievably decentered, as indeed they must be in the twentieth century: "The lie, the perfect lie, about people we know, about the relations we have had with them, about our motive for some action, formulated in totally different terms, the lie as to what we are, whom we love, what we feel with regard to people who love us and believe that they have fashioned us in their own image . . . that lie is one of the few things in the world that can open windows for us on to what is new and unknown, that can awaken in us sleeping senses for the contemplation of universes that otherwise we should never have known" (p. 213). In a work that begins with its protagonist a self-confined prisoner behind his window, this admission, this dismaying prospect of the value of human language, is the final despair and the final defeat. Only Proust's art remains, and art—as Tristram Shandy knew—is the greatest lie of all.

POSTSCRIPT

Fifteen years ago an essay like this would have been shaped, I assume, as an influence study, in which I might have tried valiantly (if fruitlessly) to prove, through verbal echoes and external evidences (letters, notes, library catalogues) that Proust was a great admirer of Sterne and consciously borrowed from him. Indeed, the two names have often been linked in Sterne scholarship, usually centered upon the literary techniques of stream-of-consciousness, although one must quickly aver that the assertions of such influence have been quite vague and unconvincing. Frankly, I find almost everything about their techniques quite dissimilar, and I do not believe for a moment that Proust learned anything about literary form or style from Sterne.

We have become increasingly aware in recent years, however, of the complexity of the concept of literary tradition as well as of some of the assumptions of critical studies, and it is one complexity in particular—that we come to a text through other texts—that I hope can justify this present effort. What I have tried to suggest is really twofold: first, that twentieth-century readers, reading the best that has been produced in their own century, come to earlier literature through that experience and cannot free their reading from it; and second, that in one specific instance, that of Proust and Sterne, a similar interest in the very fundamental human problem of male-female relations resulted in some uncanny similarities of images and concepts, the juxtaposition of which I hope has resulted in an interesting reading of both texts.

Sterne's interest in the subject, were I pushed to an hypothesis, perhaps results from his joining of a lifelong clerical role with an equally long-lived flirtatious instinct—hardly a unique combination in eighteenth-century clergy, but one I believe troubled Sterne, most particularly in the last years of his life, when continuous illness clearly foreshadowed his death. The result was, on the one hand, a troubling intensification of the sexual urge, clearly and sadly chronicled in the *Journal to Eliza,* written simultaneously with *A*

Sentimental Journey; and, on the other hand, a need to come to grips with last things, death, judgment, heaven and hell. The result was, to be sure, self-justifying, but that hardly detracts from (indeed, it might well enhance) the insights Sterne reached about human desire and divine love as the two notions struggled within his body and soul in 1766–67. And insofar as his struggle has its universality—at least within the universe of western European culture, where two centuries later the despair of human beings caught between values they cannot live up to and instincts they cannot admit is still the overwhelming question—that Marcel Proust would spend a lifetime exploring the same issues, reaching often the same conclusions, is certainly less surprising than we might otherwise wish to believe. And so it is that reading Proust does influence our reading of Sterne; and that *A Sentimental Journey* can well serve to remind us all of things yet to come.

Post Postscript

My postscript will have disappointed the reader who finds it an *unnecessary* retreat from conclusions *necessitated* by my argument. Of course. I had never any intention of doing otherwise than to disappoint the reader's belief in such necessity, the desire for a contemporary ideological closure of Sterne, one that would seem to enable us to "possess" him, to find *in* his text the things that make him "one of us." What other path is possible when we start with Proust, as we all must do in the twentieth century? The text lies passive, almost asleep before our indomitable, aggressive drive to penetrate it, to possess it. It ends, like Albertine, imprisoned within the cave of our own creating fiction—and, also like her, free to deceive us at every turn, while we stand, the Procrustean Guard, at the doors and windows protecting our possession of a necessary conclusion.

I have no doubt that a radical reading has been generated by my essay, which is all the more reason to introduce an oscillation that maintains, insists upon, the difference between ourselves and Sterne—if only to protect ourselves (and him) from the textual illusion that his struggle with desire is the same as ours. Hence, throughout the essay I have deliberately, even spitefully, I shall admit, troped upon Christian possibilities (vestiges) in Sterne, ignoring the same possibilities in Proust (it is he, after all, who talks about the "Holy Ghost"). I would prefer that my anachronistic reading lead not to a *necessary* conclusion, but only to another detour (digression), and the one I have chosen is a particularly deviant one for the lover of Sterne's modernism. To shift figures, I have in the midst of my own deceptive possession created a situation of perverse jealousy. *A Sentimental Journey,* I suspect, may well belong to someone else entirely, despite the wonderfully cooperative captive Proust and I have seemed to make of it. Indeed, I torment both myself and the unsatisfied reader by imagining a possessor as unlike the two of us as possible, a potent yet perversely gentle, shall I say feminine, religious lover, whose alien tongue may seem to perform some obscene ritual upon the body of our beautiful captive, driving it from our twentieth-century grasp, even while we droop with disappointment at yet another failure of our penetration, possession, necessity. The text flees our necessary—and predictable—understanding in order to be read—and possessed—anew. Albertine is, finally, a better "reader" than Marcel, for though the words are his, it is her world he is trying to comprehend: ". . . on n'aime que ce en quoi on poursuit quelque chose d'inaccessible, on n'aime que ce qu'on ne possede pas . . ." (*La Prisonnière*, p. 384).

Note

1. *The Captive* is cited from Volume III of *Remembrance of Things Past*, trans. by C.K. Scott Moncrieff and Terence Kilmartin (New York: Random House, 1981).

Walter Shandy, Sterne, and Gender:
A Feminist Foray

Juliet McMaster

T*ristram Shandy* is a novel (or whatever) by a man, purporting to be the auto-biography of another man, who writes mainly about still other men—his uncle, his father, the manservant of one and the man-midwife of the other. It dramatizes male obsessions and male anxieties. The novel's critics, too, have been preponderantly men. But its recurring concerns—conception, birth, sexual potency (or the reverse), and amours—are ones in which (at least half the world would agree) women deserve a say. And in fact Sterne has fairly provided standing-room for the women, if not a platform. They are indu-bitably *there,* though they seldom have a voice. Mrs. Shandy has had her champions. At least, by 1970, she had *one!* Ruth Marie Faurot published a shrewd article called "Mrs. Shandy Observed." Did this change the face of criticism? No! In fact I find, on checking a recent selected bibliography of articles on *Tristram Shandy,* that that article was selected *out,* whereas, for instance, an article of the same year, Charles Parish's "The Shandy Bull Vindi-cated," has been selected *in* (Gysin, 171–72). Now, things have come to a pretty pass if we approve vindications of the Shandy bull, but not of the Shandy wife and mother. Leigh Ehlers struck a new and powerful blow for Mrs. Shandy and the other women in an article of 1981; but, although women have been sympathetic readers of Sterne,[1] by and large the male crit-ics have fortified *Tristram Shandy* as a male preserve. Sterne's male critics have served us well in exploring "the tradition of learned wit" to which *Tristram Shandy* belongs (Jefferson, 225). 'Tis not your worships' wits I question, but your judgements; and especially on matters pertaining to the Sex. For indeed the almost exclusively male readings of *Tristram Shandy* have handed down a novel that is much more male-centred than the one Sterne wrote. Sterne wrote about an ongoing war of the sexes, and even suggested the possibility of truce and peaceful co-operation. But his male critics have written as though the war were already lost and won—lost by the women, and conclu-sively won by the men. But the war's not over yet. So, then,

Reprinted from *English Studies in Canada* 15 (1989): 441–58.

─────────────*have at you, gentlemen!*─────────────

Walter Shandy, as I believe even most men would agree, is a male chauvinist *par excellence*. His misogyny is so intricate, so ingeniously developed, that he could well stand as the patron saint of the breed. But this is not to say that Sterne, or even Tristram, shares his attitudes. Walter Shandy as misogynist is like Archie Bunker as racist, a hilarious exaggeration of latent attitudes that are meant to be discarded, purged away by a gust of laughter, as by the operation of a kind of comic catharsis. But Walter has proved too powerfully seductive for male critics. As A. R. Towers admitted in his influential "Sterne's Cock and Bull Story," "we laugh at him affectionately and perhaps with a sense of relief. The disarmed giant has become disarming" (Towers, 29). Now, sir, your affection is a sore decayer of your whoreson judgement. Against your seminal article, let me oppose an ovarian one. For it behooves the reader who finds himself (and I use the gender-specific pronoun advisedly) siding with Walter to look to his lineage, as may hereinafter appear. And yet siding with Walter is a malady most incident to males.

Take Ian Watt, for instance. In his introduction to the Riverside edition of *Tristram Shandy* he thus accounts for one of Tristram's misfortunes: "Walter insists on the letter of the marriage contract because it enables him to make a personal contribution [noble chap!] towards halting the dangerous flow of the population to London; while Mrs. Shandy [spiteful woman!], foiled of her own wishes, makes do with the local midwife and thus, one might say, cuts off her son's nose to spite her husband's face" (Watt, xxiv). Walter himself could not have put it better—and the *Attic* salt must have brought water into both their eyes, at the repartee (V.iii.421). But needless to say (or it *should* be needless!) this is a severe calumny against Mrs. Shandy (not to mention the midwife), who did all she humanly could to prevent Dr. Slop from coming near her——; and it was Slop, not the midwife, who crushed Tristram's nose. (And by the way, Walter's principles on halting the dangerous flow of the population towards London didn't hinder him from going there himself, for some three months, after getting Mrs. Shandy pregnant.) All I plead for, in this case, Sir, is strict justice (I.xviii.56).

By way of setting the record straight, let us examine some of Walter's views on generation, delivery, and some other matters on which women have some authority. Tristram and Sterne, as well as male critics after them, have provided plenty of information on the matter, and it's a pity that all the interpretation should come from one side.

☞ I have a strong propensity in me to begin this paragraph reminiscentially, and I will not balk my fancy (I.xxiii.82). When I was last working on an article on *Tristram Shandy,* I was far gone with my first pregnancy: I am in labour in the Radcliffe Infirmary in Oxford, with a brace of midwives standing by. "Pray, am I exerting four hundred and seventy pounds' pressure on the cerebellum of my baby *n*-uh-uh-*ow?*" I ask, during contractions. Such questions prompt midwives to take out their notebooks. "Four hundred and seventy pounds. Who told you that?" they counter. "Shandy, Walter Shandy? Is that *Doctor* Walter Shandy?" (The next day in Blackwell's there's a run on copies of *Tristram Shandy.*) It is a difficult labour, a forceps delivery; but my son's nose, praise be, is intact. Mrs. Shandy, I have felt with you.

Walter Shandy has strong views (I remind my critical brethren) on the delivery of the foetus. He is anxious to avoid pressure during labour on the cerebellum, because he believes that's where the soul is located. And so he wants his wife to undergo a caesarean. This solution, says Arthur H. Cash (I hope ironically) has "the simplicity of genius" (Cash, 140). We have a word for it (as C. S. Lewis said of Eve's decision to offer Adam the apple). "Its name in English is Murder" (Lewis, 125). " 'Caesarean' was synonymous with 'death sentence' " says Edward Shorter (161). Melvyn New, in his notes to the Florida Edition, records that no mother in England survived a caesarean operation until 1793. And Cash himself, the best authority on obstetrics in *Tristram Shandy,* admits "the operation in the eighteenth century was always fatal" (Cash, 141). And yet Cash, for all the fascinating material he presents, has some alarmingly pro-Walter opinions. His view is that "As a philosopher of the life sciences, [Walter] was advanced" (Cash, 142). This of a man who wants to crack his wife open like a nutshell to be thrown away, for the safer delivery of his son! (If it were a daughter he would probably think twice.)

Walter's views are not Sterne's, however. Sterne acquaints us sufficiently with the woman's angle, even though he locates most of the "opinions" among the men. Tristram's mother turns "as pale as ashes" at the very mention of a caesarean, as well she might (II.xix.179). And as Walter begins to take his measures to get his own way (delivery if not by caesarean then by "podalic version"), she summons what defences she can on her side. He turns to Dr. Slop. Tristram tells us that Slop is useful for Walter's purposes because he has written favourably on podalic version, or feet-first delivery. In changing the protestant Dr. Burton, the historical original of Dr. Slop, into a Catholic, Sterne is showing how the case is stacked against the woman.[2] For the Catholic Church, as Cash reminds us, "had long before laid down a doctrine that a child should be saved at the expense of a mother's life, if necessary" (Cash, 148). Therefore "of all men in the world, Dr. *Slop* was the fittest for my father's purpose." Walter rejects "the sisterhood" of midwives in favour of "a man of science, whom he could better deal with" (II.xix.179–80).

Mrs. Shandy's preference for the midwife, then, far from being a mere example of huffy umbrage, is a matter of life and death to her. And limited as are her resources, she finds the energy to resist her husband's arguments.

> What could my father do? He was almost at his wit's end; . . .—argued the
> matter with her like a christian,—like a heathen,—like a husband,—like a
> father,—like a patriot,—like a man:—My mother answered every thing only

like a woman; which was a little hard upon her; for as she could not assume and fight it out behind such a variety of characters,—'twas no fair match. (I.xviii.55)

Right on! She is ill equipped to match Walter's rhetorical dodges. But in this extremity, and arguing as a woman only, Mrs. Shandy still manages to achieve a draw—"that both sides sung *Te Deum.*" She is a survivor.

Sterne shows us more of the forces mustering on either side. The midwife has been alerted; Susannah is on the *qui vive;* and presently Walter spies her *running,* "as if they were going to ravish her," to fetch the midwife (II.vi.114). The war of the sexes has come to its next battleground. And again the males have a massively unfair advantage. Against Susannah running on her own two feet to fetch the old midwife, Walter sends the hairy Obadiah galloping on the big coachhorse to fetch Dr. Slop and his bag of instruments. "'Twas no fair match," Tristram might admit again. That is, Sterne fairly supplies information on both sides, and is not as partisan as some of his critics assume. He makes it plain why Mrs. Shandy prefers natural childbirth assisted by a competent midwife to caesarean section or podalic version performed by the incompetent Dr. Slop. And he shows a developed sympathy with the woman's plight in a world run by Shandy males. The old midwife, even Tristram admits, "had really some little claim to be depended upon, . . . having, in the course of her practice of near twenty years in the parish, brought every mother's son of them into the world without any one slip or accident which could fairly be laid to her account" (I.xviii.51). One wonders what is left for Dr. Slop to do. But Cash, though he acknowledges the claims of this particular midwife, takes Walter's side on the whole sisterhood, whom he characterizes as "this ignorant group of women," congenitally prone to raise a "fuss" (Cash, 145, 144).

The bonding between the women on this great occasion of birth is almost as strong as the bonding between the men on any occasion whatever; and Walter resents it accordingly. "From the very moment the mistress of the house is brought to bed," he complains, "every female in it, from my lady's gentlewoman down to the cinder-wench, becomes an inch taller for it; and give themselves more airs upon that single inch, than all their other inches put together" (IV.xii.340). Walter begrudges this brief hour of woman's glory almost as much as he begrudges paying his grandmother's jointure (III.xxxiii.260–61).

To move from Walter's theories on delivery to his theories on generation (for why should I confine myself to chronology any more than Tristram?): Walter is of course an animalculist rather than an ovist. That is—to use the information supplied in Louis Landa's fascinating article—he believes that the first "bud" of life is located in the sperm of the father, as the "homunculus" or "animalcule," rather than in the egg of the mother (Landa, 51 ff.). According to the animalculist, the mother provides only a "nidus" for the homunculus, or animalcule, which is completely formed and articulated in the *Semen Marium* before it ever leaves the father. The woman's egg as mere inanimate nest, or "place destined for his reception" (I.ii.2), is a convenient image for Walter, and for Tristram in perpetuating Walter's ideas, since it removes all procreative responsibility from the woman. Walter would like to take the whole credit of procreation to himself. As Landa shows, the debate between the ovists and the animalculists was fraught with political, legal and theological implications (Landa, 57). It is of a piece with Walter's beliefs that at the visitation dinner he is much excited by the proposition *"That the mother is not of kin to her child"* (IV.xxix.390).

Where does Tristram stand in the ovist-animalculist debate, and where does Sterne? At first glance it would seem that Tristram, at least, takes after his father in being a committed animalculist. He confirms that the "minutest philosophers"—that is, the scientists who have pursued microscopic investigations of the sperm—have "incontestably" shown the existence of the homunculus as a true fellow-creature (I.ii.2–3). But how could you, sir, be so inattentive in reading the first sentence of the book? There Tristram declares, "I wish either my father or my mother, or indeed both of them, as they were in duty both equally bound to it, had minded what they were about when they begot me" (I.i.1). In duty both equally bound: this surely argues for equal responsibility between the sexes in the act of procreation. And presently Tristram congratulates himself, "right glad I am, that I have begun the history of myself in the way I have done; and that I am able to go on tracing every thing in it, as *Horace* says, *ab Ovo*" (I.iv.5). Perhaps Tristram, and Sterne too, are ovists after all (Erickson, 202–3).

Walter as animalculist, however, takes his allegiance to the homunculus to extraordinary lengths. An early chapter of the *Tristrapaedia* is on "the foundation of the natural relation between a father and his child," which he elaborates under many headings. One of them is "procreation." Yorick is inclined to argue that the mere act of begetting, other claims aside, confers little power to the father and little obligation on the child. "You are wrong,—said my father argutely," and he proceeds to insist on the primacy of the father's role. Here his discourse moves into the asterisk mode, but it is clear that he is claiming something like a divine power of creation for the male, and deliberately marginalizing the female role: the mother is "under authority herself," and besides, *"she is not the principal agent,* Yorick," he insists (V.xxxi.468).

What he *really* wants, in fact, is to perform the act of generation all by himself. He urges Toby, when he falls in love, to remember that there are two deities of love:

the one is *rational*——
——the other is *natural*——
the first ancient—without mother——where Venus had nothing to do: the second, begotten of Jupiter and Dione—

(VIII.xxxiii.720)

(Naturally, Walter prefers the first.) He draws here on the *Symposium* (via the *Anatomy of Melancholy*): "As there are two goddesses, there must be two loves. For am I not right in asserting that there are two goddesses? The elder one, having no mother, who is called the heavenly Aphrodite—she is the daughter of Uranus; the younger, who is the daughter of Zeus and Dione, whom we call common."[3] It is no surprise that Aphrodite anadyomene, born of the sea from the potent member of Uranus, should be Walter's model for love and for procreation: the child born "without mother—where Venus had nothing to do" (the last phrase is Walter's addition, for special emphasis) is in his book generated by the ideal means.

At the Visitation dinner, soon after Mrs. Shandy has given birth, while the men are amusing themselves with the proposition that a woman is not of kin to her child, the mother is legally referred to as "venter": "*Charles* Duke of *Suffolk* having issue a son by one venter, and a daughter by another venter . . ." (IV.xxix.390). Alas, how are the mighty fallen! No longer the divine Venus genetrix, no longer the fecund Earth Mother, woman in her child-bearing capacity is reduced to mere *venter*. Pop! Out comes the baby, and the job is done.

☞ The machinery of my work is digressive, and it is progressive too (I.xxii.80–81). I am in the gynecologist's surgery. I have nothing on but a little paper tunic. Even my book I was required to leave behind with my clothes in the changing room. I am stripped of all social identity save that of female. I have nothing to do but to read the gynecologist's degrees, framed on the wall. "Be it Known to All Men," reads one, . . . that this bloke is particularly qualified to poke around in women's bodies (or words to that effect). Buster, it's not the *men* who need to know! But what consciousness has a venter? Nonentity, thy name is woman.

Since Walter can't actually conceive and give birth himself, he proceeds to do it figuratively. He is like those males in primitive cultures that the anthropologists tell us about, who lie around during their wives' pregnancies with rocks on their bellies. Immediately after Walter has begotten Tristram and (or?) Mrs. Shandy has conceived him, the two of them have a little conference in bed, "talking over what was to come" (I.xvii.49). Tristram makes it clear that both husband and wife are pregnant, she of a foetus, and he of an hypothesis about its delivery. And both pregnancies are due to reach term at the same time. The homunculus of Walter's hypothesis, unlike the other ill-starred little gentleman, has no accidents along the way to the place destined for his reception, for he has simply to stay at home.

> It is the nature of an hypothesis, when once a man has conceived it, that it assimilates every thing to itself as proper nourishment; and, from the first moment of your begetting it, it generally grows the stronger by every thing you see, hear, read, or understand. This is of great use.
> When my father was gone with this about a month . . . (II.xix.177)

Blessed hypothesis! An offspring of indubitable legitimacy, since "a man has conceived it" as well as begotten it. *O diem praeclarum!* And as Mrs. Shandy's foetus grows, nourished from her body, week by week developing limbs, and glands, and articulations, so does Walter's, nourished by ideas. By the time he is "gone with" it about a month the simple proposition about feet-first delivery takes a large stride, and turns into the developed caesarean idea, which is "six weeks" a-growing (II.xix.179). A gestation period cannot be hurried, nor an hypothesis delivered before its time. Tristram promises at the end of Volume II, "The reader will be content to wait for a full explanation of these matters till the next year,—when a series of things will be laid open which he little expects" (II.xix.181). A *series* of things, indeed. One *thing* may be his mother's, laid open, possibly, by caesarean. Tristram too is gestating, with the account of his own birth hidden in the womb of his narrative; he keeps the midwife handy, he says, "because when she is wanted we can no way do without her" (I.xiii.39). And Walter's hypothesis is evolving apace. Tristram keeps all three pregnancies going, and "with the same dash of the pen," as with the journeys through Auxerre (VII.xxviii.621–22).

We know about the delivery of Mrs. Shandy's foetus; and Volume III itself, in being published and seeing the light of day, constitutes the delivery of Tristram's. But what of the delivery of Walter's hypothesis on delivery? Tristram doesn't forget or omit the matter. Walter's pregnancy comes to term, naturally, on the same day as his wife's. He has gone into labour, unburdening himself of his views on the right and wrong end of a woman to Uncle Toby, when

> a Devil of a rap at the door snapp'd my father's definition (like his tobacco-pipe) in two,—and, at the same time, crushed the head of as notable and curious a dissertation as ever was engendered in the womb of speculation. (II.vii.118)

The rap at the door which crushes the head of Walter's foetus is delivered by Dr. Slop. The man-midwife has done it again!

Walter's longing for gestation takes a more explicit form still. At the end of his "Lamentation" on the pre-natal misfortunes of his son (which he contrives to blame on Mrs. Shandy's inward fuming about the cancellation of the trip to London [Erickson, 226]), he exclaims, "O *Licetus! Licetus!* had I been blest with a foetus five inches long and a half, like thee—fate might have done her worst" (IV.xix.355). Licetus, as Sterne's long note a few pages earlier informs us, had been born prematurely, and incubated by his father. Walter too would like to be known as "un Pere si experimenté dans l'Art de la Generation" (IV.x.338n).

Walter Shandy, in a word, has a severe case of ovary-envy. He takes no pleasure in the man's role of begetting a child—"Not a jot" (II.xii.133)— although he goes through the business with a grave face, like the Shandy bull (IX.xxxiii.808); but he secretly craves the credit of conceiving, gestating, and giving birth. He wants the child to be all his; and since he can't quite achieve this, his next choice (like podalic version if he can't have a caesarean) is to reduce the mother's role to as near nothing as possible. This is the real source, I suggest, of his misogyny.

Failing procreation, all by himself, of flesh and blood offspring, Walter is a fecund generator through language. The auxiliary verb is really more congenial to him than a wife. As Walter explains it, the mind's play with a single word is severely limited to a single idea: "When the mind has done that with it—there is an end,—the mind and the idea are at rest,—until a second idea enters:——and so on" (V.xlii.485). The rhythm is the same with Walter's "conversations" with his wife: "a discourse seldom went on much further betwixt them, than a proposition,—a reply, and a rejoinder; at the end of which, it generally took breath for a few minutes, ... and then went on again" (VI.xxxix.569). In each case, the sequence goes A, B, Z; and there's an end. But give Walter an auxiliary instead of a wife, and he can achieve momentum, and progeny:

> Now the use of the *Auxiliaries* is, at once to set the soul a going by herself upon the materials as they are brought her; and by the versability of this great engine ... to open new tracks of enquiry, and make every idea engender millions. (V.xlii.485)

After Walter has demonstrated the prolific force of the auxiliary verbs in "conjugating" (the metaphor is in-built) the White Bear, he concludes triumphantly "every word, *Yorick*, by this means, you see, is converted into a thesis or an hypothesis;—every thesis and hypothesis have an offspring of propositions" (VI.ii.492). In language he can achieve what he really wants to do—engendering millions without the trouble of a wife.

This male linguistic generation is not peculiar to Walter. The Athenian orators, Tristram tells us, consider it "a singular stroke of eloquence" to be able "to produce, pop, in the place you want it ... a tender infant" from under the mantle (III.xiv.217–18)—a process clearly analogous to childbearing (Allen, 654). And even Yorick, who regularly takes the woman's part against Walter, says of a sermon "I was delivered of it at the wrong end of me—it came from my head instead of my heart" (IV.xxvi.376–77). In the recurring analogy between creation and procreation,[4] the males long for the female role. Walter's envy so masters him that it leads to his mad misogyny.

In "Sterne's Cock and Bull Story" A. R. Towers characterized Walter as providing "the Comedy of Frustration." "Of the three Shandy males, Walter Shandy is by far the most vigorous. . . . A full account of [his] epic frustrations would encompass a major part of the novel" (Towers, 25). He went on to make it clear that he was not talking about sexual frustration; but in an article largely concerned, as its title suggests, with the sexuality in the novel, his phrase is misleading; and it has led many subsequent critics to write about

Walter as "frustrated" as a matter of course. Walter frustrated! That's a laugh. His heart sinks whenever the first Sunday of the month comes round. He is fatigued in advance, because he has a theory that women are sexually insatiable (as proven by his aunt Dinah's indiscretion with the coachman). So women are guilty on that count. Mrs. Shandy, however, has not "the least mote or speck of desire" in her eye or in her constitution (IX.i.736); but she's considered guilty on that count too. If Walter's frustration is intellectual rather than sexual, the argument goes, it is because of his wife's exasperating agreeableness. "Order it as you please, Mr. *Shandy,*" sums up her usual response (VI.xviii.529). As Ruth Marie Faurot has suggested, there is reason to believe that this response is a deliberately chosen tactic, and (given Walter's propensities) shrewdly chosen too (Faurot, 585). Because when Mrs. Shandy *doesn't* agree, as over the midwife, does he like it any better? No. He objects, too, to her lack of curiosity: "That she is not a woman of science," he complains pathetically, "is her misfortune—but she might ask a question." Tristram informs us—or rather *mis*informs us—"My mother never did" (VI.xxxix.569). But here we have another calumny, as another woman critic, Valerie Grosvenor Myer, has pointed out (Myer, 110). To our certain knowledge, Mrs. Shandy did once ask a question. "Pray, my dear, quoth my mother, have you forgot to wind the clock?" Did Walter like *that?* No! Mrs. Shandy can't win. If Walter is frustrated, either sexually or intellectually, Sterne has supplied evidence that it's not his wife's fault.

Walter is the one who has reduced the business of procreation to a boring monthly routine, cognate with the winding of the clock. His wife, says Myer, "finds his attentions . . . so boring she starts chattering *in medias res.* This would seem to be his fault" (Myer, 109). So writes a female critic. But a male critic, Gabriel Josipovici, proceeds on Walter's principle of Blame the Women, in this as in other matters:

> Mrs Shandy's one-track mind weakens, if it does not altogether stop, the natural flow [!] of Walter's semen; Susannah's faulty memory leads to Tristram's being wrongly named; the events surrounding the person of Dr Slop lead to Tristram's nose being crushed in birth. (Josipovici, 6)

A classic example, sir, of gender-discriminatory practices as documented in current research on *Seeing and Evaluating People:* "Evaluators attribute men's successes to ability, their mistakes or failures to unstable or external causes. . . . In contrast, women's failures are attributed to . . . *lack* of ability, and their successes to unstable external causes" (Geis *et al.* 5–6). In this case it's Mrs. Shandy's "one-track mind" that's to blame for Tristram's misbegetting, and Susannah's "faulty memory" for his misnaming. But when it comes to the crushing of Tristram's nose (an undoubted piece of professional bungling, since it's an obstetrician's business to know which is the front of a foetus's head, even if he has cut his thumb) it's not Dr. Slop who's to blame, but only "the events surrounding the person of Dr. Slop"! Sterne and Tristram have provided full information on each incident, and because of the "circumstances with which every thing in this world is begirt" (III.ii.187) we know that attributing responsibility is a complex matter. For the misnaming of Tristram, for instance, one could as easily blame the curate as Susannah, for dismissing her *"Tristram-gistus"* and insisting egotistically that "There is no christian name in the world . . . beginning with *Tris*—but *Tristram* . . . 'tis my own name" (IV.xiv.344). And Walter himself could have averted the catastrophe if he had bestirred himself to get to his son's christening. But Susannah is the woman, so she's the one who cops it, even a couple of centuries later. As Josipovici testifies, Sterne's characters are "'real people' for us by this time" (17)—so real that we snap into our usual habits of gender discrimination about them, as though they were job applicants, or up for tenure.

But to return to Walter, and procreation. After his monthly performances (should one say menstrual?) in bed, Walter characteristically lies "musing within himself about the hardships of matrimony" (VI.xxxix.568). He is no exception to Aristotle's rule, which he quotes, that *"omne animal post coitum est* triste" (V.xxxvi.475). In fact this rule, as other readers have pointed out (Alter, 322; Porter, 85), accounts for his aversion to the name *Tristram,* which signifies for him not the chivalric hero, but post-coital langour and depletion (all too probable in this "child of decrepitude! interruption!" [IV.xix.354]). Coition, in Walter's developed theory on "the whole secret of health," actually endangers the body by drying up the radical moisture.

For Walter, then, and for some surrounding males, the sexual act is not only undignified—in that it "couples and equals wise men with fools"; not only shameful—a deed to be compassed in the dark, and described by no decent language (IX.xxxiii.806); but dangerous as well. Indeed, sometimes mortal. Walter and Tristram between them collect a number of instances in which making love is associated with death, and sometimes even causes it (and in more ways than in the colloquial sense of "dying" as achieving orgasm). Walter's crowning instance of appropriate death is "of *Cornelius Gallus,* the prætor. . . . He died, said my father, as ************—And if it was with his wife, said my uncle *Toby*—there could be no hurt in it.—That's more than I know—replied my father" (V.iv.426). Lieutenant Le Fever's wife was killed by a musket shot while he was making love to her (VI.vii.508). In Volume VII, when Tristram is in flight from death, there is a grouping of incidents that couple love and death. The tourist attraction most interesting to him is the *"Tomb of the two lovers"* (VII.xxx.627). This pathetic pair "fly into each others arms, and both drop down dead for joy" (VII.xxxi.628). And St. Maxima's pilgrimage to touch the bones of St. Germain is made to sound very like necrophilia (VII.xxvii.620). The accumulation suggests something like a phobia.

Of course the Shandy males have reason to fear coition, because as we all know they are not very capable at it. Sour grapes, gentlemen. We've heard all about the short Shandy noses and other organs, the scattered animal spirits, the wound in the groin, the accident with the window sash; and we're very sorry for you. But does this justify your worships in trying to do without women altogether? If Walter and Tristram do what they can to take over the female role in childbearing, are they also on the lookout for a replacement for the woman in copulation?

Let us consider Phutatorius. His name means copulator, and he has written a book on keeping concubines. Here, if anywhere, we can expect to find the potent male, boldly on the rampage among the women. But Phutatorius has been absorbed by Walter's male-only world too. We meet him at the Visitation dinner, in an exclusively male gathering. And even when his genitals are warmed beyond endurance by a hot chestnut he doesn't seek the relief of "frequent use of Venus," which Burton recommends in cases of burning lust.[5] Instead, on the advice of his male friends, he proposes to wrap the part in fresh damp proofsheets from his book on concubines. Which part of the book, pray? The chapter *"de re concubinaria,"*[6] no less! (IV.xxviii.387). Here's the formula: first you reduce the woman to her thing. Then you replace her thing by a chapter on it. Now you can achieve an act of miscegenation between the signified and the signifier—a consummation devoutly to be wished, for its ingenious accomplishment of the redundancy of the female.

If Walter and some surrounding males are engaged in a mad enterprise to get along without the women, in coition, conception and birth, what of the mother's role in nurture? Walter's position here is less spectacularly eccentric, but it is nevertheless of a piece with the rest of his views. Mrs. Shandy, we can gather from the evidence presented, is a caring mother. When Tristram screams during the window-sash episode, she rushes to his side; and while Walter consults folios on circumcision rituals, she puts her mind to easing the pain (Ehlers, 64). But Walter, though he leaves Tristram in her care until he is breeched, does even this with a bad grace. He considers mothers are bad for children. To begin with, their breasts, unless flaccid, will compress and shorten the child's nose (III.xxxviii.277); and we know what *that* means. And besides, "Prejudice of education, he would say, *is the devil,*—and the multitudes of them which we suck in with our mother's milk—*are the devil and all.*" He resents what Tristram may learn from the women, and projects that the man who submits to their "prejudice" will write "nothing but a farrago of the clack of nurses, and of the nonsense of the old women (of both sexes) throughout the kingdom" (V.xvi.448). Therefore he sets out to write the *Tristra-paedia,* a work designed to substitute good male lore (his own, that is) for the clack of nurses. Hence its weighty introduction on "the foundation of the natural relation between a father and his child" (V.xxxi.467). Although the *Tristra-paedia* doesn't progress satisfactorily, Walter is impatient to take

Tristram "out of these women's hands" (VI.v.496). Certainly he tolerates little input from Mrs. Shandy on matters pertaining to their children, even such a portentous one as death. When Walter is achieving considerable relief from his grief at Bobby's death by delivering a funeral oration, he speaks, for rhetorical effect, in the person of Socrates:

> "I have friends—I have relations,—I have three desolate children," says *Socrates.*—
> ——Then, cried my mother, opening the door,——you have one more, Mr. *Shandy,* than I know of.
> By heaven! I have one less,—said my father, getting up and walking out of the room. (V.xiii.442)

That is his way of breaking the news to her of their son's death! And though we have all laughed at the misconceptions, so to speak, between husband and wife, a second look can alert us to his emotional brutality—especially as an account of Toby's gentle and sympathetic treatment of Mrs. Shandy immediately follows.

To sum up on Walter, then: Sterne has inventively presented him as a man of many hypotheses, and riding a whole team of hobbyhorses. But the unifying thread of his various original and eccentric ideas is his mad desire to free the race from woman. The ideal world of Walter's creation would be one in which the men not only beget, but conceive, gestate, deliver, nurture and educate the offspring. And since he can't achieve this, he rails against the wives, mothers, grandmothers, midwives, nursemaids, old women, and clacking nurses, because they remind him at every turn that his male universe is not potent, self-sufficient, self-reproducing.

And here's the joke about *Tristram Shandy* and the anxiety about impotence. It presents an array of males who are in a perpetual stew about their genital organs. They worry about them as vulnerable to hot chestnuts, to falling window sashes, to stones broken off from parapets. They worry about them as prey to newts and askers. They worry about them as incapable: there's doubt that Toby can make it with the widow Wadman, or Tristram with Jenny. They worry about them as too small: the short Shandy nose, which corresponds with the shortness of their other external organs, costs the family a good deal in inflated jointures; and the Shandy heir is regularly sent on the grand tour "for the sake of bettering his own private parts" (IV.xxxi.396). So here are all these men devoting their mental and physical energies towards acquiring bigger, better, and more indestructible organs— and all in order to have less and less to do with them.

Walter, says Towers, "is a formidable personage, beside whom the flighty Tristram and the benign Uncle Toby seem pliant and yielding, like jellyfish surrounding a crab" (Towers, 25). And indeed in certain ways he does dominate surrounding males by his hard-edged ideas and brow-beating articulation of them. But he doesn't always represent them. It's worth considering to what extent they share his ideas on women, and to what extent they diverge.

Uncle Toby, gentle and courteous, has none of Walter's misogyny. In his world there is room not only for flies but for women. By Tristram's testimony, Toby is outstandingly qualified for the marriage state: "[Nature] had formed him of the best and kindliest clay—had temper'd it with her own milk" (IX.xxii.776)—the female constituent in his heritage is emphasized. His view of love is simple, but effective. When Walter tries to convert his brother from *natural* to *rational* love ("ancient—without mother—where Venus had nothing to do"), Toby interrupts, "What signifies it, brother Shandy, . . . which of the two it is, provided it will but make a man marry, and love his wife, and get a few children" (VIII.xxxiii.718, 720). He sees no difficulty in getting the children (and by Trim's testimony, who ought to know, his wound in the groin doesn't incapacitate him). Nor does he show any signs of wanting to do the conceiving and gestation himself. He is like Walter and other males, however, in making his hobbyhorse a replacement for sexual activity (Alter, 317). Fortification will do instead of fornication. He posts down to his scale-model warfare like a lover to his mistress, "to enjoy this self-same thing in private" (II.v.113). The lay-out on the bowling green is even occasionally allegorized as the female body, as when the "bridge" and Bridget are simultaneously breached. Indeed, all hobbyhorses (all those of men, that is; and we're not given any examples of women's) serve the purpose of creating and satisfying sexual excitement, as "the heated parts of the rider . . . come immediately into contact with the back of the HOBBY-HORSE.—By long journies and much friction, it so happens that the body of the rider is at length fill'd as full of HOBBY-HORSICAL matter as it can hold" (I.xxiv.86). Hobbyhorses are one more substitute for women.

But if Toby's fortifications are a sublimation of sexual energy, they don't preclude the real thing, though they do delay it. The widow Wadman, by her skillful tactics in conducting a counter-siege, finally succeeds in making Toby notice and desire her. Things look propitious for Toby's amours. What goes wrong?

The widow Wadman has a healthy sexual appetite. Her lively kicking up of the blankets and corking pin constitutes a rejection of celibacy, and an energetic espousal of life and love and a full physical existence. And, since her husband had had a case of sciatica (the male equivalent of the female "headache") for the duration of her first marriage, she has a right to know if Toby is sexually capable. Who can blame her? Well, Walter can, and the male population that thinks like him. True to his principle of Blame the Women, he makes women responsible for 100 per cent of the sexual appetite of the world: he won't halve the matter amicably. And the women, blamed for it *all*, are made ashamed of having *any*. That's why the widow, when Toby suggests there may be "pleasure" in the procreation of children, replies "A fiddlestick!"

in just the timbre that will embarrass him. And that's why Toby, who has had the sexual insatiability of the Aunt Dinahs of the world dinned in his ears all his life, is shocked to discover that the widow takes an interest in his potency. "Let us go to my brother Shandy's," he says on the discovery (IX.xxxi.803). He is aware that a retreat from his amour puts him squarely in Walter's camp.

And Tristram? Tristram, like other sons, struggles both to identify himself with, and to differentiate himself from, his father. He inherits many of Walter's attitudes, including a tendency to be churlish to Mrs. Shandy. But he has some compunction about it too. When he catches her listening at the keyhole, he decides. "In this attitude I am determined to let her stand for five minutes"—as though it were wholesome discipline (V.v.427). Then, like a careless nursemaid who has locked her charge in a dark cupboard, he forgets her. "I am a *Turk* if I had not as much forgot my mother, as if Nature had plaistered me up, and set me down naked upon the banks of the river *Nile,* without one" (V.xi.438). It comes naturally to Tristram to imagine himself born by spontaneous generation, without mother. But he does reproach himself for the notion. And his fullest rejection of Walter and all his systems occurs explicitly when Walter triumphantly welcomes Toby into his misogynistic camp:

> My father . . . was demonstrating to Yorick, notwithstanding my mother was sitting by——not only, "That the devil was in women, and that the whole of the affair was lust;" but that every evil and disorder in the world of what kind or nature soever, from the first fall of Adam, down to my uncle Toby's (inclusive) was owing one way or other to the same unruly appetite. (IX.xxxii.804–5)

Tristram is pained on his mother's account; and here he voices the most hostile judgement on Walter that occurs in the book: "My father['s] . . . way was to force every event in nature into an hypothesis, by which means never man crucified TRUTH at the rate he did." Tristram renounces his father's position.

At the end of his first volume, Tristram asserts his power by declaring it's impossible for his readers to guess at what is to come: "—if you could,—I should blush; not as a relation,—not as a man,—nor even as a woman,—but I should blush as an author" (I.xxv.89). Tristram, however fleetingly, can locate himself in a woman; and he suggests that both male and female are subsumed under "author." He has in fact recurrently been seen as womanish. Towers called him "flighty," and said that Tristram had surrendered "that masculine, rational intelligence that can foresee ends and drive straight towards them" (18). (Do men, sir, have a monopoly on rational intelligence? Well, we'll let that pass.) In an interesting article on "Sexuality/Textuality in *Tristram Shandy,*" Dennis W. Allen has shown how the male model of communication, the phallic forward thrust of discourse, is shown as impotent, and associated with the doubtful virility of the Shandy males; whereas the model

for effective communication—digressive spaces fertilized by the imagination—is vaginal (Allen, 660). Shall I then, your worships, accuse Tristram of
vagina-envy as I have accused Walter of ovary-envy? I'm thinking about it.
But courage! gentle reader!—I scorn it—'tis enough to have thee in my
power (VII.vi.584).

Tristram's dallying with androgyny is different from Walter's envious
desire to displace woman and render her redundant. Tristram's is an act of
sympathy, of imagination, part of his negative capability. And *that* is a capability he has plenty of.

Leigh Ehlers has argued for a progressive evolution in Tristram's character in the direction of acquiring filial love for his mother and respect for other
women (Ehlers, 70). But his position on the relation of the sexes is present *in
posse,* as we have seen, from the first sentence of the book, where he emphasizes that the two sexes are "in duty both equally bound" to mind what they
are about in procreation. In his sexual attitudes, Tristram has two opposed
role models, his father and his uncle. His father in love, he tells us, "was all
abuse and foul language," whereas his uncle in love "took it like a lamb"
(VIII.xxvi.709–10). In his own love life Tristram bounces between one
extreme and the other. One lyrical chapter on his "earthly goddess," written
in his narrative present, reads rather like a Donne love lyric, frothing with
energy, indignation, and contrary impulses. "Curse on her! and so I send her
to Tartary . . . But as the heart is tender. . . . I instantly bring her back again."
He works himself up to a passion, until the end of the chapter:

> O Tristram! Tristram! cried Jenny.
> O Jenny! Jenny! replied I, and so went on with the twelfth chapter.
> (VIII.xi.669–71)

Jenny as woman and mistress plays the authoritative role of reconciler. Tristram treats her with tenderness and respect.

It is Tristram's role to bridge the gap between a whole series of
dichotomies in the novel, and to achieve balance: not only between his father
and mother, male and female, but also between his father and his uncle, head
and heart, mind and body, theory and practice, language and action, word
and flesh (McMaster, 53). The gaps between the elements of these
dichotomies threaten to grow ever wider, and much of the comedy of the
novel shows Tristram, according to a kind of intellectual slapstick, falling
between two stools. But it's not only with his reader that he proposes to
"halve this matter amicably" (II.xi.125). That is his role and his procedure
throughout.

Dennis Allen considers that "The use of female sexuality as a privileged
metaphor here [in *Tristram Shandy*] is surprising, given the overall misogyny of
the novel" (661n). But the novel, Sir, is not misogynist. I wish the male-reader
has not pass'd by the quaint and curious points which the female-reader has

detected. *Tristram Shandy* is *about* misogyny, and against it. As Robert Erickson has shown, Sterne's book "shows an exceptional *human* sensitivity to the feminine origins of life and creation—physical, mental, and imaginative" (Erickson, 204). Sterne is no Walter. In creating the novel, and paying close attention to such subjects as conjugal relations, childbirth, and what goes wrong with amours, he has shown himself alert (to a degree unprecedented in the history of the novel) to issues of intimate concern to women, as to men. It's not Sterne's fault if some of his male readers have found Walter, with his fertile linguistic charms, too powerfully seductive. It is to Sterne's credit that he has dramatized and articulated Walter's mad misogyny, his impulse to annihilate woman and the need for her, his desire for a monstrous progeny, begotten of itself, born of itself (like Milton's Sin); and has judged him. *Sterne* is not of the devil's party, though he understands its attraction.

Tristram Shandy isn't a notably didactic book, though it has its lasting moral seriousness as well as its immortal comedy; but for Walter and his ilk Sterne has provided the punishment that fits the crime, and fits it as its natural consequence: the Shandy family is dying out. *Tristram Shandy* is a comic version of *The Waste Land,* with Uncle Toby as its fisher king (Ehlers, 68), and Tristram as a doubtful Perceval approaching the chapel Perilous. We don't know if the rain will come at last, and fertility be restored. Walter is funny, yes. But for the good of the race we'd better laugh *at* him, rather than *with* him. Then both sides may sing *Te Deum.*

Notes

1. In the context of a discussion on a specifically female style, Phyllis Rose points out that "many women writers have liked Sterne," citing Virginia Woolf and Katherine Anne Porter; and she suggests that, if he was not actually a "feminine" writer, Sterne "was certainly not in a conventional way masculine."
2. James E. Swearingen, who does pay attention to Mrs. Shandy, erroneously states that "she is a papist," but that it doesn't matter (224). In fact she is *not* a papist, and it *does* matter.
3. From Pausanias's speech in Plato's *Symposium,* trans. Benjamin Jowett.
4. Melvyn New has identified this "concern over creativity" as "the most pervasive metaphor of the work," but in terms rather more favourable to the sexual powers of the Shandy males than they deserve: "the Shandy body and mind are in a constant state of begetting" (New, 82). So Walter would like us to believe. But in fact the metaphor for successful creation and procreation, as Dennis Allen has shown, is more usually the female one of conception, gestation, and parturition.
5. Or *"venerem saepe exercendo"* (*Anatomy of Melancholy,* III, 2, 5, 1). I use the translation in the edition of Floyd Dell and Paul Jordan-Smith, p. 768.
6. "Of the Thing pertaining to concubinage." Though "thing" may be used for either the male or female genitals, Tristram favours the female—as in the chapter on Things, and the *Argumentum ad Rem* which is balanced against the *Argumentum Tripodium* (I.xxi.79). Phutatorius's act is thus a heterosexual one.

Works Cited

Allen, Dennis W. "Sexuality/Textuality in *Tristram Shandy.*" *Studies in English Literature* 25 (1985): 651–70.

Alter, Robert. "*Tristram Shandy* and the Game of Love." *American Scholar* 37 (1968): 316–23.

Burton, Robert. *The Anatomy of Melancholy,* ed. Floyd Dell and Paul Jordan-Smith (New York: Tudor Publishing Co., 1951).

Cash, Arthur H. "The Birth of Tristram Shandy: Sterne and Dr. Burton," in *Studies in the Eighteenth Century: Papers Presented at the David Nicol Smith Memorial Seminar,* ed. R. F. Brissenden (Toronto: U of Toronto P, 1968), 133–54.

Ehlers, Leigh A. "Mrs. Shandy's 'Lint and Basilicon': The Importance of Women in *Tristram Shandy.*" *South Atlantic Review* 46 (1981): 61–75.

Erickson, Robert A. *Mother Midnight: Birth, Sex and Fate in Eighteenth-Century Fiction* (New York: AMS Press, 1986).

Faurot, Ruth Marie. "Mrs. Shandy Observed." *Studies in English Literature* 10 (1970): 579–89.

Geis, F., M. Carter, and D. Butler. *Seeing and Evaluating People* (Newark, Del.: Office of Women's Affairs, University of Delaware, 1986).

Gysin, Fritz. *Model as Motif in* Tristram Shandy (Bern: A. Francke Verlag, 1983).

Jefferson, D. W. "*Tristram Shandy* and the Tradition of Learned Wit." *Essays in Criticism* 1 (1951): 225–48.

Josipovici, Gabriel. *Writing and the Body* (Princeton: Princeton UP, 1982).

Landa, Louis. "The Shandean Homunculus: The Background of Sterne's 'Little Gentleman,'" in *Restoration and Eighteenth-Century Literature: Essays in Honour of Alan Dugald McKillop,* ed. Caroll Camden (Chicago: U of Chicago P, 1963), 49–68.

Lewis, C. S. *A Preface to Paradise Lost* (London: Oxford UP, 1942).

McMaster, Juliet. "Experience to Expression: Thematic Character Contrasts in *Tristram Shandy.*" *Modern Language Quarterly* 32 (1971): 42–57.

Myer, Valerie Grosvenor. "Tristram and the Animal Spirits," in *Laurence Sterne: Riddles and Mysteries* (London: Vision and Barnes and Noble, 1984), 99–112.

New, Melvyn. *Laurence Sterne as Satirist: A Reading of Tristram Shandy* (Gainesville: U of Florida P, 1969).

Parish, Charles. "The Shandy Bull Vindicated." *Modern Language Quarterly* 31 (1970): 48–52.

Plato. *The Symposium,* from *The Dialogues of Plato,* trans. Benjamin Jowett. 4 vols. (Oxford: Clarendon Press, 1982), I, 541–94.

Porter, Roy. "Against the Spleen," in *Laurence Sterne: Riddles and Mysteries,* ed. Valerie Grosvenor Myer (London: Vision and Barnes and Noble, 1984), 84–98.

Rivers, William E. "The Importance of Tristram's 'dear, dear *Jenny.*'" *Interpretations* 13 (1981): 1–9.

Rose, Phyllis. *Writing of Women: Essays in the Renaissance* (Middletown, Conn.: Wesleyan UP, 1985).

Shorter, Edward. *A History of Women's Bodies* (New York: Basic Books, 1982).

Swearingen, James E. *Reflexivity in* Tristram Shandy: *An Essay in Phenomenological Criticism* (New Haven and London: Yale UP, 1977).

Towers, A. R. "Sterne's Cock and Bull Story." *Journal of English Literary History* 24 (1957): 12–29.

Watt, Ian. "Introduction" to his Riverside edition of *The Life and Opinions of Tristram Shandy, Gentleman* (Boston: Houghton Mifflin, 1965).

Tristram Shandy's Consent to Incompleteness: Discourse, Disavowal, Disruption

CALVIN THOMAS

. . . sexuality as *division* and as meaning's *flight,* as contradiction and as ambivalence; the very threat, in other words of the unmastery, of the impotence, and of the unavoidable castration which inhere in *language.*

—Shoshana Felman, *Literature and Psychoanalysis,* 192

For this subject, who thinks he can accede to himself by designating himself in the statement, is no more than such an object. Ask the writer about the anxiety that he experiences when faced by the blank sheet of paper, and he will tell you who *is* the turd of his phantasy.

—Jacques Lacan, *Écrits,* 315

The single most famous comment about Sterne's most famous work is of course Victor Shklovsky's assertion that *"Tristram Shandy* is the most typical novel in world literature" (57). In their preface to the essay in which Shklovsky makes this claim, Lemon and Reis note Shklovsky's distinction between *fabula,* or story, "the temporal-causal sequence of narrated events," and *sjuzet,* or plot, "the story as distorted or defamiliarized in the process of telling" (25). In the essay itself, Shklovsky examines the revolutionary and yet "typical" way in which Sterne, by focusing the reader's attention on the text's highly distorted and defamiliarized plotting, manages to "lay bare" his own devices, and hence, for Shklovsky, those of the genre of the novel itself. But underlying Shklovsky's distinction between story and plot is a more problematic distinction between a syntagmatic or "objective" diachrony on the one hand and a paradigmatic or "subjective" synchrony on the other. Indeed, *Tristram Shandy* has often been read as the comic affirmation of the synchronous subjectivity of the narrator's mind over and against the diachronous "calendar-time" that constitutes the objective world. Implied is an ontological struggle in which identity is pitched against anonymity, self against history, presence against absence, the "essential" against the temporal, and so on—a struggle, in other words, for "mastery," and hence a distinction which underwrites a

Reprinted from *Literature and Psychology* 36 (1990): 44–62.

specifically gendered conception of the genre of the novel itself, for as Lukács puts it, "the entire inner action of the novel is nothing but a struggle against the power of time" (122).

This agonistic formulation allows us to read another meaning into the word "plot"—as a subversive design, a secret plan or clandestine scheme, a plot in the sense of "plotting against." But this meaning assumes, again, a specifically gendered connotation when a certain idea of "the feminine" or of "woman" is projected onto the temporality which the "inner action" of a novel is ostensibly plotting against, or when, as Peter Brooks has suggested, the very success of a narrative plot, of narration itself, of narrative's ability to produce "meaning," hinges upon the transmission of paternal authority and power from father to son. Given this model of narrative, the transmission of "meaning" depends upon the narrator's ability to assume a position of power, mastery, and author-ity from which to transmit such meaning, and this assumption is itself staked not only on a disavowal "of the unmastery, of the impotence, and of the unavoidable castration which inhere in *language*" (Felman, 192)—a disavowal, in other words, of that split between enunciator and enounced which *is* castration in the broadest possible sense—this assumption of mastery is also staked on a disavowal of "the feminine," of "woman," and of maternal priority in the constitution of the male subject.

But if secrecy, concealment, and subterfuge are what guarantee the success of any plot, what can be said of a plot that lays its own devices bare, announces itself and its own limitation on nearly every page, calls incessant attention to its own imposturings and impossibilities? Such plotting disrupts the disavowals upon which it is based, subverts its own subversions, acknowledges incompleteness and the failure to assume "mastery" as the grounds of its own deepest success. *Tristram Shandy* discloses such admission and consent. By revealing its own plot as a failed "plotting against"—against time, sex, "woman," death—the text recognizes and celebrates the absence around which its own discourse is organized, and designates in its own plot yet another meaning of the word: the only final place of rest, a small area of ground in which the dead are buried. As Peter Brooks suggests, "there may be a subterranean logic connecting these heterogenous meanings" of the word "plot" (12). *Tristram Shandy* disseminates itself through the cracks and fissures of this logical subterrain.

In a conversation with Richard Macksey, Jacques Lacan, clearly alluding to Shklovsky's famous comment, is reported to have called *Tristram Shandy* "le roman le plus analytique de la littérature universelle" (Macksey, 1007). Macksey paraphrases Lacan as having commented on "the peculiar way in which all of the 'characters' in the novel constitute themselves as 'modes of discourse' and the equally peculiar way in which the novel constitutes itself around a notorious 'lack.'" Macksey goes on to say that "Sterne like Lacan writes texts . . . that displace and deconstruct themselves in the very process of their production. His style, quirky, discontinuous, and deliberately odd like Lacan's inhabits time and triumphantly accepts its own incompleteness" (1007). Of course, for Lacan to accept temporality and incompletion is "to accept castration . . . to accept the primal lack which is at the center of life itself . . . a consent to incompleteness, to time and to the repetition of desire in time" (Jameson, 172). The implications of such a consent in relation to the assumption of phallogocentric "mastery" and the transmission of narrative "meaning" will become more obvious as we proceed. Macksey calls *Tristram Shandy* "an extended meditation on thwarted paternity and its consequences . . . inscribed under the sign of the death's head" (1008), and maintains that "in the opening pages the relationship of the father to the symbolic triad of the family is already one of absence" (1009). This absence, says Macksey, is quite literal: he argues that Walter Shandy is not Tristram's physical father, but that it is Parson Yorick "who in terms of appearance, temperament, and status as an author, has [the] larger claim on the role" (1010).

Macksey's arguments about Walter's dubious paternity are convincing enough, but, in terms of a Lacanian reading (which is what Macksey's piece presents itself as), such arguments are not necessary to establish in the novel the trope of the absent father. For what Lacan's theories question is not so much the fact of paternity as its fiction, the way paternal power is encoded in discourse and the absence at the heart of that power. As Lacan himself puts it, "the phallus, even the real phallus, is a *ghost*" ("Desire," 50). Thus Walter's "literal" absence as Tristram's father, though likely, is not as important as the symbolic absence that his doubtful paternity suggests, the way that absence provisionally opens up narrative desire. As Robert Con Davis says, "instituted by the discovery of absence, the desire for the father will be articulated in what is essentially a narrative" (9). But since it is clearly narrative that is questioned and subverted throughout *Tristram,* the constituting desire behind this model of narration, the desire to "fill" the absence left by the missing father, must also be subject to the text's interrogations. *Tristram* does not represent the quest for the father but deconstructs it. Through tropes of impotence, castration, and thwarted physical and symbolic paternity, the novel disrupts the fictions of male prerogative, privilege, and power, the phallogocentric transmission of "meaning" through narrative and Oedipal closure, and the disavowal of castration which is the heart of linguistic "mastery" itself.

To cite a beginning:

> I wish either my father or my mother, or indeed both of them, as they were in duty both equally bound to it, had minded what they were about when they begot me; had they duly consider'd how much depended upon what they were then doing;—that not only the production of a rational Being was concern'd in it, but that possibly the happy formation and temperature of his body, perhaps his genius and the very cast of his mind . . . Had they duly weighed and considered all this, and proceeded accordingly,——I am verily persuaded I should have made a quite different figure in the world, from that, in which the reader is likely to see me. (I.i.1)

What is most striking about this opening passage is the clear impossibility of the dream that Tristram wishes his primal scene had fulfilled: whether our parents beget us out of "domestic duty," as is certainly the case with the Shandys, or sexual pleasure, they cannot at that moment have "us" in mind as rational beings, as subjectively-ordered identities. Tristram's *cogito* is undermined by the knowledge of the *coito* of others, and his wish to rewrite the beginning of his family romance stems from the unwanted recognition that "far from constituting an indubitable premise, the self is directed by the world before it directs itself" (Swearingen, 29). Or again, Tristram realizes that, far from being the originating subject of the world he perceives, he was not even originated *as* a subject but rather has been "constituted . . . as an object since before his birth" (Wilden, 161). Later in this discussion we will see what sort of anxieties might arise from the realization that subjectivity presupposes objectivity, through what phantasmatic grid the subject views this object, or part-object, that it imagines it was. For the moment, however, we can say that Tristram's anxieties are not particularly different from anyone else's, since insofar as we are all similarly constituted, all of our troubles begin, like Tristram's, nine months before we come into the world.

In Tristram's case, however, the misfortunes are always already multiplied, his primal scene already a site of ambiguity and unmastery, a moment of disruption and disavowal:

> *Pray, my dear,* quoth my mother, *have you not forgot to wind up the clock?*——
> *Good G*—! cried my father, making an exclamation, but taking care to moderate his voice at the same time,——*Did ever woman, since the creation of the world, interrupt a man with such a silly question?* Pray, what was your father saying?
> ——Nothing. (I.i.2)

Here Mrs. Shandy's question opens up a gap in Walter's mode of discourse. Walter's consternation stems not only from having been interrupted in the apparently shaky performance of his paternal progenitive role, but also from the unwelcome intrusion of the reality of time itself into the illusion of atemporality that the discourse of sex momentarily affords. The "unhappy association" of the ideas of time and sex in Mrs. Shandy's mind leads to the unhappier association in Walter's of time, sex, "woman," and, as we shall see, death, an association that he verbally lashes out against in a frustrated attempt to reestablish his own threatened paternal priority. Conspicuously enough, he begins by invoking the Name of the Father—"*Good G*—!" Then, in a more conspicuous gesture, Walter omits the indefinite article "a" before the word "*woman,*" an omission which in effect projects onto Mrs. Shandy her status not as an individual woman but as Shandy Hall's resident feminine "property," both in the sense of attribute (as in a chemical property) and as an object to be owned, a piece of private property, a *plot* of land. On the other hand, Walter retains the indefinite article "a" before the word "man," thus laying claim to his privileged status as an individual man, autonomous subject, master of the property, owner of the plot. And yet we are told that Walter has been interrupted while saying "Nothing," one meaning of which is that he is physically impotent, while in a related sense we can say that Walter has been discovered in the abrogation of language, and of the paternal authority inscribed therein, has been caught, so to speak, in an unimpregnating silence. Quite simply, Walter has lost his phallus, in both the sexual and the linguistic sense, two losses each of which collapses into the other. The word "Nothing," dangling at the end of the chapter, lays bare the split between enunciator and enounced, the Lacanian *béance* or lack, around which Walter spends the rest of the novel trying rather ludicrously to remobilize his discourse and so recuperate himself in the power from which he has slipped, from which he slips further as each of Tristram's conspicuously logophallic catastrophes—his nasal disfigurement, his accidental circumcision, his misnaming—disrupts the "normal" flow of both paternal transmission and narrative progress (nor is it any coincidence that in each case of catastrophe a woman is "responsible").

Thus Mrs. Shandy's temporal but untimely interruption opens up a wound that never quite heals, a *béance* that reflects back onto Walter's original moment of disempowerment, of castration, and onto the other prominent "wounds" in the novel—Tristram's nose and foreskin, Toby's groin, Trim's knee, Slop's thumb, etc. One of the novel's main concerns, then, becomes the frustrated efforts of the Shandy males to establish through their various hobby-horses (the metaphor itself one of potent mastery made childish and ludicrous) the priority of their own subjective discourses over and against the objective lack represented by the association of time, sex, "woman," and death. Both this association, as well as the tragi-comic interplay between the denigration of "woman" and the frustrated attempt to establish male priority, can be made more explicit by an examination of the word "interrupt" and the importance in the novel of interruption as motif. We can see, for instance, that the word for the sexual activity that Mrs. Shandy's question disrupts, and the word which designates that disruption itself, share the same prefix—she interrupts intercourse. The "inter" in intercourse discloses both *entre* and enter, union and penetration, while the "inter" in interrupt reveals a "coming between," a severance of the self from its discourse, the opening of a rupture. Significantly though, "to inter" means to entomb or encrypt, to insert a dead body into the ground, or again, to bury something in a plot:

> We shall have a rare month of it, said my father, turning his head from *Obadiah,* and looking wistfully in my uncle *Toby's* face for some time—we shall have a devilish month of it, brother *Toby,* said my father, setting his arms a-kimbo, and shaking his head; fire, water, women, wind—brother *Toby!*—'Tis some misfortune, quoth my uncle *Toby.*—That it is, cried my father,—to have so many jarring elements breaking loose, and riding triumph in every corner of a gentleman's house. (IV.xvi.348)

Here, in Walter's list of "jarring elements," women take the all too time-honored place of earth (an identification that has more to do with traditional property relations and exchange values than with any mystified "closeness to nature"), so that once again we find feminine desire as a plot against male privilege, an elemental force that threatens to ride triumph "in every corner of a gentleman's house." The danger posed to Walter by sexuality itself is clear: intercourse with women is an interring, a burying of that part of his body with which he identifies his power into the earth, as well as an interruption, a severance, a coming between Walter and his own primary signifier, the Name of the Father, the paternal mastery inscribed within the Symbolic Order. Thus, since intercourse is for Walter already an interruption and an interring, Mrs. Shandy's question simply reveals to him, and us, the rupture that was always already there.

We can see, then, how the motif of interruption that begins, ends, and runs throughout *Tristram* opens up the question of the absence—impotence, unmastery, and unavoidable castration—at the heart of discourse itself, and of discourse in relation to the various characters' frustrated wills toward mastery. For in Shandy Hall, to interrupt is to gain power, to be interrupted is to lose it, and of course the Shandys constantly interrupt each other. Walter, naturally, hates to be interrupted by anyone ("do not—dear *Toby* . . . do not—do not, I beseech thee, interrupt me" [V.iii.422]). Uncle Toby interrupts his servant Trim quite mercilessly during the latter's story of the King of Bohemia, and despite the mutual affection between the two characters, the master-servant power-relation is inscribed within their exchange nonetheless. Toby's interruptions cause Trim to "lose" his story and thwart his will to narrative mastery, though obviously Trim, from his position as servant, could not have interrupted Toby quite so persistently. Ironically, however, the "loss" of the story of the King of Bohemia opens a space which reveals only another story, that of Trim's amours with the young Beguine, a narration which, in turn, reflects upon Toby's own amorous failures with the Widow Wadman. Thus Trim, though denied narrative mastery (as are all the characters in the novel), manages a sort of revenge.

As for Tristram himself:

> Now there is nothing in this world I abominate worse, than to be interrupted in a story——and I was that moment telling Eugenius a most tawdry one in my way, of a nun who fancied herself a shell-fish, and of a monk damn'd for eating a muscle, and was shewing him the grounds and justice of the procedure——(VII.i.576)

Significantly enough, since what stops Tristram is the sound of Death knocking at his door, interruption here quite explicitly represents the threat of interment. In his role as narrator, Tristram, of course, should be the master-interrupter; he is in the position of author-ity from which to attempt a usurpation of the role of the true master-interrupter, death itself. Further, the very success of this project seems to hinge not only on the interruption of others but, more important, on the incorporation of sexuality into discourse, a linguistic mastery of sex itself (cf. Tristram's tawdry story of the nun and monk, his desire to rewrite his primal scene, the whole effort of putting into narration his own begetting and birth). Such, indeed, is the highest goal of narration itself; to master language, to master sexuality, to possess and transmit one's own meaning, to evade interruption, to evade interment, to talk one's way out of death. But this effort, as Shoshana Felman makes clear—and as Sterne, I think, is well aware—is doomed from the beginning:

> The attempt to *master* meaning, which ought to lead to its *unification,* to the *elimination* of its contradictions and its "splits," can reach its goal only at the cost, through the infliction of a new wound, of an added split or distance, of an irreversible "separation." The seizure of the signifier creates an unrecoverable *loss,* a fundamental and irreparable *castration:* . . . Meaning's *possession* is itself ironically transformed in the radical *dispossession* of its possessor. At its final, climactic point, the attempt at *grasping* meaning and at *closing* the reading process with a definitive interpretation in effect discovers—and comprehends—only death. (174–75, emphases Felman's)

The discourse that Tristram most often interrupts is his own. We might call this a self-castrative gesture. On the other hand, Tristram's interruptions and digressions also reveal a desire to master the discourse of others (or perhaps the discourse of *the* Other). Consider, for example, Tristram's prolonged suspension of Uncle Toby's sentence in Volume I:

> I think, replied my uncle *Toby,* taking his pipe from his mouth, and striking the head of it two or three times upon the nail of his left thumb, as he began his sentence,——I think, says he:——But to enter rightly into my uncle *Toby's* sentiments upon this matter, you must be made to enter first a little into his character, the out-lines of which I shall just give you, and then the dialogue between him and my father will go on as well again. (I.xxi.70–71)

It is not until ten chapters later that Uncle Toby is permitted to finish his sentence. A more significant example of Tristram's will to mastery through interruption occurs in Volume V, just after the death of his brother Bobby, when Tristram leaves his mother suspended "in the dark along the passage which led to the parlour . . . In this attitude I am determined to let her stand for five minutes: till I bring up the affairs of the kitchen . . . to the same period" (V.v.426–27). Six chapters later, Tristram declares, "I am a *Turk* if I had not as much forgot my mother, as if Nature had plaistered me up, and set me down naked upon the banks of the river *Nile,* without one" (438).

Several gestures are at work here. First of all, the manipulation of narrative time is collapsed with the manipulation of the speech or silence, the presence or absence, of the characters themselves. The latter manipulation is, I think, rather clearly indentured to the *fort/da* game that Freud describes in *Beyond the Pleasure Principle* (*SE*, 18, 15), particularly since, in the second instance cited above, it is the body of his mother over which Tristram is exerting control. We recall, of course, that Freud interprets the child's game of throwing away a wooden spool and pulling it back by a piece of string as relating to a "staging" of the mother's disappearance and return, a staging which the child, by process of the game, brings under his own control. Freud attributes this game to "an instinct of mastery" and to a desire to move from a passive situation to a more active role. But we can read another movement here as well. I have already quoted Anthony Wilden to the effect that the human subject is in fact constituted as an object since before its birth. It is, of course, the mother who in the originary moment is the subject that constitutes the child as object, who "stages" the child's appearance (or, as in the child's own phantasmatic fears, disappearance: "can you lose me?"). In the *fort/da*, then, the movement is not only from passivity to activity but from objectivity to subjectivity, and in this reversal the mother's body assumes a status of object, hence a capacity to be represented by a wooden spool (and it should go without saying that for such active subjective mastery to be maintained, the mother's body must be constantly relegated to an objective status and represented as such). In the scene cited above, however, the narrative *fort/da* game that Tristram plays with his mother takes on a character of anal aggression: he suspends, or withholds, his mother's body in a dark passage— she becomes an object that he can either produce or retain however and whenever he sees fit. The spool, in other words, becomes stool.

We will presently have more to say about the relation between anality and the *fort/da*, between these tropes and castration, narrative, the representation of "woman," writing itself. For the moment, however, we return to Tristram's suspension of his mother's presence. It is, I think, far from coincidental that Tristram finally "remembers" his mother in terms of a metaphor that only thinly veils his desire to forget he even has a mother: "I am a *Turk* if I had not as much forgot my mother, as if Nature had plaistered me up, and set me down naked upon the banks of the river *Nile*, without one" (438). Implied is the interdependence of the will to mastery on the one hand, and on the other, the denial of maternal priority, a disavowal of the mother herself. Tristram's wishful thinking here is paradigmatic of what might be considered the main project of the Shandy males: the denigration and denial of women, of women's desires, and of women's role in the constitution of the masculine subject.

In her introduction to the Lacan volume *Feminine Sexuality*, Jacqueline Rose writes:

As the place onto which lack is projected, and through which it is simultaneously disavowed, woman is a "symptom" for the man. Defined as such, reduced to being nothing other than this fantasmatic place, the woman does not exist. Lacan's statement "the woman does not exist" [with the definite article *sous rature*] is, therefore, the corollary of his accusation, or charge, against sexual fantasy. It means not that women do not exist, but that her status as an absolute category and guarantor of fantasy (exactly *The* woman) is false (~~The~~). Lacan sees courtly love as the elevation of the woman into the place where her absence or inaccessibility stands in for the male lack . . . just as he sees her denigration as the precondition for man's belief in his own soul. . . . In relation to the man, woman comes to stand for both difference and loss. (48–49)

There are many examples in *Tristram* of how women stand for both difference and loss, of how they are differentiated and defamed. Uncle Toby's discourse on fortification is prompted by and organized around the groin wound he received at the battle of Namur, and it is to that discourse that he retreats when confronted with the reality of feminine desire as represented by the Widow Wadman. Toby, who represents more denial than denigration, does not know "so much as the right end of a woman from the wrong" (II.vii.117). Walter, on the other hand, presumably does know which end is up, but is also the novel's most vociferous misogynist. We have already seen some of his proprietorial attitudes at work. We can also see the disregard with which Walter holds his wife's health, if not her life, in his attitudes toward childbirth. Arguing in favor of the male-midwife, Dr. Slop, and against his wife's choice, the old female practitioner, Walter is loath to trust the life of his child to "the ignorance of an old woman;——and not only the life of my child, brother,—but her own life, and with it the lives of all the children I might, peradventure, have begot out of her hereafter" (II.vi.115). Despite an apparent concern for Mrs. Shandy's well-being, what this passage makes obvious is that her life is scarcely as important to Walter as her function as "venter" for his scions. Walter's callous disregard for Mrs. Shandy's health becomes more apparent when he voices his enthusiasm for the Caesarean section, for as Leigh A. Ehlers has noted, in the eighteenth century such an operation was "tantamount to matricide" (67; see also Cash, 141). Little wonder, then, that Mrs. Shandy's face turns pale at the suggestion.

Walter's misogyny is exacerbated by his anxiety over the lack of paternal presence reflected upon him by the misfortunes of Tristram's geniture, naming, and nose, an anxiety which leads him to fantasize Mrs. Shandy as "the place onto which lack is projected, and through which it is simultaneously disavowed" (Rose, 48). In this disavowal, the maternal role in the production of children is negated; the physical triad of the family romance is renounced while a wholly masculine "spiritual" dyad of father and son is privileged. In the transmission of power from father to son, in the assumption of narrative mastery, and in the production of "meaning," the mother, the woman, has no value as a presence or an agency: she exists only as a representational object, a token of exchange, an excluded absence, a phantasmatic place. We see, for example, Walter listening with "great desire" to Kysarcius's contention "*That the mother is not of kin to her child."* Consider also Walter's exchange with Yorick about the father-child relationship:

> ———I enter upon this speculation, said my father carelessly, and half shut-
> ting the book, as he went on,—merely to shew the foundation of the natural
> relation between a father and his child; the right and jurisdiction over whom
> he acquires these several ways—
> 1st, by marriage.
> 2d, by adoption.
> 3d, by legitimation.
> And 4th, by procreation; all which I consider in their order.
> I lay a slight stress upon one of them; replied *Yorick*———the act, especially
> where it ends there, in my opinion lays as little obligation upon the child, as it
> conveys power to the father.—You are wrong,—said my father argutely, and
> for this plain reason * * * * * * * * * * *
> * * * * * * * * * * * * * *
> * * * * * * * * * * * *.—I own,
> added my father, that the offspring, upon this account, is not so under the
> power and jurisdiction of the *mother*. . . . She is under authority herself . . . and
> besides . . . *she is not the principal agent,* Yorick. (V.xxxi.467–68)

Tristram himself, though less obviously misogynist than Walter, sometimes falls prey to the same sort of anti-maternal gestures and, in this sense at
least, proves to be his father's son. We have already seen his veiled wish to
have been born without a mother. Note also the strategy involved in the following passage:

> What could my father do? He was almost at his wit's end;———talked it over
> with her in all moods;—placed his arguments in all lights;—argued the mat-
> ter [of male vs. female midwife] with her like a christian,—like a heathen,—
> like a husband,—like a father,—like a patriot,—like a man:—My mother
> answered every thing only like a woman; which was a little hard upon her;—
> for as she could not assume and fight it out behind such a variety of charac-
> ters,—'twas no fair match;—'twas seven to one.—What could my mother do?
> (I.xvii.55)

Tristram's refusal to allow his mother the multiplicity of roles that he does
grant his father (or, we might say, that his father assumes through him) is a
strategy similar in effect to Walter's omission of the indefinite article before
the word "woman." Both designate the maternal body as an undifferentiated
space, reduce and elevate Mrs. Shandy to the status of an "absolute category."
She remains "exactly *The* woman" (Rose, 49).

And yet *Tristram Shandy* is not, I would argue, a misogynist text. Rather,
the text undermines its own misogynistic gestures by exposing the male characters' projections onto women as precisely that—projections that spring from
the male characters' own feelings of anxiety and lack. We can see how Walter's

various hypotheses gather themselves around losses which shake his already shaky sense of paternal presence—the loss of course, of "three-fourths" of Tristram, but more conspicuously the death of his son, Bobby, an event which exposes Walter's emotional shallowness while at the same time raising his discourse to its most hollow and pedantic (Walter tries to evade both mourning *and* melancholia). Further, Walter's attempts to deny maternal priority and establish the transcendent father-son dyad serve only to underscore his own unmastery, for if, as Yorick points out, "Mrs. *Shandy* the mother is nothing at all akin to [Tristram] . . . Mr. *Shandy,* in course, is still less than nothing" (IV.xxx.393). Similarly, Tristram's parenthetical comment holding "all misogynists to be bastards" (VI.xxx.551) explicitly designates the denigration of women as a function of male lack, rather than of anything "properly" feminine. The "absence" that "the woman" supposedly represents—that hollow bull's eye which stands as the target for the misogynist's hatred—is not really hers but rather, and exactly, the absence of the father. For what is "missing" for the bastard is that which makes him "legitimate"—i.e., the Name of the Father, which is, of course, another Lacanian trope for the phallus. The point could not be much clearer: misogyny is an effect of castration anxiety, and the disavowal of castration, the assumption of "mastery," thereby necessitates the disavowal of the feminine and the maternal, the mastery of language, sexuality, temporality, "woman," "meaning," and death.

Let us turn for a moment to the exemplary case of Dr. Slop, a minor character with major implications. Unlike Walter, who "philosophically" derides women, and Uncle Toby, who retreats from them into the fortification of his discourse on fortifications, Dr. Slop, as man-midwife, actively though ineffectively attempts to usurp women's conventional "place." As Leigh A. Ehlers points out:

> . . . man-midwifery has its classical locus in the myth of Zeus's preservation of Semele's unborn child within his thigh, from which it is later born. The result is the glorification of the father and the near exclusion of the mother. . . . [With the appearance of Dr. Slop] the pattern of male supremacy in Shandy Hall has reached its most absurd; Mrs. Shandy becomes the passive "Venter," the midwife is subordinated, and the men try to become father and womb, of course with disastrous results. Slop's "advanced" methods disrupt the natural birth process, destroy a nose, and by implication threaten the very procreativity of the Shandy family. (68)

In other words, the very effort to "secure" the transmission of meaning is what disrupts the transmission itself.

A few further points can be added about Slop. His name designates him as the contents of a chamberpot and aligns him with such other ludicrous and fecally-named authorities as Kysarcius ("Kiss-arse") and Hafen Slawkenbergius ("Chamberpot Slagheap"). The fact that Slop cuts his thumb while trying, significantly enough, to extract the forceps from his obstetric bag places him squarely under the sign of castration. More significant still is the description of Slop's first entrance into the parlour, after his fall into the mud-hole.

> *Obadiah* had led him in as he was, *unwiped, unappointed, unanealed,* with all his stains and blotches on him.——He stood like *Hamlet*'s ghost, motionless and speechless, for a full minute and a half, at the parlour door (*Obadiah* still holding his hand) with all the majesty of mud. His hinder parts, upon which he had received his fall, totally besmear'd. (II.x.123–24)

Far from being simply a throwaway comic tableau, Slop's appearance is one of the more significant scenes in the novel. Of course, it is a stock satiric device to deflate an ambitious character by causing him to fall into a mudhole, and Slop's having suffered such a fate indicates Sterne's attitude towards the doctor's intervention into the birth process. More important, however, given that very intervention, is the fact that Slop is being satirized under a rubric of infantilism. He is described as "speechless," and, of course, to be an infant means literally to be incapable of speech. Moreover, the conspicuously fecal terms used to describe Slop's fallen state (his hinder parts besmeared, unwiped) reduce him to the condition of a soiled and helpless child, with the servant Obadiah still holding his hand. Thus Slop is placed not only under the sign of castration, but, since the role of diaper-changer was then and is still predominantly female, also under the traditional emblem of maternal authority: he is reduced to the least powerful term of the process over which he, as man-midwife, is supposed to exercise "mastery." And this placement of Slop under the conventional sign of the mother is all the more significant in that it is he, again as man-midwife, who is supposed to stand as guarantor of Walter's anti-maternal fantasy of paternal autonomy and power. The doctor's unwiped hinder parts undermine Walter's fantasy and expose it as exactly that.

But we are not yet through with (out of the) Slop. The doctor is described as being not only speechless but "motionless." He becomes, for a long moment, a full minute and a half, an inert object. Thus he is not only the infant smeared with his own feces but, as his name suggests, the actual product, contents of a chamberpot, the feces itself. By the same token, we can say that Dr. Slop is not only castrated but is himself the product or effect of a castration, his own lost object, the dead severed phallus. I have already pointed out the fantasmatic association of time, sex, woman, and death. Here I will venture that this association is at least partially underwritten by another equally fantasmatic equation. Freud writes:

> . . . the handing over of the faeces for the sake of (out of love for) someone else becomes a prototype of castration; it is the first occasion upon which an indi-

vidual parts with a piece of his own body in order to gain favor of some other person he loves. So that a person's love of his own penis, which is in other respects narcissistic, is not without an element of anal eroticism. "Faeces," "baby," and "penis" thus form a unity . . . the concept . . . of "a little one" that can be separated from one's body. (*SE,* VII, 84)

Of course, the "baby" is incorporated into this unity by virtue of Freud's cloaca theory, his contention that "children are at one in thinking that babies must be born through the bowels; [that] they make their appearance like lumps of faeces" (*SE,* XVI, 319). As we have seen, Freud suggests that infants experience defecation as a giving over of a valued object, the feces as a "gift" of a part of the body (a part-object, in Klein's terms). But since this gift is rarely valued by the parent, the infant constitutes defecation as loss. In the genital stage, the male child associates that loss with the fear of castration, imagines his penis and feces might share the same fate, and so, given the childbirth-evacuation confusion already present, may come to fantasize his birth, the production of his own body, as the result or effect of a defecation/castration, the phallic mother's loss of her valued part-object. Further, since the infant imagines the production of his body as loss, and experiences defecation, his only mode of production prior to speech as loss as well, he may come to view *production itself* as loss, and anything he might produce in the future—semen, images, speech, writing—as a potential loss, as castration.

Castration, then, in its broadest sense, *is* that gap between speaker and speech, a gap that is underwritten by and indentured to the body and its productions. Speech, that guarantor of the fiction of self-presence, is always already a castration, for whatever metaphysical origins we imagine for the logos, actual speech is produced through an opening in the body, and that "loss" is only further ratified when the supposedly transcendental logos is committed to the corporeal scriptos, when the living word becomes the dead letter. This, of course, is a Derridean point, but one of which Lacan is quite well aware, for, to quote the epigraph that begins this discussion, "Just ask the writer about the anxiety that he experiences when faced by the blank sheet of paper, and he will tell you who *is* the turd of his phantasy."

Sterne, it would seem, is also aware of this collapse of phallogocentrism with scatology (or, given the stress that Lacan puts on the copula, *scatontology*), and of the implications of that collapse for writing, narration, the transmission of meaning, the representation of woman, authority itself. Consider, for example, Tristram's remarks on the author/authority Licetus:

. . . all the world knows he was born a foetus, of no more than five inches and a half in length, yet he grew to that astonishing height in literature, as to write a book with a title as long as himself——the learned know I mean his *Gonopsychanthropologia,* upon the origin of the human soul. (IV.x.337–38)

This curious concatenation of the size of a book's title and that of its author as a foetus is quite suggestive in the light of that "unity" of foetus, phallus, and feces. Here the text-as-object becomes the text-as-foetus, and thus the project of the author, of literary production itself, is placed under the sign of the mother, or rather, under the sign of the mother's denigration, for Licetus, in a re-appropriation of maternal priority, attempts to recreate or represent himself in (or as) a text: conspicuously enough, a text concerning "the origin of the soul" (we have already noted Lacan's contention that the denigration of woman is "the precondition for man's belief in his own soul"). On the other hand, this identification of the text-as-foetus opens up the association of the text as both phallus and as feces, and discloses the anxious writer as the turd of his own castrative fantasies. Upon being informed by Yorick that "the great *Lipsius* . . . composed a work the day he was born," Uncle Toby responds "They should have wiped it up . . . and said no more about it." (VI.ii.494)

These comic identifications disclose a serious interrogation of the gestures by which narrative desire struggles against the power of time, the claims of narrative "meaning" to stabilize identity, recuperate the masculine self in the face of absence, loss, death, and feminine desire. Insofar as language becomes an "object" external to its producer, language will always in its very process ratify whatever loss it attempts to deny. Writing, plotting, narration, the effort to unify, to fix meaning, are all caught up in sexual division and meaning's flight, impotence, unmastery, unavoidable castration. Sterne understands this paradox within literary production, and his text, more than simply a parody of a novel, is in fact an interrogation of Western culture's deepest convictions about literature and literary meaning itself. Holtz maintains that Tristram will be immortal "for as long as men [*sic*] read books" (138). But Tristram himself will have none of it. For him literary fame is still only "a swim down the gutter of time." He knows that his digressions, which embody his "flight from death," also embody that from which he flees, and says, "my Opinions [in other words, my *text*] will be the death of me." Tristram knows that he is interred in his own interruptions, buried in his own plot. Such is his consent to incompleteness. *Tristram Shandy* is the sanest novel in world literature.

Works Cited

Brooks, Peter. *Reading for the Plot: Design and Intention in Narrative.* New York: Vintage, 1985.

Cash, Arthur H. "The Birth of Tristram Shandy: Sterne and Dr. Burton." *Studies in the Eighteenth Century.* Canberra: Australian National UP, 1968. 133–54.

Davis, Robert Con, ed. *The Fictional Father: Lacanian Readings in the Text.* Amherst: U Massachusetts P, 1981.

Ehlers, Leigh A. "Mrs. Shandy's 'Lint and Basilicon': The Importance of Women in *Tristram Shandy.*" *South Atlantic Review* 46 (January, 1981): 61–75.

Felman, Shoshana. "Turning the Screw of Interpretation." *Literature and Psychoanalysis: The Question of Reading: Otherwise.* Ed. Shoshana Felman. Baltimore: Johns Hopkins UP, 1982. 94–207.

Freud, Sigmund. *The Standard Edition of the Complete Psychological Works.* Trans. James Strachey. 24 Vols. London: Hogarth, 1953–1974.

Holtz, William V. *Image and Immortality: A Study of Tristram Shandy.* Providence: Brown UP, 1970.

Jameson, Fredric. *The Prison-House of Language.* Princeton: Princeton UP, 1972.

Lacan, Jacques. "Desire and the Interpretation of Desire in *Hamlet.*" *Literature and Psychoanalysis: The Question of Reading: Otherwise,* ed. Shoshana Felman. Baltimore: Johns Hopkins UP, 1992. 11–52.

———. *Écrits: A Selection.* Trans. Alan Sheridan. New York: Norton, 1977.

Lukács, Georg. *The Theory of the Novel.* Trans. Anna Bostock. Cambridge: MIT Press, 1971.

Macksey, Richard. " 'Alas Poor Yorick': Sterne Thoughts." *Modern Language Notes* 48 (December, 1983): 1006–1020.

Rose, Jacqueline. Introduction II. *Feminine Sexuality: Jacques Lacan and the Ecole Freudienne.* Trans. Juliet Mitchell and Jacqueline Rose. New York: Norton, 1982.

Shklovsky, Victor. "Sterne's *Tristram Shandy:* Stylistic Commentary." *Russian Formalist Criticism: Four Essays.* Trans. Lee T. Lemon and Marion J. Reis. Lincoln: U Nebraska P, 1965. 25–60.

Swearingen, James E. *Reflexivity in Tristram Shandy: An Essay in Phenomenological Criticism.* New Haven: Yale UP, 1977.

Wilden, Anthony. "Lacan and the Discourse of the Other." *Speech and Language in Psychoanalysis.* Baltimore: Johns Hopkins UP, 1968. 159–309.

Can't Live Without 'Em:
Walter Shandy and the Woman Within

PAULA LOSCOCCO

In his sourcebook for English literature of the late Middle Ages, Robert Miller summarizes the medieval tradition of the Fall of Adam through Eve. He notes how references to "male" and "female" within this tradition operate as metaphors for the reason and flesh of each individual, male or female; the ideal for either sex is to regain the prelapsarian state of "virginity," the control of "female" flesh by "male" reason.[1] Clearly, though, the potential exists for taking these terms literally—and misogynistically—by attributing reason to men and flesh, or lust, to women. Miller refers to this literal reading of gender in the Fall story as "the antifeminist tradition" (397), and provides ample evidence of its persistence in discussions about the sexes during the Middle Ages.

Laurence Sterne's Walter Shandy describes the two sexes in ways which mark him unmistakably as a late but defiantly antifeminist reader of the Genesis story. He continually bemoans the fact "[t]hat provision . . . for continuing the race of so great, so exalted and godlike a Being as man" should be in the hands—and bodies—of women (IX.xxxiii.806). For Walter believes "not only, 'That the devil was in women, and that the whole of the affair was lust;' but that every evil and disorder in the world of what kind or nature soever, from the first fall of Adam, down to my uncle Toby's (inclusive) was owing one way or other to the same unruly appetite" (IX.xxxii.805). Walter perceives the obstacle to male self-sufficiency as deriving from a literal and ongoing Fall in which "lustful" women subvert and emasculate pure "godlike" men.

Recent feminist criticism has paid considerable attention to characterizations of gender in *Tristram Shandy*. Such criticism has attempted to determine the kinds of relationship which exist between the portrayal of the two sexes by Walter and other male characters, and the evaluation of gender constituted by and constituting the novel as a whole. Leigh Ehlers represents the view that sees Sterne, or the novel, as a corrective to the misogynistic limitations of Walter and all the Shandy men, including Tristram. "Sterne's novel is

Reprinted from *The Eighteenth Century: Theory and Interpretation* 32 (1991): 166–79.

indeed very much of a 'woman's book,' in which women are invested with considerable, though untapped, restorative powers," she writes: "Sterne's attitude towards women diverges from Tristram's hasty condemnation of them. A similar case may be made for Mrs. Shandy's role as a satiric norm for revealing the shortcomings of Walter, Toby, and particularly Tristram."[2]

Ruth Perry convincingly refutes Ehlers's claims, arguing the illegitimacy of separating Sterne from the misogyny expressed in his book. "*Tristram Shandy* . . . [is] a man's book if ever there was one," she declares,[3] and her evidence for this claim is the virtual absence of women in the novel:

> Despite the valiant attempts of Ruth Faurot and Leigh Ehlers to demonstrate Mrs. Shandy as a vivid presence and beneficent antidote to the obsessive Shandy men, she and the other women barely exist in the narrative except in their concern for the phallus. As Tristram himself avers, "all the SHANDY FAMILY were of an original character throughout;—I mean the males,—the females had no character at all." (34)

Perry argues that the male "marriage between Toby and Trim is the emotional center of the book" (37); she also notes that it would be difficult to read the Shandy males' frustrations as "symptomatic of the cosmic irony of human life," since "the overtones are comic rather than tragic, and women are the butts of the joke" (32).

To argue, however, as both Ehlers and Perry do, that *Tristram Shandy* takes a stand about women, pro or con, is to do precisely what Walter Shandy does: namely, to take the terms of the lapsarian metaphor literally, to read "woman" (vs. human flesh or lust) when Sterne writes "female," and "man" (vs. human reason) when he writes "male." In other words, the readings of Ehlers and Perry are equally "antifeminist," in Miller's sense of being literal and therefore gender-specific. I am not denying that *Tristram Shandy* compels this kind of literal, sex-differentiating reading. But I am asserting that failure to examine this compulsion has caused critical discussion to remain unselfconsciously within the novel's antifeminist paradigm of a woman-provoked Fall of man, trying to decide whom to blame for the misogynistic portrayal of women,[4] instead of understanding why the novel hampers us as it does from any continuous grasp of that paradigm as a gender-neutral metaphor or allegory.[5] What is the point, in other words, of making us no more able than a misogynist like Walter Shandy to read the metaphors of the Fall story figuratively?

I answer this question by exploring the connection that *Tristram Shandy* establishes between characterizations of gender on the one hand, and habits of reading and interpretation on the other. I focus primarily on Walter Shandy, a misogynist whom the novel clearly presents as being prone to specific interpretive habits, a man who "reads" the two sexes literally and who is only fleetingly aware of the metaphoric possibilities of the words "male" and "female." The clarity with which *Tristram Shandy* depicts Walter's ways of interpreting gender is balanced, however, by its care never explicitly to censure him. We as readers, on the other hand, come in for critical attack all through the novel, a fact which suggests that our ways of reading differ from Walter's. Yet this apparent distinction conceals a real similarity: the portrait of Walter as a literal reader strikingly resembles the ways in which Tristram portrays us as readers all through the novel.[6] Again and again Tristram reprimands us for making the error of interpreting his book literally and bawdily, for paying more attention to the literal and sexual than to the metaphoric and platonic possibilities of his text. Of course, even as it exhorts us to avoid nonmetaphoric interpretation, *Tristram Shandy* prevents us from doing otherwise. We are systematically compelled to make literal interpretative choices, and so to develop characteristically "Shandean"—i.e., sex-specific and therefore misogynistic—readings of gender. But the fact remains that our habits of reading are characterized by Tristram as wrong-headed. I suggest, consequently, that to the extent that our maligned interpretive habits resemble Walter's, the novel implicitly defines his antifeminist ways as erroneous.

I suggest as well that the literalness and sexual specificity of Walter's habits of perception are matched only by the vociferousness of his denial of connection to all things literal and sexual. He betrays the presence in himself of that which he most denies. And it is in precisely this way that Tristram most closely resembles his father. While he denies responsibility for literally gendered or sexual meaning (blaming others—us—for that instead), Tristram at the same time constructs his narrative on the basis of a distribution of "male" reason and "female" flesh to men and women respectively. Tristram, in short, reads (and writes) gender literally—just as he says we do. And to the extent that his narrative habits resemble those of the reader which he most condemns, he implicitly defines his own antifeminism as mistaken.

The book, then, is what Perry claims it to be—a "man's book": it blames or dismisses women, cherishes and prioritizes men, and compels the reader to do the same. But, contrary to Perry, I argue that the novel presents itself not only as a man's book, but as both a man's book and a mistaken or failed book. *Tristram Shandy* notoriously refers to itself as a failure, an incompletion. It repeatedly describes itself, its characters, and its readers as impotent or unable: literally and bawdily unable to "integrate" the two sexes, but also, as a consequence of this obsession with sexuality, finally and seriously unable to develop a metaphoric sense of the individual self as both "male" and "female." *Tristram Shandy* thus presents itself as unable to regain what Miller calls the ideal prelapsarian state of metaphorical "virginity." In the final analysis, the book portrays its own pervasive antifeminist literalism as "fallen," a consequence of the Fall.

In a sense, then, this essay does what cannot be done within the parameters of the novel itself, by character, author, or reader: it articulates an "unfallen" sense of the sexes and of sexuality as gender-neutral metaphors. Only from this perspective, a perspective that *Tristram Shandy* demands that we recognize and recognize our distance from, can we see how Sterne, Tristram, Walter, and the reader all "fall" to literal definitions of gender. This perspective may not redeem the novel's misogyny: misogyny, springing as it does in the novel from antifeminist roots, is represented as universal, inevitable, and a source of considerable if rueful pleasure and amusement. But this perspective does provide the context that *Tristram Shandy* requires for considering and evaluating its own rampant antifeminism.

Walter Shandy's antifeminist tendencies are perhaps nowhere so dramatically clear as in the procreation scene which opens *Tristram Shandy*. There Walter tries hard to believe in the possibility of pure masculine rationality by screening out the distractingly carnal presence of his wife, Elizabeth. Perhaps the most striking aspect of Walter's notions about procreation, as they are reported in I.i–ii by Tristram and developed throughout the novel by Walter, is their perfect maleness. His "animal spirits" are "transfused from father to son"; the child is never presumed to be other than a boy; the mother does not once feature in his thoughts; and when Elizabeth does make her presence known, it is considered to be a terrible "*interrupt*[ion]" (2) and "accident" (3).[7] Paradoxically, Walter so excludes women from his thinking here that, though he is in fact fully engaged sexually, he is at the same time advocating continence, even celibacy—as if he were a medieval ascetic and not a man actively involved in "family concernments" (I.iv.6). This same mixed message recurs in his letter to Toby in VIII.xxxiv. There, in counsel ostensibly geared towards the conduct of a successful courtship of the Widow Wadman, Walter firmly steers his brother away from sexual interaction with her. Take "cucumbers, melons, purslane, water-lillies, woodbine, and lettice" (728), he tells Toby, prescribing a Burtonian diet conducive to chastity. Walter's stance here and in I.i may well be of practical use to a man overcome with and seeking to restrain his passion. But his conspicuous silence in both cases about women, presumably the end of the processes described, suggests a curious commitment to male celibacy under the least likely of circumstances.

Walter's ideas about proper procreation, however, feature an even more telling prescription: it should be done in silence. Again, in an anecdote about what happened "*nine months before ever {Tristram} came into the world*" (I.iii.4), a man's desire for silence in order to maintain control of himself may seem reasonable enough, especially when an interruption of that silence by his partner provokes a "scatter[ing]" and "dispers[ion]" of liquid "spirits" (2). But Walter elsewhere claims a different and peculiarly linguistic reason for his preference for silence under these particular circumstances. Walter wants quiet, he explains, because he distrusts words' carnality: no words, he believes, are "clean" enough to convey the idea of human genesis—or any other idea, for that matter—without calling up the sexual act. "For what reason is it," he asks, "that all the parts thereof . . . are so held as to be conveyed to a cleanly mind by no language, translation, or periphrasis whatever?" (IX.xxxiii.806).

Walter's distrust of language's carnality falls squarely within the Augustinian hermeneutic tradition; a brief elaboration of that tradition clarifies the link between Walter's attitudes about gender and his linguistic habits. In Section III.5 of his Biblical commentary, *On Christian Doctrine,* Augustine stresses the need to guard against literal uses of language:

> You must be very careful lest you take figurative expressions literally. What the Apostle says pertains to this problem: "For the letter killeth, but the spirit quickeneth." That is, when that which is said figuratively is taken as though it were literal, it is understood carnally. Nor can anything more appropriately be called the death of the soul than that condition in which the thing which distinguishes us from beasts, which is the understanding, is subjected to the flesh in the pursuit of the letter. He who follows the letter takes figurative expressions as though they were literal and does not refer the things signified to anything else. . . . There is a miserable servitude of the spirit in this habit of taking signs for things, so that one is not able to raise the eye of the mind above things that are corporal and created to drink in eternal light.[8]

In the interests of figurative reading, Augustine defines literal reading (the "letter") as carnal, fleshly, a mere thing or body, and figurative reading (the "spirit") as of the soul or understanding, a sign pointing beyond itself to the "light." In a tradition in which men tend to be equated with understanding and women with carnality, however, Augustine's terms at the very least fail to hinder an explicitly antifeminist hermeneutics that equates men with the ideas or "sense" referred to by language, and women with actual language itself. For just as Walter seeks to block out the unsettling presence of women, so he betrays a profound uneasiness towards what he sees as their linguistic counterparts—words. III.xxxvii offers the exception that proves the rule when Walter actually does arrive at "clean" language, though he does so only by excising the offending "word" to get the "sense" pure. "My father," Tristram writes,

> read [Erasmus' dialogue] over and over again with great application, studying every word and every syllable of it thro' and thro' in its most strict and literal interpretation,—he could still make nothing of it, that way. Mayhaps there is more meant, than is said in it, quoth my father. . . .——I'll study the mystic and the allegoric sense,——here is some room to turn a man's self in, brother. . . .
> [H]e had got out his penknife, and was trying experiments upon the sentence, to see if he could not scratch some better sense into it.—I've got within a single letter, brother *Toby,* cried my father, of *Erasmus* his mystic meaning. . . . I've done it,——said my father, snapping his fingers.—See, my dear brother

Toby, how I have mended the sense.—But you have marr'd a word, replied my uncle *Toby.* (III.xxxvii.271–72)

Only the removal of the actual word, Augustine's carnal "letter," can satisfy Walter's hunger for the "mystic and the allegoric sense" that is appropriate to a "man's self."

Tristram, very much his father's son,[9] echoes Walter's conceptions about language to a significant degree, and nowhere more clearly than in those passages where he instructs us as readers how to interpret his book. In I.xx he condemns literal reading as both bawdy and female, and applauds "reflective" reading as both pure and male. He then rebukes the "vicious taste" of his pointedly female reader "of reading straight forwards, more in quest of the adventures, than of the deep erudition and knowledge which a book of this cast, if read over as it should be, would infallibly impart with them.——The mind should be accustomed to make wise reflections, and draw curious conclusions as it goes along." This "vile pruriency for fresh adventures," he goes on, has made us

> so wholly intent . . . upon satisfying the impatience of our *concupiscence* that way,—that nothing but the gross and more *carnal* parts of a composition will go down:—The subtle hints and sly communications of science fly off, like *spirits,* upwards. . . .
>
> I wish the *male-reader* has not pass'd by many a one, as quaint and curious as this one, in which the *female-reader* has been detected [italics added]. (65–66)

But Tristram then goes on to subvert his own admonitions here. He sends "Madam" reader back to I.xix to find the "subtle hint" that Elizabeth was not a papist; the reader comes back to be chidden, unable to pick up a clue so obscure as to defy "reflective" reading: "Then, Madam, be pleased to ponder well the last line but one of the chapter, where I take upon me to say, 'It was *necessary* I should be born before I was christen'd.' Had my mother, Madam, been a Papist, that consequence did not follow*" (Sterne's asterisk). The literalness of the footnote immediately following, on christening a child in utero by injection ("Anglicé, *a squirt*"), then compels the literal or "concupiscent" reading that Tristram has just professed to abhor. To the extent, then, that we must read "pruriently," we find ourselves prevented from and therefore incapable of "reflective" thinking. This fact in turn identifies us within the antifeminist interpretive tradition as literal-minded and carnal women, "Madam readers." Not coincidentally, this characterization of the reader as female is precisely what allows Tristram to assert his own freedom from any taint of femininity.

Another feature of Walter's ideal of procreation is refraining from action. Elizabeth's question in I.i, as noted earlier, interrupts the process and causes Walter to "scatter . . . and disperse . . . the animal spirits." But if Walter perceives "scattering" as an "accident," then arguably his idea of safe conduct involves maintained concentration, continued retention. He seems to have in mind an ideal of suspension, of remaining in transit, of hesitating on the brink of action in a moment of pure and perfect conceptualization. Walter's letter to Toby corroborates his commitment to this ideal. "A just medium prevents all conclusions," Walter writes: "Leave . . . as many . . . things as thou canst, quite undetermined" (VIII.xxxiv.726–27). Suspension, indeterminacy, potential: Walter savors the moment of undiluted and implicitly masculine thought, devoting all his energies to forestalling "conclusive" action.

Once again, Tristram can be found to echo Walter even as he exposes him, corroborating and making explicit the implications of Walter's antifeminist linguistics. For as Patricia Spacks notes, indeterminacy is a central feature of Tristram's narrative style: "Uncle Toby remarks that Mrs. Shandy may not choose to let a man come so near her * * * *. All conceivable ways of completing the sentence will evoke distinct response; incomplete, it remains provocative, potential—the state of being for which Tristram himself always yearns" (144). An example particularly pertinent to this discussion occurs prior to the naming in IV.ix–xiii, when Tristram genially allows Walter to savor the sweetness that a moment so richly male and abstract has for him by a mock profession of his own powerlessness to keep his story moving: "Holla!—you chairman!—here's sixpence—do step into that bookseller's shop, and call me a *day-tall* critick. I am very willing to give any one of 'em a crown to help me with his tackling, to get my father and my uncle *Toby* off the stairs, and to put them to bed" (IV.xiii.340–41). Walter's "conception" of Trismegistus reaches its fulsome peak during this slowing down or suspension of time that Tristram so generously provides. We can point to a parallel between Walter's desire in I.i indefinitely to prolong his son's "conception" and Tristram's narrative strategy here, detecting the bawdiness of the former in the apparent "cleanliness" of the latter. Once again, though, perceiving a "carnal" level of meaning in the passage would immediately identify us as concupiscent "female-readers," leaving Tristram as free to protest his masculine purity as Walter does in I.i. Walter and Tristram betray a marked family resemblance in their heated denials of any connection to things "female."

Yet clearly, by thinking of procreation as a masculine and cerebral concern, Walter is trying desperately to deny the reality of his situation. He not only engages in sexual activity while disciplining his thoughts to remain utterly asexual—a practical temporary measure, perhaps—but also engages in sexual activity while trying to believe that he is not actually doing so. A "transfusion" occurs which is denied to have anything whatsoever to do with sex. And the homunculus takes a "journey" from which things physical, sexual, and female are conspicuously absent: the "little gentleman" will eventually settle in the "place destined for his reception" (I.ii.2–3). Throughout the novel, Walter attempts to claim that his conduct in connection to Tristram's genesis is purely rational: "Brother *Shandy,* answer'd my uncle *Toby* . . . you do increase my pleasure very much, in begetting children for the *Shandy* Family at your time of life.——But, by that, Sir, quoth Dr. *Slop,* Mr. *Shandy* increases his own.——Not a jot, quoth my father. . . . My brother does it, quoth my uncle *Toby,* out of *principle*" (II.xii–xiii.133–34). Walter's denials permit him perfectly to dissociate his "reason" and "flesh." He then claims the former as male and therefore his own, while both denying the latter in himself and projecting it onto Elizabeth as something female and carnal: "the devil was in women, and . . . the whole of the affair was lust" (IX.xxxii.805).[10]

But the question now arises: if Walter could have his way and exclude women and sex, words and action from his ideal of child-begetting, how would he propose to generate a child? It is hard to tell, since the "accident" of Elizabeth's presence in I.i cuts his plans short. But there are hints scattered throughout the novel as to how Walter would proceed if he could, and it is these hints that I wish to pursue, since they lead to the central contradiction in Walter's habits of reading gender.

Tristram Shandy offers several suggestions that Walter sees himself as some sort of Old Testament divinity: *Tristram Shandy* begins, notoriously, *in the beginning* both of the book and of the character; Walter's asexual theories of procreation suggest a myth of a single male parent; Walter explicitly refers to "the creation of the world." Given this context, we might hypothesize that what Walter would like to effect is a single Genesis-style fiat: a fully conceived idea in the mind of the man-god, a verbal progenerative act, a creation of a son in his own image.[11] It perhaps bears remarking that Walter favors the Spanish proverb " '*That talking of love, is making it*' " (IX.xxv.787). Walter, then, may wish that his "word" could be made into purified flesh through the power of his immaculate "conception." Walter's general theory about names, and his particular attempt to name his child "Trismegistus" in IV.xiv, bear out this hypothesis in interesting and pertinent ways.[12]

Like his theory of procreation, Walter's theory of names is patently antifeminist. It is, to begin with, exclusively male in its orientation. Walter, in his various speculations on names (I.xix; IV.viii, xi), never consults Elizabeth or considers any name but that of a boy. As with procreation, moreover, Walter treasures his idea, the "sense," of the name. Prior to the pronouncement of the name itself after the child's birth, Walter plays with his idea of Trismegistus either in his head or in the safely male world of uncommitted speculative discussion. There Trismegistus is for Walter unfallen man, man as he was originally meant to be: "This *Trismegistus* . . . was the greatest . . . of all earthly beings—he was the greatest king—the greatest lawgiver—the greatest philosopher—and the greatest priest" (IV.xi.339). In the moment between thought and definitive verbal action, a moment suspended in time, what might be seems like what could—and should—be.

The crucial point about the naming in Volume IV, however, is that here, as in Volume I's procreating, Walter betrays a wish that the mere pronouncing of the name will realize his entire conception of Trismegistus and make it fact. Earlier on, Walter insisted on "a strange kind of magick bias, which good or bad names . . . irresistibly impress'd upon our characters and conduct" (I.xix.57–58). This theory about names suggests an ideal in which the *name-word* fully embodies a "good or bad" *idea,* which "irresistibly" becomes who a *person* is. Not only does Walter understand the signifier "Trismegistus" fully to embody the signified idea of Trismegistus, but he also seems to wish that a person—actual flesh—can "embody" the unified signifier/signified. In terms of the Augustinian hermeneutic tradition, Walter apparently imagines a conflation of the "letter" and "spirit" such that the literal and figurative sense of the word coincide at the level of the figurative. The "letter" in effect becomes perfectly "spiritualized."

Yet in this thinking about the potency of his own speech-act, Walter violates what he himself has defined as his own (purely rational and purely masculine) nature. For in crediting the antifeminist equation of masculinity and reason, and so assuming the possibility of an abstraction embodied (a "male" man), he transgresses against his own tradition's cardinal hermeneutic premise: "He who follows the letter takes figurative expressions as though they were literal and does not refer the things signified to anything else." In granting the word, "Trismegistus," the power fully to embody his idea, Walter eliminates the word's ability to function as a signifier: if the word contains what it means then it can only signify itself, and the word, then, is a thing, an object. "There is," Augustine notes, "a miserable servitude of the spirit in this habit of taking signs for things." And as an unadulterated object, the word is necessarily utterly carnal.[13] The movement of "Trismegistus" in IV.xiv shows this to be true with a vengeance.

As far as Susannah knows, "Trismegistus" is a word, a verbal object, a thing. She therefore quite reasonably treats the name only in terms of its physical characteristics. When the curate suggests that the name is *"Tristram,"* she counters with *"Tristram-gistus,"* matter-of-factly sensing that "Tristram" is inadequate (344); she recognizes a decline from the fullness of the name's original dimensions. Needless to say, the "concupiscent" possibilities of such a carnal handling of the word are endless. Walter's ideal child, Trismegistus, has translated into reality as some *thing* rather inadequate, plus some empty space. And that space, given the receiving presences of Susannah here and Elizabeth in I.i, is clearly female—and "carnal"—space. The same principle lies behind the blank page in VI.xxxviii, by far the most obscene page in the book. For the page reserved for the "concupiscible" Widow Wadman, "which MALICE will not blacken, and which IGNORANCE cannot misrepresent," is literally a hole in the text.[14]

By defining the human ideal as both "male" in the sense of being rational or abstract, and "male" in the sense of being a specific gender, a male, Walter reads himself literally, carnally, "like a woman." In so doing, and to the extent that he desires to embody anything, he betrays the presence of the "female" *in* himself. He experiences gender, in other words, not as an actual distinction of sex but as a metaphor for conflicting aspects of his own being—despite his protestations and denials to the contrary. Walter himself is the carnal, female obstacle in the path of his own masculinely idealist dreams. His own being—as opposed to his scapegoat of choice, woman's body—is what dooms his antifeminist ambitions to frustration.

Walter, naturally, strenuously resists this kind of metaphoric gender-neutral understanding of the terms "male" and "female." In IV.xiv, as in I.i, he blames the flawed ("leaky") female body, here Susannah, for his impotence: "But stay—thou art a leaky vessel *Susannah,* added my father; canst thou carry *Trismegistus* in thy head, the length of the gallery without scattering—Can I? cried *Susannah,* shutting the door in a huff—If she can, I'll be shot, said my father, bouncing out of bed in the dark, and groping for his breeches" (344). And, as in I.i, it is clearly the consequences of his own conflicting premises that doom Walter's ideas to their imperfect and fleshly conclusions. But even Walter, though only at rare moments and then much to his chagrin, does find himself compelled to acknowledge his own carnal predilections. When Elizabeth wishes "to look through the key-hole out of *curiosity*" (VIII.xxxv.729), Walter, complacent in his assumptions about her female carnality and his own male spirituality, rather smugly reproaches her for harboring a "different impulse":

> Call it by it's right name, my dear, quoth my father—
> *And look through the key-hole* as long as you will.

But "he had scarce got to the last word of this ungracious retort, when his conscience smote him": "[A]s he turned his head, he met her eye————Confusion again! he saw a thousand reasons to wipe out the reproach, *and as many to reproach himself*————a thin, blue, chill, pellucid chrystal with all its humours so at rest, the least mote or speck of desire might have been seen at the bottom of it, had it existed————it did not" (IX.i.735–36; italics added). Walter's momentarily lucid perception that the locus of "desire" lies entirely within himself is indeed "confusion," at least as far as his antifeminist characterizations of gender are concerned. For to "reproach himself" for concupiscence is dimly to understand "female" not as a literal "other," a reassuringly separate gender, but as a metaphor for something within and of himself.

The closest Walter could ever have come to his antifeminist sense of the human ideal, incidentally, would have been to do what he finds so impossible: never to "speak," verbally or sexually. To the degree that he finds himself again and again so speaking, Walter himself at times recognizes his distance from this ascetic ideal. "My dear brother Toby," he writes:

> What I am going to say to thee, is upon the nature of women, and of love-making to them. . . .

> Had it been the good pleasure of him who disposes of our lots—and thou no sufferer by the knowledge, I had been well content that thou should'st have dipp'd the pen this moment into the ink, instead of myself; but that not being the case————Mrs. Shandy being now close besides me, preparing for bed. (VIII.xxxiv.725)

Walter signals a reluctant involvement in the world of Augustine's "letter" by this candid admission of his knowledge of verbal and sexual "pen-dipping." He envies but cannot imitate the largely silent and perpetually celibate Toby.

Yet if Walter resists the presence of the "female" in men and tries to project it onto women, Toby in his retreat to perfect masculinity effectively denies its existence altogether, in either sex. This denial fuels his many difficulties with the Widow Wadman, since he has left himself no means for suspecting or detecting "female" desire in himself or in others. Nothing, as a result, comes of the affair: courtship based exclusively on one gender—in effect, no gender—can involve no engendering.

Toby's may not be the only kind of sterility that *Tristram Shandy* asks us to consider. A fully metaphoric or, in Miller's terms, prelapsarian understanding of gender would, arguably, be equally barren (in the sense of incapable of physical reproduction): an individual in possession of both "male" and "female" aspects would be androgynous, self-contained, self-sufficient. But the possibility of self-sufficiency and closure is just what *Tristram Shandy* categorically denies itself, its characters, its narrator, and its readers. The "female" in Walter craves an actual body—if not his own then at least that of a son. But because he has denied the body for himself and projected it instead onto Elizabeth, Walter finds himself quite unable to "embody" his own desires. He is consequently impelled against his will towards a woman to get what he insists that he does not have and she does: a body, a child, a son. The ensuing literal fusion of two sexes—the literal, antifeminist parody of the prelapsarian metaphoric fusion of gender within the individual—is, of course, literally generative: "True *Shandeism*, think what you will against it, opens the heart and lungs, and like all those affections which partake of its nature, it forces the blood and other vital fluids of the body to run freely thro' its channels, and makes the wheel of life run long and chearfully round" (IV.xxxii.401). Had the "other vital fluids" of Walter's body not "run freely" in I.i–ii, had they not poured out into the "leaky vessel," Susannah, in IV.xiv, Tristram would have been neither created nor named. *Tristram Shandy,* in other words, locates (reproductive) life in the antifeminist misapprehension of gender. Whatever existed beforehand, life as we know it, according to *Tristram Shandy,* began with the Fall. Misreading gender, we engendered; fallen, we replaced our lost individual self-sufficiency with sufficiency of the race.

This equation of "life" with the antifeminist misreading of gender has provoked much of the feminist critical debate about *Tristram Shandy*. While the novel makes it clear that the literal division of gender into two different sexes is an error, a "fall" from an ideally metaphoric understanding of gender, it makes it equally clear that this error is the source and definition of life. Without this error we would die out, sterile; with it "the wheel of life run[s] long and chearfully round." Does Sterne then present such a Fall as fortunate (the source of cherished life being the division of "male" and "female" into two sexes) or unfortunate (an error in the reading of gender which represents a devastating reduction of original self-sufficiency)? Are we to applaud him for recognizing antifeminism as an error, or hiss him off-stage for exploiting and delighting in that error? It is hard, perhaps impossible, to say: "think what you will against it," *Tristram Shandy* insists intransigently on the *fact* of the antifeminist *error*.

Notes

1.   Robert P. Miller, *Chaucer: Sources and Backgrounds* (New York: Oxford UP, 1977), 400–401:

> The Christian community which succeeded the Roman Empire regarded the presence of death and all our woe, in what Saint Augustine called this our "penal condition," as the fatal consequence of Adam's consenting to the temptation of Eve. This also was widely understood as the dissolution of *virilitas* into "effeminacy" (*muliebritas*), whether the story was interpreted literally or allegorically. Literally, Adam the first husband abrogated his responsibility when he allowed his moral authority to be swayed by Eve. Allegorically, Reason consented to the seductions of the Flesh. In either case the natural order of Paradise was abandoned, and the descendents of Adam have been consigned to live with the weakness which he willed to them.
>
> An emphasis on the "restoration" of the depraved image of man led to widespread asceticism in the early Christian Church, and the ascetic ideal was respected, though not always practiced, throughout the Middle Ages. To restore the image betrayed by Adam, one sought to subjugate the Flesh again to the authority of Reason. In secular circles this effort was symbolized by the good "horsemanship" of the chivalric man, who controlled the "reins of reason's rule." Among solitaries we frequently find men who, in addition to abstinence from food, drink, sleep, and the like, absolutely forbid themselves the sight of women. . . . The ascetic, however, was not concerned with the evil of women so much as with his own evil which the sight of a woman might arouse. . . .
>
> Saint Jerome, in his famous *Epistle Against Jovinian* (393 A.D.), was working in this tradition. . . . Marriage, he pointed out, . . . is better than fornication, but inferior to the state of virginity, which most closely approximates the state of innocence lost through Adam's uxoriousness. Women as well as men are called to the virgin life; in the purity of their will both can conquer their *muliebritas,* as far as the fallen state of human nature allows.

2.   Leigh A. Ehlers, "Mrs. Shandy's 'Lint and Basilicon': The Importance of Women in *Tristram Shandy,*" *South Atlantic Review* 46 (1981):61–73; 61–62. See also Ruth Marie Faurot, "Mrs. Shandy Observed," *Studies in English Literature* 10 (1970): 579–89. Juliet McMaster has joined Ehlers and Faurot in arguing for a distinction between a misogynistic Walter Shandy

and a non-misogynistic Sterne or *Tristram Shandy:* "Sterne is no Walter," she declares, and *"Tristram Shandy* is *about* misogyny, and against it" ("Walter Shandy, Sterne, and Gender: A Feminist Foray," *English Studies in Canada* 15 [1989]:456 [reprinted in this collection]).

3. Ruth Perry, "Words for Sex: The Verbal Sexual Continuum in *Tristram Shandy,"* *Studies in the Novel* 20 (1988):27–42; 29.

4. Melvyn New brings attention to this problem when he states that Perry's "real thesis, namely, that Sterne is a sexist," reduces critical debate to "an exercise in either/or ideology" (*The Scriblerian* 22 [1989]:33).

5. It could be argued that misogyny persists even in a metaphoric reading of gender, since it is the individual's "female" flesh that is a problem that needs to be addressed. But since this way of understanding "male" and "female" has equal consequences for actual men and women, it is, for my purposes here, adequately androgynous.

6. Since I am arguing that the novel shows antifeminist habits of reading to be an inescapable component of lapsarian sexuality and language, I do not perceive significant differences between the novel, Sterne, or Tristram, subject as they all are in the book to these habits.

7. H.W. Matalene argues that the Shandys' lovemaking in Volume I is far more mutual than twentieth-century criticism has assumed (372). Matalene, however, finds no discrepancy between this conjugal mutuality and what he himself identifies as the exclusively rational and "patriarchal" orientation of Walter's reproductive designs ("Sexual Scripting in Montaigne and Sterne," *Comparative Literature* 41 [1989]:360–77; 373).

8. Saint Augustine, *On Christian Doctrine,* trans. D. W. Robertson, Jr. (New York: Macmillan, 1986), 84.

9. See Patricia Meyer Spacks, *Imagining a Self: Autobiography and Novel in Eighteenth-Century England* (Cambridge, Mass.: Harvard UP, 1976), 127–57. Spacks elaborates on the father-son resemblance between Walter and Tristram, and extends it as well to the family resemblance between the reader and the Shandys.

10. See Juliet McMaster, " 'Uncrystalized Flesh and Blood': The Body in *Tristram Shandy,"* *Eighteenth-Century Fiction* 2 (1990):197–214. McMaster comments in passing on Walter's joint antipathies to women and bodies: "just as Walter as male is committed to a mad enterprise to do without women, so Walter as mind, committed to cerebral activity, is also madly trying to dispense with the body" (213).

11. McMaster (1989) comes to a similar conclusion: Walter, in V.xxxi, "is claiming something like a divine power of creation for the male, and deliberately marginalizing the female role . . . What he *really* wants is to perform the act of generation all by himself" (445–46).

12. See Robert A. Erikson, " 'Tis *Tris*-Something': Fatherhood and Naming in *Don Quixote* and *Tristram Shandy,"* *Pacific Coast Philology* 21 (1986):54–59.

13. In his influential essay, Sigurd Burckhardt explores the "messy fatality [that] attends the falling bodies of the novel": "they always land on the genitals" ("*Tristram Shandy*'s Law of Gravity," *English Literary History* 28 [1961]:70–88; 72).

14. See Alain Bony, "Terminologie chez Sterne," *Poétique* 29 (1977): 28–49. Bony draws on Lacan to argue that woman represents a "hole" of silence that man, as language-user, forever tries and forever fails to fill.

A Sentimental Journey, or "The Case of (In)delicacy"

MADELEINE DESCARGUES

"The world has imagined, because I wrote Tristram Shandy, that I was myself more Shandean than I really ever was."[1] Sterne's declaration, made in a 1767 letter and seemingly as much a defense of the purity of his present intentions as a denial of past shandean indiscretions, was at best only half sincere. It was, in part, designed to help work himself into the right mood to write his new work; more essentially, it was aimed at the future reading public of *A Sentimental Journey* and initiated the launching of an advertising campaign for the new book. In such a context, Sterne was only too willing to pass as a person far more sentimental in the eyes of the world than he really ever was: "My Sentimental Journey will please Mrs. J[ames], and my Lydia. . . . It is a subject which works well, and suits the frame of mind I have been in for some time past—I told you my design in it was to teach us to love the world and our fellow creatures better than we do—so it runs most upon those gentler passions and affections, which aid so much to it" (*Letters,* 400–401).[2] Leaving behind the lustier days of the Shandy saga, during which he had indeed often claimed an identity with his hero Tristram (in his correspondence, he alternated between identifying with Tristram and Yorick), Sterne hoped to work out a compromise among the competing claims of his desire for redemption, his need for success, recognition, and money, all of which had failed him for some time since the decline of interest in *Tristram Shandy,* and the public's growing taste for sentiment.[3] He had already been advised by some reviewers, for example Ralph Griffiths in the *Monthly Review,* to follow his inclination for the "pathetic" rather than the bawdy. As noted by Gardner D. Stout in his introduction to *A Sentimental Journey,* "Although the influence of Griffiths' advice should not be exaggerated, it is difficult to believe that it was lost on a shrewd opportunist like Sterne, particularly when he needed funds" (*ASJ,* 10).[4] In short, Sterne felt and appreciated the fact that sentiment and sensibility were more in favor than smutty talk and double entendre in 1768, when *A Sentimental Journey* was published.

This translation (by the author) of "*A Sentimental Journey,* ou le cas d'indélicatesse" (*Études Anglaises* 46 [1993]: 407–19) appears here for the first time.

My point in recalling the context of the *Journey*'s publication, however, is precisely not to treat it as the second work of a chastened writer, which would not do it sufficient justice. *A Sentimental Journey* has suffered from diametrically opposed critiques: for some, its sentiment is not pure enough, and Yorick is guilty of unchaste or equivocal feelings; for others, its wit is defective because the Sternean discourse is held in check in order to accommodate pathos. In either case, Sterne's exercise in sentiment has generally been deemed too affected, too self-consciously maudlin, and hence flawed.[5]

Rather than further investigate the evolution of Sterne's sentiment as a clue to his novel, I would prefer to explore certain textual evidences that argue Sterne's continuation of the reflections on aesthetics that marked his earlier fiction. Another light might in this way be thrown on such epistolary protestations of innocence as cited earlier, and which continues: "If it is not thought a chaste book, mercy on them that read it, for they must have warm imaginations indeed" (*Letters*, 403). Sterne here echoes Tristram's own elaborate attempts to whitewash his bawdy insinuations in *Tristram Shandy*; in that work, as in *A Sentimental Journey*, the narrator wishes to depend, as Tristram phrases it, "upon the cleanliness of [his] reader's imaginations" (*TS*, III. xxxi.258). Yorick raises the same point when he abstains from describing the Piedmontese lady's and his own undressing in the *Journey*'s final sequence: "that I leave to the reader to devise; protesting as I do it, that if it is not the most delicate in nature, 'tis the fault of his own imagination—against which this is not my first complaint" (*ASJ*, 289–90). The feigned strictures of Yorick, Tristram, and Sterne on the reader's imagination, a device used explicitly to effectuate equivocal or self-reflexive textual potentialities in Sterne's fictions, would seem then to offer an adequate model for the double denial that binds reader and narrator in Sterne's writing. There is also a double measure of ambivalence, as purity is (dis)claimed by the same rhetorical trick, a trick the reader is at once congratulated and upbraided for interpreting rightly. Further, the reader must consent to be implicated in the process of understanding what the text may imply if the well-extended shandean gamut, sentimental or not, is to take effect at all.

This makes it impossible to conceive of Yorick as a tame Tristram. The difference between the two, rather, lies in their handling of narration. Compared with Tristram's masterly flippancy, Yorick's attitude is inspired by a tormenting wish for reliable self-observation and analysis, a wish that bears significantly on the difficulties of writing about oneself in the form of a narrative. Not that the question is about the author's greater or lesser autobiographical credibility in the text of *A Sentimental Journey*. Rather, Yorick's attempt at total sincerity can be read as a parable about the autobiographical predicament, as Sterne exposes him to the ironic treatment of his introspective narration and makes him stumble in the faithful representation of himself he wishes to project. In this way, Sterne demonstrates the difficulty of the coincidence of author and narrator in the perspective of autobiographical confession.[6]

THE WILES OF NARRATIVE TECHNIQUE

The narrative technique of *A Sentimental Journey* may appear less complex than that of *Tristram Shandy* because of the reduced exuberance of digressions, the fewer dialogues and competing narratives or protagonists, and perhaps most important, the choice of one privileged persona, Yorick, through whose exclusive viewpoint the story is continuously told. Yorick's speech in the first person is deceptively simple, however, because in the course of the narrative it illustrates the difficulties of being the subject of one's own discourse. His *authority*, not to mention his *authorship*, is contested. In the first place, in whose name is he speaking? Where Tristram laughingly dodges the question of identity ("And who are you? said he.——Don't puzzle me; said I"; *TS*, VII.xxxiii.633), Yorick is made to struggle, albeit playfully, for an identity: "there is not a more perplexing affair in life to me, than to set about telling any one who I am—for there is scarce any body I cannot give a better account of than of myself" (*ASJ*, 221). He first uses the recommendation of Shakespeare to make good the lack of a passport (215), to which the Count objects: "Shakespear is full of great things—He forgot a small punctillio of announcing your name—it puts you under a necessity of doing it yourself" (220). In response, Yorick's name will do, spelled out in "the grave-diggers scene in the fifth act" (221) and reminding the reader of the literary filiation and textual character of all narrative heroes.

As glib a talker as Tristram, Yorick is made to focus his conversational energies on the task of disclosing the secrets of his mind to a willing partner, the narratee, as he gradually unveils them to himself. Here again his good intentions send him to purgatory at the very least. When Parson Yorick mentions "nakedness" in the profane conversations of which he is so fond, and then specifies that he means "of the land" (217), he triggers the Count's allusion to female nakedness: "*Hèh bien! Monsieur l'Anglois,* said the Count, gaily—You are not come to spy the nakedness of the land—I believe you—*ni encore,* I dare say, *that* of our women—But permit me to conjecture—if, *par hazard,* they fell in your way—that the prospect would not affect you" (217). Yorick blushes and invokes the nakedness of hearts, but in truth, and despite his rhetorical agility, he cannot escape his own disclosure, the denuding of his design. His innocence and straightforwardness must be appreciated with that "*grano salis*" that Tristram recommends for sound reading (*TS*, II.iv.104).

Similarly, though in a different tone, Sterne had demonstrated from the pulpit the impossibility of knowing oneself, in the sermon entitled "Self knowledge":

> To know one's self, one would think could be no very difficult lesson;—for who, you'll say, can well be truly ignorant of himself and the true disposition of his own heart. If a man thinks at all, he cannot be a stranger to what passes there—he must be conscious of his own thoughts and desires, he must remember his past pursuits, and the true springs and motives which in general have directed the actions of his life: he may hang out false colours and deceive the world, but how can a man deceive himself? That a man can—is evident, because he daily does so.... [H]e is as much, nay often, a much greater stranger to his own disposition and true character than all the world besides. (*Sermons*, 31–32)

Not that Yorick is unaware of his own duplicity: he himself gives his good conscience a severe check in such episodes as "The Monk" (*ASJ*, 70–75), "Montriul" (132–34), and "Paris" (261–66), not even concealing with his smile—his smirk, some might say—the seriousness of the discredit he brings on himself. He does not hesitate to let us see through his generous impulses, which at one point he implies are to be credited to the invigorating qualities of French burgundy. He confesses to outrageous meanness toward the poor monk (72–75), and then seems to aggravate it with the petty sentimental calculation that presides over his redeeming gesture, his desire to captivate a beautiful woman's attention: "I set myself to consider how I should undo the ill impressions which the poor monk's story, in case he had told it her, must have planted in her breast against me" (98). In the end, he admits to not knowing himself how to discriminate between his reasons for crying: is it sadness or the sting of nettles—or both (102–3)?

Yorick spares no harsh words to describe some of his emotions—"Every dirty passion, and bad propensity in my nature, took the alarm . . . AVARICE . . . CAUTION . . . COWARDICE . . . DISCRETION . . . HYPOCRISY . . . MEANNESS . . . PRIDE" (104–5)—and he entertains no more illusions about his charity toward beggars (132–34) than about the extreme servility to which he feels reduced when prison is looming: "How many mean plans of dirty address . . . did my servile heart form! I deserved the Bastile for every one of them" (207). In short, Yorick is also pleased, on occasion, to draw a quite dark self-portrait.

He sits at his darkest in the episode of the practiced beggar, whose method—reckless flattery—he uses to earn a few meals in Parisian salons (261–66). The joke is so unscrupulous, in fact, that it might contaminate even the validity of the faith that Yorick calls to witness in the conversational contests he relishes. His rhetorical ardor in dispute with a deist coquette convinces her that she still needs religion as a guardian to her virtue: "there is need of all restraints, till age in her own time steals in and lays them on us" (265). But this is not only a successful piece of satire on the vanity of the French woman; it is also a disquieting proof, even to himself, that this self-same religion on which he founds his moral principles owes its even temporary triumph—"she put off the epocha of deism for two years" (265)—exclusively to his opponent's coquetry. Even latitudinarian realism does not like to flirt so blatantly with proclaimed cynicism, and Sterne, having let Yorick throw a good deal of suspicion on the integrity of his religious convictions, makes him put a halt to this "prostitution" of himself (266), thus concluding the sulfurous chapters and reestablishing religion and its prerogatives.

That Yorick should playfully endeavor to write what he can construe of his motivations defines his central flaw of self-complacency. This misled Virginia Woolf's analysis of his rambling introspection, in which she conflated the narrator with the author: "Indeed, the chief fault of *A Sentimental Journey* comes from Sterne's concern for our good opinion of his heart."[7] Yorick is indeed concerned to give a "good opinion of his heart" in his narration, but Sterne does not necessarily share the same concern. Yorick's moral failure is to be proven guilty of cultivating altruism and humility for his own satisfaction and to be found enjoying the vertiginous delights of confession. His failure is, of course, fortunate, a fortunate fall from ideal narration that serves his author's purpose, to expose readers in a pleasurable manner to the rhetoric of a self-conscious narrator and lead them ultimately to question the assumption that the narrator is reliable.

An awareness of Sterne's project in this regard helps us make better sense of the numerous instances during which Yorick betrays himself or, rather, is betrayed by the text he is supposed to elaborate, under the control of the author's shaping hand, concerning most particularly his protestations of chaste motives. Yorick has a genius for uncovering the bawdy in the purest of intentions and for allowing his confusions to be teased, as if he had forgotten Tristram's warning: "Chastity, by nature the gentlest of all affections—give it but its head—'tis like a ramping and a roaring lion" (*TS*, V.i.414). In Yorick "the *extreams* of DELICACY, and the *beginnings* of CONCUPISCENCE" (415) rejoin.

The reader finds it difficult to forget what Yorick is about when he compulsively lays his finger on delicate matters, even while simultaneously declaring himself ignorant of the world's wickedness. In the *opéra comique,* he finds it difficult to account for the injunction of the "parterre": "*Haussez les mains, Monsieur l'Abbe*" (*ASJ,* 180). "And can it be supposed, said I, that an ecclesiastick would pick the Grisset's pockets? The old French officer smiled, and whispering in my ear, open'd a door of knowledge which I had no idea of—" (180). On the occasion of his discovery of the "*grossierte*" of French ways, Yorick turns pale—merely blushing would not be proportionate, obviously, to the seriousness of the sin that exposes the appetites of the papists, already disliked and distrusted by Yorick and his compatriots. "Is it possible," he asks, "that a people so smit with sentiment should at the same time be so unclean, and so unlike themselves—*Quelle grossierte!*" (180). The old French officer then reacts with equanimity to the Englishman's sense of outrage, thus deflating Yorick's exaggerated reaction and making it seem a jot too spectacular to be trusted.

A typical exercise in ambiguity, requiring close, even suspicious, reading occurs in the episode of the fair "*fille de chambre.*" By failing to come to an easy resolution of the conflict between his conscience and his passions, Yorick seems more dependable in this episode. He simply confesses to fleeing instead of attempting to resist the devil's temptations: "I give up the triumph, for security; and instead of thinking to make him fly, I generally fly myself" (235). Yet the measure of time makes Yorick's unreliability very clear: the timing of the episode counters his version of it. The time needed for his disquisition on "clay-cold heads and luke-warm hearts" in the ambiguously entitled chapter "The Conquest" (237) does not cover the narrative gap of two hours revealed by the intervention of a character who is minor but whose clockwise authority, nonetheless, the text corroborates. The master of the hotel would like Yorick to decamp: "How so? friend? said I.—He answer'd, I had had a young woman lock'd up with me two hours that evening in my bed-chamber, and 'twas against the rules of his house" (241). To make matters clearer—and worse—the master of the hotel offers to pimp for him by providing a "Grisset." She indeed pays a visit to Yorick, who buys her laces and ruffles—and nothing more. "I have only paid as many a poor soul has *paid* before me for an act he *could* not do, or think of" (243) is his wry conclusion, throwing yet another light on the nature of his protracted abstinence with the *"fille de chambre."* At this moment, the reader may well remember Yorick's exalted description of a woman's eyes in another passage of the novel: "she had a quick black eye, and shot through two such long and silken eye-lashes with such penetration, that she look'd into my very heart and reins" (168–69); perhaps the reasons that it took two hours for his performance with the *"fille de chambre"* to remain purely textual are not, after all, moral reasons.

Yorick's introspective rhetoric allows the attentive reader to hear a second voice in the background of the apparently all-encompassing monologue. That is to say, his monologic narration is continually impinged on by an implied author who questions the truth claim of the narrator's explanation. *A Sentimental Journey* thus elicits a double set of questions and answers: those of the narrative voice and those that implicitly dislodge Yorick from his central position of enunciation and thus suggest a competition for narrative power, stimulating alternative versions or explanations. In this doubleness, Yorick, as the questioned subject of his own fiction, is instrumental: he is the instrument of the questioning, and he is an instrument put by the author into the hands of the reader. The narrator's delicate task is to give birth to the well-informed reader *in utero* in the narratee.

Socrates' maieutic, that is, the dialectical art of making minds give birth to concepts, is an apposite model here to account for these narrative wiles. The idea of a Socratic approach to truth in Sterne's fictions was broached by John Traugott in his analysis of *Tristram Shandy:* "The very process of rhetorical dialectic, as the rhetorician proposes question and answer, shifts his ground, communicates with his respondent, leads him to self-implication and exposure—the very process makes Socratic irony which can shade from wry realization to paradox to buffoonery."[8] The narrative technique in *A Sentimental Journey* provides the shifting ground that allows for readerly "self-implication and exposure" and that puts in question Yorick's command over his own fiction by suggesting a competing fiction to be devised by the reader. The midwifery of *A Sentimental Journey,* to pursue the Socratic analogy, gives birth to a truth that is not Yorick's, a good illustration of the ironic distance existing in the relationship between the text and the alleged subject of its elaboration, or the writing of the self and the living reality of that same self.[9]

Delicacy and Indelicacy

The narration of *A Sentimental Journey* enacts the theory of ambivalence formulated in *Tristram Shandy:* "here are two roads . . . a dirty and a clean one, ——which shall we take? (*TS,* III.xxxi.258). It is the essence of Sterne's writing that the two roads have to be kept open and that they can cross: "hence, although sentimentality was a favorite eighteenth-century way to deny sexuality, in Yorick the two can never be distinguished."[10] Either Yorick chooses purity, knowing that renouncement may be tainted with impure wishes, or he yields to temptation and must therefore construct the rhetoric of a guilty conscience, as illustrated by the hypothetical clause in "The Conquest": "YES ——and then—Ye whose clay-cold heads and luke-warm hearts can argue down or mask your passions—tell me, what trespass is it that man should have them? or how his spirit stands answerable, to the father of spirits, but for his conduct under them?" (*ASJ,* 237).

The devil—rather fled from than confronted—is everywhere: "there is nothing unmixt in this world; and some of the gravest of our divines have carried it so far as to affirm, that enjoyment itself was attended even with a sigh—and that the greatest *they knew of,* terminated *in a general way,* in little better than a convulsion" (228). Erotic response is the choicest expression of Yorick's sensitive awareness of the ambivalence of any experience, open to delicate or indelicate interpretation.[11] The conversation with the beautiful Flemish woman (96–98, 110–12), the feeling of the "Grisset's" pulse (164–67), the step danced with the "Marquesina di F***" (172–73),[12] are just so many experiences, culminating in the final case of delicacy, in which the erotic game instigates a substantial encounter of reader and text through the exposure of indelicacy. The text's and the reader's indelicacy must be exposed, a necessary stage in the process of initiation into mature reading and a crucial device of Yorick's intellectual midwifery.

That is why, far from being purer than that of *Tristram Shandy, A Sentimental Journey*'s style is deliberately impure, "typical of Sterne's most mature writing—a virtuoso mingling of heretofore incompatible intentions, most obviously the pathetic and the bawdy."[13] When Yorick meets the pretty and available "Janatone," whom Tristram had met before him, her father rejoices over the "*ecu*" given her by an English gentleman: "*Tant pis, pour Mad^{lle} Janatone,* said I" (121). "*Tant mieux,*" the father thinks it proper to correct, "supposing I was young in French" (122), a commentary on both father's and daughter's morals. Naturally a fictional text so loaded with multiple ironies is also open to misinterpretation, of which the numerous sentimental (mis)-translations of *A Sentimental Journey* are an ironic example.[14]

The delicate inscription of indelicacy in the text of Sterne's novel insinuates itself into the reader's mind. It rests on a mode of writing in which sense cannot be born without traversing the "dirty" road of desire. On the level of plot, circumstances never stop throwing the men and women of the *Journey* into one another's arms. Fundamentally, the masculine narrator's rhetoric is always in search of something that seems best supplied by female characters. The interlocutors who best set off Yorick are women. In *Tristram Shandy,* the function of such heroines as Mrs. Shandy or Widow Wadman is, in great part, to prove the weakness of male rhetoric with unanswerable riddles, silent or voiced. In *A Sentimental Journey,* setting aside for the moment the case of Eliza—a character who does not belong to the story proper and whose part can be likened to that of Jenny in *Tristram Shandy*[15]—the female characters have become endowed with the undisputed value of positive heroines and inspiring muses; they are the dispensers of pleasures and the means of moral reflection as well, mediators between the human and the divine, consolers and redeemers.

From *Tristram Shandy* to *A Sentimental Journey,* Madam reader, that most quarrelsome version of a muse, has journeyed from the outside to the inside of the narrative, so to speak. The search for a soul mate motivates the novel. Ultimately, female characters are ontologically necessary to the narrator, whom they reestablish within the rich consciousness of his faith. Thanks to Maria, and despite a jest or two at her expense, Yorick can declare, "I am positive I have a soul" (*ASJ,* 271). The "great SENSORIUM of the world" (278) manifests itself in a dance mingling men and women, propitious to the expression of religious feeling (283–84).

It is in this sense that Yorick's amours have a platonic intent: "having been in love with one princess or another almost all my life . . . I hope I shall go on so, till I die, being firmly persuaded, that if ever I do a mean action, it must be in some interval betwixt one passion and another" (128–29). But seeking the ever-renewed female interlocutor, the multiple muse of the *Journey,* does not proceed without certain pangs of conscience. Yorick cares as much for fidelity (147–48) as for the portrait of Eliza, "the little picture which I have so long worn, and so often have told thee, Eliza, I would carry with me into my grave" (67), and indeed as much as he cares for himself. The theme of redemption through constancy, running through the text alongside the dominant theme of the multiplicity of encounters, enables Sterne to approach the vexed question of fidelity to oneself. His perspective would seem to argue that constant faith and faith in love are able to define and stabilize the moving center of the self, despite the ebb and flow of constant and inconstant human loves.

A Sentimental Journey is the product of a balance between several desires. Yorick's tormented but accepted inconstancy, "if they will but satisfy me there is no sin in it" (129), is anchored in the fluidity of his search for sentiment, in a journey that subsumes the fickleness of sentiment within the constancy of the pursuit. His progress depends on a reader's reciprocal appreciation to achieve its metaphorical value of a journey toward the other. Yorick's introspection, the study of his fleeting self, is self-revealing to the reader: it is a digressive narrative that leads in reality to the reading other. Instead of celebrating digression provocatively, as Tristram used to do, Yorick uses it sentimentally, as the paradigm of all communication.

Sterne, "Harlequin Shandy," as Griffiths called him,[16] is too humble, too Christian, too classical to believe in the transparency of his own discourse. Not trusting himself, he attempts to elaborate this discourse shaped as a journey toward the other through the dialectic of digression. In his novel, Yorick, the narrator-character, illustrates the fact that self-identity is impossible because self-knowledge is at best fleeting. Yet he also serves to illustrate the struggle to approximate autobiographical verities, despite which efforts truth is endlessly pursued by fiction, as in the story of the "Fragment," the missing sheets of which have been used to wrap a bouquet that is extraneous to the story in the novel: "And where is the rest of it, La Fleur? said I" (*ASJ*, 255). The strength of his digressive verities is to touch and move his alter ego, leaving it for the reader to appropriate a coherence other than fictional, in which the missing sheets of autobiographical truth can contain defining reflections.

The narrative strategy of the *Journey* bears on the lesson in Christian humility it encapsulates. The author's didactic purpose in the novel is achieved perversely, by means of the immodest unveiling of Yorick's soul. Yorick's eloquence is at its best in the scabrously sentimental mode, and Sterne, the artful moralist, teaches his moral lesson through Yorick's confession of his immorality. Such a lesson can be taught only to a reader who accepts Sterne's invitation to give birth to Yorick's wicked thoughts in the text—and, indeed, to endorse them. For the *Journey*'s rhetoric teases narrator and reader alike, just as Sterne's pulpit eloquence jostled his parishioners out of their good conscience into reflection.[17] The precariousness of the moral guidance the work presents is qualified by the persistence of the goodness inspired by faith and unrestricted by doubt in Sterne's classical (Christian) thinking. Through the Socratic exploration of Yorick's (in)delicate game of questions and answers, *A Sentimental Journey* pursues the moral reflection of Sterne the preacher and novelist. Its putting forward the platonic intent of

Yorick's quest is another way of considering the pursuit of fidelity to oneself and to others, when infidelity and fickleness stand at the very core of self-consciousness.

Notes

1. *Letters of Laurence Sterne,* ed. Lewis Perry Curtis (Oxford: Clarendon Press, 1935), 402–3.

2. Lydia was Sterne's daughter. Mrs. James was a common friend of Sterne and Eliza Draper; as Rufus Putney observes: "Mrs. Draper filled a gap—to which I think Mrs. James, had she been willing, would have been elected—in the procession of Sterne's ladies" ("Alas, Poor Eliza!" *Modern Language Review* 41 [1946]: 413).

3. The desire for redemption is forcefully expressed in his *Journal to Eliza.* Despite its title, the *Journal* was not so much a daily accounting addressed to Eliza Draper, one of Sterne's most famous passions, who was at the time returning to an ungracious husband in India, as it was a diary for the purposes of self-observation. To a certain extent, it served a cathartic aim and made it possible for Sterne to traverse a deeply depressed period and to recover enough peace of mind to write *A Sentimental Journey,* the composition of which shadows that of the *Journal.*

4. "Better take a friend's advice," Griffiths had written (*Monthly Review* 32 [February 1765]) in response to volumes VII and VIII of *Tristram:* "I am inclined to think that, all this while, you have not sufficiently cultivated your best talents. . . . One of our gentlemen once remarked . . . that he thought your excellence lay in the PATHETIC. I think so too" (quoted from *Sterne: The Critical Heritage,* ed. Alan B. Howes [London: Routledge and Kegan Paul, 1974], 167).

5. Throughout the nineteenth century, the repeated publications of *The Beauties of Sterne,* a selection of the passages Sterne had written that could be deemed purely sentimental—a perilous undertaking for any editor—contributed to the reputation of affectation incurred by Sterne, culminating in Thackeray's famous fulminations.

6. Although the word "autobiography" was first used by Southey in 1803, the usage seems apposite here in that Sterne poses the problem of the ambiguity of the autobiographical performance long before our own age's reflections on what Philippe Legeune terms the "autobiographical pact."

7. Virginia Woolf, introduction to *A Sentimental Journey through France and Italy* (London: Oxford University Press, 1928), xiv.

8. *Tristram Shandy's World: Sterne's Philosophical Rhetoric* (Berkeley: University of California Press, 1954), 80–81.

9. Through Yorick's example, Sterne does not seem to support the view that the narrator can be equated with the author or that transparency to oneself is a possibility, despite all attempts at sincerity. A famous exponent of the principles of just that transparency and sincerity is, of course, Jean-Jacques Rousseau in his *Confessions.* The belief in the possibility and the efficacy of sincerity is indispensable to the autobiographical perspective, which is therefore less prone to ironic detachment than the art of novel writing. This would be confirmed by Sterne's *Memoirs,* a short and properly autobiographical text, that is, one in which the author speaks about himself in his own name and in which the tone, contrary to that of *A Sentimental Journey,* is totally deprived of irony.

10. Melvyn New, "Proust's Influence on Sterne: Remembrance of Things to Come," *MLN* 103 (1988): 1034 (reprinted in this volume).

11. It takes no more than a bird's vitality to arouse the learned Bevoriskius's interest:

'Tis strange! . . . but the facts are certain, for I have had the curiosity to mark them down one by one with my pen—but the cock-sparrow during the little time that I could have finished the other half this note, has actually interrupted me with the reiteration of his caresses three and twenty times and a half.

How merciful, adds Bevoriskius, is heaven to his creatures! (*ASJ,* 228–29)

By an intertextual effect, namely a most suggestive and subtle lexical echo, Yorick's feigned confusion—"Ill fated Yorick! that the gravest of thy brethren should be able to write that to the world, which stains thy face with crimson, to copy in even thy study" (229)—is evocative of his sensuous temptation in the episode of the *fille de chambre* a few pages later (234): "crimson" there is the rich color of the curtains and of the sunset, before it becomes the color of the blush on the cheeks of both Yorick and the "fair *fille de chambre.*"

12.   Stout attempts to account for the initial by referring to real names (*ASJ,* 343–44). One suspects, nevertheless, that "F***" is not quite pure.

13.   New, "Proust's Influence," 1032.

14.   See Serge Soupel, "Voyage bibliographique parmi quelques traductions et trahisons du *Voyage sentimental,*" *Trema* 9 (1984): 133–42.

15.   In *Tristram Shandy,* Jenny is often taken to represent the singer Catherine Fourmantel, Sterne's dulcinea at the time; in *A Sentimental Journey,* Eliza is Eliza Draper, Sterne's last(?) passion. From one work to the other, the function of Sterne's heroines becomes more comprehensive, whether they are inside or outside the narrative. Those who have an intradiegetic status tend to play a more creative role in the emotional economics of the text.

16.   Howes, 181.

17.   Traugott suggests that Tristram's fictional rhetoric borrows its effectiveness from Sterne's pulpit experience: "Just as he [Sterne] argued the cause of a worldly morality to his parishioners by exciting their sentiments, vexing them, and then pointing to their motives for those sentiments, so Tristram speaks as a preacher, arguing not for sentiment or cynicism or whimsicality, those supposedly Shandean touchstones, but for the recognition of their real influences in our pharisaical rationales. Writing, properly managed, our author seems to say, is warfare with the reader" (xiii).

THE ETHICAL STERNE

◆

Sterne's Novels: Gathering Up the Fragments

Elizabeth W. Harries

Gather up the fragments that remain, that nothing be lost.

—John 6:13

He that gathereth not with me scattereth.

—Luke 11:23

I

Tristram Shandy, as one of its earliest critics suggested, has "more the air of a collection of fragments, than of a regular work."[1] Sterne emphasizes the desultory, disjointed character of his novels by including sections he labels as fragments: the section on whiskers and word contamination in the first chapter of Volume V of Tristram Shandy; the story of the Abderites in A Sentimental Journey (which includes a genuine classical fragment from Euripides' lost Andromeda); the beginning of the "history of the decayed gentleman" that Yorick finds under his breakfast butter and translates in Volume II of A Sentimental Journey. These identified fragments are only the most obvious of the many tantalizing, unfinished strands that dangle in both works: Slawkenbergius' dwindling tale, Trim's story of the King of Bohemia, the story of Yorick's encounter with the fair fille de chambre. The fragments could even be said to be miniatures of the novels in which they appear. Tristram Shandy, though it begins ab ovo or even ab semine, ends—if it ends—with a remark about a cock-and-bull story. A Sentimental Journey begins with a fragment of a dialogue and ends—if it ends—with a broken sentence and a double entendre.

Another of Sterne's early readers maintained that Sterne's "collection of fragments" was just that, that there was no figure in the random design of the carpet:

Reprinted from ELH 49 (1982): 35–49 and New Casebooks: Tristram Shandy, ed. M. New (London: Macmillan, 1992), 94–110.

I have been much diverted with some people here who have read it. They torture their brains to find out some hidden meaning in it, & will per force have
all the Starts—Digressions—and Ecarts which the Author runs out into, &
which are surely the Excellencies of his Piece, to be the constituent members of
a close, connected Story. Is it not provoking to meet with such wise acres who
. . . will pretend to seek for connection in a Work of this Nature.[2]

In his reply, Sterne suggests that he is equally impatient with this kind of
"philosophizing" about his novel: "they all look too high—tis ever the fate of
low minds."[3] The debate between the high and low lookers has continued
ever since. No one has seriously suggested that *Tristram Shandy* or *A Sentimental Journey* has an Aristotelian structure or is a "close connected story." But
some maintain that *Tristram Shandy* is really a complete work, while others see
it as deliberately unfinished. Some see the novels as the last development of
Augustan wit and order, while others see them as the expression of a shat-
tered world syntax, a confusion with more buzz than bloom.

In order to resolve, or dissolve, this debate, we must see Sterne's fragments in their context. What did Sterne mean by the word "fragment"?
What other kinds of fragments would he have known and what might have
inspired him to fragment his own works? What aesthetic ideas might have
contributed to his strategies of order (or disorder)? I will sketch some of the
contexts that have been suggested before, all of which do play some part in
Sterne's novels. But then, recognizing the danger of looking far too high, I
will comment on a resonance of the word "fragment" that most of us no
longer hear today, a Biblical echo suggested in my two epigraphs. Sterne's
fragments, I hope to show, require the examination of a context that has usually been neglected, the Biblical and even liturgical framework that was
always a part of his life and thought. This context can help us re-examine,
and perhaps reconcile, the dichotomies between various current perceptions
of Sterne's "Starts—Digressions—and Ecarts."

II

The eighteenth century was of course particularly aware of antique and
"Gothick" fragments, the remains of previously perfect works. The excavations at Herculanaeum and Pompeii and all the new antiquarian interests had
drawn attention to the "*Frusts*, and *Crusts*, and *Rusts* of antiquity," as Sterne
called them (VII.xxxi.628). Though Uncle Toby "had as little skill, honest
man, in the fragments, as he had in the whole pieces of antiquity" (V.iii.423),
Walter Shandy is more typical of the magpie tendency of his time. His delight
in the bits and scraps and extracts that he exhumes on every possible occasion
mirrors the delight of his contemporaries in the ruins and literary remains of
past civilizations. In this delight the joy of rediscovery and the pathos of

decay are inextricably mingled. These fragments "afford that pleasing melancholy which proceeds from a reflection on decayed magnificence."[4] Tristram's search for the monument of the two lovers in Volume VII is typical of this response.

Sterne designed his own fragments, dashes, and digressions to elicit a similar mixed response, the oscillation between the comic and pathetic that is so characteristic of his work. Like many of his contemporaries, he *produces* fragments—works which have not become incomplete, but that have been planned and executed as incomplete. (Friedrich Schlegel comments on this trend in 1798 in his Athenaeums-fragment 24: "Many works of the ancients have become fragments. Many works of the moderns are fragments at the time of their origin.")[5] These artificial fragments, like the artificial ruins that were constructed in many eighteenth-century gardens, emphasize the interplay of chance and design, of the work of nature and the work of the artist.[6] Like artificial ruins, they suggest this interplay in a contrived, completely *made* form. They are neither remains of earlier complete works, nor unfinished sections of longer works that have been abandoned, nor extracts from longer, more complete works, but rather planned fragments, creations that are intended to be partial. Sterne's broken-off forms, like the crumbling walls of the ruins, call our attention to their deliberate incompleteness.

Why do Sterne and his contemporaries turn to this fragmentation? Why does Tristram insist that things are "as certainly . . . convey'd to the mind by three strokes as three hundred" (II.ix.121) or insist on giving us "little books . . . instead of many bigger books" (IV.xxii.359)? In part, Sterne, his contemporaries, and Tristram are relying on the principles of affective aesthetics and its corollary, the *non-finito* (though, as Marcia Allentuck points out, that term was not used in England in the eighteenth century).[7] Gradually, throughout the century, the reader or spectator became more and more important in aesthetic theory and artistic practice. The urn was no longer simply wellwrought, according to external or internal principles, but wrought to elicit a participatory response—sometimes more, sometimes less defined—from its beholder. As Aulay Macaulay said, in 1778, "an ordinary writer spins out his thoughts, if I may so express myself, to the last dregs; but it is the one great mark of an original genius, to give scope to the invention of his reader, and to make one thought give rise to a whole train of ideas."[8] The lines actually on the canvas, the words actually on the page are synecdoches; the beholder or reader expands and "finishes" their suggestive, unfinished forms. The more indistinct or incomplete their forms, the more the beholder is required to do.

As always, Sterne pushes these ideas to a logical, literal, and comic extreme. His asterisks and dashes constantly "give rise" to our bawdy powers of invention. Sometimes they seem to be suppressions of the unseemly: "Cannot you contrive, master, quoth *Susannah,* . . . for a single time to **** *** ** *** ******?" (V.xvii.449). Sometimes they allow us to create our own indiscreet version of Walter Shandy's abstract reasoning on concrete subjects, as in his conversation with Yorick about "the natural relation between a father and his child" (V.xxxi.467). The supreme instance of this kind of aesthetic foolery is, of course, Tristram's invitation to his readers to draw their own portraits of the widow Wadman in the space he has thoughtfully, artfully left blank:

> To conceive this [the "concupiscible" allure of widow Wadman] right,—call for pen and ink—here's paper ready to your hand.——Sit down, Sir, paint her to your own mind——as like your mistress as you can——as unlike your wife as your conscience will let you. (VI.xxxviii.566)

But Sterne does not merely trifle with the possibilities of the *non-finito*. His familiar comment about the necessary, complementary activity of the reader takes on a new, enriched meaning when seen in this context:

> Writing, when properly managed, (as you may be sure I think mine is) is but a different name for conversation: As no one, who knows what he is about in good company, would venture to talk all;—so no author . . . would presume to think all: The truest respect which you can pay to the reader's understanding, is to halve this matter amicably, and leave him something to imagine, in his turn, as well as yourself.
> For my own part, I am eternally paying him compliments of this kind, and do all that lies in my power to keep his imagination as busy as my own. (II.xi.125–26)

Though somewhat disingenuous (Tristram goes on to thwart any attempt his readers might make to form their own pictures of Dr. Slop), this comment shows that Sterne was alert to the central meaning of the *non-finito,* the way that an aesthetic of the unfinished leads to an aesthetic (and, ultimately, an ethic) of participation. Like the desultory conversations of the Shandy brothers, the "conversation" between Tristram and his readers depends on the oscillating conflicts and correspondences of their associative "trains" and emotional reactions. As Mrs. Barbauld remarked (1810),

> It is the peculiar characteristic of this writer, that he affects the heart, not by long drawn tales of distress, but by light electric touches which thrill the nerves of the reader who possesses a corresponding sensibility of frame. . . . He resembles those painters who can give expression to a figure by two or three strokes of bold outline, leaving the imagination to fill up the sketch; the feelings are awakened as really by the story of *Le Fevre* (*sic*), as by the narrative of *Clarissa*.[9]

Mrs. Barbauld may have been oblivious to the self-conscious irony of Tristram's account of Le Fever's death; but, in her description of Sterne as a master of the sketch, she suggests the source of the "electric" power of his unfinished forms. Tristram's attempts to galvanize the reader, to make the reader a partner in the production of the text, are subtle indications of Sterne's interest in and dependence on the *non-finito*.[10] His blanks, asterisks, and outlines (of characters, of scenes, of gestures) are designed to let "the imagination fill up the sketch."[11] Like the contemporary interest in ruins, the torso, and the sketch (as we see it in Diderot's *Salons* or Reynolds's *Discourses*), Sterne's novels depend on the "fertile . . . obscurity" (II.ii.100) of the unfinished.

Sterne also suggests, however, another related aesthetic model for his work, the "image made by chance." Throughout both *Tristram Shandy* and *A Sentimental Journey,* Tristram and Yorick insist on the unplanned, random nature both of their lives and of the books they are making out of them. Prefaces and dedications appear in the middle of the novels; chapters are reversed or omitted; stories are interrupted or "lost," as Trim says to Uncle Toby in Volume VIII. Yorick insists on his freedom to shift from scene to scene, or even country to country, without much warning; Tristram maintains that his pen, not he himself, governs his writing. In the middle of one particularly random chapter in Volume IX, which is all one unfinished sentence, Tristram claims "——That whatever resemblance it may bear to half the chapters which are written in the world, or, for aught I know, may be now writing in it—that it was as casual as the foam of Zeuxis his horse" (IX.xxv.785). As James Work points out, Tristram has muddled his reference to Pliny, since it was Nealces, not Zeuxis, who finally was able to produce the effect he wanted by throwing his sponge at his painting of a horse. But Sterne may also have been thinking of Montaigne's discussion of Protogenes, whom Nealces was actually copying: "Fortune guided the throw with perfect aptness right to the dog's mouth, and accomplished what art had been unable to obtain."[12]

Several art historians have pointed out the sudden reappearance of the "image made by chance," common in the workshop talk of the Renaissance but then apparently forgotten until the later eighteenth century.[13] All of them point to Alexander Cozens's blot technique, his *New Method* for teaching drawing by beginning with the chance images made by random blots on the page. Cozens describes his method in this way: "To blot, is to make varied spots and shapes with ink on paper, producing accidental forms without lines, from which ideas are presented to the mind. . . . To sketch, is to delineate ideas; blotting suggests them."[14] Like the *non-finito,* this theory is grounded in the idea of imaginative expansion, but Cozens suggests that even the sketch is too definite, too circumscribed by invention and will. Only the fortuitous shapes formed by blots will lead to an original exercise of what he calls, apparently interchangeably, "invention" and "imagination."

Twenty years earlier, Sterne apparently came to much the same conclusion. Although his random chapters and eccentric divisions are in part "parables of preconception,"[15] designed to counter rigid literary expectations, they are also celebrations of the artistic value of chance and the natural. Sterne might have quoted Shakespeare, as Cozens did:

This is an Art
Which does mend Nature, change it rather; but
The Art itself is Nature.

(*Winter's Tale* IV.4.95)

Sterne constantly, self-consciously calls our attention to the artlessness of his performances, the blot-like nature of his novels. We interpret them much as we would the blots of a Rorschach test—and, he suggests, reveal just as much of ourselves in the process. His emphasis on chance, on improvisation rather than on working from a pre-conceived plan, is, as always, part paradox, part parody. But his virtuosity in transforming chance into design, or design into apparent chance, shows their interplay in a particularly compressed and accessible way. "The foam of Zeuxis his horse" is another "motly emblem" (III.xxxvi.268) of Sterne's fragmentary works.

It is possible to trace several other strands in the fabric of ideas that led to the fragmentary. Sterne constantly plays with the discrepancy between the artist's vision and his ability to realize that vision. Tristram will always grow up faster than Walter Shandy can formulate the *Tristra-paedia*—or than he himself can compose his autobiography. Gines de Pasamonte says, while discussing his autobiography, *The Life of Gines de Pasamonte,* in *Don Quixote,* "How can it be finished, if my life isn't?" (Part I, Ch. 22). Tristram pushes that paradox still further by maintaining that he lives "364 times faster" than he can write (IV.xiii.342). But this comic preoccupation suggests the pathos of unfinished works, sexual acts, and lives that pervades the novels, a pathos that is akin to the pathos of ruins, or of memorials, or of the black, opaque page that marks Parson Yorick's death in the first Volume of *Tristram Shandy.*

The fragmentary also suggests the pathos of the inarticulate and of the inadequacy of words. Words tend to separate the characters in Sterne's novels, while gestures and glances unite them. Yorick's mastery of the *"short hand"* of gesture, "the several turns of looks and limbs with all their inflections and delineations" (*ASJ,* p. 171) makes it possible for him to see Paris more clearly than the traveller who has mastered French. Uncle Toby's *aposiopeses* are more telling than Walter Shandy's diatribes. Such fragments of speech become Sterne's equivalent for an inexpressibility topos: what is important cannot be said. (Sterne also suggests the reverse: what is said cannot be important.) The expressive silences of the novels, the gaps in verbal communication, mirror their formal "breaks and gaps" (VI.xxxiii.558). Both suggest the dangers of words and of false coherence.

These four related strands—the *non-finito,* the "image made by chance," the pathos of the unfinished, the pathos of the inarticulate—were all part of the intellectual context in which *Tristram Shandy* and *A Sentimental Journey* were written. To separate them as I have, and several other critics have before me, is artificial and difficult, since they constantly underline and reinforce each other. Together they form part of the dense web of circumstances and ideas that

Sterne often referred to: "the circumstances with which every thing in this world is begirt, give every thing in this world its size and shape" (III.ii.187). These strands contribute to the fragmentary form of Sterne's novels.

III

So far, however, no one has noticed another strand in Sterne's fragmentary fabric, "a large uneven thread, as you sometimes see in an unsaleable piece of cambrick, running along the whole length of the web, and so untowardly, you cannot so much as cut out a ** . . . but it is seen or felt" (VI.xxxiii.558). It seems "uneven," because it comes from a realm that is seldom considered when we think about Sterne. But, like the "large uneven thread" in Tristram's brain, it becomes both central and unavoidable once we see it. For Sterne, as for many of his contemporaries, the word "fragment" was inextricably bound up with the passage in which, after the miracle of the loaves and fishes, Jesus tells the disciples to "gather up the fragments that remain, that nothing be lost. Therefore they gathered them up together, and filled twelve baskets with the fragments of the five barley loaves, which remained over and above unto them that had eaten" (John 6:12–13). Anyone steeped in the Bible, as Sterne was, would have heard an echo of this passage every time he heard or thought of the word "fragment."[16] The fragmentary was always connected with the notion of overflow—or plenitude in apparent dearth; with the command to collect that overflow—or the significance of the apparently insignificant; and ultimately with the Eucharist—a memorial that is also a renewal. (The passage "I am the bread of life" comes later in that section in John; the language of the earlier passages is echoed in the *Didache* as well as in a passage from the Anglican Order for Holy Communion: "We are not worthy so much as to *gather up* the *crumbs* under Thy table.")

Sterne nowhere refers to this passage directly. But when he was still a quite orthodox, conscientious, Latitudinarian parish minister, he would have read it at least three times a year in each of his parishes: on the Feast of St. Philip and St. James, on the Monday after the twenty-second Sunday after Trinity, and particularly on the Fourth Sunday in Lent. There, in the *Book of Common Prayer*, it is juxtaposed as the Gospel reading with the Epistle, Gal. 4:21, an allegorical promise of a new Jerusalem. In his *Rationale upon the Book of Common Prayer*, a book that is in the sale catalogue of Sterne's library, Anthony Sparrow describes that Sunday in this way:

> This is called *Dominica Refectionis;* for the Gospel, St. John 6:1 tells of Christ's miraculous feeding and satisfying the hungry souls, that hunger after Him and his doctrine; and the Epistle, Gal. 4:21, tells us of a Jerusalem that is above. . . . Thus holy Church mixes joy and comfort with our sorrows and afflictions.[17]

The day is a day of rejoicing within sorrow, of light within the gloom of Lent. The "fragments that remain" are remnants of a surprising and joyful occasion; they bring to mind an unexpected fullness, a feeding that went beyond the actual requirements of the five thousand. A modern interpretation echoes and clarifies Anthony Sparrow's:

> If the incident . . . was more in the nature of a prophetic symbol, then we may see . . . the fragments collected as symbolic language from the evangelists. Jesus, who feeds them now in token of the impending Kingdom and the Messianic feast, will never fail to feed them. There is enough and to spare.[18]

This is indeed "high" language, but Sterne would have been quick to catch the hope that the fragments gathered up by the disciples offer. They are not mere scraps left from a feast, but rather signs that point beyond themselves to an ungraspable fullness.

Sterne must also have been familiar with other, extended uses of the passages. Many religious writers he knew fall easily and naturally into echoes of its language and of its meaning. Jeremy Taylor, in *The Great Exemplar,* uses it effortlessly to describe one of the functions of a minister of the church:

> yet the mercy of God, besides this great feast [mercy through baptism] hath fragments, which the apostles and ministers spiritual are to gather up in baskets, and minister to the after-needs of indigent and necessitous disciples.
> And this we gather, as fragments are gathered, by respersed sayings, instances, and examples of the divine mercy recorded in holy scripture.[19]

The gathering up of the fragments here becomes a metaphor for the collection of scattered Biblical passages in order to show—as the miracle of the loaves and fishes showed—the wideness of God's mercy. By Sterne's time, it had begun to be used in a purely literary way—by his German near-contemporary Herder, for example, who describes the addition of some new parts to his *Uber die neuere deutsche Litteratur. Erste Sammlung von Fragmenten* (1766) in 1768 using the language of Luther's translation of John: "So the crumbs have been gathered conscientiously enough, so that nothing be lost. All, however, is still a fragment."[20] Herder, possibly influenced by Sterne, sees his work as a collection of crumbs or fragments within a larger structure that is itself a fragment. He points to the necessary incompleteness of his enterprise, the way the fragmentary scraps of analysis and commentary are related to the fragmentary nature of the whole. The formal structure of his essay—or apparent lack of it—reflects the tentative nature of his conclusions.

I do not want to argue that Sterne knew these particular instances. (He couldn't, in fact, have known the Herder.) What I do want to suggest, however, is that the reverberations of that Biblical passage were in the air, both in religious and in more purely literary circles (partly, of course, because the distinction was then largely less clear-cut than it is today). For Sterne, who was both the Parson Yorick of the novels and sermons and the scriptomaniac Tristram, the passage became a subterranean metaphor for his procedure in his novels and for their meaning. They are rather like the disciples' baskets, baskets in which he "gathered up the fragments" of learning and of the quotidian that came his way. By emphasizing the bric-a-brac of scholarship and the "little serpentine tracks" of the daily, he indicates their comic insignificance—but also their ultimate meaning in a larger and more flexible context. As he says, in his dedication of the second edition of *Tristram Shandy* I and II to William Pitt:

> . . . I live in a constant endeavour to fence against the infirmities of ill health, and other evils of life, by mirth; being firmly persuaded that every time a man smiles,—but much more so, when he laughs, that it adds something to this Fragment of Life.

Sterne was interested in collecting the flotsam and jetsam of literature and of daily life, but not in a whimsical or merely antiquarian spirit. His formal gaps and leaps—most striking perhaps in those sections he actually labels as fragments—point to the necessary incompleteness of our attempts to make sense of life's fragments and of life itself as a fragment, but also to the expanding and ultimately liberating power of those attempts. Life itself is merely a fragment, but a fragment, as the Biblical resonance of the word suggests, is also a sign of something higher, wider, and more encompassing. As Alan D. McKillop remarked long ago, Sterne "blends the use of a symbol that might be taken as degrading or ludicrous with the assertion of its dignity and significance, the implication that the low things of the earth may surpass the great, and the humble things confound the mighty."[21] By giving us fragments and thwarting ordinary coherence, Sterne forces us to contemplate a different kind of order—an order not governed by "any *man*'s rules" (I.iv.5, emphasis mine) but by rules more inscrutable and divine.

A consideration of this "Biblical connection" should help us revise our current understanding of Sterne's project. Recently, Sterne, Yorick, Tristram, and the inhabitants of Shandy Hall have been taken more and more often as types and forerunners of a new modern subjectivity and consciousness, following Earl Wasserman's remarks in *The Subtler Language* (1959). He uses the Shandy family and their misunderstandings, as well as Tristram's "vain struggle for meaningful form,"[22] as symptoms of the collapse of the analogical ordering systems that gave life and meaning to Renaissance and Augustan literature. The Shandy universe becomes at best a system of interlocking solipsisms; nothing can mediate between them. Tristram's paronomasia is at best a battle with the meaninglessness of language, an early instance of Eliot's despair: "Words strain, / Crack and sometimes break, under the burden, / Under the tension, slip, slide, perish" ("Burnt Norton"). According to Wasserman, Sterne is like the associationist, whose only real interest is in "the free play of a chain of associations whose endless and directionless movement is his only conception of order" (p. 171). Wasserman treats Sterne and the Shandys as figures that lead to Romantic isolation, to a new world struggling to be born.

But I think we should attend to Denis Donoghue's quiet observation that Sterne "is a man of his time, though he complicates our sense of that time."[23] Sterne was peculiarly alive to all the currents of his age; like the "great—great SENSORIUM of the world" (*ASJ*, p. 278), he vibrates to many different stimuli. On the one hand, as I indicated in section II, he was alert to the implications of contemporary aesthetics, currents that led to—though always remained distinct from—Romantic aesthetics. On the other hand, however, he was still deeply dependent on the continuing and still coherent Christian syntax of his time. His fragments suggest the subjective character of contemporary aesthetic theory and psychology, but in an older, deeply analogical context. His novels are not outgrowths of skepticism or solipsism or mere aesthetic play. Rather they reflect his acceptance of the fragmentary character of our experience and the conviction that there is a matrix for that experience.

IV

A stubbornly material fragment in *A Sentimental Journey* may help us see the nature of Sterne's treatment of fragments more clearly. As Yorick travels from the Bourbonnais to Savoy, he is travelling from a land of plenty to a land of scarcity, from a land overflowing with wine and music "where Nature is pouring her abundance into everyone's lap" and everything is "pregnant with adventures" (268), to a land where Nature "in the midst of [her] disorders" is "still friendly to the scantiness [she has] created" (285). The land of fullness, harvest, and vintage is at first shadowed by the image of the mad Maria: "in every scene of festivity I saw Maria in the back-ground of the piece, sitting pensive under her poplar" (277). But an accident leads to the happy union and *agape* with the peasant family and the dance that is both grace and benediction: "In a word, I thought I beheld *Religion* mixing in the dance" (284).

Yorick has hardly entered the land of scarcity when he and his fellow travellers meet their first obstacle:

> Let the way-worn traveller vent his complaints upon the sudden turns and dangers of your roads—your rocks—your precipices—the difficulties of getting up—the horrors of getting down—mountains impracticable—and cataracts, which roll down great stones from their summits, and block his road up.—The peasants had been all day at work in removing a fragment of this kind between St. Michael and Madane. (285)

The presence of this massive fragment forces Yorick to spend the night in a small inn. But the fragment, obstructive though it is, is nothing compared to the mutual embarrassment of Yorick and a lady traveller when they discover that they must share the same small bedroom: "There were difficulties every way—and the obstacle of the stone in the road, which brought us into the distress, great as it appeared whilst the peasants were removing it, was but a pebble to what lay in our ways now" (287–88). This greater obstacle is accompanied by insistent words of separation (cut off, separate, barrier) and words of warfare (surrender, negotiation, proviso, articles, treaty of peace, hostilities). And yet this hostile separation leads to a connection, perhaps random and accidental, yet unmistakably there:

> . . . she had got herself into the narrow passage which separated them [the beds], and had advanc'd so far up as to be in a line betwixt her mistress and me—
> So that when I stretch'd out my hand, I caught hold of the Fille de Chambre's
>
> END OF VOL. II.   (291)

Sterne's characteristic break obscures and complicates our sense of an ending, perhaps violates it as well, but, wherever Yorick's hand has landed, some contact has occurred. The imagery of separation has been superseded by a connection, brought about—though not defined—by the equivocal syntax and vocabulary. Even in the land of scarcity and embarrassment, on his "journey of caution" (285), Yorick breaks through the barriers of decorum and reserve. The fragment in the road has led to another comic conjunction, more strained and dubious than the earlier feast of love, but also an overcoming of doubt, distance, and disaster. Both episodes confirm Sterne's description of the book as a *"Work of Redemption."*[24]

The ending of *A Sentimental Journey*, like the ending of Volume IX of *Tristram Shandy*, is ambiguous, uncertain, and open-ended. Though Sterne remarked in a letter to Garrick that "plots thicken toward the latter end of a piece,"[25] he gives us no sense of that thickening in either novel. The equivocal syntax of the last sentence of *A Sentimental Journey* and Yorick's remark about "A COCK and a BULL" (IX.xxxiii.809) suggest possible continuation at least as much as *Finis*. This openness has of course left room for controversy: is either novel really finished? would Sterne have continued them if he had lived?[26] Framing this question in a different way, however, may help us to see its implications more clearly: are the novels themselves as fragmentary as so many of their parts?

Like Marcia Allentuck, I would answer yes—but for rather different reasons. Sterne certainly is responding to and embroidering on the implications of the aesthetic of the *non-finito* and its many corollaries. He was interested in activating the imaginative powers of his readers, in part, of course, by blocking and thwarting them. He was also interested in suggesting the ways that the artificial and natural are intertwined, the necessity of artifice in suggesting and even creating the natural, the necessity of chance and the natural in creating the effects of art. But the fragmentary for Sterne always had Biblical over- tones, overtones that suggested the importance of the fragment as a gesture toward a greater fullness and as a reminder of a more perfect communion.

As Sterne says in one of his sermons, "consider the beginnings and end of things, . . . how they all conspire to baffle thee" (*Sermons,* 415). Sterne's beginnings and endings are abrupt, irregular, baffling. His novels are sketchy, incoherent, fragmentary. But the fragments are not despairing, solipsistic ges- tures toward an empty world; rather they are a response to what Sterne called "the distress of plenty" (*ASJ,* p. 268), his limitations faced with the overflow- ing and ungraspable fullness of the world. Saint Paraleipomenon, the patron of things left out (III.xxxvi.268), does indeed watch over Sterne's novels, with the God Muddle. But Sterne's gaps, leaps, blank pages, and fragments are a comic fulfillment of the command "that nothing be lost."

Notes

1. John Ferriar, *Illustrations of Sterne* (1797; rpt New York, 1971), p. 4.
2. Letter from the Reverend Robert Browne (Geneva, 25 July 1760) to John Hall Stevenson, *Letters of Laurence Sterne,* ed. L. P. Curtis (Oxford, 1935), pp. 432–33.
3. *Letters,* p. 122.
4. William Shenstone, "Unconnected Thoughts on Gardening" (1764) in *The Genius of the Place: The English Landscape Garden 1620–1800,* ed. John Dixon Hunt and Peter Willis (London, 1975), p. 289.
5. *Dialogue on Poetry and Literary Aphorisms,* trans. Ernst Behler and Roman Struc (Uni- versity Park, Pennsylvania, 1968), p. 134.
6. On eighteenth-century ruins—both artificial and natural—see Jean Starobinski, *The Invention of Liberty 1700–1789,* trans. Bernard C. Swift (Geneva, 1964), pp. 180–98, and Martin Price, *To the Palace of Wisdom* (New York, 1964), pp. 388–89.
7. "In Defense of an Unfinished *Tristram Shandy:* Laurence Sterne and the *Non-Finito,*" in *The Winged Skull: Papers from the Laurence Sterne Bicentenary Conference, University of York, 1968,* ed. Arthur H. Cash and John M. Stedmond (Kent, Ohio, 1970), p. 149.
8. Quoted from *Essays on Various Subjects of Taste and Criticism* by Eric Rothstein in his article " 'Ideal Presence' and the 'Non-Finito' in Eighteenth-Century Aesthetics," *Eighteenth- Century Studies,* 9 (1976), 307.
9. From "The Origin and Progress of Novel-Writing" in her edition of *The British Nov- elists;* quoted in *Sterne: The Critical Heritage,* ed. Alan B. Howes (London, 1974), p. 332.
10. Sterne was also aware of the dangers inherent in this technique. This explains, I think, some of his constant warnings to his readers—and also a passage in his sermon on "The Levite and his concubine": ". . . give but the outlines of a story,——let *spleen* or *prudery* snatch the pencil, and they will finish it with so many hard strokes, and with so dirty a colouring, that *candour* and *courtesy* will sit in torture as they look at it" *Sermons,* 167–68.
11. John Preston, in Chapter 7 of *The Created Self: The Reader's Role in Eighteenth Century Fiction* (London, 1970), discusses the effects, though not the sources, of this technique. Ronald Paulson, in *Emblem and Expression: Meaning in English Art of the Eighteenth Century* (London,

1975), explores the relationship between Sterne's invitations to the reader to participate and Capability Brown's gardens (p. 136) or Gainsborough's "dashes and daubs" (pp. 229–30).

12. "Fortune is often met in the path of reason" (I, 34), in *Essays,* trans. Donald M. Frame (Stanford, 1948), p. 164. For an excellent discussion of their relationship, see Jonathan Lamb, "Sterne's Use of Montaigne," *Comparative Literature,* 32 (1980), 13–15.

13. See particularly Ernst Gombrich, *Art and Illusion: A Study in the Psychology of Pictorial Representation* (Princeton, 1960), pp. 190–91, and H. W. Janson, "The Image Made by Chance in Renaissance Thought," in *16 Studies* (New York, 1973), pp. 55–69.

14. *A New Method of Assisting the Invention in Drawing Original Compositions of Landscape* (1785–1786), in A. P. Oppé, *Alexander and John Robert Cozens* (London, 1952), p. 170.

15. I borrow this phrase from Howard Anderson, "Tristram Shandy and the Reader's Imagination," *PMLA,* 86 (1971), 966–73.

16. For a brief reference to the literary implications of this passage as reflected in the Latin title of Petrarch's Rime, *Rerum vulgarium fragmenta,* see Robert M. Durling's introduction to *Petrarch's Lyric Poems* (Cambridge, 1976), p. 26. For a fuller and more searching discussion, see Ernst Zinn's article "Fragmente über Fragmente" in *Das Unvollendete als künstlerische Form,* ed. J. A. Schmoll, gen. Eisenwerth (Bern, 1959), pp. 161–69. Zinn also quotes one of the rare reverberations of the passage in the twentieth century, A. E. Housman's epitaph for a Salvation Army officer run over by a train:

> "Hallelujah!" was the only exclamation
> That escaped Lieutenant-Colonel Mary-Jane
> When she tumbled off the platform of the station
> And was cut in little pieces by the train.
> "Mary-Jane, the train is through yer . . . !"
> "Hallelujah! Hallelujah!"
> We will gather up the fragments that remain.

17. Anthony Sparrow, *Rationale upon the Book of Common Prayer* (1657; rpt Oxford, 1839), p. 122.

18. Quoted from the note on Matthew 14:20–21 (which echoes John 6:12–13 in retelling the miracle of the loaves) in *The Anchor Bible: Matthew,* ed. W. F. Albright and C. S. Mann (Garden City, NY, 1971), p. 178.

19. *The Great Exemplar of Sanctity and Holy Life,* Part II, Sect. XII (1649; rpt London, 1872), p. 361.

20. "So sind ja fleissig genug die Brocken gesammlet, auf dass nichts umkomme. Alles bleibt indessen nur Fragment." (Translation mine.) *Sämtliche Werke* II, ed. Suphan (Berlin, 1879), p. 4. In German, as Zinn points out, the word "Fragment" was also always heard in connection with 1 Cor. 13:9. Luther translates "ex parte" as a substantive, "Stückwerk," which is often used in connection with "fragment." This, however, is not the case in English.

21. *The Early Masters of English Fiction* (Lawrence, Kansas, 1956), p. 186.

22. *The Subtler Language: Critical Readings of Neoclassic and Romantic Poems* (Baltimore, 1959), p. 169.

23. In *The Winged Skull,* p. 58.

24. *Letters,* p. 398, n. 3.

25. *Letters,* p. 234.

26. See particularly Wayne Booth, "Did Sterne Complete *Tristram Shandy?*" *Modern Philology,* 48 (1951), 172–83, and Marcia Allentuck's "In Defense of an Unfinished *Tristram Shandy.*"

Sentimentality as Performance:
Shaftesbury, Sterne, and
the Theatrics of Virtue

ROBERT MARKLEY

At the beginning of the second volume of *A Sentimental Journey*, Sterne's narrator encounters a chambermaid in a Parisian bookstore. While flirting with her, Yorick slips a crown into her purse with this advice: "be but as good as thou art handsome, and heaven will fill it" (*ASJ*, 188). In this line, Sterne articulates concisely the ideological values of his sentimental narrative; the woman's goodness, beauty, and piety merit a reward that literally puts a price on her virtue. Yorick's demonstrative generosity to the chambermaid is cast in a language that is explicitly mercantile—and ideological—rather than pristinely moral or poetic. The crown he gives her, as he recognizes, is not an innocent token of his admiration but a talisman, a symbol of the values that define their relationship hierarchically: he is the freeborn English gentleman who may flatter, bribe—or even command—the French chambermaid. Money becomes the sentimentalist's medium of exchange, a palpable, materialist manifestation of good nature as a commodity.

Yorick's scene with the chambermaid is characteristic of a self-confessedly sentimental narrative that implicitly assumes and explicitly asserts the values of a middle-class culture intent on demonstrating the naturalness and benevolence of its moral authority. Instances of Yorick's charity and generosity abound in the novel; whenever Sterne wants to dramatize his hero's benevolence he has him give away his money—to chambermaids, beggars, and wandering monks. Sterne's foregrounding of the equation of money and virtue, however, seems a deceptively simple solution to a complex ideological problem: as a sentimental novelist, he attempts both to assert the "timeless" nature of a specific historical and cultural construction of virtue and to suppress his reader's recognition of the social and economic inequalities upon which this discourse of seemingly transcendent virtue is based. Like most eighteenth-century sentimental narratives, *A Sentimental Journey* suppresses

Reprinted from *The New Eighteenth Century*, ed. Felicity Nussbaum and Laura Brown (London: Methuen, 1987): 210–30.

questions about how one acquires the wealth to be able to afford one charitable act after another. The poverty and social inequality that Yorick encounters on the Continent are not described as the result of any specific economic or political conditions, any authoritarian strategies of repression, or any conscious malevolence abroad in the world; they are simply presented as opportunities for him to demonstrate his "natural," innate virtue. Paradoxically, however, the novel's commodification of "good nature" reveals the strategies it employs to ascribe an absolute and ahistorical value to particular cultural forms of self-congratulation and mystification. By emphasizing the theatrics of Yorick's generosity and by highlighting the equation of money and virtue, Sterne testifies to—and dramatizes—both his own difficulties as a half-hearted apologist for sentimentality and the tensions that inhere in a genre that is both assertive and self-consciously defensive about its claims to moral authority. In this respect, Sterne the Christian moralist coexists uneasily with Sterne the propagandist for bourgeois sensibility. Although, as many of the novel's admirers note, A Sentimental Journey comically questions naive forms of sentimental benevolence, it ultimately neither subverts nor transcends the ideology that upholds them. Unlike Tristram Shandy, it comes close to sentimentalizing the conditions of its own performance; it does not mock its generic history and narrative strategies, nor does it demythologize the genealogy of sentiment. Instead it remains caught within the ideological contradictions of sensibility—at once alert to the excesses of the genre yet seemingly powerless to offer a sustained critique of them.

I

Sentimentality—the affective spectacle of benign generosity—emerges early in the eighteenth century less as a purely "literary" phenomenon than as a series of discursive formations that describe what amounts to an aesthetics of moral sensitivity, the ways in which middle- and upper-class men can act upon their "natural," benevolent feelings for their fellow creatures. It is, as G. S. Rousseau and John Mullan have demonstrated, at least in part a masculinist complex of strategies designed to relegate women to the status of perpetual victims, biologically constrained by their hypersensitivity and emotionalism to passive suffering and sociopolitical docility. Yet at the same time sensibility valorizes masculine sensitivity as a virtue, as an indication of a "natural" sympathy possessed by men of feeling.[1] The ideology of sentiment also explicitly promotes narrowly conservative and essentialist views of class relations, implicitly identifying the victims of social inequality—men, women, and children—with "feminine" powerlessness. This strategy of rendering the victims of sentimental ideology as politically and symbolically impotent becomes a crucial means of mystifying the class prejudices and ideological imperatives that underlie the workings of sensibility. Yet this subtly coercive strategy of defusing class conflict by sentimentalizing its victims offers us a way to investigate how and why sentimentality developed as it did during the eighteenth century and to explore its myths of "natural" benevolence and class-specific virtue.

The strategies which, taken together, might be described as constitutive of sentimentality have a complex genealogy. Donald Greene's long-needed attack on R. S. Crane's "The Genealogy of 'The Man of Feeling' " has left critics of eighteenth-century sentimentality in a bind; no longer able to allude to a vaguely-defined latitudinarian tradition in the seventeenth century as the definitive origin of sensibility, we have been put in the position of having to account anew for the rise of the phenomenon we study.[2] The genealogy Greene invokes as an alternative to Crane's is, for students of eighteenth-century moral philosophy, a familiar one—he argues that sentimentality gets its start in the deistical idea of a self-sufficient virtue advocated by Anthony Ashley Cooper, Third Earl of Shaftesbury, and later by Francis Hutcheson.[3] Yet neither Greene nor other historians of sensibility have explained how Shaftesbury, a deist who mocked Christian pieties and a tireless defender of aristocratic privilege, became a seminal figure in the development of an affective, bourgeois sensibility that often explicitly invokes Christian verbal formulae, if not latitudinarian theology. Shaftesbury is no doubt a crucial influence on the development of sentimentality as both a rhetoric and a "system" of values. However, those critics who read him as a dispassionate "moral philosopher," a proponent of republican (read Whiggish) principles, or a protoromantic ignore or obscure the ideological origins of sentimentality, its genesis in the complex and uncertain relationships between aristocratic and bourgeois characterizations of virtue, power, social privilege, and moral worth. These competing reconstructions of idealized values figure prominently in the adaptation of Shaftesbury's discursive strategies by writers less interested in defending upper-class privilege than in pressing their own claims to the social status of gentlemen.

Despite the overtly polemical intentions of his work, Shaftesbury, the aristocrat and ideologue, is usually ignored by modern critics or transformed into a disinterested observer of a transhistorical human nature. Many of the twentieth-century readings of Shaftesbury one encounters are relentlessly ahistorical; they succeed in salvaging him as a "thinker" or "philosopher" only by removing him from his historical context, ignoring the two-thirds of his work given to snobbish defenses of aristocratic privilege, downplaying the warmed-over truisms of his literary criticism, and avoiding any discussion of his political and social biases.[4] By obscuring the fundamentally conservative bias of Shaftesbury's thought (or for that matter of many of the seventeenth-century latitudinarians), critics of his work and of the "men of feeling" who populate a number of eighteenth-century novels distort what Shaftesbury calls the "Sentiment of MORALS."[5] As an aristocrat, idealist, and Whig,

Shaftesbury is a historically important figure because he shifts discussions of morality and virtue away from the traditional rhetoric of religious orthodoxy to secular discourses of ideological power and privilege. In effect, he depoliticizes the seventeenth-century languages of religious conflict and helps to convert the rhetoric of goodness, tolerance, and generosity into the languages of political and moral authority, into defenses of an innate—literally, for Shaftesbury, inborn—and demonstrable virtue.

In his *Inquiry Concerning Virtue,* Shaftesbury celebrates what he perceives as the cultural and ideological bases of moral behavior. He begins by defining "virtue" in ahistorical, universal, and absolute terms; it is not a "personal" attribute of individuals but, in effect, an essential, informing principle of creation. There is, Shaftesbury asserts, "no such thing as real ILL in the Universe, nothing ILL with respect to the Whole" (II.9). Man therefore is naturally, instinctively good; social and civil order are maintained by his "natural Esteem of *Virtue,* and Detestation of *Villainy*" (II.65) rather than by the Christian fear of punishment, a belief that Shaftesbury frequently attacks. Having established the beneficence of man as a social creature, he goes on to declare that it is "the *private Interest* and *Good* of everyone, to work towards the *general Good*" (II.175). However, Shaftesbury's ideas of "everyone" and "the *general Good*" are determined, as the author acknowledges, by his aristocratic biases. Far from being disinterested ruminations on innate virtue and proper political governance, the *Inquiry,* like his other works, delimits carefully the responsibilities and privileges of "the better sort." The audience Shaftesbury envisions for his writings is, he states, "the grown *Youth* of our polite World . . . whose *Taste* may yet be form'd in *Morals;* as it seems to be, already, *in exteriour Manners and Behaviour*" (III.179). His comparison of "*Morals*" to "*Manners*" is a revealing one that echoes throughout his published and unpublished works. In *The Moralists,* for example, he characteristically equates the timeless virtues of theistic enthusiasm and his own social and political values: "To *philosophize,* in a just Signification, is but To carry *Good-Breeding* a step higher. For the Accomplishment of Breeding is, To learn whatever is *decent* in Company, or *beautiful* in Arts: and the Sum of Philosophy is, To learn what is *just* in Society, and *beautiful* in Nature, and the Order of the World" (III.161). Polished language, "*Good Breeding,*" "*Manners,*" social grace, aesthetic perfection, natural harmony, innate virtue, and universal order form a natural circuit in Shaftesbury's mind. The vocabulary that he uses to define his conception of innate goodness—the civilized man living in a just society—is frankly idealistic and insular: "The real *Honest Man* . . . is struck with that *inward* Character, the Harmony and Numbers of the Heart, and Beauty of the Affections, which form the Manners and Conduct of a truly *social* Life" (III.34). Virtue, for Shaftesbury, becomes the inward manifestation of an "aesthetic" response to life that celebrates stability and harmony within a closed, paternalistic society.

Even as he invokes an idealized realm of a society bonded by "natural Affections," then, Shaftesbury defines personal virtue and social justice as the natural prerogatives of aristocratic existence. He argues that moral authority inheres in a social structure that elevates the well-bred above "the common World of mix'd and undistinguish'd Company" (II.224). Whatever unconventional views one might want to attribute to Shaftesbury—particularly his deriding of Christianity—are ultimately a function of his unshakeable faith in an irrevocable, "natural," and transhistorical system of social stratification that has, in effect, preemptively decided questions of individual value, virtue, and responsibility, of political, economic, and cultural power. The *Characteristicks* attempts without apology to inscribe an aristocratic system of values—based on the equation of birth and worth—in the "natural" order of the universe. In this respect, the rhetoric of "republican" principles in Shaftesbury's work (frequently taken out of context and duly celebrated by his modern critics) emerges only against a backdrop of his defenses of upper-class interests and prejudices.

Consequently, Shaftesbury's statements of idealistic principle scattered throughout his works must be read contextually as part of his ideological project. In his essay on wit, for example, he describes "common sense," rather stirringly, as the *"Sense of Publick Weal,* and of the *Common Interest;* Love of the *Community* or *Society,* Natural Affection, Humanity, Obligingness, or that sort of *Civility* which rises from a just *Sense of the common Rights* of Mankind, and the *natural Equality* there is amongst those of the same Species" (I.104). But this rhetoric is hedged by its very contingency: *"Society," "Civility," "Equality,"* and his other high-sounding terms are not ahistorical ideals but culturally-specific concepts. To my mind, the more concretely Shaftesbury defines "republican" concepts like *"common Rights"* and *"Equality,"* the more they seem extensions of old-line aristocratic values. Shaftesbury's talk of liberty, for example, did not prevent him from supporting the Qualifying Bill of 1696 restricting the franchise.[6] His characteristic attitude toward his social inferiors is at best condescending, at worst frankly manipulative: "The Publick is not, on any account, to be laugh'd at, to its face; or so reprehended for its Follys, as to make it think it-self contemn'd. And what is contrary to good Breeding, is in this respect as contrary to Liberty. It belongs to Men of slavish Principles, to affect a Superiority over *the Vulgar,* and to despise *the Multitude"* (I.75–76). His argument here with ill-bred oligarchs is not over definitions of "Liberty" but over strategies to placate and control *"the Vulgar."* The "natural Affections" that he frequently invokes to justify man's capacity for goodness are, in this regard, a generic redaction of what is best in human nature, typified by the gentlemen who gather on a country estate in *The Moralists* "to talk Philosophy in . . . a Circle of good Company" (II.182); men such as these constitute "the Standard of good Company, and People of the better sort" by which writers must learn to "regulate [their] Stile" (II.165). The setting is idyllic, the exclusive nature of the company assured, and the style and substance of the dialogue correspondingly decorous. For Shaftesbury, civility, humanity, and common rights can be realized only in a harmonious, benevolent—that is, hierarchical—society. His concepts of "Liberty" and "freedom" depend on a strong aristocracy capable of checking the threats posed, on the one hand, by power-hungry monarchs, high Church clergymen, high Tory Jacobins, and Catholics; and, on the other, by the leveling tendencies of those descendants of seventeenth-century radicals for whom challenges to religious and political orthodoxies also mean challenges to hereditary privilege and the established structures of political and economic power.

Shaftesbury's rhetoric—his defense of aristocratic political and cultural authority—aspires to what Mikhail Bakhtin terms a monologic, single-voiced language. It seeks to suppress the sociopolitical differences that structure historical utterances, to restrict the dialogic nature of language to an authoritative voicing of absolute principles.[7] As one might expect then, the ideology that Shaftesbury promotes and defends is similarly holistic, ahistorical, and—from his point of view—unproblematic. Although it is relatively simple for us to demystify the ideological strategies that he promotes, we should be wary of imposing upon Shaftesbury our own sophisticated, postmodern notions of ideology—or of attributing to him any particular insight into the complex processes by which an oligarchic society sustains both its political power and the fictive constructions that support it. Unlike the radicals of the late seventeenth century (like Henry Stubbe) or the late eighteenth century (like Blake),[8] Shaftesbury champions rather than resists the fictions of univocal authority. His appeal to his contemporaries lies in his single-voiced and even simplistic defenses of privilege, his contention that power is "naturally" held by those who by birth are worthy to hold it. In this sense, his philosophical project is to educate the up-and-coming rulers of the "polite" world, to facilitate the operations of hegemonic power. Paradoxically, however, it is precisely his emphasis on educating the ruling classes that makes him an appealing figure to his bourgeois successors.

II

Shaftesbury's championing of the hegemonic cultural and political authority exercised by "the better sort" poses both ideational and rhetorical problems for his contemporaries of less exalted social standing, particularly those figures like Addison and Steele whom we associate with the "rise" of bourgeois literature in the eighteenth century. His Whiggish sentiments, his vigorous defenses of English liberty and the "ancient Constitution" provide a convenient, indeed at times seminal, vocabulary for writers as different as Hutcheson and Steele precisely because they are manifestations of a profound conservatism, a belief in the status quo as a self-generating and self-regulating ideal.[9] It is easy enough to make Shaftesbury seem a reactionary dolt by isolating snippets of his snobbish, self-congratulatory rhetoric. But, paradoxically, his equation of morals and manners holds open the possibility of enlarg-ing the ranks of "the better sort" by tacitly offering to admit those of demon-strated "virtue." At one point Shaftesbury asserts "that the Perfection of Grace and Comeliness in Action and Behaviour, can be found only among the People of a liberal Education" (II.190). It would probably be a mistake to read the last phrase as a retreat from his customary class prejudice, as any-thing other than a rephrasing of "the better sort" or "our polite World." But coming from a former student and patron of Locke, the notion that "Grace" can be acquired by "People of a liberal Education" encourages a selective mis-reading of Shaftesbury's political intentions by those writers eager to advance their claims morally and socially to the status of "the better sort." Through-out the eighteenth century, Shaftesbury is read by Thomson, Shenstone, Cowper, and others as the proponent of a virtue that mediates and, to use the word in a very narrow sense, deconstructs the differences between the mer-cantile and upper classes.[10]

If Shaftesbury assumes that generosity and sentiment are hallmarks of aristocratic privilege, his rhetoric nonetheless allows Steele and Addison, for example, to appropriate, redefine, and reapply his vocabulary for their own ideological purposes—expanding the social parameters of politeness, virtue, and moral leadership. As Terry Eagleton has argued, the *Spectator* and the *Tatler* are the "catalysts in the creation of a new ruling bloc in English society, cultivating the mercantile class and uplifting the profligate aristocracy"; they attempt to promote a "historical alliance" between the middle and upper classes that is at once political, economic, and cultural.[11] In cultural terms, sentimentality stakes the claim of the middle class to playing the role of En-gland's moral conscience. Sentiment thus represents the bourgeois usurpation of and accommodation to what formerly had been considered aristocratic pre-rogatives; in the plays of Steele, for example, it becomes a literary manifesta-tion of an ongoing attempt to reconcile aristocratic systems of value based on innate worth and patrilinear inheritance to middle-class conceptions of value based on notions of individual merit and worthy deeds. In *The Conscious Lovers,* for example, Bevil Junior, Steele's exemplary hero, is described by his father in terms that disclose both his status, as a member of the landed gen-try, as the heir to a large estate and his "bourgeois" desire to make his own way in the world: "my Son has never in the least Action, the most distant Hint or Word, valued himself upon that great estate of his Mother's, which, according to our Marriage Settlement, he has had ever since he came to Age" (I.i.34–37).[12] Sentimentality, however, has no particular claim to being the only register of this accommodation between classes. Throughout the seven-teenth and eighteenth centuries, aristocratic and mercantile classes fought, intermarried, blurred, and redefined the always unstable demarcations between old wealth and new, country landholders and urban mercantilists.[13] In this respect, sentimentality is not a simple indication of the "rise" of a monolithic bourgeois ideology but a register of the literary complexities arising from the need to come to terms with class relations seemingly perpetually in turmoil. Sentimentality manifests the anxiety of a class-stratified society trying both to assert "traditional" values and to accommodate as "gentlemen" increasing numbers of economically—if not always politically—aggressive merchants, professionals, small landowners, and moneymen. In the case of Sterne's *Sentimental Journey,* Eagleton's "historical alliance" is effected only by the middle class's trying to outrefine the aristocracy by embracing the conservative biases of a hierarchical social system, and by actively demonstrating their claims to the same kind of innate, ahistorical moral authority that had been, for Shaftesbury, the exclusive preserve of the upper classes.

Eighteenth-century sentimentalists, in this regard, must negotiate the distance between the aristocratic equation of birth and worth and the middle class's celebration of upward social and economic mobility. The similar strategies of writers otherwise as different as Steele, Sterne, and Mackenzie attempt to universalize Shaftesbury's "natural Affections," to expand the ranks of the innately virtuous and good-natured to include merchants, minor clergymen, the minor gentry, technocrats, and writers. These strategies do not subvert, radically undermine, or fundamentally realign the hereditary bases of wealth and power but seek to expand them. The class struggle between the aristocracy and the mercantile classes blurs into an accommodation that reformulates the problematic of birth and worth as a celebration of qualities that both can share. For many middle-class authors, sentimentality—the generosity of feeling—becomes their claim to a cultural power-sharing based on a liberal interpretation of "Breeding" that equates hereditary power and moral sensitivity. Steele, for example, frequently engages in rhetorical juggling acts to balance hereditary and bourgeois claims to virtue:

> I think a Man of Merit, who is derived from an Illustrious Line, is very justly to be regarded more than a Man of equal Merit who has no Claim to Hereditary Honours. Nay, I think those who are indifferent in themselves, and have nothing else to distinguish them but the Virtues of their Forefathers, are to be looked upon with a degree of Veneration even upon that account, and to be more respected than the common Run of Men who are of low and vulgar Extraction.
>
> After having thus ascribed due Honours to Birth and Parentage, I must however take Notice of those who arrogate to themselves more Honours than are due to them on this Account. The first are such who are not enough sensible that Vice and Ignorance taint the Blood, and that an unworthy Behaviour degrades, and disennobles a Man, in the Eye of the World, as much as Birth and Family aggrandize and exalt him.
>
> The second are those who believe a *new* Man of an elevated Merit is not more to be honoured than an insignificant and worthless Man who is descended from a long Line of Patriots and Heroes.[14]

Steele's rhetoric suggests something of the ideological complexity of his argument. Images of innate and acquired worth interpenetrate: the *"new* Man" is
"elevated" and "honoured"; the degenerate aristocrat "degraded" and "disen-
nobled," effectively stripped of the honor with which he was born. The rigid
class structure of Shaftesbury's thought is thus complicated, contorted, and
opened to new kinds of misreadings by writers who acknowledge hereditary
privilege but, in the course of defending its prerogatives, assert their own
claims to "elevated Merit." In this regard, if a writer cannot lay an hereditary
claim to an innate, Shaftesburian virtue, he must demonstrate that he indeed
possesses it; he must, as Steele implies, dramatize his worthiness. Yet, trapped
in the mystifications of a rhetoric that celebrates innate virtue, he cannot
allow his performance to seem—even to himself—to be a calculated act, a
put-on role; instead it must sustain the fiction that it is a "natural" expression
of his "true" self as it is manifest in the seemingly irrepressible eloquence of
his feelings and physiology.

Sentimentality, then, is neither solely a literary nor philosophical phenomenon, but a form of moral self-promotion that manifests itself in the discursive practices of a variety of literary and nonliterary genres: the novel,
moral conduct books, philosophical discourse, and, as Rousseau and Mullan
argue, medical literature.[15] What unites these disparate forms is their
authors' ideological preoccupation with emerging middle-class virtues of sensitivity, generosity, natural sympathy, health, and physical beauty. As Mullan
has demonstrated, eighteenth-century medical writers and novelists share a
common vocabulary that virtually equates hypochondria and moral sensitivity. Nervous, even debilitating, psychosomatic symptoms paradoxically
become a natural, praiseworthy demonstration of the middle- or upper-class
male's moral fitness. As a cultural phenomenon, hypochondria translates
moral polemic into an affective semiology that makes palpable the mind's
sensitivity to the body's "natural Affections." In this respect, hypochondria
becomes a half-willed performance, a theatrics of the bourgeois soul. For a
number of writers, including Steele, Richardson, and, in a different way,
Sterne, sentimental distress and affection become the outward signs—the
body's performances—of its inner virtues. Sentimentality, therefore, cannot
be reified as an abstract system of values or disembodied as passive sympathy;
it is manifest only in the concrete particularity of a noble or generous action
or in physical symptoms: tears, blushes, and palpitating hearts.

The problem that the theatrics of sentimentality raises, however, is obvious: how consciously does the sentimental actor perform his role? how voluntary (or involuntary) are his sighs, tears, and flutterings of the heart? G. A.
Starr notes that the sentimental hero is a "natural" innocent, "subjected to
ordeals and stresses of various kinds, but not to the pressure of having his
character made dependent on training, habit, and . . . other contingencies of
experience."[16] But the problematic of acting, of displaying one's "true"
nature, can never be simple or pristine. Tears and sighs, as Fielding comically

demonstrates in *Shamela,* can also be read as strategies of manipulation, as challenges by the supposedly powerless to the aristocratic structures of power that—as in Richardson's first two novels—allow the predatory Mr. B—and Lovelace to terrorize their innocent victims. Richardson, though, must face ideological problems that never trouble Shaftesbury. For the latter, style *is* nature: good breeding, manners, morals, aesthetic grace, and political authority are of a worldview compact, validated by an aristocratic ideology that verges on a metaphysic. But bourgeois sentimentality represents a deformation of this holistic ideology into an attempt to equate natural virtue with a rejection of worldly, political power. In its own terms, it cannot answer the question "Pamela or Shamela?" because its affective semiotics, its assumption that the body and soul always work in unison, cannot account for the inequalities—the discrepancies between merit and reward—of the society in which it flourishes. Richardson, for example, may try to reproduce Shaftesburian assumptions about innate virtue—Pamela is a "natural" aristocrat raised to her "rightful" place as a lady of demonstrated virtue—but without advocating an explicit form of socioeconomic validation (worth equals birth) he has no way of assuring the Fieldings among his readers that his heroine is what she seems. Like Steele, he ends up trying to straddle the claims of hereditary privilege and natural goodness; the result is that he ends by celebrating the class distinctions that the novel, at first, had seemed either to disavow or conceal.

In *A Sentimental Journey* Sterne attempts to resolve the problems of championing bourgeois virtue in a hierarchically structured society by using money as a way of assigning and confirming value. For Yorick and more problematically for his creator, cash becomes a way of suggesting a one-to-one correspondence between sentimental and monetary values, between moral worth and its outward, demonstrable, material signs: the crowns that the hero passes out to those who stir his "natural Affections." This equation of money and benevolence marks a sophisticated deployment of the ideology of class privilege, but it also complicates and extends that ideology in ways not anticipated by Steele and Richardson. Yoking money and sentimental good nature, for Sterne, is less a strategy to celebrate privilege or deceive *"the Vulgar"* than a means to dramatize and paradoxically mystify the complicity of the sentimental actor in social injustice and inequality. In one respect *A Sentimental Journey* marks the passage of sensibility from self-conscious and self-interested celebrations of hereditary privilege to the comic questioning of these biases; in Sterne's wry, satiric deflating of Yorick's pretensions to goodness we are at least part way to Blake's "mind forg'd manacles," to a recognition of the self-policing and self-repressing strategies of ideology as described by Michel Foucault.[17] But this "questioning" is hardly clearcut or self-evident. If Shaftesbury is a straightforward defender of the aristocratic faith, Sterne seems both a propagandist for bourgeois good nature and its critic; if Shaftesbury's philosophical mouthpieces are simple propagandists, Yorick seems both a virtuous innocent and a naive butt. How we define the relationship between author and narrator in *A Sentimental Journey* ultimately determines how we view its display of sentimental attributes—as straightforward, satiric, or, as I shall argue, as a complex interweaving of both.

III

Virtually all critics of *A Sentimental Journey* explicitly or implicitly describe their tasks as finding a vocabulary suitable to explaining what is going on in the novel or to justifying its status as a canonical text. In general, critics have tried one of three basic strategies: comparing the novel to *Tristram Shandy* and attacking its excesses of sentimental self-interest, as Virginia Woolf does; defending it as a satire of sentimentality, as Arthur Cash, Melvyn New, and John K. Sheriff do; or celebrating its narrative sophistication, a tactic favored (in different ways) by Jeffrey Smitten, Joseph Chadwick, and Michael Seidel.[18] None of these views, however, demystifies the coercive aspects of sentimental ideology, although Woolf's reading of the novel comes closest when she calls attention to the self-dramatizing aspects of Sterne's narrative. "His mind," she argues, "is partly on us [the readers], to see that we appreciate his goodness," and she adds that the "chief fault" of the novel "comes from Sterne's concern for our good opinion of his heart" (xiv). As Woolf recognizes, the act of writing a sentimental narrative is a kind of self-advertisement, a manipulation of the reader's response. Sentimentality, as it is culturally deployed, is paradoxically a collusive and impersonal response to the display of exemplary virtue. Our appreciation of the author's goodness makes us his collaborators: if we respond as he does, then we can appreciate not only his goodness but our own; if we applaud Yorick's generosity to the chambermaid, we also must applaud our sensitivity to his virtue. Woolf, for one, remains skeptical of this self-congratulatory aspect of *A Sentimental Journey*: "instead of being convinced of the tenderness of Sterne's heart—which in *Tristram Shandy* was never in question—we begin to doubt it. For we feel that Sterne is thinking of himself" (xiii). For Chadwick, Lamb, and Seidel, the discourses of sentimentality frequently elicit a similarly ambiguous response; all three argue, albeit in different ways, that *A Sentimental Journey* suspends the reader between recognizing the hero's innocent virtue and the novelist's skillful manipulation, between passion and theater. As they suggest, the problems of interpretation are crucial in the novel, but these difficulties are less the result of narrative technique than of the ethical and ideological quandaries that define the sentimental novel.

In his sermons, Sterne frequently calls attention to the disparities between the injunctions of Christian religion and the ways of an imperfect world. As Cash and Sheriff argue, Sterne preaches a traditional brand of ethics:

> Could christianity . . . engage us, as its doctrine requires, to go on and exalt our natures, and, after the subduction of the most unfriendly of our passions, to plant, in the room of them, all those (more natural to the soil) humane and benevolent inclinations, which, in imitation of the perfections of God, should dispose us to extend our love and goodness to our fellow-creatures, according to the extent of our abilities;—in like manner, as the goodness of God extends itself over all the works of the creation:—could this be accomplished,—the world would be worth living in. (*Sermons*, 384)

Henry Mackenzie, the author of the often misunderstood and disparaged novel, *The Man of Feeling,* makes explicit the practical problems that arise from trying to live according to both the dictates of Christian ethics and the demands of social existence. This "war of duties," he argues, produces the unrealistic and potentially dangerous "species [of the novel] called sentimental" that subordinates socially-constructed "truth and reason" to idealistic visions of sensibility: "The virtues of justice, of prudence, of economy, are put in competition with the exertions of generosity, of benevolence, and of compassion."[19] Significantly, this "competition," as Mackenzie's phrasing implies, must elevate the bourgeois, capitalist virtues of "justice," "prudence," and "economy" over sentimental virtues that in themselves are admirable but that, as he demonstrates in *The Man of Feeling,* are naive and impractical in a postlapsarian world.

For Sterne, the discrepancies between Christian and capitalist values in *A Sentimental Journey* are not easy to reconcile. In some respects, his dilemma is characteristic of the competing reconstructions of Christianity that emerge in seventeenth and eighteenth-century England; religious debate from the reformation through the nineteenth century is the site of often overt ideological battles among the upper, middle, and lower classes. Christian doctrines are invoked, depending on the speaker's or writer's political leanings, to justify conservative defenses of the status quo, liberal apologies for gradual socioeconomic "progress," and calls to radical social action. Anglican theology in the late seventeenth and eighteenth centuries is used to justify both the fictions that equate birth and worth and those that assert that virtue is acquired rather than inborn.[20] In the context of Sterne's theological concerns, the problems of interpretation posed by *A Sentimental Journey* reflect the ideological ambiguities that result from the internal divisiveness of the ideology of sentiment, its attempt to hold on to Christian ethics and to promote the kind of materialist virtues that Mackenzie celebrates. The fact that both Christian ethics and capitalist virtue are themselves the sites of ideological conflict between notions of aristocratic prerogative and bourgeois merit only complicates Sterne's narrative problems in *A Sentimental Journey* further.

The very ambiguity that the novel engenders encourages the author to try to "resolve" these conflicts by repeating his litanies of the hero's sentimental acts. For Sterne, the accumulation of Yorick's gestures of sympathy and generosity becomes a deliberate strategy to reassure those of us who, like Woolf, begin to doubt the sincerity of a character who keeps telling us how sincere he is. But this strategy is itself double-edged: it calls attention to both the hero's generosity and to the inequalities of a fallen world that renders acts of charity as marginal or ineffective attempts to embody a radically idealized Christian ethics. Sterne's theatrics of bourgeois virtue, then, are devoted paradoxically to demonstrating the sensitivity of a culture that shies away from acknowledging its responsibility for inflicting upon its victims the very injuries that it mourns and pities but does little to alleviate. The novelist cannot resolve the contradictory bases of sentimental ideology but only restage and restate them. Therefore, the more uncomfortable the reader feels about the tendentious display of sentimental affection, the more necessary it becomes for the reader to witness additional demonstrations of sentimental morality in operation.

I would read *A Sentimental Journey,* then, as a series of strategies designed to mystify the contradictory impulses of sentimentality, to celebrate and mock Yorick's faith in human nature, and to attempt to reconcile ideas of innate virtue with demonstrations of moral worth. One of the primary means that Sterne employs to effect this reconstruction is to recast traditional forms of discourse, turning, for example, the rhetoric of courtly address to the task of dramatizing his hero's good nature. In his encounter with the chambermaid, Yorick describes their relationship in the outmoded forms of feudal rhetoric: she pays him "submissive attention" and offers him "more a humble courtesy [curtsy] than a low one" (188, 189).[21] Yorick's use of this language of courtly submission emphasizes the self-centered and exaggerated aspects of his sentimental affection; his rhetoric blinds him to her "true," sexually-experienced nature. He turns his "feelings" into a form of discourse incapable of registering departures from a simple-minded benevolence. His apostrophe to the peasants of Savoy near the end of the novel indicates that the only way he can describe social inequality and suffering is to invoke a warmed-over Shaftesburian rhetoric that trivializes what it describes: "Poor, patient, quiet, honest people! fear not; your poverty, the treasury of your simple virtues, will not be envied you by the world, nor will your vallies be invaded by it"(285). These "simple virtues" are, in effect, the rationalization of a middle-class culture that cannot reconcile its virtuous self-image with its dependence on economic inequality. Yorick's moral intentions are perhaps laudable, but Sterne, like Mackenzie, implies that moral idealism does not translate into the active, bourgeois virtues of justice, prudence, and economy.

The self-absorption implicit in the hero's narrative voice limits the responses—both individual and cultural—that his brand of sentimentality calls forth. On his way to Paris, Yorick is accosted by a group of beggars. One by one, he describes the beggars and gives some of them a sous each in what he describes as "the first publick act of my charity in France" (132). When he thinks he has finished, however, he finds that he

> had overlook'd a *pauvre honteux,* who had no one to ask a sous for him, and who, I believed, would have perish'd, ere he could have ask'd one for himself: he stood by the chaise a little without the circle, and wiped a tear from a face which I thought had seen better days—Good God! said I—and I have not one single sous left to give him—But you have a thousand! cried all the powers of nature, stirring within me—so I gave him—no matter what—I am ashamed to say *how much,* now—and was ashamed to think, how little, then: so if the reader can form any conjecture of my disposition, as these two fixed points are given him, he may judge within a livre or two what was the precise sum. (133–34)

Our attention in this passage, as throughout the scene, is focused on the mind and "nature" of the sentimental hero, not on the objects of his generosity. Significantly, Yorick leaves the exact amount he gives to this *"pauvre honteux"* up to the reader. By judging correctly the sum that Yorick gives, we are implicated in his act of charity and implicitly asked to judge our own moral goodness by the amount of our estimate. We are subtly but effectively coerced into sharing in the hero's demonstrative triumph over the forces of miserly ill nature.

The object of Yorick's charity, though, seems carefully selected. He has no name, no independent existence other than as the recipient of the hero's generosity, and, unlike the other beggars, he remains silent and suitably embarrassed by his poverty (note that *"honteux"* may carry the double meaning of ashamed and disgraced). In this regard, he is the perfect sentimental victim—inarticulate, passive, and anonymous—less an individual than an idealized object of pity. Yet he touches Yorick's heart precisely because he seems once to have "seen better days"; he is the victim of an unnamed bad fortune that, significantly, Sterne chooses to leave unexplored. As a man without a history, this figure becomes an embodiment of the disgrace of poverty: he is not simply an outsider but a projection of the narrator's unstated fears, a nightmare image of the sensitive, generous individual stripped of his only means—money—of demonstrating his goodness in a mercantile society. Left penniless, this apparently good individual becomes pathetic rather than noble, his good nature imprisoned by his poverty.

The gift of money, then, assumes a complex double function: it provides a seemingly straightforward economy of sentiment, the value of the charitable act serving as an indication of the sentimentalist's nature, and it ensures that the transaction, the exchange of currency, allows both giver and receiver to retain their anonymity. In Sterne's sentimental economy, money replaces the reciprocal obligations (at least in theory) of feudal, aristocratic society that to some extent are still resonant in Shaftesbury's kid-gloves treatment of *"the*

Vulgar." The anonymity of his cash transactions serves to distance Yorick from the objects of his charity, like the *"pauvre honteux,"* even as he proclaims his sympathy for them. In one sense, his sentimental generosity allows him to assent tacitly to the bourgeois fiction that one's comparative wealth is a valid indication of both one's moral worth and social value. Yet neither Yorick nor the reader can persist in this daydream for long; paradoxically the ideological function of sentimental charity must be seen to be imperfect to justify its existence: if possessing money were an unambiguous indication of each individual's intrinsic worth, there would be no moral obligation for the sentimentalist to give away anything. Sterne's narrative, in this regard, works to disclose as well as to conceal the ideological workings of charity, leaving Yorick open, as in his encounter with the chambermaid, to the reader's suspicions that he is acting out of self-interest or hopes for sexual profit. His acts of charity at once construct and demystify the middle-class sentimentalists's fictions of depoliticized virtue in a society still ruled, to a large extent, by hereditary privilege.[22]

There is, then, in Sterne's depiction of his hero's encounters with the beggars a necessary suppression of political consciousness, a generic lack of interest in the causes of poverty. Yet we must again be careful to distinguish between the author and narrator. Sterne allows his readers to see that his hero's responses, however good-natured, are inadequate to the task of correcting the misfortunes he encounters; yet the novelist can provide no vocabulary to redress the social and economic injustices that he depicts. Sterne the Christian moralist can offer only a naive sentimentality that he implies is insufficient, yet that can never transcend limited and limiting acts of isolated, individual charity. Yorick, when he fears that his lack of a passport may land him in the Bastille, admits his inability to imagine the suffering of the poor as anything but an individual misfortune:

> I was going to begin with the millions of my fellow creatures born to no inheritance but slavery; but finding, however affecting the picture was, that I could not bring it near me, and that the multitude of sad groups in it did but distract me.—
>
> —I took a single captive, and having first shut him up in his dungeon, I then look'd through the twilight of his grated door to take his picture. (201)

The description that follows portrays the prisoner in gothic dejection, although the tone of the passage wryly undercuts the narrator's stance by making him too moved to continue with his imaginative rendering: "But here my heart began to bleed—and I was forced to go on with another part of the portrait" (202). The prisoner's plight, however, makes sense to Yorick only as it affects him emotionally. The portrait, like the description of the beggars, generates sympathy in direct proportion to the helplessness and passivity of the victim. Sentimentality here operates by a straightforward calculus: the more pathetic the victim, the greater the hero's generosity, and the more affecting the scene.

The hero's imaginary prisoner is an apt image of the isolation and powerlessness of suffering in *A Sentimental Journey*. Yorick cannot bring the sufferings of "millions of [his] fellow creatures" close to home because he—and Sterne— are ideologically constrained by a culture which refuses to acknowledge the legitimacy of a vocabulary to describe large-scale political oppression. The prisoner must be romanticized and isolated from his "millions" of fellow creatures because otherwise he would lose his status as a helpless victim: one unfortunate individual engenders sympathetic tears; "millions" pose a threat to the class-based ideologies of the mid-eighteenth century that seek to identify privilege with both hereditary nobility and demonstrated bourgeois virtue. As the representative of "the multiple of sad groups" excluded from political and economic power, Yorick's "single captive" presents a more complex image—and more of a potential threat to social stability—than the faceless multitude that Shaftesbury assumes it is his birthright to outwit. That this individualized victim is imprisoned not only makes him a pitiable victim but also effectively isolates him from his fellow "millions," from any possibility of concerted and collective political action. His isolation, therefore, testifies to the radical potential of the bourgeois ideology of individual merit: if no individual is innately superior to another, then the unpropertied and unfortunate classes of Europe have as good a claim as their "betters" to a share of wealth and political power. Yorick's "millions" can no longer be consigned to servitude solely because they are low-born; and, in an important sense, the ideology of sentiment may be seen as a complex network of relationships designed to guard against the revolutionary implications of middle-class justifications for social climbing. To move, then, from Shaftesbury's condescension to *"the Vulgar"* to Sterne's sympathy for an individual captive is implicitly to reject aristocratic arguments for the "natural" hierarchy of class relations; but what the latter cannot do is to transform his imaginary prisoner into "millions." To do so would be to move from sentiment to social injustice, from pity to either outrage or fear, and from passive sympathy to the spectres of outright repression and revolutionary action.

In this sense, sentimentality can exist, in whatever narrative forms it assumes, only in societies in which money and power are unequally distributed, only where persons of potential moral "worth" suffer "unjustly," that is without regard to their (potential) intrinsic merit. Yorick feels most pity for those who have fallen from a state of bourgeois grace: "to see so many miserables, by force of accidents driven out of their own proper class into the very verge of another, which it gives me pain to write down" (174–75). If sentiment does not have a victim to pity it must, in effect, create one hyperbolically. In a passage which seems comically to recall Shaftesbury's effusions Yorick offers an apostrophe to hypersensitivity:

—Dear sensibility! source inexhausted of all that's precious in our joys, or costly in our sorrows! thou chainest thy martyr down upon his bed of straw— and 'tis thou who lifts him up to HEAVEN—eternal fountain of our feelings!— 'tis here I trace thee—and this is thy divinity which stirs within me——not, that in some sad and sickening moments, *"my soul shrinks back upon herself, and startles at destruction"*—mere pomp of words!—but that I feel some generous joys and generous cares beyond myself—all comes from thee, great—great SENSORIUM of the world! which vibrates, if a hair of our heads but falls upon the ground, in the remotest desert of thy creation. (277–78)

The ambiguity, the problems of interpretation that Chadwick locates at the center of our experience of reading Sterne's novel seem, in this passage, to spring from ironies of disproportion and exaggeration. The metaphors which undergird this passage are economic—"precious" and "costly"—and they subtly belie the narrator's attempt to elevate sensibility to a divine hypersensitivity to falling hairs. The trivial nature of the final image brings us back to the problem of value: "sensibility" can only affix value by hyperbole, the debts and credits of small acts that carry the narrator "beyond" himself but that ironically confirm his role in a hierarchical society. The theatrics of sentimental virtue preclude any action to alleviate the suffering of the poor beyond doling out money and self-consciously recording the amount to keep one's accounts in order in the "divine" ledger book of bourgeois morality.

IV

Given the divided and divisive ideological structure of sentimentality noted by Mackenzie, it is hardly surprising that the narrative structure of *A Sentimental Journey* is, as Seidel argues, itself problematic. The class biases of sentiment—evident in Hume's bald-faced assurance that the "skin, pores, muscles, and nerves of a day-labourer are different from those of a man of quality: So are his sentiments, actions, and manners"[23]—has a profound effect on the artistic forms in which sensibility is couched. In the drama sentimentality reflexively validates its claims to moral authority, often by yoking bourgeois sensitivity to the ideology of patrilineal privilege. In *The Conscious Lovers,* to take only one example, the action onstage is designed to confirm Bevil Junior's intrinsic worth, his ability to transcend the social clichés of dissolute idleness and sexual irresponsibility that had defined his rakish ancestors on the late seventeenth-century stage. In the Prologue (written by Steele's friend, the poet Leonard Welsted) the audience is told " *'Tis yours* [that is, your responsibility], *with Breeding to refine the Age / To Chasten Wit, and Moralize the Stage,"* and later that the sentimental hero is *"the Champion of your Virtues"* (27–28, 30). Like most sentimental comedies in the early eighteenth century, *The Conscious Lovers* works hard to flatter its audience by reassuring them of their virtues and, in effect, telling them what they already know. It does not interrogate the bases of Bevil Junior's heroism; it simply offers him as an exemplar of virtue, a model for the audience to emulate.[24]

In the novel, however, repetitive demonstrations of the man of feeling's good nature quickly grow wearisome; as Mackenzie notes, sentimentality is interesting not primarily in and of itself but in its effects and contexts, in the clash between the values of idealistic self-absorption and capitalist self-interest.[25] In *A Sentimental Journey,* Sterne's device of the journey works against the generic clichés of the private spaces of the sentimental novel by thrusting his hero into the world, a tactic Mackenzie also employs in *The Man of Feeling.*[26] Yorick is, at least part of the time, a picaresque hero, who delights in the unexpected and the comic: "I count little of the many things I see pass at broad noon day, in large and open streets.—Nature is shy, and hates to act before spectators; but in such an unobserved corner, you sometimes see a single short scene of her's worth all the sentiments of a dozen French plays compounded together" (257). The result in *A Sentimental Journey* is a marriage of convenience between picaresque imitations of nature and sentimental displays akin to the kind of Christian idealism that Sterne preached on Sunday mornings. The theory underlying Sterne's experiment is articulated by the old French Officer whom Yorick meets at the opera: "there is a balance . . . of good and bad every where; and nothing but the knowing it is so can emancipate one half of the world from the prepossessions which it holds against the other—that the advantage of travel, as it regarded the *sçavoir vivre,* was by seeing a great deal both of men and manners; it taught us mutual toleration; and mutual toleration . . . taught us mutual love" (181). But this ideal, which the narrator enthusiastically embraces, inverts the picaresque tradition that Sterne had found and admired in Cervantes. The notion of the sentimental traveler transforms the cunning of the picaresque hero into something approaching the innocence of Candide. But Sterne, unlike Voltaire, cannot bring himself to play innocence strictly for laughs. In his novel sympathetic observation displaces satiric critique; a self-centered moral sensitivity apparently implies a kind of epistemological lethargy on the narrator's part. It is tempting to say that *A Sentimental Journey* ends where Yorick had first "ended" at the beginning of *Tristram Shandy*—at the black page. If sentimentality is not a dead end, it is a discrete moment that can provide the impetus only for reflection, not action. Like Yorick, whose death in *Tristram Shandy* marks a temporary exit, the sentimental moment is always waiting in the wings for Sterne to bring it back onstage. Sentimental theatrics verge on idylls of benevolence; precisely because they seek to suppress the contingencies on which their values depend, they have no history, no means of investigating the interstices of character and ideology. They provide only the kind of repetitive tableaux we find presented in both *A Sentimental Journey* and *The Man of Feeling.*

Sterne's decision to inscribe the sentimental novel in a parody of the picaresque mode is an ideologically revealing one; it suggests strongly that sensibility lends itself only to paratactic structures that undermine the fictions of socioeconomic and technological progress promoted by the Whiggish ideology of Addison, Steele, and Locke. Because Yorick's travels provide neither a satiric anatomy of society's foibles nor an epistemological quest for self-knowledge, his narrative can reach no conclusion; it can only stop. Had Sterne lived to write another two or ten volumes of *A Sentimental Journey,* the narrative "end" would likely have been the same. Generically, the only conclusions that sentimental novels can reach are either the hero's death (*The Man of Feeling*) or the improbable conversions of bourgeois "prudence" and "economy" into the millenarian Christian ethics that Sterne envisions when he imagines his parishioners acting "in imitation of the perfections of God" (Dickens's *A Christmas Carol,* for example). Ideologically, there is no other option. This may sound as though I have junked a dialogic, Bakhtinian notion of "ideology" for a more deterministic reading of the relations between eighteenth-century socioeconomic conditions and literary products. I do not think I have. The ideological constraints upon the sentimental novel in general and upon *A Sentimental Journey* in particular limit what can be done in the genre. Committed to defending the ideological structures of class prejudice, Sterne and Mackenzie can dramatize their heroes' benevolence but cannot convince either themselves or their readers that good nature is sufficient to correct the ways of a corrupt and unjust world.

Sentimentality may at times seem to represent the cry for a soul in a mechanistic age, but it also demonstrates, as Mackenzie maintains, the powerlessness and impracticality of the very benevolence it attempts to valorize. Sterne is less vocal than Steele, for example, in proclaiming that virtue is a function of social class, but the implications of *A Sentimental Journey* are that the radical ethicizing of Sunday morning sermons does not lead to selfless charity but to self-absorbed and self-congratulatory mystifications of inequality. In this respect, sentimentality represents the displacement of Christian ethics into Shaftesburian class prejudices, into myths that the world is as it should be and that individual actions, however nobly intended, matter very little when it comes to the "millions" of victims of poverty and injustice. Both Sterne and Yorick are confronted by the paradoxical impasse of sentimental morality: the more you give, the more virtuous you become, although your actions leave you with less and therefore limit your capacity to keep on demonstrating your virtue. His generosity dramatizes the sentimentalist's dilemma: his gifts do more to ennoble him than to assist those who receive his money. The tragic, rather than pathetic, undercurrents in *A Sentimental Journey* may lie in Sterne's implicit recognition that however much he would like to distance himself from his hero's naive benevolence, he can suggest no alternative to an ideology that can neither interrogate nor change the socioeconomic injustices that its "virtues" promote.

Notes

1.   See G. S. Rousseau, "Nerves, Spirits and Fibres: Towards the Origin of Sensibility," in R. F. Brissenden, ed., *Studies in the Eighteenth Century III* (Canberra: Australian National University Press, 1975), pp. 137–57; and John Mullan, "Hypochondria and Hysteria: Sensibility and the Physicians," *The Eighteenth Century: Theory and Interpretation* 25 (1984): 141–74.

2.   Donald Greene, "Latitudinarianism and Sensibility: The Genealogy of the 'Man of Feeling' Reconsidered," *Modern Philology* 75 (1977): 159–83. R. S. Crane's article, "The Genealogy of 'The Man of Feeling,' " appeared in *ELH* 1 (1934): 205–30. Greene had been attacked and Crane defended by Frans de Bruyn, "Latitudinarianism and Its Importance as a Precursor of Sensibility," *JEGP* 80 (1981): 349–68; de Bruyn, however, redefines "latitudinarianism" so broadly—as a "widespread 'supra-denominational' influence" (352)—that it encompasses virtually all forms of moderate and liberal Christianity. John K. Sheriff in *The Good-Natured Man: The Evolution of a Moral Ideal, 1660–1800* (University, Ala.: University of Alabama Press, 1982) notes perceptively that, given their differing descriptions of "latitudinarianism," the views of Greene and de Bruyn are "not necessarily contradictory" (105n). As my discussion indicates, I am sympathetic to Sheriff's account of the tensions that exist between traditional Christian emphases on an active virtue and the sentimental self-absorption in one's own "good nature" as an end in itself. On this problem see also Louis Bredvold, *The Natural History of Sensibility* (Detroit: Wayne State University Press, 1962).

3.   See Sheriff, *Good-Natured Man,* pp. 1–18; and Chester Chapin, "Shaftesbury and the Man of Feeling," *Modern Philology* 81 (1983): 47–50.

4.   I have noted my disagreements with some of these critics in "Style as Philosophical Structure: The Contexts of Shaftesbury's *Characteristicks,*" in Robert Ginsberg, ed., *The Philosopher as Writer: The Eighteenth Century* (Cranbury, N.J.: Associated University Presses for Susquehanna University Press, 1987). Two recent works are representative of this approach to Shaftesbury's work: Robert Voitle's biography, *The Third Earl of Shaftesbury, 1671–1715* (Baton Rouge: Louisiana State University Press, 1984) and David Marshall's study, *The Figure of the Theater: Shaftesbury, Defoe, Adam Smith, and George Eliot* (New York: Columbia University Press, 1986), pp. 13–70. One valuable exception to these readings of Shaftesbury is Lawrence Klein, "The Third Earl of Shaftesbury and the Progress of Politeness," *Eighteenth-Century Studies* 18 (1984–85): 186–214.

5.   All quotations from Shaftesbury's published works are from the sixth edition of *Characteristicks of Men, Manners, Opinions, Times,* 3 vols. (London, 1737–38), and will be cited by volume and page number in the text. This edition follows the authoritative second edition and includes the late but significant "Letter Concerning Design."

6.   See Voitle, *Shaftesbury,* pp. 75–76.

7.   See Mikhail Bakhtin, *The Dialogic Imagination,* ed. Michael Holquist; trans. Caryl Emerson and Michael Holquist (Austin: University of Texas Press, 1981), esp. pp. 264–66, 298–300. There are numerous discussions of Bakhtin's writings on the relationship between discourse and ideology. See particularly Susan Stewart, "Shouts on the Street: Bakhtin's Anti-Linguistics," *Critical Inquiry* 10 (1983): 265–69; Caryl Emerson, "The Outer Word and Inner Speech: Bakhtin, Vygotsky, and the Internalization of Language," *Critical Inquiry* 10 (1983): 245–64; Laurie Finke, "The Rhetoric of Marginality: Why I Do Feminist Theory," *Tulsa Studies in Women's Literature* 5 (1986): 251–72; and Robert Markley, *Two-Edg'd Weapons: Style and Ideology in the Comedies of Etherege, Wycherley, and Congreve* (Oxford: Clarendon Press, 1988), chap. 1.

8.   On Stubbe, see J. R. Jacob, *Henry Stubbe: Radical Protestantism and the Early Enlightenment in England* (Cambridge: Cambridge University Press, 1983). On Blake, see particularly David Gross, " 'Mind-Forg'd Manacles': Hegemony and Counter-Hegemony in Blake," *The Eighteenth Century: Theory and Interpretation* 27 (1986): 3–25.

9. See Francis Hutcheson, *An Inquiry Concerning the Original of Our Ideas of Virtue or Moral Good* (London, 1725) for a defense of Shaftesbury's doctrine of innate goodness. Shaftesbury's *Characteristicks* went through eleven editions before 1790. For his influence on James Thomson, William Shenstone, and John Gilbert Cooper, see Chapin, "Shaftesbury and the Man of Feeling," pp. 47–50.

10. See Chapin, "Shaftesbury" pp. 47–50; and Sheriff, *Good-Natured Man,* pp. 6–10, 16–17.

11. Terry Eagleton, *The Function of Criticism: From "The Spectator" to Post-Structuralism* (London: Verso, 1984), p. 11.

12. *The Plays of Richard Steele,* ed. Shirley Strum Kenny (Oxford: Clarendon Press, 1971).

13. The literary implications of this process in the eighteenth century have been studied by a number of critics. See particularly Ian Watt, *The Rise of the Novel: Studies in Defoe, Richardson, and Fielding* (London: Chatto & Windus, 1957); Maximillian Novak, *Economics and the Fiction of Daniel Defoe* (Berkeley: University of California Press, 1962); James H. Bunn, "The Aesthetics of British Mercantilism," *New Literary History* 11 (1980): 303–21; Michael McKeon, "Marxist Criticism and *Marriage à la Mode,*" *The Eighteenth Century: Theory and Interpretation* 24 (1983): 141–62; and Richard Braverman, "Capital Relations and *The Way of the World,*" *ELH* 52 (1985): 133–58.

14. *The Guardian* 137, 18 August 1713.

15. See Rousseau, "Nerves, Spirits and Fibres," esp. pp. 137–48; and Mullan, "Hypochondria," pp. 141–74.

16. G. A. Starr, "Sentimental De-Education," in *Augustan Studies: Essays in Honor of Irvin Ehrenpreis,* ed. Douglas Lane Patey and Timothy Keegan (Cranbury, N.J.: Associated University Presses for Delaware University Press, 1985), p. 254.

17. See particularly Michel Foucault's arguments in *The Order of Things* (New York: Pantheon, 1970), and Volume One of *The History of Sexuality,* trans. Robert Hurley (New York: Pantheon, 1978).

18. Virginia Woolf, introduction to *A Sentimental Journey* (rpt. London: Oxford University Press, 1967), pp. v–xvii; Arthur Cash, *Sterne's Comedy of Moral Sentiments: The Ethical Dimension of the Journey* (Pittsburgh: Dusquesne University Press, 1966); Melvyn New, *Laurence Sterne as Satirist: A Reading of "Tristram Shandy"* (Gainesville: University of Florida Press, 1969), pp. 43–46; Sheriff, *Good-Natured Man,* esp. pp. 49–53, 77–81; Jeffrey Smitten, "Spatial Form as Narrative Technique in *A Sentimental Journey,*" *Journal of Narrative Technique* 5 (1975): 208–18, and his "Gesture and Expression in Eighteenth-Century Fiction: *A Sentimental Journey,*" *Modern Language Studies* 9, 3 (1979): 85–97; Joseph Chadwick, "Infinite Jest: Interpretation in Sterne's *A Sentimental Journey,*" *Eighteenth-Century Studies* 12 (1978–79): 190–205; Michael Seidel, "Narrative Crossings: Sterne's *A Sentimental Journey,*" *Genre* 18 (1985): 1–22. For other important views of the novel see Eve Kosofsky Sedgwick, "Sexualism and the Citizen of the World: Wycherley, Sterne, and Male Homosocial Desire," *Critical Inquiry* 11 (1984): 238–44; Jonathan Lamb, "Language and Hartleian Associationism in *A Sentimental Journey,*" *Eighteenth-Century Studies* 13 (1980): 285–312; Arnold E. and Cathy N. Davidson, "Yorick contra Hobbes: Comic Synthesis in Sterne's *A Sentimental Journey,*" *Centennial Review* 21 (1977): 282–93; and Gardner Stout, Jr., "Yorick's *Sentimental Journey:* A Comic 'Pilgrim's Progress' for the Man of Feeling," *ELH* 30 (1963): 395–412.

19. *The Lounger,* 18 June 1785; cited in Sheriff, *Good-Natured Man,* p. 82. Sheriff provides a valuable reading of *The Man of Feeling* as a critique of sentimental excess, pp. 81–87.

20. See particularly Gerald R. Cragg, *The Church and the Age of Reason, 1648–1789* (New York: Atheneum, 1961); and, for the seventeenth-century background, Christopher Hill, *The World Turned Upside Down: Radical Ideas during the English Revolution* (rpt. Harmondsworth: Penguin, 1975).

21.   On the survival of courtly forms of address in the eighteenth century see Carey McIntosh, *Common and Courtly Language: The Stylistics of Social Class in Eighteenth-Century British Literature* (Philadelphia: University of Pennsylvania Press, 1985), pp. 69–101.

22.   See John Cannon's revisionist account of class relations in the eighteenth century, *Aristocratic Century: The Peerage of Eighteenth-Century England* (Cambridge: Cambridge University Press, 1984).

23.   David Hume, *A Treatise of Human Nature,* ed. P. H. Nidditch (Oxford: Clarendon Press, 1978), p. 402. Seidel also calls attention to this passage.

24.   On the problem of how audiences were intended to respond to dramatic characters in the late seventeenth and eighteenth centuries, see Rose Zimbardo, "Imitation to Emulation: 'Imitation of Nature' from the Restoration to the Eighteenth Century," *Restoration* 2 (1978): 2–9.

25.   See Mackenzie's letter to Elizabeth Rose of 18 July 1769; quoted in Sheriff, *Good-Natured Man,* p. 89.

26.   On the "private spaces" of the eighteenth-century novel see Christina Marsden Gillis, "Private Room and Public Space: The Paradox of Form in Clarissa," *Studies on Voltaire and the Eighteenth Century* 176 (1979): 153–68.

The Pentecostal Moment in
A Sentimental Journey

Elizabeth Kraft

Toward the end of Laurence Sterne's *A Sentimental Journey,* a section entitled "The Act of Charity" finds Yorick deriving, he says, a moral lesson from a short scene enacted by a beggar and "two upright vestal sisters" in a passage near the opera. These women at first resist the beggar's appeal for charity, but in the end they each give him a "twelve sous piece" (*ASJ,* 258). As Yorick discovers, what changes their minds, what softens their hearts, is the "delicious essence" of flattery (260). Sometimes, Yorick notes, such a scene is "worth all the sentiments of a dozen French plays compounded together"; sometimes, he admits, "I . . . make my sermon" out of such a scene (257). "[A]nd for the text," he reveals, "'Capadosia, Pontus and Asia, Phrygia and Pamphilia'—is as good as any one in the Bible" (257). For most readers today, I imagine this passage is fairly meaningless, and even eighteenth-century readers, though they at least heard the text read during Whitsunday services once a year, may have had few emotional or spiritual associations with the list of geographical names that comprises Acts 2:9–10.[1] Both then and now, readers of *A Sentimental Journey* would be justified in finding Yorick's comment simply an assertion that many verses in the Bible can serve as the text for a sermon about charity. To extract that general sense of the passage does not require musing over the biblical text.

In any event, we are soon distracted by the act of charity itself, performed because the beggar compliments the women: "What is it but your goodness and humanity which makes your bright eyes so sweet, that they outshine the morning even in this dark passage? and what was it which made the Marquis de Santerre and his brother say so much of you both as they just pass'd by?" (*ASJ,* 259). What is such charity, we are led to wonder, but self-indulgence, selfish vanity? Such flattery may indeed make the self-centered charitable, but it may also make the chaste unvirtuous: "the beggar gain'd two twelve-sous pieces—and they can best tell the rest, who have gain'd much greater matters by it" (260).

This essay was written specifically for this volume and appears here for the first time.

In revisiting the opening situation of Yorick's journey, in which he himself is moved to a charitable act by sexual attraction, this scene with the beggar and the women seems to offer a repudiation of the notion, advanced in the opening episode and in other scenes throughout, that love (self-love or sexual love that is in part born of selfish desire) is a sure foundation for acts of charity. In his definitive statement of this principle, Yorick maintains, "if ever I do a mean action, it must be in some interval betwixt one passion and another: whilst this interregnum lasts, I always perceive my heart locked up—I can scarce find in it, to give Misery a sixpence; and therefore I always get out of it as fast as I can, and the moment I am rekindled, I am all generosity and good will again; and would do any thing in the world either for, or with any one, if they will but satisfy me there is no sin in it" (*ASJ*, 128–29). But in this later scene we are led to wonder, can there be no sin in such self-flattery? Are not acts of charity that are the byproducts of desire invalid and unreliable by definition? I believe these questions—and, indeed, the broader question of Sterne's serious moral purpose in what he labeled his "*Work of Redemption*"—can best be answered by exploring the themes of Pentecost to which we are directed by Yorick's invocation of Acts 2.[2]

PENTECOST AND THE EIGHTEENTH CENTURY

The story of Pentecost, related in the second chapter of Acts, tells of the apostles gathered "with one accord in one place": "Suddenly there came a sound from heaven as of a rushing mighty wind, and it filled all the house where they were sitting" (2:1–2). Tongues of fire descend on the disciples "and they were all filled with the Holy Ghost, and began to speak with other tongues, as the Spirit gave them utterance" (2:4). The story of this miracle soon draws a crowd:

> And there were dwelling at Jerusalem Jews, devout men, out of every nation under heaven. Now when this was noised abroad, the multitude came together, and were confounded, because that every man heard them speak in his own language. And they were all amazed and marvelled, saying one to another, Behold, are not all these which speak Galileans? And how hear we every man in our own tongue, wherein we were born? Pärthians, and Medes, and Elamites, and the dwellers in Mesopotamia, and in Judea, and Cappadocia, in Pontus, and Asia, Phrygia, and Pamphylia, in Egypt, and in the parts of Libya about Cyrene, and strangers of Rome, Jews and proselytes, Cretes and Arabians, we do hear them speak in our tongues the wonderful works of God. (2:5–11)

Some mock the apostles, saying they must be drunk, but Peter denies the charge, delivering a sermon extempore, as it were. He tells the Jews that the "last days," days of prophecy, visions, dreams, wonders, have arrived (2:17). The day of the Lord shall come, Peter assures them: "And it shall come to pass, that whosoever shall call on the name of the Lord shall be saved" (2:21). Peter goes on to exhort the Jews, telling them of the resurrection of "Jesus, whom ye have crucified," and he urges them to "repent, and be baptized . . . in the name of Jesus Christ for the remission of sins, and ye shall receive the gift of the Holy Ghost" (2:36, 38). That day, according to Acts 2:41, "there were added unto them about three thousand souls." These converts followed the apostles' doctrine; they "sold their possessions and goods, and parted them to all men, as every man had need" (2:45). And they continued together in fellowship: "breaking bread from house to house, [they] did eat their meat with gladness and singleness of heart, Praising God, and having favour with all the people" (2:46–47). The second chapter of Acts concludes, "And the Lord added to the church daily such as should be saved" (2:47).

In our own era, the term *pentecostal* is synonymous with *charismatic* and refers to a variety of religious denominations that emphasize the ecstatic experience of possession by the Holy Spirit. Very early in the Christian tradition, however, there seems to have been disagreement about the significance of the particular pentecostal moment described in Acts 2. Was it to be regarded as a unique or at least rare occurrence occasioned by the special needs of the early apostolic mission? Or were visitations of the Holy Spirit and glossolalia, its sign, to be common among Christians? The mainstream Christian tradition would de-emphasize speaking in unknown tongues, viewing it as a "sign . . . to them that believe not," having no place in the Church itself (1 Corinthians 14:22). Nevertheless, the practice of speaking in tongues survived in dissenting traditions.[3]

The eighteenth-century established Church was notoriously suspicious of fanaticism and "enthusiasm." One might expect, therefore, an avoidance of the subject of Pentecost, perhaps even a hostility toward the notion of possession by the Holy Spirit, especially since pentecostal images—wind, fire, the babel of languages—are common satiric tropes in writings against perceived religious excesses. "Enthusiasm," religious or cultural, was seen as dangerous and self-flattering, born of appetite disguised as spirituality or creativity.

Yet our expectation may in fact elide categories the eighteenth century itself found distinct. After all, the story of Pentecost is not only crucial to the story of Christianity; the season is also part of the Church calendar, as it was in the eighteenth-century Anglican Church. The miracle itself was commemorated annually in Whitsunday services, and Pentecost was traditionally the season for the sacrament of baptism. The descent of the Holy Spirit, the possession of the apostles, the miracle of speaking in tongues—none of these components of the Pentecostal narrative was viewed as the product of "enthusiasm" or delusion or irrationality. In fact, quite the opposite is true.

For a standard eighteenth-century reading of this text, we can turn to John Tillotson's sermon "Of the Gift of Tongues conferred on the Apostles."[4]

The text is Acts 2:1–4, but in the course of his remarks Tillotson touches on all the elements of the narrative outlined in the previous paragraphs. For Tillotson Pentecost represents the fulfillment of Old Testament typology. As he explains, the "giving of the Law" to the Jews "was to be a type of the Christian Church, and of the Dispensation of the Gospel by the Son of God."[5] It is "therefore no Wonder, if . . . the Divine Providence should so order the Event of Things, that the Seasons of dispensing the great Evangelical Blessings should happen at the same Times, when the great Blessings of the Law, which were the Types of them, were dispensed and commemorated" (278). This season coincides with the "Season that the Law was delivered to the *Jews* from Mount *Sinai,* and the first Covenant establish'd" (278). The typological correspondences Tillotson enumerates confirm for him the belief that the visitation of the Holy Spirit on the day of Pentecost represents a second covenant between God and his chosen people.

It is thus that the miracle of Pentecost seems highly "reasonable" to Tillotson. Such a miracle occurred, he argues, because it was necessary for the propagation of Christianity. It was a miracle particularly suited for such a task because the apostles had been residing for some time in Jerusalem and were known to be "simple and illiterate" men (281); it was well known, therefore, not only what language but what dialect they spoke. Their sudden and miraculous command of other languages was itself powerful evidence, Tillotson argues, of the presence of the Holy Spirit—so powerful and persuasive an event that 3,000 people were converted to Christianity and began to practice and teach the precepts of the new religion. Because the converts came from many different places, having, like the apostles, come to Jerusalem for Pentecost, they assured a wide dissemination of the gospel. No other circumstance, no other miracle could have suited the divine purpose as well, both logistically and symbolically.

Finally, Tillotson speculates, the miracle could occur again. The "Conversion of Infidel Nations" might very well require it, "for as the Wisdom of God is not wont to that which is superfluous, so neither is it wanting in that which is necessary"; further, "the Necessity seems to be much the same that it was at first" (284). He concludes the sermon by asserting that he is not claiming another Pentecostal miracle will occur, but merely articulating a "probable Divinity; no-wise contrary to Scripture, and very agreeable to Reason" (284).

Orthodox Anglicanism did not repudiate the story of Pentecost, but "inspiration" in eighteenth-century contexts was associated primarily with dissenting sects regarded as dangerous to the stability of church and state. Nevertheless, Tillotson's interpretation of the Pentecostal narrative is in no way contradicted by those who viewed "enthusiasm" as a political and spiritual evil. Swift, the most familiar opponent of enthusiasm to the modern reader and a source for much of Sterne's wit and many of his perceptual biases, directly invokes Pentecost in "Mechanical Operation of the Spirit," an attack on "enthusiasm," or "fanaticism," in learning and religion. Enthusiasts,

Swift maintains, "proceed in general upon the following Fundamental: That *the Corruption of the Senses is the Generation of the Spirit*."[6] Fanatics address their auditors "to divert, bind up, stupify, fluster, and amuse the *Senses* . . . and while they [i.e., "the *Senses*"] are either absent, or otherwise employ'd, or engaged in a Civil War against each other, the *Spirit* enters and performs its Part" (176).

Swift notes that modern enthusiasts differ from the apostles at Pentecost on three counts: (1) unlike the apostles, modern saints are never "*gathered together with one accord,*" and in fact it is impossible to find two fanatics who agree (177); (2) modern saints do not speak in tongues and indeed do not know even their own language; and (3) modern saints keep their hats on in worship, thus precluding the Holy Spirit's approach, as on the day of Pentecost, in the form of cloven tongues over the heads of the apostles. These discrepancies are easy enough to explain, however, for modern enthusiasts mean something different by *spirit* than was meant in the second chapter of Acts. There *spirit* signified "a supernatural Assistance, approaching from without," but to the modern fanatic, "*Spirit* . . . proceed[s] entirely from within" (177).

Swift goes on in "Mechanical Operation," as he does in the Aeolist section of *A Tale of a Tub,* to equate enthusiastic inspiration with base and profligate carnality. He tells the story of the "*Banbury Saint*" who discovered the art of "*Snuffling,*" which, as William Wotton's note points out, refers to the tone of canting preachers.[7] "Upon a certain Day, while he was far engaged among the Tabernacles of the *Wicked,*" this saint "felt the Outward Man put into odd Commotions, and strangely prick'd forward by the Inward; An Effect very usual among the Modern Inspired" (184). Ultimately, the "saint" undergoes a cure for venereal disease that drives his ailment "from its Post . . . into his Head," causing a new intonation, somewhat like the "*Snuffle* of a Bag-pipe" and leading to "wonderful Success in the Operation of the *Spirit*" (184–85). The suggestion is, of course, that the inspiration of canting preachers is a displacement of their sex drive and that it works on the members of their congregations by exciting and displacing their carnal impulses as well.

"Mechanical Operation of the Spirit" ends with a rather direct discussion of the confusion between sexuality and spirituality that Swift attributes to modern enthusiasts. He notes, first of all, "how unaccountably all Females are attracted by Visionary or Enthusiastick Preachers, tho' never so contemptible in their *outward Men*" (189). Such an attraction "is usually supposed to be done upon Considerations, purely Spiritual, without any carnal Regards at all," but the case may be altogether different than it is commonly assumed to be. Perhaps the women "form a truer Judgment of Human Abilities and Performings, than we our selves can possibly do of each other" (189). No doubt, in other words, the attraction is sexual after all. Swift concludes:

however Spiritual Intrigues begin, they generally conclude like all others; they may branch upwards toward Heaven, but the Root is in the Earth. Too intense a Contemplation is not the Business of Flesh and Blood; it must by the necessary Course of Things, in a little Time, let go its Hold, and fall into *Matter*. Lovers, for the sake of Celestial Converse, are but another sort of *Platonicks* who pretend to see Stars and Heaven in Ladies Eyes, and to look or think no lower; but the same *Pit* is provided for both; and they seem a perfect Moral to the Story of that Philosopher, who, while his Thoughts and Eyes were fixed upon the *Constellations,* found himself seduced by his *lower Parts* into a *Ditch.* (189–90)

Swift thus thoroughly reduces the separation of spirit and matter to absurdity and modern enthusiasts to orgiasts and sensualists.

In Sterne's time, the enthusiasm against which Swift argued was still a subject of concern, having taken a new form—Methodism. In fact, as Melvyn New has pointed out, "the use of Restoration polemics [attacking dissent] against the perceived enthusiasms of Methodism is commonplace throughout the middle of the century."[8] Borrowing much of his language from the Restoration divine George Hickes, for example, Sterne found occasion in two of his sermons—"Humility" and "On enthusiasm"—to censure what he considered to be the spiritual pride of these new fanatics.[9] "Spiritual pride," he says in "Humility," "is the worst of all prides" (*Sermons,* 241). And in "On enthusiasm," he describes the religious enthusiast as behaving "ostentatiously," "arrogantly," in "boasting of extraordinary communications with the God of all knowledge" (365). Sterne does not deny God's participation in the affairs of men, even individual men. Indeed, he asserts that "the influence and assistance of GOD's spirit . . . does enable us to render him an acceptable service," but, he insists, it does so in a way imperceptible to us:

in what particular manner this is effected, so that the act shall still be imputed ours——the scripture says not: we know only the account is so; but as for any sensible demonstrations of it's workings to be felt as such within us——the word of GOD is utterly silent; . . . As expressly as we are told to pray for the inspiration of GOD's spirit,—there are no boundaries fixed, nor can any be ever marked to distinguish them from the efforts and determinations of our own reason; and as firmly as most Christians believe the effects of them upon their hearts, I may venture to affirm, that since the promises were made, there never was a christian of a cool head and sound judgment, that in any instance of a change of life, would presume to say, which part of his reformation was owing to divine help,——or which to the operations of his own mind, or who, upon looking back, would pretend to strike the line, and say, "here it was that my own reflections ended;——and at this point the suggestions of the spirit of GOD began to take place." (*Sermons,* 241–42)

Yet "enthusiasts" of the past spoke of the *"in-comings, in-dwellings,* and *out-lettings* of the Spirit"* that, they claimed, imbued every word they said, every action they performed, with spiritual significance (242). Moreover, although Methodists have not yet adopted the language of their enthusiastic forbears, insofar as "we have not yet got to the old terms of the in-comings and in-dwellings of the spirit," they are, nonetheless, quite eager to "tell you the identical place,——the day of the month, and the hour of the night, when the spirit came in upon them, and took possession of their hearts" (243).

There is no arguing with enthusiasts; if one is unconvinced by their assertion of spiritual possession and asks for evidence, "they will tell you, 'They feel it is so'" (243). To enthusiasts, past and present, "faith, the distinguishing characteristick of a christian, is defined . . . not as a rational assent of the understanding, to truths which are established by indisputable authority, but as a violent persuasion of mind, that they are instantaneously become the children of God" ("On enthusiasm," *Sermons,* 366). Such "faith," Sterne concludes, is the product of "an heated imagination," a "disorder . . . in the head" that "call[s] for the aid of a physician who can cure the distempered state of the body, rather than one who may sooth the anxieties of the mind" (366). Like Swift, Sterne is suspicious of an enthusiasm that attempts to claim for the spirit what more properly belongs to the body.[10]

The Methodists, like the enthusiasts Swift castigated, insist on a personal conviction of spiritual possession. Although John Wesley agrees with Swift and Sterne that enthusiasm may be a "religious madness arising from some falsely imagined influence or inspiration of God," he does not consider the personal conviction of a special "possession" by the Holy Spirit to be "falsely imagined."[11] Indeed, for Wesley, true Christians are those who "walk after the Spirit": "Being filled with faith and with the Holy Ghost, they possess in their hearts, and show forth in their lives, in the whole course of their words and actions, the genuine fruits of the Spirit of God" ("The First Fruits of the Spirit," 1:69). The imagery of Pentecost—addressed to the conversion of 3,000 in Acts 2—is characteristically employed by Wesley to describe individual conviction of personal salvation. His emphasis on the felt, continual presence of the Holy Ghost is one of his primary quarrels with mainstream Anglican thought, as the following passage from his sermon "Scriptural Christianity" suggests: "how few of you spend, from one week to another, a single hour in private prayer! How few have any thought of God in the general tenor of your conversation! Who of you is, in any degree, acquainted with the work of his Spirit, his supernatural work in the souls of men? Can you bear, unless now and then, in a church, any talk of the Holy Ghost? Would not you take it for granted, if one began such a conversation, that it was either hypocrisy or enthusiasm?" (1:44). For Wesley, clearly, the significance of Pentecost is not that the apostles, already Christian, were enabled by a possession of the Holy Spirit to perform a miracle that converted thousands; what he instead finds significant is the infusion of the Holy Ghost into the converts themselves.[12]

This interpretation is not only sustained by the biblical text itself, but is advanced in standard Anglican commentary on Acts 2:38, in which the converted are told by Peter, "ye shall receive the gift of the holy Ghost." Matthew Poole, for example, says that this gift signifies both "internal gifts, confirmation, and strengthning in the faith" and "external gifts, as that of speaking with tongues. . . ; both, or either of these, according to their conditions or stations."[13] But what Poole and other Anglican commentators cite as occurring for *these* converts must, Wesley insists, occur for every true Christian. Where the Anglican priests of the eighteenth century believed that baptism sufficed to confer on the individual "remission of his sins by spiritual regeneration," Wesley believed that a personal sense of the Holy Spirit's presence was necessary for salvation.[14]

As G. J. Barker-Benfield has noted, the rise of Methodism coincided with the emergence of "the culture of sensibility": "Adherence to both Methodism and the cult of sensibility was demonstrated by the capacity to feel and to signify feeling by the same physical signs—tears, groans, sighs, and tremblings."[15] Both were also characterized by "a striking combination of a rigid [sexual] code and intense emotional release."[16] As Barker-Benfield has persuasively argued, although the culture of sensibility emerged from a celebration of the body's materiality, particularly its eroticism, it came to represent a contrary taming of the erotic impulse in favor of the body's response to emotion, to feeling. Rousseau's Emile, for example, learns to desire a woman's virtue and thus to temper his sexual passion:

> His heart opens itself to the first fires of love. Its sweet illusions make him a new universe of delight and enjoyment. He loves a lovable object who is even more lovable for her character than for her person. He hopes for, he expects a return that he feels is his due. . . . This supreme happiness is a hundred times sweeter to hope for than to obtain. One enjoys it better when one looks forward to it than when one tastes it. O good Emile, love and beloved! Enjoy a long time before possessing. Enjoy love and innocence at the same time. Make your paradise on earth while awaiting the other one.[17]

For Sterne as for Swift, such a formulation smacks of hypocrisy and self-delusion. It is this "transformation" of bodily impulses into spiritual essences that both writers find so offensive. Yet in Sterne's view, the offense would seem to lie in claiming not only too much for the spirit but, equally offensive, too little for the body. The body has erotic impulses, and to act on those impulses is often quite pleasurable. But the body is also, in the conventional Christian view Sterne would have held, the "temple of the spirit." As such, its responses—even, perhaps especially, its erotic responses—speak to moral and spiritual truth.

With these significances of the story of Pentecost to eighteenth-century Anglicanism in mind, we are better able to perceive how Yorick's invocation of Acts 2 guides us toward a clearer understanding of Sterne's musings on eroticism, charity, and language—the three central motifs of the *Journey* and of the Pentecostal narrative as it had been formulated in eighteenth-century debate between Anglicans and "enthusiasts" of various sorts.

EROTICISM

Throughout *A Sentimental Journey,* Yorick experiences a number of what we could term "Pentecostal" moments—that is, moments when he transcends the limitations of language to perceive the spiritual "truth" of eternal life; more often than not, he does so through the agency of sexual desire. It is important to remember that when Sterne wrote *A Sentimental Journey* he was very ill most of the time, acutely aware of his body, its limitations, its mortality. Yet he was also acutely aware of its desires, its sexuality, its physical response to emotion. After all, during the writing of *A Sentimental Journey* Sterne underwent a cure for syphilis and also carried on a "sentimental" affair with Eliza Draper.[18]

In his *Journal to Eliza* Sterne speaks of his love for Eliza in biblical terms that emphasize bodily and spiritual oneness. Although he calls her the "Goddesse of this temple," his "help-mate," and says he hopes to inhabit "Elysium" with her, Sterne's impulses are clearly erotic.[19] Thus, he describes his meeting with Eliza as catching "fire at each other" (*JE,* 166), and he feels their bodies are in such sympathetic alignment that were something to happen to her on her way to India, he would feel "some monitory sympathetic Shock within me, which would have spoke like Revelation" (*JE,* 154). Moreover, he feels this powerful attraction must be approved by God: "assuredly—God made us not for Misery and Ruin—he has ordered all our Steps—and influenced our Attachments for what is worthy of them—It must end well—Eliza!" (*JE,* 160).

It did not, of course. Eliza Draper did not (apparently) return Sterne's passion in full measure, and the *Journal* ends abruptly some months before Sterne's death. We can also, if we wish, dismiss Sterne's sentimental prose in the *Journal* as the expression of the excessive and rather pathetic emotions of a sick and lonely man. Yet the intensity of erotic longing that informs the *Journal,* and the consistent return to biblical themes and texts to express that longing may alert us to a similar pattern in *A Sentimental Journey,* a pattern elaborated in that work with more emotional distance and greater clarity.

Yorick's initial encounter in France presents the argument of the entire narrative. As he sits in Calais after his dinner, pondering the illogic of animosity toward the French, he congratulates himself on what his spirit of benevolence suggests about the state of his soul. He feels charitable, "at peace with man"; he "pulls out his purse, and . . . looks round him, as if he sought for an object to share it with" (*ASJ,* 68). He notes his body's responses to this generosity: "I felt every vessel in my frame dilate—the arteries beat all chearily together, and every power which sustained life, perform'd it with so little friction, that 'twould have confounded the most *physical precieuse* in France: with all her materialism, she could scarce have called me a machine" (68–69). Here Sterne invokes the debate outlined in the preceding paragraphs and, like Swift, opposes the notion that body and soul are two separable entities.

Yet Yorick's repletion, his full stomach, his self-satisfaction, do not—despite his theories to the contrary—open his purse to the needy. For as he tells us, "I had scarce utter'd the words, when a poor monk of the order of St. Francis came into the room to beg something for his convent. . . . The moment I cast my eyes upon him, I was predetermined not to give him a single sous" (70). Yorick again describes his reaction in bodily terms: "there is no regular reasoning," he says, "upon the ebbs and flows of our humours; they may depend upon the same causes, for ought I know, which influence the tides themselves" (70). The explanation Yorick offers to the monk for his refusal to respond charitably is chauvinistic in both a national and a religious sense: "I have left thousands in distress upon our own shore . . . But we distinguish . . . my good Father! betwixt those who wish only to eat the bread of their own labour—and those who eat the bread of other people's, and have no other plan in life, but to get through it in sloth and ignorance, *for the love of God*" (73–74).

Although Yorick realizes almost immediately that he has "behaved very ill," his "hardness of heart" is significant (75); when he finally opens his purse, and his heart, to the monk, it is in response to sexual desire.[20] Madame de L*** effects the "miracle" self-satisfaction could not produce. Yorick's desire for her, which in turn prompts a desire to appear worthy in her eyes, leads to a reconciliation between Yorick and Father Lorenzo. That a moral act emanates from the desires of the flesh is quite natural to Sterne, as a later remark illustrates. After his "conquest" of either the *fille de chambre* or his desire for her (the text, of course, sustains both readings), Yorick draws this conclusion:

> If nature has so wove her web of kindness, that some threads of love and desire are entangled with the piece—must the whole web be rent in drawing them out?—Whip me such stoics, great governor of nature! said I to myself—Wherever thy providence shall place me for the trials of my virtue—whatever is my danger—whatever is my situation—let me feel the movements which rise out of it, and which belong to me as a man—and if I govern them as a good one—I will trust the issues to thy justice, for thou hast made us—and not we ourselves. (237–38)

This philosophizing, with its movements, its risings and its issues, is thoroughly erotic, but no more so, as Gardner Stout has pointed out, than certain passages in Sterne's sermons that address a similar theme (237n). In "The

Levite and his concubine," for example, Sterne expresses the sentiment in language as sensual if not as playfully suggestive as that in *A Sentimental Journey:* "let me be wise and religious——but let me be M A N: wherever thy Providence places me, or whatever be the road I take to get to thee——give me some companion in my journey, be it only to remark to, How our shadows lengthen as the sun goes down;——to whom I may say, How fresh is the face of nature! How sweet the flowers of the field! How delicious are these fruits!" (*Sermons*, 170).

The conjoining in this passage of the sensual and the spiritual speaks to Sterne's awareness of mortality and of the morality by which we (in Sterne's orthodox Christian view) will be judged in the afterlife; and, as well, to a proper enjoyment of the sensual pleasures of this life, given perhaps more poignancy, more piquancy by the knowledge that they are temporal and temporary. Sterne, like the Anglican divines to whom his theology is indebted, can be described as latitudinarian in his insistence that a proper enjoyment of the world's sensual pleasures does not run counter to true spirituality and the spirit of Christianity—a position that legitimated certain kinds of pleasure and thereby encouraged (or at least did nothing to hamper) consumerism.[21]

Sterne's notion of pleasure, however, is not focused on the enjoyment of artificial stimulants, such as the tea, coffee, chocolate, and tobacco that fueled the eighteenth-century economy. After all, these particular goods—none of them consciousness altering—stimulate the body alone. Sterne's notion of proper pleasure originates in the more complicated desire one human being has for another human being—his (or her, though Sterne, logically enough, writes from the male perspective) longing for "companionship," as the sermons would have it, for sexual union, as *Tristram Shandy* and *A Sentimental Journey* more bluntly maintain. This is a pleasure he does not view as merely a physical pleasure. Indeed, for Sterne sexual desire is both physical urge and spiritual longing. For him, erotic urges signify a longing for completeness in a physical and a spiritual sense. Sexual desire certainly speaks to carnal impulses, but it also speaks to the human need for "society, help and comfort."[22] Where one begins and the other ends, Sterne is not prepared to say.

That Father Lorenzo and Yorick exchange snuffboxes as a pledge of mutual forgiveness and esteem is fitting, for in addition to containing a stimulant for the body, the snuffboxes remind the men of their affection for one another. As Yorick presents his tortoise box to the monk, he says, "when you take a pinch out of it, sometimes recollect it was the peace-offering of a man who once used you unkindly, but not from his heart" (*ASJ*, 99). And he reverences the horn snuffbox presented to him by Father Lorenzo: "I guard this box, as I would the instrumental parts of my religion, to help my mind on to something better" (101).

In all his writings, from *Tristram Shandy, The Sermons of Mr. Yorick*, and *A Journal to Eliza* to *A Sentimental Journey*, Sterne suggests that physical health and erotic desire are inevitably linked. Uncle Toby's placidity with regard to sexual matters is an effect of his wound; Tristram's own impotence signals the onset of disease. If the absence of desire is an indicator of an ebbing vitality, erotic renewal can actually bring health, while governing eroticism by mistaken principles can have the opposite effect. Even though Madame de L*** has a beneficial moral effect on Yorick in his encounter with Father Lorenzo, when the two meet again in Amiens, Yorick decides not to accompany her to Brussels, despite his desire to comfort and (the text implies) make love to her: "with what a moral delight will it crown my journey, in sharing in the sickening incidents of a tale of misery told to me by such a sufferer? to see her weep! and though I cannot dry up the fountain of her tears, what an exquisite sensation is there still left, in wiping them away from off the cheeks of the first and fairest of women, as I'm sitting with my handkerchief in my hand in silence the whole night besides her" (*ASJ*, 145–46). Although Yorick maintains that "there was nothing wrong in the sentiment," he reveals that he "instantly reproached [his] heart," for he had only three months earlier "sworn . . . eternal fidelity" to Eliza (146–47). He then decides, on principle, to go to Paris instead: "Eternal fountain of happiness!" he says, kneeling on the ground, "be thou my witness—and every pure spirit which tastes it, be my witness also, That I would not travel to Brussels, unless Eliza went along with me, did the road lead me towards heaven" (148). The problem is, of course, that there are no pure spirits among mortal men. As Tristram puts it, "REASON, is half of it, SENSE; and the measure of heaven itself is but the measure of our present appetites and concoctions" (*TS*, VII.xiii.593). Yorick reaches a similar conclusion after his apostrophe to the "Eternal fountain of happiness": "In transports of this kind, the heart, in spite of the understanding, will always say too much" (*ASJ*, 148).

CHARITY

Arthur H. Cash has chronicled Sterne's attraction to sickly women.[23] Sterne met and courted Elizabeth Lumley when she was very ill, and Eliza Draper was also in poor health when he became infatuated with her; similarly, the women in *A Sentimental Journey* who receive the most profound erotic and emotional attention from the narrator are ill. Madame de L*** is grieving; Maria of Moulines is insane. This circumstance has led some critics, most notably Ann Jessie Van Sant and Eve Kosofsky Sedgwick, to read *A Sentimental Journey* as a repudiation or reification of sexual desire. From Van Sant's point of view, Yorick (and indeed Sterne) is impotent, and thus his "sensation seeking is, finally, intellectualized."[24] Sedgwick sees *A Sentimental Journey* as a narrative that is not so much about sexual desire as about a masculine power that translates all gender and class relations into sexual terms.[25] Van Sant's and Sedgwick's arguments are predicated on wildly dissimilar Yoricks—the impotent, introspective Yorick versus the Yorick of dominant and domineering masculine drives. Both readings unite, however, in ignoring important aspects of the female others whom Yorick encounters on his journey. After all, the *fille de chambre* and the *grisset,* although of a lower social class, seem to equal—if not surpass—Yorick in desire, and Madame Rambouliet and the woman with whom Yorick shares a room at the end of the narrative are his social equals, if not betters.

Yet the sickly, weak women are particularly important, for through them Sterne is able to connect benevolence with erotic desire, a linkage that would otherwise remain obscure. As he presents Yorick's reactions to Maria de Moulines and Madame de L***, Sterne suggests that the charitable impulse and the erotic impulse are not in fact different. The same longing for comfort, help, and companionship is expressed in both.

In those sermons that Sterne preached in order to recommend charity to his parishioners, he presents compassion as a human attribute. In "Elijah and the widow of Zerephath," for example, he observes: "GOD certainly interwove that friendly softness in our nature to be a check upon too great a propensity towards self-love" (*Sermons,* 43); as even Epicurus acknowledged, "the best way of enlarging human happiness was, by a communication of it to others" (49). Further, "the very body of man is never in a better state than when he is most inclined to do good offices:—that as nothing more contributes to health than a benevolence of temper, so nothing generally was a stronger indication of it" (49). Sterne continues: "And indeed, setting aside all abstruser reasoning upon the point, I cannot conceive, but that the very *mechanical motions* which maintain life, must be performed with more equal vigour and freedom in that man whom a great and good soul perpetually inclines to shew mercy to the miserable, than they can be in a poor, sordid, selfish wretch, whose little, contracted heart, melts at no man's affliction; but sits brooding so intently over its own plots and concerns, as to see and feel nothing" (49). Although there are such individuals with contracted hearts (Yorick shows himself to be one at the beginning of his sentimental journey), Sterne maintains in "Philanthropy recommended" that compassion is so "universally and deeply . . . planted in the heart of man . . . that from the general propensity to pity the unfortunate, we express that sensation by the word *humanity,* as if it was inseparable from our nature" (28–29).

The argument that compassion is natural to "man" is, in both "Elijah and the widow of Zerephath" and "Philanthropy recommended," offered in opposition to the view that man is fundamentally selfish—a view that, as Sterne says elsewhere, threatens to "untie the bands of society, and rob us of one of the greatest pleasures of it, the mutual communications of kind offices" ("Vindication of human nature," 67).[26] Sterne repudiates the Hobbesian view, in other words, by the argument that, body and soul, we are disposed to charity by the design of God.

Anglican commentary on the final verses of Acts 2, wherein the new converts are described as having "all things [in] common" and selling "their possessions and goods," giving to "all men, as every man had need," empha-sizes the extraordinary charity these converts exhibited. There is no need, says Matthew Henry, for "all Christians in all places and ages" to sell their homes and belongings and distribute the money to the poor.[27] Matthew Poole denies that even these Christians went so far: "And these, *all things* which they had in common, must either be restrained to such things as every one freely laid aside for the poor; or that it speaks the extraordinary charitable disposi-tion of those new Converts, that they would rather have parted with any thing, nay, with their *all*, than that any of their poor brethren should have wanted."[28] The commentators do not wish to read the verse as a challenge to the inviolability of private property, and indeed Poole says specifically that "Christs Gospel does not destroy the Law"; "*meum* and *tuum*" are still opera-tive concepts, as other scriptural passages, before and after Acts 2, attest. This commentary serves, of course, to endorse the status quo by denying the obvi-ous challenge the biblical text would seem to sustain.

Predictably, Sterne's notion of charity does not depart from the orthodox Anglican view. As Robert Markley has pointed out, the kind of charity *A Sen-timental Journey* endorses is far from a radical or even effective means of solving the social problem of poverty, the inequities arising from the uneven distribu-tion of wealth that characterizes both a patriarchal, feudal society and the emergent capitalist economy. Markley correctly perceives that Sterne's con-cern is not so much to offer a practical solution to social ills as to elaborate a flattering theory of human nature that in a very real sense militates against active reform. In his assessment, *A Sentimental Journey* is an example of "the rationalization of a middle-class culture that cannot reconcile its virtuous self-image with its dependence on economic inequality."[29]

Sterne, of course, could not foresee the kinds of social problems that would arise with industrial growth—the nature of poverty, like the nature of wealth, would change in the nineteenth century, becoming more impersonal, more widespread, and more conspicuous. For Sterne, charity is still a matter of parish duty, of personal encounters with beggars of various sorts. As Patri-cia Meyer Spacks has argued in answer to Markley's charges, Sterne does make a powerful case for "taking feelings seriously."[30] Although she admits that Yorick, like most sentimental protagonists, "dramatize[s] altruism's futility, its incapacity to produce sustained, complex action," she also sees a challenge to power in the very language of benevolence, a language often focused on objects of charity—the weak, the wounded, and the poor.[31]

LANGUAGE

Yorick's ability to communicate with the French in their native tongue is lim-ited. He often finds their language amusing; he seems to revel, for example, in the appropriateness of the term *"Desobligeant"* (*ASJ*, 78, 85) and the phrase *"Rien que pisser"* (182). At other times, however, he is confused by what he hears, as when he misinterprets the cry *"Haussez les mains"* at the opera (180); and at still other times, he is simply frustrated. His attempt to write Madame de L*** a letter results in a torn and blotted sheet of paper and an impatient oath: *"Le Diable l'emporte!"* (151).[32] Yet, like the Jews on the day of Pentecost, Yorick does understand the strangers he meets; he discovers in the language of feeling a universal passport by means of which he can transcend cultural differences. Although often the "speaker" of this language is a woman, Yorick is also moved by a dwarf he sees at the opera, a peasant and his dead ass, and a starling in its cage. With all, especially the last, there is a measure of self-identification, but self-identification is not necessarily selfishness. To see in the plight of another our own fate or possible fate may be less commendable, in idealistic terms, than to sympathize without self-identification. Kenneth MacLean has argued as much, suggesting that Sterne, like Adam Smith, would have viewed such "translation" as sentimental chicanery.[33] Yet such a reading insists on the very dualism that, as we have seen, Sterne rejected. To view self and other as separate is to deny the common human bonds that link us all, just as viewing body and soul as separate denies the irrevocable union of spirit and matter that characterizes human life. We are limited creatures, in Sterne's orthodox Christian view, limited by our sinfulness, our appetites, our self-concern. But those very limitations are also sources of our strength. Because of our sinfulness, we experience the grace of God; our appetites and desires provide us a glimpse of heaven; our self-concern teaches us to love one another.

At Pentecost, the Holy Ghost made it possible for the apostles to speak fluently languages unknown to them for the purpose of converting 3,000 Jews who had gathered in Jerusalem. The event was extraordinary, a miracle. The limitations of language were overcome by a special dispensation that transformed a mass of strangers into a community. *A Sentimental Journey,* in which language is shown to be similarly limited, records more ordinary miracles as time and again Yorick finds in cultural difference a common human bond.[34]

Moreover, in direct analogy to the converts in Jerusalem, Yorick occasionally hears his own language spoken in France with such fluency, such power, as to strike him with the force of revelation. The starling that cries, in English, "I can't get out—I can't get out" reveals to Yorick the importance of a liberty he has undervalued (*ASJ*, 198). And it does so by prompting an imaginative identification with the oppressed. He imagines "a single captive," starving, pale, marking the days of his confinement with "a little calendar of small sticks" (201–2). The pathetic scene reduces Yorick to tears, and he sets out with La Fleur to procure the papers he needs to avoid similar confinement.

Yorick's search for credentials leads him to an interview wherein English literature serves as his ambassador, mediating his relationship with the Count de B****, whose admiration for Shakespeare prompts him to value one he takes to be the King of Denmark's jester.[35] Left alone by the count, who has gone to prepare a passport, Yorick passes the moments by reading *Much Ado about Nothing* and meditating on the value of literature itself. It is, in Yorick's view, an occasion for forging bonds of sympathy and compassion. He remembers, particularly, the emotion with which he read as a schoolboy the story of Dido, for whom he still grieves: "I lose the feelings for myself in hers" (225). He has, he tells us, "a clearer idea of the elysian fields than of heaven" (225), but the terms with which he describes his compassionate reaction forge a connection between the two, a connection severed—as Sterne surely knew—by St. Augustine in his *Confessions*. To respond with emotion to Dido's plight was, Augustine argued, to sin against God. In weeping for Dido, he says, "I committed fornication against Thee . . . *for the friendship of this world is fornication against Thee*."[36]

In Sterne's own time the Augustinian rejection of Dido had been echoed by Bishop William Warburton, who also found offensive any imaginative sympathy with the spurned Queen of Carthage. In *The Divine Legation of Moses,* Warburton speaks of Dido as one who represents an "unruly passion" that temporarily distracts Aeneas from his pious duty. The episode is a warning against the "voluptuous weakness" that may create "public mischiefs" if indulged in by those in power.[37] While more political in tone than the Augustinian gloss on the Virgilian text, Warburton's remarks serve similarly to insist on the separation of imagination and duty to God. Sterne, as we have seen, disagrees.[38] Language, though a human attribute and therefore imperfect and limited, can at times speak to our common humanity, just as our bodily desires can reveal to us the union of body and soul.

The final episode of *A Sentimental Journey,* entitled "A Case of Delicacy," finds Yorick struggling with his erotic desire and a sense of moral obligation. Having agreed to share his room with two female travelers, a lady and her *fille de chambre,* Yorick promises to sleep clothed and to remain silent, except for saying his prayers. Yet the situation is provocative. Yorick is stimulated, disturbed, aroused by the presence of the woman in the next bed. He thrashes about restlessly "till a full hour after midnight," at which point he exclaims, "O my God!" (*ASJ,* 290). When the lady chastises him for breaking his silence and his word, he tells her that "it was no more than an ejaculation" (290). In this episode's thorough confounding of religion, eroticism, and sensibility, we have Sterne's view of human life and human nature. Driven by desires, longing for union with others, for caring, concern, sexual satisfaction, mergings of all kinds, human life is, like Yorick's journey, a state of incompleteness, but an incompleteness that offers glimpses of completeness to come, prefigured in moments when longing is fulfilled—in acts of compassion, of communication, and yes, of erotic pleasure.

In *A Sentimental Journey,* Sterne offers a rebuttal to both the mechanical theory of the body and the culture of sensibility. The narrative insists that it is to human beings, to sinners, not saints, that God offers redemption. It insists that through our bodily lives we experience the grace of God, the gifts of the spirit and the promise of salvation. In his sermon to the converts on the day of Pentecost, Peter enjoined: "He who calls upon the name of the Lord will be saved." And, not coincidentally, among Yorick's last spoken words in *A Sentimental Journey* are "O my God!" He speaks these words in the context of an erotic longing so intense that it has produced an "ejaculation." And most important, he speaks these words from erotic pleasure as much as from spiritual need, as much from the body as from the soul. For in this life, Sterne maintains, it is impossible to say just where one begins and the other ends.

Notes

1. *The Book of Common Prayer*'s text for Whitsunday services is Acts 2:1–11.

2. Sterne so labeled *A Sentimental Journey* in a letter to Richard Griffith. *Letters of Laurence Sterne,* ed. Lewis Perry Curtis (1935; rpt. Oxford: Clarendon, 1962), 399 n.

3. For a review of the place of glossolalia in the Christian tradition, see *The Oxford Illustrated History of Christianity,* ed. John McManners (Oxford: Oxford University Press, 1990), 585, and for a more thorough discussion of the theological and literary significance of "the gift of tongues," see *A Dictionary of Biblical Tradition in English Literature,* gen. ed. David Lyle Jeffrey (Grand Rapids, Mich.: William B. Eerdmans Publishing Co., 1992), 596–601, 770–71.

4. Melvyn New points to Tillotson's centrality for eighteenth-century Anglicanism in general and Sterne in particular in his introduction to *The Sermons,* V:24–25 and n. 56. On Tillotson's popularity with a general readership in the eighteenth century, see J. Paul Hunter, *Before Novels: The Cultural Contexts of Eighteenth-Century English Fiction* (New York: W. W. Norton, 1990), 249.

5. Sermon CXLIII, "Of the Gift of Tongues conferred on the Apostles," in *The Works of the Most Reverend Dr. John Tillotson, Late Lord Archbishop of Canterbury,* 2 vols. (London, 1712), 2:277.

6. "A Discourse Concerning the Mechanical Operation of the Spirit in a Letter to a Friend," in *A Tale of a Tub with Other Early Works 1696–1707* (Oxford: Basil Blackwell, 1957), 176.

7. Wotton's note, not included in the Blackwell edition of Swift's work, is printed in other editions, including the Oxford Authors, *Jonathan Swift,* eds. Angus Ross and David Woolley (Oxford: Oxford University Press, 1984), 175 n.

8. "Some Sterne Borrowings from Four Renaissance Authors," *Philological Quarterly* 71 (1992): 306. Of course, both Swift and Sterne, as Anglican priests, would have considered enthusiasm a political as well as spiritual danger. In objecting to the enthusiast's theoretical severing of body and soul, both writers speak metaphorically of the turbulence of the preceding century—Swift referring to a "Civil War" ("Mechanical Operation," 176), Sterne to an "interregnum" (*ASJ,* 129).

9. See New's discussion of Sterne's specific borrowings from Hickes in "Some Sterne Borrowings," 306–10.

10.   For a discussion of Sterne's place in the shift from "mechanical" theories of the body to "materialistic" theories, see John A. Dussinger, "The Sensorium in the World of 'A Sentimental Journey,' " *Ariel* 13.2 (1982): 3–16, which places Sterne's views in the intellectual context of eighteenth-century opposition to dualistic theories of the self.

11.   Wesley, "The Nature of Enthusiasm," in *Sermons on Several Occasions*, 2 vols. (New York: Carlton and Lanahan, 1800), 1:331.

12.   Among Wesley's sermons is one preached at St. Mary's, Oxford, for Whitsunday services in 1736 (2:530–39, "On the Holy Spirit"). It is very similar, it must be said, in tone and theme to Tillotson's sermon, and in fact ends with the "excellent collect of our church" included in the *Book of Common Prayer* for Whitsunday.

13.   *Annotations Upon the Holy Bible. Wherein the Sacred Text Is Inserted, and Various Readings Annex'd, Together with the Parallel Scriptures*. 2 vols., 3d ed. Corrected and amended by Samuel Clark and Edward Veale (London, 1696), s.v. Acts 2:38.

14.   *Book of Common Prayer*, "Public Baptism of Infants."

15.   G. J. Barker-Benfield, *The Culture of Sensibility: Sex and Society in Eighteenth-Century Britain* (Chicago: University of Chicago Press, 1992), 268.

16.   Barker-Benfield, 268.

17.   Jean-Jacques Rousseau, *Emile, or On Education,* ed. Allan Bloom (New York: Basic Books, 1979), 419.

18.   Although Sterne underwent a mercury cure for a condition diagnosed as syphilis, he was probably misdiagnosed, as Arthur Cash points out. Still, as Cash also notes, Sterne's "willingness to risk [the cure] indicates that he thought the diagnosis was correct"—and that he had reason to think so. *Laurence Sterne: The Later Years* (1986; rpt., London: Routledge, 1992), 290.

19.   *Journal to Eliza,* in *A Sentimental Journey Through France and Italy by Mr. Yorick with The Journal to Eliza and A Political Romance,* ed. Ian Jack, the World's Classics (Oxford: Oxford University Press, 1969), 160, 136, 137.

20.   See Jacques Berthoud, "The Beggar in *A Sentimental Journey*," *Shandean* 3 (1991): 37–47, for a contrastive reading of this scene. Berthoud questions the extent to which sexual attraction is responsible for Yorick's change of heart.

21.   For discussions of the relationship between latitudinarianism and a market economy, see Margaret C. Jacob, *The Newtonians and the English Revolution* (Ithaca, N.Y.: Cornell University Press, 1976), 51–56; Colin Campbell, *The Romantic Ethic and the Spirit of Modern Consumerism* (Oxford: Basil Blackwell, 1987), 88–89; Michael McKeon, *The Origins of the English Novel, 1600–1740* (Baltimore: Johns Hopkins, 1987), 198–200; and G. J. Barker-Benfield, 68–69.

22.   "The Form of Solemnization of Matrimony," *Book of Common Prayer*. See Melvyn New's examination of this perennial human need—one that links Sterne and Proust—in his "Proust's Influence on Sterne: Remembrance of Things to Come," *MLN* 103 (1988): 1031–55; reprinted in this volume.

23.   *Laurence Sterne: The Early and Middle Years* (London: Routledge, 1975), 83–84.

24.   *Eighteenth-Century Sensibility and the Novel: The Senses in Social Context* (Cambridge: Cambridge University Press, 1993), 110.

25.   "Sexualism and the Citizen of the World: Wycherley, Sterne, and Male Homosocial Desire," *Critical Inquiry* 11 (1984): 226–45.

26.   Cf. "Philanthropy recommended," where Sterne asserts that those who evidence "an utter insensibility of what becomes of the fortunes of their fellow-creatures" seem "not partakers of the same nature, or [have] no lot or connection at all with the species" (*Sermons,* 23).

27.   *Matthew Henry's Commentary on the Whole Bible,* 6 vols. (1706–1721; rpt., Peabody, Mass.: Hendrickson, 1991), 6:24.

28.   Poole, s.v. Acts 2:44.

29.   Robert Markley, "Sentimentality as Performance: Shaftesbury, Sterne, and the The-atrics of Virtue," in *The New Eighteenth Century: Theory, Politics, English Literature,* ed. Felicity Nussbaum and Laura Brown (New York: Methuen, 1987), 224; reprinted in this volume.

30.   Patricia Meyer Spacks, *Desire and Truth: Functions of Plot in Eighteenth-Century English Novels* (Chicago: University of Chicago Press, 1990), 130.

31.   Spacks, 132.

32.   Sterne's own facility with the French language was limited, as Cash notes: "he never mastered [French] in its spoken form, though his written French may have been respectable" (*The Later Years,* 131).

33.   "Imagination and Sympathy: Sterne and Adam Smith," *Journal of the History of Ideas* 10 (1949): 399–410.

34.   For a discussion of the way *A Sentimental Journey* explores "the possibilities and limi-tations of communicating with others," see Keryl Kavanagh, "Discounting Language: A Vehi-cle for Interpreting Laurence Sterne's *A Sentimental Journey,*" *The Journal of Narrative Technique* 22 (1992): 136–44.

35.   J. Paul Hunter has discussed Sterne's "confusion between the world of fiction and the world of fact" in terms that suggest that, on this front too, Sterne opposed dualism. Hunter describes this confusion as "an important aesthetic and philosophical statement, about the relation of life and art, a statement that refuses to draw the line, a decision to live and write along the margin, somewhere between genes and imagination" ("Clocks, Calendars, and Names: The Troubles of Tristram and the Aesthetics of Uncertainty" in *Rhetorics of Order/Order-ing Rhetorics in English Neoclassical Literature,* ed. J. Douglas Canfield and J. Paul Hunter [Newark: University of Delaware Press, 1989], 195).

36.   *The Confessions of Saint Augustine,* trans. E. B. Pusey (London: Dent, 1907), 13.

37.   *The Divine Legation of Moses Demonstrated,* 10th ed., 3 vols. (London: Thomas Tegg, 1846), 1:240.

38.   For the complex relationship between Sterne and Warburton, see Melvyn New, "Sterne, Warburton, and the Burden of Exuberant Wit," *Eighteenth-Century Studies* 15 (1982): 245–74.

Levinas and Sterne:
From the Ethics of the Face to
the Aesthetics of Unrepresentability

Donald R. Wehrs

Sterne's *A Sentimental Journey* is constructed around a series of episodic face-to-face encounters between Yorick and his foreign interlocutors, encounters that are likely on a first reading to strike one as remarkable for their lack of narrative consequence and for their ambiguous teetering between appeals for sentimental identification and displays of self-ironic, witty distance.[1] Because the pleasures that Yorick derives from these encounters often seem to depend on aestheticizing his compassion for the poor or aestheticizing his erotic receptivity to the charms of sexually vulnerable working-class young women, the question arises of whether Yorick's encounters have a predatory, exploitive dimension that undercuts their evocations of fine feeling.[2] Judith Frank argues that when Yorick expresses the desire to "spy the *nakedness* of [French women's] hearts, and through the different disguises of customs, climates, and religion, find out what is good in them to fashion [his] own by" (*ASJ*, 217–18), his "wish is a typically sexualized version of the sentimental traveler's project: the spying of the hearts of others in the service of bourgeois self-improvement and self-empowerment."[3] The distresses of others may become so much material for the construction of a complex, nuanced, but unjustly privileged individuality.

Our unease with Yorick may lead to unease with a novel that invites us to participate imaginatively in his sentimental experiences; that unease has led many in Victorian and contemporary times to find in Sterne and in the sentimental mode something not quite proper.[4] Terry Eagleton notes that the aesthetic is "a contradictory, double-edged concept": on the one hand, "it figures a genuinely emancipatory force—as a community of subjects now linked by sensuous impulse and fellow-feeling rather than by heteronomous law"; on the other hand, "the aesthetic signifies what Max Horkheimer has called a kind of 'internalised repression,' inserting social power more deeply into the very bodies of those it subjugates, and so operating as a supremely effective

This essay was written specifically for this volume and appears here for the first time.

311

mode of political hegemony."[5] Eagleton argues that moral-sense philosophy and the sentimental evocation of sensibility created a supposedly "natural" basis for consensus and social harmony in an early capitalist Britain, where the legacy of sectarian, ethnic strife and congealing class exploitation generated a deep need (and political utility) for the belief that Britons could "experience right and wrong with all the swiftness of the senses, and so [moral sense] lays the groundwork for a social cohesion more deeply felt than any mere rational totality. . . . The body has its reasons, of which the mind may know little. . . . To follow out our self-delighting impulses, provided they are shaped by reason, is unwittingly to promote the common good."[6]

To the extent that we view Sterne as one of the fathers of the novel, unease with Yorick may feed into current suspicions that novels naturalize a "violence of representation," a violence that reinforces existing power relations and contains otherness within safe, predetermined boundaries.[7] Frank argues that by linking "the acts of surveillance, discipline, and characterization, then, *A Sentimental Journey* suggests that the sentimental novel is itself a form of social control. . . . [T]he scenario of disciplinary pathetic literature functions as a symbolic domestication of the lower classes in the service of the benevolist's self-empowerment."[8] Therefore, the novel's generic susceptibility to fostering the internalization of Foucauldian surveillance and to serving as a vehicle of Gramscian hegemony reinforces and is reinforced by the sentimental tradition's naturalization of class and gender condescension, and by the sentimental tradition's evocation of the position of an impartial spectator as one of ethical insight and epistemological privilege. In Adam Smith's *Theory of Moral Sentiments* (1759), for example, the sentimental spectator both imagines himself in the situation of the suffering other and observes his response to that suffering.[9] Therefore, even in the act of being moved by what he sees, the subject of what Timothy Dykstal calls "Smith's spectatorial ethics" remains detached from and above what he sees; relation to others through "imagination," through aesthetic appropriation and emotive fellow-feeling, has the paradoxical effect of reinstating the isolated *cogito*, the confluence of self-consciousness and identity, and the subject/object epistemology Cartesian rationalism and British empiricism share: with reason, the sentimental tradition saw itself as the heir of Locke.[10]

Viewing Yorick's encounters in the light of Emmanuel Levinas's ethics of the face, however, may allow one to negotiate the tension between, on the one hand, taking seriously, as Martin Battestin has recently done,[11] Yorick's insistence that the responsiveness of his feelings to his interlocutors constitutes a refutation of Hobbesian/French egocentric materialism, and, on the other hand, pursuing, as Frank has done, the implications of selfishness in Yorick's representation of the pleasure he derives from his fleeting encounters and in Sterne's own mocking treatment of the genre he masters. According to Frank, "the sentimental novel is systematically represented as a degraded object throughout *A Sentimental Journey*," and Yorick is "as diligently acquisitive as any eighteenth-century entrepreneur" and is "a virtual imperialist of sensibility."[12] If we turn, however, to a specific episode, Yorick's encounter with the monk at Calais, we find contemporary concerns about the potential for imperialistic appropriations of others to our own self-empowering, self-enclosing projects unnervingly close to the surface of Sterne's text.

The monk appears immediately after Yorick, carried away by a sentiment of goodwill toward the French and their king, declares that he is in a charitable mood. Battestin notes that this scene "dramatize[s] the materialist view of man expounded by the *philosophes*. . . . To La Mettrie, for instance— the state of the soul being entirely dependent on the condition of the body— our generous sentiments are the inevitable consequence of a good dinner."[13] But no less striking than the materialistic basis of Yorick's good mood is his viscerally hostile response to the monk's arrival at that moment to ask for alms, which he experiences both as an intrusion on his private enjoyment and as a rather nasty joke by the fates at his expense: "No man cares to have his virtues the sport of contingencies—or one man may be generous, as another man is puissant . . . for there is no regular reasoning upon the ebbs and flows of our humours; they may depend upon the same causes, for ought I know, which influence the tides themselves" (70).

Although Yorick parodies materialist arguments in claiming that he finds his own "humours" unaccountable because the deterministic, mechanistic causality that explains their "ebbs and flows" is too minute for his discernment, he is predisposed against the monk because, in Levinas's terms, the monk is an Other who calls him away from enjoyment (*jouissance*). Levinas notes that what we enjoy in enjoyment is not satisfaction of needs, but liberation from need: delight in the physical substances of life when we are not in need "delineates independence itself, the independence of enjoyment and of its happiness, which is the original pattern of all independence." We enjoy the feeling of independence because we feel self-sufficient and self-created: "Enjoyment . . . is an independence *sui generis*, the independence of happiness."[14] In other words, what we enjoy in enjoyment is precisely the sense of being detached from and above a world of need, the position that allows the sentimental hero to indulge in condescending empathy, a materially generated sense of independence that, by placing us into an aesthetic relation to exteriority, allows us to enjoy the illusion that we are God.

Levinas emphasizes that this sense of independence is an illusion; we live *from* life, exist by means of matter.[15] So Sterne emphasizes, in Yorick's irritation at the monk's unexpected appearance while he is enjoying *both* just having had a fine meal *and* contemplating the goodness of his sentiments, that we resent having the illusion of independence broken: "No man cares to have his virtues the sport of contingencies." The reason we don't "care" for this is that it disrupts the illusion that our virtues are instruments for our self-making, and that the external world is there for us to enjoy—to bring into our comprehension and to serve as material for our themes, to be culled by us for self-improvement and self-empowerment. In other words, the illusion that is broken and that causes Yorick a paroxysm of irritation is the illusion that we can be imperialists of sensibility, that an acquisitive, appropriative relation to the external world can be sustained without disruption.

Such a view is implied by what Charles Taylor calls "Locke's punctual self," an ideal of disengagement and self-making predicated on "a radical rejection of teleology, of definitions of the human subject in terms of some inherent bent to the truth or to the good," so that standing "back from ourselves and our existing 'relish' . . . allows us the possibility to remake ourselves in a more rational and advantageous fashion. . . . To take this stance is to identify oneself with the power to objectify and remake, and by this act to distance oneself from all the particular features which are objects of potential change. . . . [T]he real self . . . is nowhere but in this power to fix things as objects."[16] Levinas suggests that intentionality, thematization, and representation often function as cognitive/conceptual equivalents of sensual enjoyment, and that the intellectual pleasures embedded in such functioning ultimately flow from the body's delight in the illusion of self-sufficiency;[17] similarly, Sterne portrays Yorick assimilating the monk into *his* story, seeing him as violating a space he has colonized, and Sterne links Yorick's initial aggressive response to physiological impulses ("the ebbs and flows of our humours") in a way that, as in Levinas, ties the mind to the body so as to bring home the truth of our nongodlikeness at the very moment we are upset by not being God. In this way, as Battestin argues, Sterne is able to dramatize "the materialist view of man" in such a way as to "reconcile with the doctrines of his religion those elements of [materialist systems] that seemed to him persuasive."[18]

Both Sterne and Levinas argue that our material being, our corporeality, is inseparable from our spiritual life—but both do so, paradoxically, to argue against the dominant forms of materialism of their times. Where Sterne confounds "the most *physical precieuse* in France: with all her materialism" (69),[19] Levinas disputes the totalizations that inscribe the human into conceptual systems in ways he likens to war: "The visage of being that shows itself in war is fixed in the concept of totality, which dominates Western philosophy. Individuals are reduced to being bearers of forces that command them unbeknown to themselves (*à leur insu*)" (*TI*, 21; x). Materialism, for Levinas as for Sterne, participates in the dehumanizing totalizations figured by war: "To place the Neuter dimension of Being above the existent which unbeknown to it this Being would determine in some way, to make the essential events unbeknown to the existents, is to profess materialism" (*TI*, 298–99; 275). By theorizing materiality in a radical way, Sterne and Levinas articulate vindications of transcendence consistent with, but not philosophically dependent on, the religious doctrines each writer elsewhere, within devotional genres, advocated and explicated—those of latitudinarian Anglicanism and Talmudic Judaism respectively.[20]

Yorick is in a charitable mood when the monk appears because his unease with the French (as foreigners) and with the French king (who embodies, in Yorick's conventional ideological imagination, European tyranny as opposed to British liberty)[21] has just been mollified by French food and wine, and by his reckoning that the spiritual expense of material covetousness is not worth it: "[W]hat is there in this world's goods which should sharpen our spirits, and make so many kind-hearted brethren of us, fall out so cruelly as we do . . . ?" (68). Sterne's narration suggests the interpenetration of spiritual and material causality: "When man is at peace with man . . . he pulls out his purse, . . . looks round him, as if he sought for an object to share it with—In doing this, I felt every vessel in my frame dilate—the arteries beat all chearily together" (68). The passage moves from a mixture of physical and philosophical contentedness to a desire to share with others to a physiological benefit, a movement that underscores both the interpenetration of the spiritual and the material, and the dependence—in this world—of the former on the latter: without vessels and arteries, no sentiments are possible. At the same time, however, Sterne rejects a one-way causal sequence, from materialist cause to emotive-psychological effect, and thus underscores the implicit narrowness of the modern materialism of Hobbes and the *philosophes* by affiliating Yorick's experience with Hellenistic and Renaissance traditions of considering philosophy to be medicine for the soul, of linking the health of the mind to the health of the body, both through extended analogy and through tracing direct effects of the tenor of the mind on the tone of the body.[22]

A similar recognition of interpenetration is inscribed in the description of Yorick's encounter with the monk: the narrative moves from Yorick's annoyance that the monk has disturbed his enjoyment of his own material and spiritual well-being to the observation that "there is no regular reasoning upon the ebbs and flows of our humours." We are opaque to ourselves because our internal life is subject to external influence and because we cannot know ourselves well enough to reduce to scientific clarity the motions of our passions; we can be neither Locke's "punctual self" nor Smith's "impartial spectator" because our relations to others cannot be resolved into "the power to fix things as objects" and because we cannot disengage ourselves from ourselves sufficiently to see ourselves undistorted by egotistic self-love (a central theme of many of Sterne's sermons).[23] We are, then, in two ways ungodlike (neither self-moving nor all-knowing), but as Yorick determines to seize control of his story, not to allow his virtues to be the sport of contingencies, he is "predetermined not to give [the monk] a single sous" and so "set[s] [himself] upon [his] centre" (70).

By setting himself upon his center, Yorick attempts to seal himself off from the sources of ethical motion that lie outside him, sources that call him into an ethical relation by speaking, as it were, behind his consciousness directly to his sensibility: the monk made his appeal for alms "with so simple a grace—and such an air of deprecation was there in the whole cast of his look and figure—I was bewitch'd not to have been struck with it— —A better reason was, I had predetermined not to give him a single sous" (72). Yorick seeks to shield himself from being diverted from his intention; indeed, to aspire to an engagement with the external world in which that "world" is always already refracted by one's predetermination or intentionality—one's "fore-understanding"—is to predispose oneself to the sorts of "bewitchments" that will secure one from being "struck," from vulnerability. So Levinas notes that "Intentionality remains an aspiration to be filled and fulfilment, the centripetal movement of a consciousness that coincides with itself, recovers, and rediscovers itself . . . rests in self-certainty, . . . thickens into a substance."[24]

Therefore, we experience the ethical relation, "[t]he order that orders me to the other," as a disruption, a digression: "The signification of my responsibility for what escapes my freedom is the defeat or defecting of the unity of transcendental apperception" (*OTB*, 140, 141; 179). Through the defeat of the unity of transcendental apperception, the defeat of the self detached from and above the world grasped in representation, we experience a radical lack of autonomy, "the extraditing of the subject that rests on itself, to what it has never assumed," a lack that—paradoxically—discloses transcendence: "I, the same, am torn up from my beginning in myself, my equality with myself. The glory of the Infinite is glorified in this responsibility. It leaves to the subject no refuge in its secrecy that would protect it from being obsessed by the other. . . . The glory of the Infinite is the anarchic identity of the subject flushed out without being able to slip away" (*OTB*, 144; 184). Yorick becomes obsessed, involuntarily, by the monk as soon as he rebuffs him: "MY heart smote me the moment he shut the door—Psha! said I with an air of carelessness, three several times—but it would not do: every ungracious syllable I had utter'd, crouded back into my imagination" (75). This "crowding back" that is neither solicited nor escapable is a sort of persecution; this "irremissible guilt with regard to the neighbor is like a Nessus tunic my skin would be" (*OTB*, 109; 139).

The position that Yorick occupies at this point is far from that of Smith's impartial spectator; indeed, the illusion that such a position could mediate human relations, and that socioeconomic privilege or ethnic-sectarian difference could consolidate it, has been torn away, to Yorick's considerable discomfort. Just as the ethical relation discloses, for Levinas, the delusive self-centeredness of Husserlian intentionality and Heideggerian ontology—in which the only intelligible world is one preformed by our projects—so the ethical relation discloses, for Sterne, the bewitching nature of predeterminations that have as their motive a freedom from disturbance that connects the egotistical anthropology of Hobbesian/French materialism to the detachment of both the sentimental observer and the Lockean self. Such a relation also connects all three modern "schools" to the aspiration shared by the three major schools of Hellenistic philosophy—freedom from disturbance (*ataraxia*) and liberation from vulnerability (*tuchê*) as the way to happiness (*eudaimonia*).[25]

Levinas and Sterne share the conviction that the effort to escape vulnerability, to secure godlike equanimity or self-production, to which much of the Western philosophical tradition, ancient and modern, is committed, is like Cain's flight, a vain attempt to escape from the relation that confers humanity upon us. The Epicurean Metrodorus writes, "I have gotten in ahead of you, O Tuchê, and I have built up my fortifications against all your stealthy attacks," and Lucretius presents Epicurus's school as one that is building an impregnable fortress (*De Rerum Natura*, II: 7–8).[26] Although Sterne, of course, understands well the human proclivity for fortifications, he suggests in Yorick's engagement with the monk and elsewhere that it is in the perilous experience of having our fortresses penetrated, and in the consequences of the inevitable breaching of our defenses, that our humanity is engendered and sustained.

Just as the scene with the monk moves toward a recognition of the self as placed within orders of obligation beyond the self, so Levinas emphasizes that what is brought home to us through the ethical relation is that "the one-for-the-Other [the ethical relation] is not a commitment," not an "engagement" in the Sartrean sense of the radically free subjectivity's gratuitous assumption of responsibility,[27] but rather is anterior to the possibility of any commitment: "As a result of a decision freely taken or consented to . . . commitment refers . . . to an intentional thought, an assumption, a subject open upon a present, representation, a logos" (*OTB*, 136–37; 174). The ethical is not for Levinas, as it tends to be for Derrida and for postmodern thought generally, a matter of recognizing difference, of not doing violence to the other's difference (and freedom) by letting the other be;[28] rather, the ethical is to be called in a way that demands response, demands action, and so brings home to us that we are not situated in contexts that are *only* culturally constructed, and so arbitrary, or remissible, or illicit (just as, in Sterne, when the nakedness of the heart is revealed, it discloses something behind variations in customs and manners that commits us—that obliges imitation rather than displays options): "The non-indifference to the other as other and as neighbor in which I exist is something beyond any commitment in the voluntary sense of the term, for it extends into my very bearing as an entity. . . . Responsibility, the signification that is non-indifference, goes one way, from me to the other. In the saying of responsibility, which is an exposure to an obligation for which no one could replace me, I am unique" (*OTB*, 138–39; 176–77). Because we are called to the ethical relation rather than choose it, we know we are not God; as in Sterne, the ethical relation is mediated through materiality in a way that reveals the illusoriness of Western modernity's various promises of independence or disengagement (various modern ways of carrying on ancient philosophy's struggle against vulnerability), based on the delusion that human beings need only negative liberty to be happy and fulfilled— a delusion that may be said to inform both the liberal individualism of Sterne's day and the postmodern ethics of Levinas's.[29]

Through Yorick's encounter with the monk, Sterne traces how, in Levinas's terms, sensibility undercuts thematization, how saying disrupts the said. Yorick responds to the monk's request for alms with an elaborate anti-Catholic speech, a rhetorical set piece built around an extended periodic sentence (a grammatical fortress), in which Yorick argues that he has finite resources for charity, that the English poor have first claim to his purse, that the foreign poor may have some claim,[30] but that "we"—that is, the English—distinguish "betwixt those who wish only to eat the bread of their own labour—and those who eat the bread of other people's, and have no other plan in life, but to get through it in sloth and ignorance, *for the love of God*" (74). Clearly, Yorick attempts to "fix" the monk within nationalistic, sectarian discourses that will reduce him to an instance of all he dislikes about Catholicism.[31]

Even as Yorick makes the speech, however, the monk's concrete particularity contests the interpretative/assimilative categories to which Yorick would colonize him. What shows through in the precise but polysemic physical descriptions for which Sterne is celebrated is not simply how the pursuit of determinacy is frustrated or even how the other exceeds our conceptualizing grasp, but how the exposure of the other's materiality and vulnerability issues in sensibility: "The monk, as I judged from the break in his tonsure, a few scatter'd white hairs upon his temples, being all that remained of it, might be about seventy—but from his eyes, and that sort of fire which was in them, which seemed more temper'd by courtesy than years, could be no more than sixty—Truth might lie between—He was certainly sixty-five; and the general air of his countenance, notwithstanding something seem'd to have been planting wrinkles in it before their time, agreed to the account" (71). Frank argues, drawing on Foucault, that such descriptions subject the body "to a discipline whose primary purpose is to render it visible; once the body becomes permanently visible . . . knowledge can be obtained about it."[32] In such descriptions, however, precision of detail often does not yield certain knowledge (the monk's age remains conjectural, as do the particulars of his story), and what becomes visible is not knowledge *about* the other but one's own obligation *to* the other inscribed, as it were, in the other's exposure and sensibility.[33] Levinas defines sensibility as "this changing of being into signification, . . . the subject's subjectivity, or its subjection to everything, its susceptibility, its vulnerability . . . exposure to outrage, to wounding, passivity more passive than all patience" (*OTB*, 14–15; 17–18).

The description of the monk reveals that sensibility is neither something we project on the world nor something we can evade; to see the monk at all is to be placed in an ethical relation because the exposure that yields sensibility fuses cognition and concern. By calling the reader to sensibility, Sterne's novelistic discourse refutes the thesis that description and prescription belong to separate "value-spheres," that the worlds of *is* and *ought* are categorically distinct. As Hilary Putnam has observed, "Just as we criticise a describer who does not employ the concepts of *table* and *chair* when their use is called for, so also, someone who fails to remark that someone is *considerate* or *spontaneous* may open himself to the criticism that he is imperceptive or superficial; his description is not an adequate one."[34] The novel's capacity for descriptive precision, which Sterne was certainly among the first to master, may render visible all that we habitually render invisible in order to see others as objects of knowledge. Indeed, Yorick immediately knows that he has acted wrongly because the monk's response to his speech does not counter one ideological inscription, or fortress, with another: "The poor Franciscan made no reply: a hectic of a moment pass'd across his cheek, but could not tarry—Nature seemed to have had done with her resentments in him; he shewed none—" (74). The monk's response is a "saying" that discloses to Yorick the violence of his "said," a "said" whose views on monks, Catholics, and foreigners Sterne's contemporaries were likely to share: "Saying uncovers, beyond nudity, what dissimulation there may be under the exposedness of a skin laid bare. It is the very *respiration* of this skin prior to any intention. . . . The one is exposed to the other as a skin is exposed to what wounds it, as a cheek is offered to the smiter" (*OTB*, 49; 62–63).

Sterne portrays Yorick's ability to apprehend and respond to the other in the dimension of saying as invariably and necessarily intermittent; the aestheticizing of his encounters and the return from the other to private pleasure involve a placing of the other in the realm of the said and a reiteration of thematization, a reinstatement of the unity of transcendental apprehension. What is ethically ambiguous about Sterne's text is also what saves its sensibility from sentimentality. When Yorick, in repentance, offers the monk his tortoise-shell snuffbox, he receives from the monk his horn snuffbox in exchange. This exchange suggests that we receive something back for our acts of kindness (that social- and self-love are not mutually exclusive), but Yorick's physical appropriation of something from the monk seems to suggest sentimental appropriation as well. When Yorick, on his return journey, visits the monk's grave and opens the snuffbox, the issue arises of whether Yorick "appropriates" his encounter with the monk, and the monk's death, as an occasion for self-refinement, transforming the encounter into a type of affective capital. The likening of sentimental exchanges to commercial exchanges, the uneasy affiliation of sensual, spiritual, and monetary forms of profit, has been much remarked[35] and has long contributed to what Frank calls "the question of the novel's tone, . . . whether Sterne intended it to be a straightforward sentimental novel or a satire of sentimentalism."[36]

Since the scene at the grave is a set piece of the sentimental mode, one might wonder whether Sterne implicates the reader in an appropriative activity analogous to Yorick's. When Yorick describes "a nettle or two" on the monk's grave striking "so forcibly upon [his] affections" that he bursts into "a flood of tears," attention is turned away from the monk to Yorick himself as a gender-inflected object for aesthetic consumption: "but I am as weak as a woman; and I beg the world not to smile, but pity me" (102–3). If the monk becomes a sentimental commodity for Yorick, and Yorick presents himself as a sentimental commodity for the reader, Sterne may be suggesting that our relations with others can only momentarily step beyond an egocentric and perhaps sexist economy. As David P. Haney notes, for Levinas the "saying," the "manifestation of infinite spirit as human mortality," is "in a necessary relation of interdependence with totalizing representational structures"; therefore, "the 'saying' is not simply expressed, but is necessarily given by the 'said': we cannot help but see the world in terms of meaningful entities. . . . The saying, as the realm of the infinite, goes beyond the said, but also dies into the said."[37] So Yorick, and by implication the reader, cannot avoid assimilating others into structures of meaning, into thematizations that, like sentimental genre conventions, are inherently distorting, partial, colonizing, and unjust.

The best defense against being subsumed into the partiality and injustice of the said is to acknowledge its constitutive deficiency through irony, through the refusal signaled by tone to align oneself unreservedly with the said's internal drive for closure and adequation. Thus Sterne's irony, his wavering between straightforward sentimental fiction and satire of sentimentalism, his invitation for affective participation at the very moment of calling attention to its exploitive dimension, may be seen as a transposition into novelistic discourse of the ancient Skeptics' rhetorical device of *isostheneia*—that is, presenting opposing claims of equal persuasive force in order to produce a state of suspension (*epochê*) derived from recognizing the partiality, the injustice, in each argument that calls forth univocal or totalizing representational schemes.[38] Through irony, Sterne can insist simultaneously on the inevitability, for humans, of the reversion of the saying into the said and still keep the said from congealing into a totality, into the walls of a fortress.

The question of whether Sterne implicates the reader in Yorick's appropriative relation to the world comes up again, with special urgency, in the scenes with working-class young women, in which Yorick may be seen as responsive enough to the "saying" inscribed in the face not to exploit the sexually vulnerable, but still "man" enough to relish the temptation and his self-conquest. Here also the male reader is placed in a similarly ambiguous situation: an affective participation in Yorick's story enacts his compromise. In the sexual tease, for example, of "the fair *fille de chambre*" showing Yorick "the little purse" to hold his "crown" (236), the reader shares Yorick's feeling of "something at first within [him] which was not in strict unison with the lesson of virtue" (235). At the same time, the materiality of sexual desire is emphasized—"There is a sort of a pleasing half guilty blush, where the blood is more in fault than the man" (234)—not to excuse an appropriative relation, as in libertine and materialist traditions, but to suggest, in opposition to both modern and ancient philosophical aspirations to godlike impenetrability, the cognitive value of the emotions and the ethical value of vulnerability: "If nature has so wove her web of kindness, that some threads of love and desire are entangled with the piece—must the whole web be rent in drawing them out?—Whip me such stoics, great governor of nature! . . .—Wherever thy providence shall place me for the trials of my virtue—whatever is my danger—whatever is my situation—let me feel the movements which rise out of it, and which belong to me as a man—and if I govern them as a good one—I will trust the issues to thy justice, for thou hast made us—and not we ourselves" (237–38). Commenting on this passage, Battestin observes, "Of the passions that serve our self-interest there was one, in Sterne's view, that, if properly understood and cultivated, could lead us out of the prison of the self: this was sexual desire."[39] If this is the case, it is so only because to "feel the movements which rise out of" the dangerous "situation" that belongs to "a man" brings home to us the ethical necessity of "govern[ing]" those movements as a good man; acknowledging one's vulnerability to being swept away by exploitive projects is to acknowledge one's ungodlike, unself-created condition—and the impiety of the aspiration for it to be otherwise.[40]

When the internal momentum of seeing the other within conventional gender and class categories that solicit totalizations by "fixing" an object for condescension and exploitation is abruptly arrested through "conquest" of self, such scenes reveal precisely what is disclosed to Yorick in those moments when his encounters yield a "saying": Yorick comes to self-consciousness through self-reproach, through recognizing, as with the monk, that he has been on the way toward violently appropriating the other. Indeed, Sterne's novel suggests that genuine self-consciousness involves a recognition of the aggressivity, invasiveness, and hence injustice of consciousness itself; in our egocentric "use" of the world in representing it to ourselves as a repository of themes and pleasures *for us*, we are, as one might expect an Anglican divine to affirm, by nature sinful. So Levinas argues, "The consciousness of any natural injustice, of the harm caused to the Other, by my ego structure, is contemporaneous with my consciousness as a man. The two coincide" (*DF*, 16). Sexual temptation and gender exploitation are perhaps so frequently entwined in Yorick's encounters because sexuality may bring home for Sterne with particular immediacy the ego structure's constitutive aggressivity. In this respect, Sterne follows Augustine's analysis of sexuality's affinity for sinfulness in its promotion of selfishness even as he stresses, in tracing how potentially sexual encounters may open the way for self-denying solicitude, the Erasmian (and Protestant) tradition of redeeming sexuality through emphasizing its affinity for sociability.[41]

Since the ego structure that grounds representation is broken in upon by the other, by "saying," it might seem that Sterne and Levinas would call on representation only to indict or subvert it. When Yorick is brought to a sense of his own injustice, it is invariably through an interjection of speech that disrupts a silent visual assimilation of object to subject: either another person says something unexpected, or an internal dialogue breaks out. With the monk, Yorick "consider'd his grey hairs—his courteous figure seem'd to re-enter and gently ask me what injury he had done me?—and why I could use him thus?" (75). When Yorick suspects that M. Dessein might cheat him in the price of a coach, he begins to assimilate him into a succession of increas-ingly negative ethnic stereotypes until a counter-voice breaks in, freeing Yorick from a self-impoverishing, internal inertial momentum: "I looked at Monsieur *Dessein* through and through—ey'd him as he walked along in pro-file—then, *en face*—thought he look'd like a Jew—then a Turk—disliked his wig—cursed him by my gods—wished him at the devil— —And is all this to be lighted up in the heart for a beggarly account of three or four louisd'ors, which is the most I can be overreached in?—" (89). The breaking up of Yorick's text and consciousness with a proliferation of voices, and the way in which Yorick's encounters suggest that what is expressed is valuable largely as a necessarily inadequate approximation of what is inexpressible (as, similarly, the exchange of snuffboxes says what cannot be said), might lead us to con-clude that Sterne (and perhaps Levinas) aspires to an aesthetics of unrepre-sentability, a view that depends on the notion that what discourse can pre-sent—like metaphysics in Derrida's account—is always tainted with a violence and exclusiveness that cannot be overcome but only undermined, locally, from within, as through Sterne's irony.

But what separates Sterne and Levinas from a postmodern ethics also sep-arates them from Lyotard's equation of the unpresentable with the sublime.[42] The Sterne-Levinas critique of modern subject/object epistemology is part of a broader critique of the metaphor of vision as the privileged source of knowledge that, unlike apparently similar postmodern critiques, considers the metaphor as transgressive of the distance between man and God. The egotism implicit in the unity of transcendental apperception reveals the human tendency to forget that one is not God, a tendency that Sterne and Levinas both suggest receives reinforcement from the Western philosophical tradition, which from its incep-tion has contained the danger of replacing God as absolute knower with the human philosopher whose "system" is the true creation. Stanley Rosen argues that "the difference between Genesis and the major myth of the *Phaedrus*" lies in there being "no creation or production" in the latter: "The soul, as directed toward the Ideas, is silent. However, the book of Genesis, as a writing, is poste-rior to the speech of creation it records. The speech of the *Phaedrus*, as a Platonic writing or monologue, *is* the speech of creation. Platonic monologue orders the cosmos after a silent vision of the good, which transforms the pretheoretical understanding of the world. . . . Human beings must take Jehovah's word for His goodness, and hence for the goodness of His creation. In the case of Plato, they can see for themselves (if they have eyes to see). But they must do so silently, and this is their *imitatio dei.*"[43]

To the extent that contemplation (*theoria*) has as the object of vision not trace, nor distorted image, but presence, man as contemplator assumes the role of God—a tendency that reaches its peak when man is the unity of his self-constructed world (what is transcendentally apprehended). The modern disengaged, spectatorial, punctual self may be seen as renewing the epistemological confidence of Cicero's Stoic Lucilius, for whom contemplation allows one to discern intelligible order, just as an ideal of impartial scientific observation, codified by the transparent "plain style" of Hobbes, Locke, and the Royal Academy, may be seen as renewing Stoic confidence that one can "grasp" firmly objects of knowledge in such a way that their truth and significance become "self-evident" in their visibility.[44] As Fielding notes when he jokingly refers to himself as the creator of a little world, the novel as a genre may have theocidic tendencies in the way that it relies on the silent contemplation of print to make visible an objectified world produced by a solitary creator, thereby aspiring (potentially, at least) to the effacement and thus naturalization of its own rhetoric.[45] Sterne may work against these tendencies by disrupting silent contemplation/appropriation with intersubjective, dialogic, rhetorical speech—speech traceable to the traditions of classical and Renaissance humanism, which insist on the mediation of understanding through rhetoric in ways that stress the human inability to "grasp" unmediated truth, the human need for an education of the affections and desire as well as for reason, or both.[46]

Neither Sterne nor Levinas, however, sees representation *as such* as violent; rather, violence lies in the false assumption that representation is primary or sufficient. As Melvyn New has pointed out for *Tristram Shandy*, Sterne does not simply celebrate indeterminacy; determinate things happen and they matter in determinate ways.[47] Moreover, the ability to narrate in determinate ways, to come to some reasoned conclusions, is as much a constitutive part of humanity as is the inevitability of insufficient knowledge and ambiguities: "Our narratives are 'truths' in so far as they make life possible for us. The inner compulsion not to contradict these truths, the instinct to narrate our stories to some useful conclusion, would seem inbred in our use of language."[48] Without rational predication and without the principle of non-contradiction, the irony of opposing claims with equal force (*isostheneia*) would be impossible to convey or appreciate. The dependence of the saying on the said, the dying of the former into the latter, should not be seen as merely negative, as a descent into "inauthentic" being. Levinas argues that absolute responsibility for the other passes into a concern for justice when a third party enters the picture; justice involves "comparison, coexistence, contemporaneousness, assembling, order, thematization" (*OTB*, 157; 200), and thus representation: "Out of representation is produced the order of justice, moderating or measuring the substitution of me for the other. . . . It is thus that the neighbor becomes visible, and, looked at, presents himself, and there is also justice for me. The saying is fixed in a said, is written, becomes a book, law and science" (*OTB*, 158–59; 202).

Instead of representation being of necessity an order of violence—something I must escape to affirm a difference that, as unrepresentable, can involve no determinate claims or obligations—Levinas suggests that the irre-missibility of the ethical grounds the possibility of the political. In this way, Levinas does not argue for, as Christopher Norris suggests, an "idea of ethics as a discourse of radical alterity [that] would in effect close off the very prospect of any . . . intersubjective appeal to the other's knowledge and expe-rience."[49] Rather, the possibility of intersubjective appeal—of claims of rea-son, freedom, pluralism—depends on being able to appeal to shared encoun-ters with exposure and sensibility—to a common constitution through the irremissibility and radical anteriority of the ethical: "[T]hat all men are broth-ers is not added to man as a moral conquest, but constitutes his ipseity. . . . The relation with the face in fraternity, where in his turn the Other appears in solidarity with all the others, constitutes the social order, the reference of every dialogue to the third party by which the *We* . . . encompasses the face to face opposition, opens the erotic upon a social life, all signifyingness and decency" (*TI*, 279–80; 257); "Reason and freedom seem to us to be founded on prior structures of being whose first articulations are delineated by the metaphysical movement, or respect, or justice—identical to truth" (*TI*, 302–3; 279).

Similarly, what emerges as determinate in Yorick's encounters with the monk and the *fille de chambre* is the co-extensiveness of recognizing ethical claims upon the self—recognizing, in Levinas's terms, that freedom needs to be justified (*TI*, 303; 280)—and recognizing the answerability of our cultural categories to the dimension incarnate in the other's face that will not release us from obligation and that cannot be "grasped" by our partisan, partial cate-gories, whatever their validity (Yorick and Sterne have no intention of renouncing "reasoned" opposition to Catholicism); that which is incarnate in the other's face is not merely "produced" by other, potentially inferior cul-tural categories (as with the monk), nor is it merely the "effect" of general-ized, materially grounded desire (in which case exchanging sex for money with the *fille de chambre* would be to follow nature). Rather, in the theological language that Sterne and Levinas share, what is incarnate in the face of the other is the image of God; all our notions and projects must arise from and answer to the predication of our ipseity upon the ethical relation that incarna-tion will not allow us to evade.

To affirm the determinate, however, in no way unsays the primacy of saying over said. In seeking to answer the objection of skepticism (or Derrida) that his argument's very dependency on language betrays it to the said, Lev-inas notes that the "reference to an interlocutor permanently breaks through the text that the discourse claims to weave in thematizing and enveloping all things" (*OTB*, 170; 217).[50] Similarly, when Yorick imagines the monk reply-ing to his insulting speech, he takes back the violence of what he has said, but offers at least the possibility that attending to the saying of the monk will constitute a determinate step in his learning how to be more just: "I have behaved very ill; said I within myself; but I have only just set out upon my travels; and shall learn better manners as I get along" (75). If we may see the journey as a metaphor for life, the implication is that our encounters may be progressive, may have narrative consequence, because they disturb the stories we would make of ourselves; and that learning "better manners," being acculturated through intersubjectivity into civility, need not be a violence against the self, but rather can be an antidote to the self's propensity for violence. In this way, *A Sentimental Journey* may stand apart from the sentimental fiction that Dykstal sees as being ethically defective through a "lack of narrative coherence": "Narrative provides the context that permits a sentimental hero's actions to be judged."[51] Dykstal argues that sentimental fiction's displacement of narrative coherence in favor of disjointed episode is of a piece with its reliance on something like Martha Nussbaum's ethics of "intuitive perception and improvisatory response" as opposed to an ethics of rule, law, established principle, which, drawing on Geoffrey Galt Harpham, Dykstal associates with the "law of the text," or plot and narrative.[52]

In the case of Sterne and Levinas, however, the fixing of the saying in the said, in book and law, allows the episodic incarnational encounter to ground and return one to principled coherence, to the fidelity of narrative continuity, even to institutional and national histories. For Levinas, the child, as both "my own and not-mine," is at once self and other, and relates us to "a future, irreducible to the power over possibles, [that] we shall call fecundity" (*TI*, 267; 245); through the child our "personal I" is related to society and time even as "[t]ranscendence is time and goes unto the Other" (*TI*, 269; 247). Thus, "[t]he intersubjective reached across the notion of fecundity opens up a plane where the I is divested of its tragic egoity, which turns back to itself, and yet is not purely and simply dissolved into the collective" (*TI*, 273; 251). Children consecrate time and thus make its content a matter for politics, for the reasoned pursuit of justice. In Sterne's case, the putting into question of Yorick's assumptions and the straining of his rectitude by his sentimental encounters serve to reinforce his fidelities—to Eliza, to the Shandys, to Anglican Christianity, to civil discourse, to good humor and humane forbearance.

To orient oneself to the incarnational moment is not the same as to seek escape from the meditated, ambiguous, "fallen" temporal human condition. Such an effort, which Sterne understood as enthusiasm and Levinas as ecstasy, is a doomed quest to achieve the status of the divine by absorption into "the spirit" or "Being," in ways that would forfeit the estrangement that makes our identity human.[53] When Yorick, near the end of Sterne's narrative, observes a peasant family dancing after supper, he notes, "I fancied I could distinguish an elevation of spirit different from that which is the cause or the effect of simple jollity.—In a word, I thought I beheld *Religion* mixing in the dance—but as I had never seen her so engaged, I should have look'd upon it now, as one of the illusions of an imagination which is eternally misleading me, had not the old man . . . said, that this was their constant way; and that all his life long he had made it a rule" (283–84). What distinguishes religious "elevation of spirit" from mechanical "cause or effect" is not that the inertia, folly, and egotism of ordinary life are abrogated in transport, rupture, or fusion, but that a "constant way" that "all [one's] life long" has been "a rule," a pattern of narrative coherence, reiterates into habit and sentiment the ability to "feel some generous joys and generous cares beyond [ourselves]" (278), an ability that ceases to be self-aestheticization when it rests, in Levinas's terms, on the "reverting of heteronomy into autonomy" (*OTB*, 148)—that is, when the encounter with otherness rests on the discovery, as in Yorick's encounter with the monk, that the other's claim upon us does indeed make our virtues the sport of contingencies, and through such contingencies the "divinity" that "sensibility" "stirs within" us "lifts [us] up to HEAVEN" (277), not by incorporating us, in this life, into an inhuman world of ceaseless perfection, but by incarnating in us the intermittent transcendence of all the isolating, colonizing worlds within which we are apt to situate ourselves, and of whose immanent laws we are apt to take ourselves and others as merely "products" or "effects."

Notes

I wish to thank Lorna Wood for her help with this essay.

1. The "perilous balance" of Sterne's tone between "irony and seriousness" has been well described by W. B. C. Watkins in *Perilous Balance: The Tragic Genius of Swift, Johnson, and Sterne* (Cambridge: Boar's Head, 1960); this is a balance that, in *Tristram Shandy*, has led to a succession of "dark," existential, or absurdist readings on the one hand and comic, playful, "postmodern" readings on the other hand.

2. For critiques of class and gender condescension in sentimental fiction, see Lucinda Cole, "'(Anti)feminist Sympathies: The Politics of Relationship in Smith, Wollstonecraft, and More," *ELH* 58 (1991): 107–40; Robert Markley, "Sentimentality As Performance: Shaftesbury, Sterne, and the Theatrics of Virtue," in *The New Eighteenth Century: Theory, Politics, English Literature*, ed. Felicity Nussbaum and Laura Brown (New York: Methuen, 1987), 210–30 (reprinted in this volume); Carol McGuirk, "Sentimental Encounter in Sterne, Mackenzie, and Burns," *SEL* 20 (1980): 505–15. For the aestheticization of ethics, see Robert E. Norton, *The Beautiful Soul: Aesthetic Morality in the Eighteenth Century* (Ithaca, N.Y.: Cornell University Press, 1995), 9–54.

3. Judith Frank, "'A Man Who Laughs Is Never Dangerous': Character and Class in Sterne's *A Sentimental Journey*," *ELH* 56 (1989): 97.

4. For accounts of the decline of the sentimental mode and current unease with its attributes, see Timothy Dykstal, "The Sentimental Novel As Moral Philosophy: The Case of Henry Mackenzie," *Genre* 27 (1995): 59–60, 77–78.

5. Terry Eagleton, *The Ideology of the Aesthetic* (London: Basil Blackwell, 1990), 28.

6. Eagleton, 34; see also pp. 31–66.

7. See especially Paula R. Backscheider, *Spectacular Politics: Theatrical Power and Mass Culture in Early Modern England* (Baltimore: Johns Hopkins University Press, 1993); Nancy Armstrong and Leonard Tennenhouse, "Introduction: Representing violence, or 'how the west was won,'" in *The Violence of Representation*, ed. Nancy Armstrong and Leonard Tennenhouse (London: Routledge, 1989), 1–26; John Bender, *Imagining the Penitentiary: Fiction and the Architecture of Mind in Eighteenth-Century England* (Chicago: University of Chicago Press, 1987).

8. Frank, 112, 114.

9. See Dykstal, 71; see also D. D. Raphael, "The Impartial Spectator," *Essays on Adam Smith*, ed. Andrew S. Skinner and Thomas Wilson (Oxford: Clarendon Press, 1975), 83–99.

10. Dykstal, 71; on the debt to Locke of Shaftesbury and Hutcheson, see Charles Taylor, *Sources of the Self: The Making of the Modern Identity* (Cambridge: Harvard University Press, 1989), 248–65.

11. See Martin C. Battestin, "Sterne among the *Philosophes:* Body and Soul in *A Sentimental Journey*," *Eighteenth-Century Fiction* 7 (1994): 17–36.

12. Frank, 114, 120.

13. Battestin, 28–29; see also Julien Offray de La Mettrie, *La Mettrie's "L'Homme Machine": A Study in the Origins of an Idea*, ed. Aram Vartanian (Princeton, N.J.: Princeton University Press, 1960), 154–55.

14. Emmanuel Levinas, *Totality and Infinity: An Essay in Exteriority*, trans. Alphonso Lingis (Pittsburgh: Duquesne University Press, 1969), 110, 115; *Totalité et infini: Essai sur l'extériorité*, 2nd ed. (La Haye: Martinus Nijhoff, 1965), 82, 87; hereafter cited in the text as *TI*, with page numbers from the translation (cited first) and the original separated by a semicolon.

15. See *TI*, 110–14; 82–86.

16. Taylor, *Sources of the Self*, 164, 170, 171, 172.

17. See especially *TI*, 35–40, 109–10, 122–42; 5–10, 81–82, 94–116.

18. Battestin, 28.

19. See Battestin, 19–30; Arthur H. Cash, *Laurence Sterne: The Later Years* (London: Methuen, 1986); and Alice Green Fredman, *Diderot and Sterne* (New York: Columbia University Press, 1955), for accounts of Sterne's friendship and intellectual engagement with the leading materialist *philosophes*.

20. See Melvyn New, "Sterne As Preacher: A Visit to St. Michael's Church, Coxwold," *Shandean* 5 (1993): 160–67, and New, "Laurence Sterne's Religion," *Studies on Voltaire and the Eighteenth Century* 303 (1993): 453–54. See also Levinas, *Difficult Freedom: Essays on Judaism*, trans. Seán Hand (Baltimore: Johns Hopkins University Press, 1990); henceforth cited in the text as *DF*.

21. Yorick's anxiety that, were he to die in France, all his personal effects would be forfeited to the king underscores conventional British assumptions that the state on the Continent is invasive in a way that British traditions of natural rights and liberty preclude. See Linda Colley, *Britons: Forging the Nation, 1707–1837* (New Haven: Yale University Press, 1992).

22. For extensive treatment of the medical analogy in Hellenistic philosophy, see Martha C. Nussbaum, *The Therapy of Desire: Theory and Practice in Hellenistic Ethics* (Princeton, N.J.: Princeton University Press, 1994). Nussbaum notes that in Aristotle and in the three main Hellenistic schools (Epicureanism, Skepticism, and Stoicism) emotions "are forms of *intentional awareness . . . directed at* or *about* an object" that have "a very intimate relationship to beliefs, and can be modified by a modification of belief" (80); thus philosophy can heal an emotionally ravaged mind by rationally persuading one to see, and hence feel, in ways that wean one from self-destructive beliefs.

23. See especially "The abuses of conscience considered"; see also "Self knowledge," "Self-examination," "Pride," and "Trust in God," in *Sermons*, 255–67, 31–39, 132–39, 225–34, and 322–30.

24. Levinas, *Otherwise Than Being or Beyond Essence*, trans. Alphonso Lingis (The Hague: Martinus Nijhoff, 1981), 48; *Autrement qu'être ou au-delà de l'essence* (La Haye: Martinus Nijhoff, 1974), 62; hereafter cited in the text as *OTB*.

25. For Levinas's critique of Husserl and Heidegger, see especially *TI*, 42–48; 12–18. For the relation of *ataraxia* to *eudaimonia*, see Nussbaum, 102–39, 280–315, 316–58.

26. Quoted in Nussbaum, 121, 280. See Lucretius, *De Rerum Natura* II:6–7: "sed nil dulcius est, bene quam munita tenere / edita doctrina sapientum templa serena . . ." ("But nothing is more delightful than to possess well fortified sanctuaries serene, built up by the

teachings of the wise . . .") (Lucretius, *De Rerum Natura,* trans. W. H. D. Rouse [New York: Putnam, 1924], 84–85).

27.   For Sartrean commitment or engagement, see Jean-Paul Sartre, *Being and Nothingness: A Phenomenological Essay on Ontology*, trans. Hazel E. Barnes (New York: Washington Square Press, 1956), especially 619–29.

28.   On the postmodern ethics of radical alterity, see Christopher Norris, *Truth and the Ethics of Criticism* (Manchester, England: Manchester University Press, 1994); Simon Critchley, *The Ethics of Deconstruction: Derrida and Levinas* (Oxford: Blackwell, 1992); Richard J. Bernstein, *The New Constellation: The Ethical-Political Horizons of Modernity/Postmodernity* (Cambridge, Mass.: MIT Press, 1992).

29.   For critiques of negative liberty, see Charles Taylor, "What's Wrong with Negative Liberty," in *Philosophy and the Human Sciences: Philosophical Papers 2* (Cambridge: Cambridge University Press, 1985), 211–29; William M. Reddy, *Money and Liberty in Modern Europe: A Critique of Historical Understanding* (Cambridge: Cambridge University Press, 1987). For critiques of postmodern ethics' renewal of negative liberty, see Bernstein, 31–78, 142–229; Critchley, 188–247; John McGowan, *Postmodernism and Its Critics* (Ithaca, N.Y.: Cornell University Press, 1991). Nussbaum notes in *Therapy of Desire* that a radical critique of how we have been "constructed" by society is central to both Epicurean and Stoic philosophical healing (see 102–39, 316–58).

30.   This argument parallels Adam Smith's remarks in "Of the Order in which Individuals are recommended by Nature to our Care and Attention," in Adam Smith, *The Theory of Moral Sentiments* (1759), ed. D. D. Raphael and A. L. Macfie (Oxford: Clarendon Press, 1976), 219–27.

31.   Similar efforts by Yorick to "fix" women by employing conventional categories are explored by Melinda Alliker Rabb in "Engendering Accounts in Sterne's *A Sentimental Journey*," in *Johnson and His Age*, ed. James Engell (Cambridge, Mass.: Harvard University Press, 1984), 531–58.

32.   Frank, 106.

33.   Frank's primary example of how Sterne's description links visibility to apprehending the other as an object of knowledge—the portrait of the victim of the Inquisition on the rack in "The abuses of conscience" sermon as placed in *Tristram Shandy* (II.xvii.161–63)—is problematic for two reasons. First, the description does not render up the "truth" about the victim, but illustrates that "true religion" provides us a "rational" way out of ideological, egotistical self-enclosure through the "rule": "By their fruits ye shall know them." Second, the description's rhetorical function in the sermon's argument suggests that Sterne and Yorick are working within a tradition in which appeals to sensibility, to the rhetoric of Ciceronian humanism, are not only vehicles of theological exposition, but central to theological hermeneutics, to the rational determination of doctrine. Sterne thus affiliates himself with Anglican versions of the Erasmian Christianity described in Manfred Hoffman, *Rhetoric and Theology: The Hermeneutic of Erasmus* (Toronto: University of Toronto Press, 1994).

34.   Hilary Putnam, *Reason, Truth and History* (Cambridge: Cambridge University Press, 1981), 139.

35.   See, for example, Rabb, 534.

36.   Frank, 119–20. Frank notes that much criticism argues for a synthesis of these alternatives (124 n. 44).

37.   David P. Haney, *William Wordsworth and the Hermeneutics of Incarnation* (University Park, Penn.: Pennsylvania State University Press, 1993), 39.

38.   See Nussbaum, 285–86; Sextus Empiricus, *Outlines of Pyrrhonism*, trans. Rev. R. G. Bury (New York: Putnam, 1933), 1:8. For Sterne's relation to the Skeptical tradition, see Donald R. Wehrs, "Sterne, Cervantes, Montaigne: Fideistic Skepticism and the Rhetoric of Desire," *Comparative Literature Studies* 25 (1988): 127–51; for a discussion of the centrality of Skeptical thought to eighteenth-century British intellectual and literary discourse, see Harry M.

Solomon, *The Rape of the Text: Reading and Misreading Pope's* Essay on Man (Tuscaloosa: University of Alabama Press, 1993).

39. Battestin, 30–31.

40. The criticism of the "impiety" of Stoic epistemological hubris, as well as the rejection of the Stoic aspiration to achieve a godlike impassivity through the "extirpation of the passions" (see Nussbaum, 359–401), has a long tradition in Christian theology. See Marjorie O'Rourke Boyle, *Rhetoric and Reform: Erasmus' Civil Dispute with Luther* (Cambridge, Mass.: Harvard University Press, 1983); Marcia L. Colish, *The Stoic Tradition from Antiquity to the Early Middle Ages, Vol. 2: Stoicism in Christian Latin Thought through the Sixth Century* (Leiden, Netherlands: E. J. Brill, 1985), 9–91, 221–25.

41. For Augustine's account of the egotism inherent within postlapsarian sexuality, see St. Augustine, *Treatise on Marriage and Other Subjects*, trans. Charles T. Wilcox, M. M., *The Fathers of the Church*, vol. 27 (New York: Fathers of the Church, 1955), 9–51; St. Augustine, *City of God*, trans. Henry Bettenson (Harmondsworth, England: Penguin, 1972), 566–94. For Erasmus's rehabilitation of sociability in sexuality, see Erasmus, *Encomium matrimonii*, in *Opera Omni Desiderii Erasmi*, vol. 1/5 (Amsterdam: North Holland Publishing, 1975). Erasmus draws on the linking of marriage and friendship (*philia*) that Plutarch articulates in *Coniugalia praecepta* (*Moralia*, vol. 2, trans. Frank Cole Babbitt [New York: Putnam, 1927], 298–343). For apostolic and patristic disassociations of sexuality from sociability, see Peter Brown, *The Body and Society: Men, Women, and Sexual Renunciation in Early Christianity* (New York: Columbia University Press, 1988).

42. See Jean-François Lyotard, *The Lyotard Reader*, ed. Andrew Benjamin (Oxford: Basil Blackwell, 1989), 196–211, 402–6.

43. Stanley Rosen, *Hermeneutics As Politics* (Oxford: Oxford University Press, 1987), 63–64; see also Taylor, *Sources of the Self,* 115–26.

44. See Cicero, *De Natura Deorum* II: ii and *Academica* I: xi, in Cicero, *De Natura Deorum and Academica*, trans. H. Rackham (New York: Putnam, 1933), 124–25, 448–51. For the Royal Society's ideal of "plain speech," see Michael McKeon, *The Origins of the English Novel, 1600–1740* (Baltimore: Johns Hopkins University Press, 1987), 65–89.

45. Henry Fielding, *The History of Tom Jones, A Foundling*, ed. Martin C. Battestin (Middletown, Conn.: Wesleyan University Press, 1975), 524–25.

46. For Sterne's debt to and saturation in these traditions, see *TS: The Notes;* for similar borrowing in *A Sentimental Journey* and the *Sermons*, see Melvyn New, "Some Sterne Borrowings from Four Renaissance Authors," *Philological Quarterly* 71 (1992): 301–11. Of particular importance to Sterne's ironic style is the reception of Lucian among Renaissance humanists. See Michael O. Zappala, *Lucian of Samosata in the Two Hesperias: An Essay in Literary and Cultural Translation* (Potomac, Md.: Scripta Humanista, 1990); R. Bracht Branham, *Unruly Eloquence: Lucian and the Comedy of Traditions* (Cambridge, Mass.: Harvard University Press, 1989); Walter M. Gordon, *Humanist Play and Belief: The Seriocomic Art of Desiderius Erasmus* (Toronto: University of Toronto Press, 1990).

47. Melvyn New, "Sterne and the Narrative of Determinateness," *Eighteenth-Century Fiction* 4 (1992): 315–29 (reprinted in this volume).

48. New, "Narrative," 318.

49. Norris, 57.

50. See Jacques Derrida, "Violence and Metaphysics: An Essay on the Thought of Emmanuel Levinas," in *Writing and Difference*, trans. Alan Bass (Chicago: University of Chicago Press, 1978), 79–153.

51. Dykstal, 72–73.

52. Dykstal, 61, 74; Geoffrey Galt Harpham, *Getting It Right: Language, Literature, and Ethics* (Chicago: University of Chicago Press, 1992).

53. See "On enthusiasm," in *Sermons*, 357–67; Levinas, *TI*, 70–81, 203–9, 294–99; 42–44, 177–84, 270–75.

Index

♦

The Volume Editor

Melvyn New is professor of English at the University of Florida. He has been writing about Laurence Sterne for 30 years, most recently publishing a scholarly edition of Sterne's sermons, which comprise volumes 4 and 5 of the *Florida Works of Sterne* (1996), and the new Penguin Classics edition of *Tristram Shandy* (1997). *Telling New Lies: Essays in Fiction, Past and Present* (University Press of Florida, 1992) and *Tristram Shandy: A Book for Free Spirits* (Twayne, 1994) are his most recent works of critical commentary.

The General Editor

Zack Bowen is professor of English at the University of Miami. He holds degrees from the University of Pennsylvania (B.A.), Temple University (M.A.), and the State University of New York at Buffalo (Ph.D.). In addition to being general editor of this G. K. Hall series, he is editor of the James Joyce series for the University Press of Florida and the *James Joyce Literary Supplement*. He is the author of six books and editor of three others, all on modern British, Irish, and American literature. He has also published more than one hundred monographs, essays, scholarly reviews, and recordings related to literature. He is past president of the James Joyce Society (1977–1986), former chair of the Modern Language Association Lowell Prize Committee, and currently president of the International James Joyce Foundation.